A COMIC VISION
OF
GREAT CONSTANCY

Stories about Unlocking the Wisdom of Everyman

BY ALAN GRIESINGER

For Julie, Peter, and Michael,
with love

A Comic Vision

of

Great Constancy

Stories about Unlocking the
Wisdom of Everyman

by Alan Griesinger

CONTENTS

The Knight's Tale

A Midsummer Night's Dream

PREFACE

It's only fair to advise the reader that my recreations of these texts are closer to poetry than to scholarship. I approach them with a great longing to understand the world and myself and so read them the way they live in me. While writing the book, I watched and listened one evening as my friend Jonathan played piano works by Bach at an Eastman School of Music recital. He was reading for himself and for us—with fingers, arms, body, mind, and heart—the composer's musical legacy. Long after their composition, live performances of Bach's scores still create a complicated yet harmonious musical world for their audiences, and it occurred to me at the time that I was attempting something like this—a performance of Chaucer's and Shakespeare's texts that has the effect of complicated but harmonious music. Just as Bach embodied a comic vision in his scores, these authors embodied a comic vision in their tales and plays. Now that I'm retired from teaching, writing these essays has reminded me of what can be gained from an active engagement with them. In a live performance Chaucer's and Shakespeare's texts bring to life a comprehensive pattern of experience that opens the way for comic resolutions.

I begin my book with Chaucer's vision in "The Knight's Tale" of the wisdom unlocked by a fall to earth. He is making the case that this experience is the basis for relationships that survive and prosper. Given the difficulties of relationships in any time or place, there's always a need for this. The survival of a text written over six hundred years ago is still a kind of miracle; to better understand why it has survived, I have gone to some lengths to study and interpret Chaucer's story for our own time. In addition to outlining traditional comic themes, I'll argue that his tale offers a refuge and a counter argument (for someone who needs an argument) against those who claim that the human mind and its many forms of speech can't accurately record reality. There have been skeptics about this throughout the history of the West, but for most part they were writing within a classical and Christian culture that assumed the existence of a logos, a rational principle governing the universe. Starting with Heraclitus, philosophers saw a deep correspondence between the logos of the mind and the logos of the world, and so they thought and wrote with confidence that what they thought and wrote was a meaningful inquiry.

Modern thought, however, has attacked the bedrock belief that timeless archetypes give form and meaning to experience. Instead, it's a world where "anything goes" as Cole Porter's madcap passengers sing. Modern philosophers have met the enemy, and they are grand narratives. No doubt, these writers advocate for this position out of a great dedication to the truth, but literature from ancient times has illustrated that anything goes as a final word on the subject tends to fracture our social life as much as it liberates; this is an important theme in Homer's *The Odyssey*. Also, there's an inherent inconsistency in a grand narrative dedicated to the deconstruction of grand narratives. This may seem to be a debate for intellectuals, a tempest in a teacup, but it's a question that Everyman confronts at some level of awareness without specific instruction in it. People may not know that philosophers, scientists, social scientists, and artists have extensively argued for anything goes in books, but when someone reacts to an assertion or a situation with a cool "Whatever," it's a sign that person has absorbed, at some level, the need in modern thought to hedge a response to life. For the one saying "Whatever," the miracle of Chaucer's tale has ceased to exist.

Comedy is not just an intellectual matter or a clever manner of speaking. Like the claim of anything goes, it's a form of power and vision. As an integral agent of the life force, comedy aims at setting ideas and ideologies free from being mistaken as reality, and to that end, it employs a certain magic that unlocks the mind's enchantment with them in a short but sharp observation. A comic strip I remember from growing up in the 50s is a case in point. It depicts a sidewalk at night illuminated by a single street light. In the little pool of light, a boy bends over to look for something. Another boy comes along and asks him what he's doing, and he explains that he's trying to find a quarter he dropped. So the two bend over there to look together. After a while, the one asks where exactly he dropped it, and the other replies, "Oh, I dropped it over there," (gesturing toward the darkness), "but the light is better here."

For all its brevity, this little parable illuminates much. For example, modern philosophy and science were born out of a passionate quest for certainty. The case is best illustrated by Descartes who put such faith in the power of rational structures. He famously found the illumination he was looking for, and the laws of mechanics he helped to champion have led to many scientific and technological discoveries. But what if the "something" he lost when the ancient and medieval cosmos of his childhood fell apart for him, not an objective certainty necessarily but an intuitive and wholehearted love of life, is still back there in the dark where he'd prefer not to look. It's just a little comic strip, but it also illustrates in a simple way the task Chaucer set for himself in writing *The Canterbury Tales*. Long before Descartes, Chaucer wrote about characters and for readers who would live their lives in the certainty of what they know. The light of what his characters know, however, tends to mislead them.

Just as the narrative of the comic strip actually begins in the darkness where the quarter was dropped, the opening lines of Chaucer's poetic world begins in the darkness underground of a dormant seed or root. This darkness is the starting point of Everyman's narrative, for no individual can say anything scientific about the source from which he was born and to which he will return. After introducing this seed or root underground, every tale is designed to draw our attention to it. At the end of "The Knight's Tale" Theseus' speech begins with the source that draws "all that is engendered" forth into being. He calls it the "First Great Cause", and the whole tale (culminating in the speech) is an attempt to make the reader as aware of it as he would be of a quarter he lost on a sidewalk. A rational record of things-as-they-are, the poet warns, cannot lose sight of this darkness, the vast expanse of what we don't know.

In Act I of *A Midsummer Night's Dream*, the unhappy Helena puts in a single sentence what Shakespeare learned from Chaucer about why relationships fail. Helena's disappointments in love lead her to conclude that "Love looks, not with the eyes, but with the mind." For Helena, looking with the mind is at the heart of her problem; it's what has exiled her to present loneliness. On the surface of it, her formulation is a baffling dualism, and Shakespeare has made it the business of his play to come to terms with it. Without commenting on it further here, I mention simply that her line about the way love "looks" provides a frame of reference for calling this reading of Chaucer and Shakespeare's stories *A Comic Vision of Great Constancy* as Shakespeare built his vision on the foundation he found ready-made in Chaucer. These two together have constructed an ark for transporting its living cargo through perilous floods, and it's as well-built and seaworthy as any we are like to know.

To keep extensive footnotes from interrupting the text, I acknowledge those writers and books that have significantly influenced the shape and direction of the book in an Afterword.

THE
KNIGHT'S
TALE

THE BUSINESS OF COMEDY

An incident from Dore's illustrations of Dante's *Commedia*

And the earth was without form, and void; and darkness was upon the face of the deep. And the spirit of God moved upon the face of the waters.

And God said, Let there be light: and there was light.

~ Genesis 1:2-3

***

When dawn came, fresh and rosy-fingered, Nestor the Gerenian charioteer got up from his bed, went out, and seated himself on a smooth white bench which stood, gleaming and polished, in front of his lofty doors. Here his father Neleus used to sit and give counsel as wise as the god's; but he had long since died and gone to Hades' Halls. So now Nestor of Gerenia sat there in his turn, sceptre in hand, a Warden of the Achaean race.

~ Homer, The Odyssey

To Restore Amends

The poet of *The Odyssey* begins that work by calling on his Muse for aid in the rendering of Odysseus' adventures:

> *Tell me Muse, the story of that resourceful man who was driven to wander far and wide after he had sacked the holy city of Troy...Tell us this story, goddess daughter of Zeus, beginning at whatever point you will.*[1]

I, too, would invoke the muse that inspired *The Odyssey* and other priceless texts. I also recognize the resourcefulness of a man driven into exile by wars and storms at sea, for it is through his resourcefulness that he will eventually find his way home. Like Homer appealing to the muses and like Dante relying on the poet Virgil, I am content to be guided by a larger intelligence in the telling of this comic vision.

For centuries literature in the West has evolved out of the Hebrew and Greek cultures represented by the opening quotes, and I draw on these texts to introduce my theme. The second and third verses of the Bible set the stage and frame the action for everything else to come. First there is darkness, and then there is light. This is a pattern that expresses the Bible's deepest structure. It's also a pattern that the medieval poet Dante recognized as *The Divine Comedy* in his passionate and encyclopedic account of a pilgrim exile who is guided through the darkness of error into the light of redemption. Likewise, with the light of a new day pouring over the land and pushing night steadily westward with its fingers, old Nestor passes through the lofty doors of his palace to sit on the smooth white bench of true judgment. It's a comic vision of a well-ordered household waking up once more to be governed by the light of clear seeing and wisdom.[2] It's the place an exile seeks, where family and friendships flourish.

At the end of *A Midsummer Night's Dream*, the trickster Robin closes Shakespeare's comic vision with a promise as we go forth from the theater that this place, which is less a place than a state of being, exists. Everything in the play lays a foundation for Robin's assurance that "we shadows"—the fairy company, the natural world they regulate, and the comic vision of which they are a part—represent real and present powers for good in our lives:

And, as I am an honest Puck,

If we have unearned luck

Now to scape the serpent's tongue,

We will make amends ere long;

Else Puck a liar call.[3]

Their representation of this power, unlike the serpent's tongue, is true and faithful. Since he's a fairy, Robin is so small he's almost invisible, and like ordinary human beings, he can make mistakes because he doesn't know everything. Thanks to the magic of the stage, however, we see him large as life, and we hear him now modeling for us a willingness to make amends for the disruptions that attend his limitations. A serious misstep or a trick that gets out of control can make anyone, even a fairy, feel small in the scheme of things. In keeping with the comic vision that has created him, though, Robin counts himself lucky to be alive and wholly himself. This is the essence of his honesty, and in this honesty, despite the littleness of his time and place in our lives, there's room for the amends that maintain a relationship.

If those in the audience suspend judgment and absorb the play of an honest Puck and his creator, he vouches for the healing effect of its performance, and in keeping with this effect he makes an emotional appeal:

So, good night to you all.

Give me your hands, if we be friends,

And Robin shall restore amends.

He promises the mending of a life that has been an exile from friendship; he promises a restoration of relations with a trickster who, on the whole, means well. If we make friends with him, if we give him our hands, then ere long we may look at the world with the lightness and freedom that he does.

As I present it here, comedy is not just a light entertainment. While lively and fun, it's also informed by a deep sense of wonder and purpose. Some comic moments are characterized by a moment of complete attention as when something unexpected or beyond one's powers of comprehension suddenly clears the mind of its habitual chatter; this is a characteristic of stories in the Bible. There are wonders in the *The Odyssey* as well, but the figure of Odysseus also represents a comic relish for people and places and adventures of all kinds. Each stop and every woman who cares for him is like a gift that speeds him on his way to Ithaca. More seriously, ancient writers have shown that the power of a comic vision sees people through the grief of a tragic loss. Chaucer represents this in "The Knight's Tale" as the mindfulness of Theseus when the great tournament he devised as a vehicle for judgment ends in an untimely death. Theseus deeply grieves the loss of his knight, but he never loses sight of his function as a comic sensibility and center for his people. He honors the dead with suitable rites, but in all he does he continues to serve the living. From ancient times writers have consistently represented for us the pattern of comedy, and since Chaucer thousands of comic plays, movies, novels, and TV shows have added to our literature characters who adapt to life, make new forms for life, and create new life.

A comic state of being keeps people going, but it's not blind willfulness. While a comic story may include instances of unconscious impulses and instincts, in its overall effect it's a literary form for representing attention, an unobstructed vision of things-as-they-are. Comedy is that moment in Genesis when suddenly there is light, and unconditioned vision is the primal first act in creating a space fit for human life. *The Odyssey* also depicts the vision Odysseus gains from his adventures to restore order in his home for his father, his wife, his son, his servants, and himself. He never loses sight of his goal, and that deep purpose forces him to pay close attention to every situation along the way. He may be lost in a strange world, but he keeps his wits about him. In separation from his home and in the quest to return, Odysseus is Everyman. Everyone lives in a world of constant change and conflict that seems to draw one centrifugally away from a comic center, and, like Odysseus, everyone seeks a return to that center. It's a quest that's renewed in every generation, and, more immediately, it's a quest that's renewed from moment to moment for anyone who would be aware of things-as-they-are.

The Wake-Up Call

Call me a reader. Literature was the great sea on which I set forth. After taking a degree in literature as a graduate student, I taught English to junior high students for ten years, but then my principal asked me to teach the advanced placement course in English literature offered to seniors. I'll mention as well that I coached the boys' junior high soccer team for twenty-two years because this job plays a role at a critical point in my narrative of "The Knight's Tale." Much of the material in these essays was developed over the eighteen years that I taught AP. From the start, the course was constructed around a simple informing principle: my students and I studied stories about the comic errors and mishaps that unlock the wisdom of Everyman. People have been making mistakes for thousands of years, and Western literature often makes these errors its subject. It's a truism at the heart of comedy that people learn most from their mistakes. Along the way I added my own missteps into the mix for good measure, and so did my students. Nobody's perfect. Kids, I discovered, need to put their own stamp on things, but they also want order and direction in the classroom. If I moved ahead with them in exploring this theme, it was because they recognized it as something of value and worked to understand it.

Comedy has much to do with children, for they carry life forward.

Greek comedies that still survive from the classical period undoubtedly derive from even more ancient fertility rites. These plays were originally performed in celebration of Dionysus, the god of wine and a divine catalyst for lustiness. When there were gods for so many other phenomena like volcanoes, sudden storms at sea, the death and rebirth of plants in winter and spring, it makes sense there would be gods and ceremonies concerned with the renewal of human life. Then and now the inception and birth of new life, for all our knowledge about the facts of life, is a mystery. My wife and I were graduate students when we learned that we were going to be parents. The news took us by surprise. We were in the process of preparing for a family by getting an education and then landing a job, but the child on the way wasn't going to wait until we were perfectly ready. In retrospect, I doubt whether anything other than the child himself could have made me ready to be a father.

In his poem "My Heart Leaps Up," Wordsworth writes how the child is father to the man:

My heart leaps up when I behold

A rainbow in the sky:

So was it when my life began;

So is it now I am a man;

So be it when I shall grow old,

Or let me die!

The child is father of the man;

And I could wish my days to be

Bound each to each by natural piety.

These lines celebrate the radical innocence, the natural piety of childhood that responds wholeheartedly to the beauty of this world, and the poet hopes that this inner child will continue to "father" a spontaneous love of nature as he grows older. In my life, the child has been father of the man but not from a focus on an inner child. I still recall that moment when I finally realized what the swelling of my wife's belly meant. I wouldn't say that my heart "leapt up"—that's just an expression—but I know for a fact that my heart was changed forever. I borrow Wordsworth's assertion that the child is father of the man to affirm an old-fashioned piety that the prospect of becoming a father was the most sobering and salutary event of my life to that point.

It wasn't a proud moment, and it didn't involve the contemplation of beauty. It was like a loud, sudden sound that stopped me in my tracks and made me wonder, *What was that?* Once stopped, I had to consider my situation, my readiness for whatever it was that had stopped me. A moment's attention told me that there were some things that had to change if I was going to care for a baby. With the life of a child on the line, I had no more excuses. The reality of the child that grew in my wife's womb induced a radical sense of my own life and the extent to which my life and the life of the child were in my hands for better or for worse.

My child was not a dream or poetic self-expression. Even before he was born, he dictated a new way of life. Behind these changes was a constant concern, something like the respect that I imagine people long ago had for the powers of earth, air, fire, and water, which they could see and touch and hear but could not comprehend. The ancients, nevertheless, learned something of the gods from the effects their actions had on human beings, and this is borne out in the many stories told about them. In my case, this child moved me to do for him what I might not have done for myself because the old ideas about how to pass my days no longer applied; I began with more seriousness to govern myself instead of leaving it to others or to habitual behavior. Even though the nonstop attention to the needs of a baby may not sound much like comedy, the experience enforced a comic state of seeing things-as-they-are and doing what needs to be done.

The Work

I was a father before I was a public school teacher. After we finished graduate school, there weren't many job openings so I felt lucky to finally get a position. The feeling changed when the duties and responsibilities of the job, like the experience of becoming a father, brought me to a full stop time and time again in situations I had never faced before. By becoming a father, I had been forced to more constructively govern my own unhelpful behaviors. By becoming a teacher, I was forced to learn the governing, not just of myself but of a large, volatile group of people. There's a notion, which was common back then and is still said today, that self-knowledge and self-government come from introspection. In my work experience introspection played a role after the fact. First something would happen in the classroom or out on the playing field that would cause me to stop and wonder how I was going to solve a problem that sometimes was of my own making. It was another rite of passage (a long one) where the world of work served as the sternest of taskmasters. Children have generic needs that can be reasonably anticipated, and teachers go to school to learn about these needs. At the same time, children are sovereign selves who can reveal their autonomy in the blink of an eye. It's the teacher's job to deal with this, but kids will test even a highly trained and experienced teacher if they sense a weakness or a blind spot.

To be an effective teacher, I had to discover what sort of government would help me do my job. Since it was a time when education was undergoing radical shifts in standards of all kinds, teachers in our building employed a variety of disciplinary styles that reflected conflicting political theories and practices. It was the best of times and the worst of times to be speculating about government in the classroom. In my first few years on the job, our principal and older teachers sometimes paddled students who didn't respond to other corrections. This was before the state outlawed the practice. At the other extreme, some teachers employed a school-without-walls style of instruction where students initiated their own learning and governed themselves.

I have no doubt that my government of students in a classroom impacted them as much as their response to my government impacted me. We all have to figure out how to live in the world. That's our work. While I was learning to manage my situation, they were busy learning to manage their own. Day after day in countless relationships and interactions with young people I learned the hard way that some ideas—in this case about what and how to teach—were better than others. Children, even from an early age, are acute observers and critics of those responsible for their care. It's a negotiated relationship. Whether it succeeds or not ultimately depends on the child's own judgment about that government and the reliability of what is being taught. Everyone knows from personal experience that often enough the negotiations of that relationship break down.

The story of mankind in the Bible begins with the rebellion of Adam and Eve. Even King David suffered the rebellion of his son, Absalom. Clearly, for human beings government is an active, dynamic process. Some parts of our country were originally settled by pilgrims who refused to observe the forms of worship enforced by state-sponsored churches in the Old Country. Just as they sought liberty of conscience in church matters, from the first these pilgrims chose their own leaders and governed themselves in their own councils and assemblies. With this history of individualism and independence, it's no wonder that nineteenth-century Americans admired and imitated the free spirits they read about in German and English Romanticism, but the lure of America for Europeans had a much more significant impact and influence.

Throughout our history people have come to the United States because they heard that Americans had created a framework of laws within which a process of political and economic freedom could take place. My ancestor, Andreas, was a case in point. Like many Germans, he emigrated after the failed revolution in 1848 when it was clear that the old country would continue to suppress individual aspirations. For him and for millions of others, the American Dream represented a pragmatic opportunity for working and prospering in an enterprise. Andreas was a cobbler. He settled in a small Ohio town and eventually built a shoe store that supported him and his family. The building still stands. It's a dream made manifest and one that many others in our own time are still realizing. For example, there's a woman in our neighborhood who escaped from Vietnam after the war. She went into business giving manicures, raised her family, and put all three of her children through college. Her dream of a better life became a reality through great courage and single-mindedness of purpose. That was her work.

Lately, though, especially in popular culture, the American Dream appears to be more like an actual dream than a realistic program for creating a better life. A culture that encourages dreaming for dreaming's sake without a regard for the ordinary processes of providing for oneself and one's family runs the risk of Everyman setting up as the ruler of a sovereign power, and children are quick to learn this from the adults around them. Some wonder if government is possible at all in such times.[4] It's a trend toward anarchy similar to that in the seventeenth century when people understood Luther's teachings to mean that Everyman was his own priest, and political activists at the time extended this to mean that Everyman was his own king. Since anarchy is not a viable form of government, history has repeatedly shown that a breakdown in public order leads to the seizure of power by a strongman. A classroom may be only a small sample on which to base a generalization, but I learned firsthand from experiences there that anarchy and the rule of a strongman share a loss of freedom for all parties, and this loss, if one values freedom, makes them essentially the same.

Comic literature as I define it here imagines a more hopeful prospect. It models for everyone in the audience a wake-up call from wishful thinking and illustrates a significant pattern of human behavior. Everyman is a dreamer, and this can lead to both tragic and comic mistakes. In comedy, characters strive to live the good life, but their experience needs a structure, like that provided in a comedy, for this potential to be realized.

The wisdom of comedy is not the exclusive property of a special intelligence or a highly educated class of people. Because it contains the experiences of countless generations, a comic worldview expresses an archetypal form as accurate and as germane for the continuation of human life as any ever devised. As I indicated in my Preface, this essay on the relation of comedy to government is subjective and is more like poetry than scholarship. It points not to a government so much as to self-government, the precondition—as human beings have long known— for a civilized social order. It's a narrative that's based on my own experiences in husband/wife, parent/child, teacher/student, and teacher/principal relationships, but, less subjectively, I borrow its overarching structure from the narratives of traditional comedy which tell much the same story over and over: a character in a social context encounters frustrating obstacles, but in the end the difficulties are resolved in such a way that both the character and the society are enriched. These stories, which have been preserved and retold for thousands of years, express the deepest hope a parent has for a child, and they continue to deeply inform an intuitive sense of that which guides people in the direction of a better life. Admittedly, some people and some conflicts are intractable, but they are not the subjects of comedy. Comedy is about insight and adaptability.

Once I resolved on something important to teach, the questions about government largely took care of themselves. It was the seventies, and the spirit of the time questioned authority at every level of government and in every discipline. One thing, though, was certain—it was my job to maintain order in a classroom, not give in to the breakdown of it. Comedy, I discovered, provided a form for containing both the questioning of and the need for authority. A comedy delights in revealing the smallness and absurdity of a character's ideas and actions (often enough the ideas of those in authority), but the trials that inevitably follow from these absurdities eventually free the character to live a happier, more grounded life within a social context. Comedy gets to have it both ways: it can be a cutting-edge, smart-aleck critic about the status quo even as it seeks to establish healthy and enduring relationships. It allows an anarchic display on a deeply rooted stage.

Governments, both small and large, stand a better chance of survival when the play of ideas is given a stage like that in comedy. The audience watches as a character takes a closely held idea about himself and others out for a test drive only to discover that a bad idea doesn't get him where he wants to go. While frustrating, this is his moment of truth; he experiences disappointment but gains insight into the limited nature of his idea. This pattern of experience describes a basis for enduring, real-life relationships. I suspect, half seriously and half whimsically, that our own government has succeeded for as long as it has because our political thinkers, who were thoroughly familiar with English law and literature, constructed a constitution and a government that was shot through with (what I would call) comic reality checks. With two of the greatest comic poets, Chaucer and Shakespeare, available to them in their own language, English literature is a school for a comic sensibility.

An egalitarian worldview reigns in comedy. It laughs without discrimination at all pretenses of power and sets the stage for human happiness without regard to age, race, religion, education, gender, political persuasion, or income. It's a timeless mission. Twenty-five hundred years after his plays were performed, Aristophanes still "speaks to power" in the twenty-first century. Because the ancients didn't have cell phones and jet airplanes and all the rest, there's a tendency to dismiss them and their culture as primitive and intellectually undeveloped. Aristophanes would have laughed at such an attitude just as hard as he laughed at Socrates in *The Clouds*. In this now timely play, a spendthrift young man's gambling on horses has thrown his whole household deep into debt. The father eventually enrolls him in The Thinkery of Socrates so he can learn how to talk his way out of anything, including the claims of creditors. Emboldened by this new weapon, the father throws a big party and contemptuously sends his creditors away. Unfortunately for him, it's obvious that, even as the creditors go away, the father's problems are not going away. This becomes clearer when, for all the care and expense of sending his son to The Thinkery, the son physically beats the father in a dispute and then calmly argues why it is proper for a son to beat a father.[5]

The records of Aristophanes and other comic writers remind us that the way to secure life, liberty, and happiness in this world is difficult to find (especially when so-called experts cloud the issue), but it can be discovered, if not right away then gradually in the school of hard knocks. The comic stories that have come down to us since then suggest that ordinary people for thousands of years have attended that school and leaned what it takes to make a world that's fit and full of promise for the children we bring into it.

Like others, I dealt with the world as I found it. I found my work and my way in the school of hard knocks. The actions I took in the classroom were driven by the circumstances of my position. I accepted that position because I needed work, and it was the first that had been offered in a time when few jobs were available. There was much I didn't know about teaching. For example, to get the job I had to agree to teach Latin to ninth graders even though several years of Latin classes in junior high were the extent of my training in the subject. It was a case of sink or swim. I quickly discovered that I disliked disorder in the classroom because it made me feel like I was not doing my job. My principal reinforced this impression since that was his job. Over time I learned by trial and error what and how to teach. After the usual probationary period during which I was closely observed and evaluated, I had more freedom to develop programs for my students, but this freedom also made me even more responsible for my own mistakes. In junior and senior high school, students will let a teacher know right away if a lesson falls flat. If it worked, I kept it. If it didn't, I changed it or threw it out. My students' appreciation for a good lesson drove me from day to day.

The course I designed was a risky venture so I was relieved when the students responded so well to a study of comic literature. A comic ordering of the world and people's interest in it, I have come to believe, are as fundamental to human nature as students who do what a teacher asks them to do and students who don't. It's like the sun, which is always shining, but for those of us on earth circumstances here below will often take it from our view. Sometimes the earth itself keeps us from seeing it, sometimes clouds obstruct, and sometimes we don't notice it even if it's up there blazing away with light and energy.

The Holding Cell: Antechamber of Insight

The wisdom of comedy contrasts significantly with the knowledge model dominant in modern times. Out of respect for the healing power of these older texts, it's important to outline this difference and to acknowledge that a tension or a competition for attention in schools has developed between them.

Since the rise of science during the sixteenth and seventeenth centuries, its method and spectacular success have shaped a worldview that rivals and even surpasses the success of that sanctioned and propagated by the medieval church. The scientific knowledge model and its resulting technologies have achieved a dominant position in what is now a global culture. Developed to replace superstitions and pointless customs with empirical evidence, it's a method that has directed people to inquire into the nature of reality by subjecting it to an experiment and drawing conclusions from data. The experiment has to be conducted in such a way that the observer does not influence what is being observed. For example, when I went to graduate school classes to get my teacher's certificate, we observed a classroom through a one-way window so that the students and the teacher on the other side of the glass couldn't see us or be influenced by our presence. The ultimate goal of the new method aimed at a quantifiable result expressed in a rigorous form which could then be tested and retested by other scientists to verify that it did in fact describe reality. Newton's laws of gravitation set the gold standard for scientific inquiry. Simple and expressed in mathematical terms, these laws explained observable phenomena precisely and objectively, and they opened up the heavens in a way no one had ever opened them up before. People at the time thought that Newton's genius and the method behind it represented the beginning of a new creation. Alexander Pope said of him:

Nature and nature's laws lay hid in night.

God said, "Let Newton be!" and all was light.

In scientific experiments, people are strictly sidelined as observers, but even science has now discredited the notion that an observer has no influence on what is observed. Wisdom reflects an older consensus that puts human beings in the middle of the action. The goal is not an abstract, intellectual formula but rather the awareness and the strength a person develops from ever-changing experiences in order to survive and prosper. As a teacher I learned the hard way—from my mistakes. It would be nice to draw abstract conclusions in a comfortable, clinical environment where the real world lies on the other side of a one-way window, but that's not how it worked for me. I had to go through that window, mix it up with the students, and stick around for twenty-eight years to live through the consequences of my experiments. It was, and still is, sink or swim, a constant immersion in an unfinished work.

Nothing in this book is intended to diminish the importance and the value of the scientific worldview. All of us have a loved one whose life has been prolonged by modern medicine, a life that would have been cut short not so long ago by a now manageable illness. This is just one example of its many contributions. Nevertheless, there are limits to what science can do to enrich human life, and this "cutting edge" needs to be explored. The remarkable technological achievements of the West are directly related to the way the globe, our bodies, matter, and the universe have opened up to our understanding since the rise of science. We fly through the air like birds; we have walked on the moon; we have mapped the genetic makeup of the human body; we can clone animals; we can blow up a city and even a country at the push of a button; we can talk to people on the other side of the globe with a little handheld device. These miracles make it easier to sell the world view of science to all and sundry. But even as the saving of a life and modern plumbing and space travel and all the benefits our technological cornucopia has poured out into the modern world, all these technological breakthroughs and conveniences have not solved the problem of human fear and insecurity. Disease, old age, violence, and death—all are still problems. How is it that fear can pass so easily through all the security systems our technology can devise? How is it that, with so much scientific knowing to fortify them, individuals still suffer from paralyzing anxieties and societies still suffer from the occasional, highly destructive mass panic?

To put the case into a scenario that I sometimes dealt with in the classroom, science does not have a ready answer for the young adult who embarks on a nihilistic program of aggression or who falls into depression. Experts and researchers in mental health, philosophers of the mind, and social scientists may have important explanations as to why this happens. As a layman who had to deal with this problem in the everyday duties of my work, I discovered that the study of literature to which I had dedicated my attention for so many years provided a structure for coming to terms with the hopelessness and anger of alienated students. The great comic texts of our literature specifically address this alienation with countless examples and always with an eye to how the alienation could be mended. Given the challenges I faced, these authors and their works were great company, and so, quite naturally, I borrowed their diagnosis of the problem and their prescription for it. Then and now my comic vision focuses on the individual, not abstractions about society, and argues that both the aggressive nihilism and the depression spring from an obsessive, habitual idea that life is a form of solitary confinement, a holding cell for meaninglessness and death. This is also a worldview.

The image of life as a prison has an ancient pedigree, for prison experiences have figured prominently in spiritual traditions. Egypt was a prison before Moses led his people out of bondage into the Promised Land.

For Christians, death was a prison before Jesus broke out of his tomb after three days and nights and was resurrected. A prison severely limits a person's interactions with the world, so it's no wonder that the prison experiences of ordinary people lend themselves to explorations and revelations of the spirit. For example, Boethius wrote *The Consolation of Philosophy* in prison after he was put there by King Theodorus the Great in 524 AD. Boethius had been one of the king's most trusted advisors, but Fortune suddenly frowned on him (the story goes that it was through no fault of his own) and changed his situation. Since he was a Christian as well as a classical scholar, his unjust imprisonment casts doubt on a divine ordering of things. Why, he wonders, would God punish a good man?

To dramatize this conflict, Boethius imagines that Philosophy herself comes to him in his cell and addresses his doubts. Fame and wealth are transitory, she reminds him. If that is the case, Philosophy, unlike worldly securities and pleasures, is the one true good. In prison he discovers that happiness comes from within and that this inner strength or virtue triumphs over whatever Fortune can give and take away. But the insight is tied to the encounter he had with the emperor who imprisoned him; the shock of the emperor's power opened his eyes to a radical freedom he previously hadn't seen.

There are many examples from different spiritual traditions that advocate for the power of mind the way Philosophy does for Boethius in his cell. Consider, for example, the story about two barefoot travelers who had to walk a hundred miles over an uneven and rocky country. One of the travelers wanted a road built. The other suggested that they find shoes to wear. Both suggestions solve the problem, but they also highlight two very different ways of dealing with the difficulties and the pain of living in the world. The one involves a huge expense of men and resources directed by a large and impersonal government while the other requires only a minimal change in how the travelers walk on the earth that's easily within their own powers to achieve.[6]

The consolation of Philosophy and the simple solution of the barefoot traveler point to the sovereign power of the human mind. As William

Blake's poem "London" movingly suggests, the mind is at the heart of the matter in that the mind alone can unfasten the "mind-forged" manacle of viewing one's life as a holding cell. Blake's famous phrase points out, however, that the mind is also the agent that fashions the manacle in the first place.[7] Sometimes, therefore, the mind has a strange, vested interest in maintaining a reign of alienation and fear.

The nihilistic aggression and depression that afflict some young people at a critical point in their development point to the flip side of every mind's sovereign freedom. In these cases, the mind's sovereignty becomes a critical challenge not just for a teacher or a parent, but also for the young person in question. No amount of persuasion can change a mind that is dead set against being changed; an idea that is fixed in the mind can be as hermetically sealed up as the gold in Fort Knox. An idea, which is strangely valued as the person would value life itself, is his or her "precious."[8] Despite the efforts of parents and other authority figures to solve the problem, subjective opinions, even when they are dead wrong or plainly unhelpful, can still rule the lives of human beings. A person who embraces an aggressive nihilism or who falls into a depression has drawn a conclusion from what he or she knows about the world. It is not particularly difficult for this person to see life as a meaningless holding cell, and if, in the modern way of thinking about it, the world and knowledge of it exist apart from the observer as an isolated factual thing, like a lonely planet in deep space, there is nothing to be done. The observer is trapped in an unpleasant and hopeless existence. Recent incidents have shown that a person like this may seek an end to it in violence against himself and others.

What can science do for a person like this? Can these negative thoughts be resolved with talk therapy and chemical suppressants? From what I can gather, consciousness is a field of study that continues to elude the grip of science. So how can a doctor or a scientist observe or cure that which is still a mystery and which, some say, may not even exist. A person suffering from alienation and depression may well be helped by the ministrations of modern medicine, but the therapies and their effects are often a matter of trial and error. They lack the precision that's the hallmark of science.

Comedy as Insight

Anyone who has ever experienced a day of doubt and confusion probably has also experienced that these dark states can be dispelled by a glimpse of the truth or a loving touch. Due to the transforming power of these experiences, people eventually devised literary works to celebrate and transmit them. Odysseus' epic journey home after the Trojan War illustrates the pattern.

The fictional world of *The Odyssey* is surrounded and sometimes immersed in water, a liquid, changeable stuff that's similar to the liquid, streaming character of the human mind. The otherworldly character of the one-eyed men, the many-headed monster, and the beautiful women who have supernatural powers add to an impression that the dreaming mind is at the center of things. This worldview has much in common with the subjectivity of nineteenth- and twentieth-century Romanticism. For Homer, though, there most certainly is a world "out there," and it is governed by definite laws. He builds his poem around the tension between the dreaming mind and insight into the power of these timeless laws. In the end, the world is not a subjective dream or a malleable bit of clay that can be interpreted or molded by a man into any shape he desires. The world, like the human body, has a structure that limits human behavior. People who force the body to do what it can't do end up getting hurt, and in this world people who act on the basis of a counterfactual dream end up getting injured by those powers that obey natural laws. Sometimes, therefore, the wake-up call is painful.[9]

The suitors in *The Odyssey* vividly illustrate Homer's focus on the mind, its missteps, and the suffering that comes from misconceptions. While Odysseus is absent for twenty years fighting at Troy and striving to return home, hundreds of young men court his wife, Penelope, year after year lusting after her beauty and his kingdom, lounging around his palace, and wasting his food, his wine, and the labor of his servants. It is convenient for them to assume that Odysseus is dead. It allows them to take advantage of his absence by throwing a nonstop party at his expense. Since the reader knows that Odysseus is in fact alive, we observe that the suitors are living in a dream. They flagrantly abuse the rites of hospitality, enforced by Zeus himself, that constitute the heart of their social order, and they compound this abuse by trying to assassinate Odysseus' son. As sure as night follows day, these men suffer for their misconceptions. Their mistakes are willful, mental errors, not accidents. The suitors stubbornly claim that Odysseus is dead without real proof that this is so, and they disregard as well sensible, well-established customs to boast that might makes right. They learn the hard way that their boasts are empty and powerless to save them when Odysseus, stringing his bow effortlessly, reveals himself in the doorway of the only exit.[10] The suitors recognize him in the instant of an arrow's flight, a fatal reckoning for a lifetime of folly. The nature of things turns tables on each one as if to say, "Rather than telling tales about life and death, taste it now in the flesh."[11]

The suitors are only a part of Homer's design; they are not the focus.[12] In the end, the story is about Odysseus reestablishing order in his kingdom, and it leads us to a bracing conclusion: tragedy is not our business.[13] Our business is to learn, as Odysseus does, what the laws are, what happens when you cross them, and what the chances are that the whole adventure will end in a night of pillow talk in bed with the one you love. In both the works attributed to him, Homer's depiction of the gods suggests that even they had only a vague knowledge of the laws, and often enough they have to learn (the hard way) what they are. These gods don't stay on Mount Olympus where they can observe dispassionately. Instead, they get involved, they act and react with people and with other gods, and sometimes they are outsmarted or made to look like complete fools.

Even though they may go about it in different ways, science and comic literature seek the continuing and the prospering of human life by describing reality accurately. Once the laws of a scientific inquiry are established, as in Einstein's famous equation showing the relationship of energy to matter, that knowledge can then be applied to a practical use. Just as science does, *The Odyssey* teaches in narrative form that there is a world out there with definite laws. Unlike hard science, though, which concerns itself with abstract, physical laws, Homer's tale describes how people *interact* with natural laws, like those that govern the behaviors of host and guest. The tale would show that people who defy those laws pay a heavy price, but it makes the case as well that they suffer because they have willfully substituted their own ideas about the laws in place of the real ones. Here's the comic opening, for it holds out the possibility that the mind lies at the root of virtue (strength) and a good life. The life of the mind, as Philosophy tells Boethius, is at the heart of the matter.

Knowledge, we have been taught, is power, so it's no wonder that people lay siege to knowledge the way the suitors lay siege to Odysseus' wife and kingdom. Success in every form of work depends on knowledge. Even as a person revels in obtaining the power that knowledge confers, once possessed it can have an effect of alienation. The knower is now different, for example, from those who don't know. As it is for kings and presidents, this kind of power has its perks and its perils. The upside of knowledge is obvious and needs no public relations campaign, but knowledge that is false has a dangerous downside as the suitors find out when they confront the living Odysseus.

A mind that prides itself and basks in the power of knowledge is dangerously vulnerable to those times when the brightness of knowing goes dark, and the mind knows only nihilism, aggression, and despair. This knowledge tends to be confused with what people call facts, and the power of knowledge to destroy a person's will to live tends to be excused or ignored by those attached to the power of knowledge. The aggressive nihilism or depression of a loved one, close friend, or coworker, though, is difficult to ignore. Unhappy themselves, they are hard to be around. Still, the idea that one is powerless to dispel the fog and the weight of alienation may have an odd sort of attraction for them. The idea that "life sucks and then you die" is a depressing thought, but those who put that message on their bumper must derive a certain pleasure in doing so. The negative effect of the gloomy picture apparently is outweighed by the pleasure of certainty and of the emotions that color and dramatize the situation. This is why soap operas are so popular even though they tell very sad stories. They exercise the emotions and keep the excitement of them strong.

Comedy takes a different and, you could say, a counterintuitive path, for the business of comedy is to pull the rug out from underneath what we know. It finds that universal banana peel and sets it in the way of the unmindful pedestrian. In the days of vaudeville, the pedestrian is reading the newspaper as he is walking on the sidewalk. These days he could be reading his BlackBerry, but the situation is the same. The pedestrian has the idea, even if the words are painting a gloomy picture, that he lives in a world that's secure and full of meaning as he absorbs the glib confidence of the writer, of the machine, and of the whole media universe. His reading, however, has distracted him from the reality of the banana peel. As in this little miniature, comedy paints pictures of self-deception, of someone living in a dream.

Now let's picture our pedestrian, his foot swept from under him and his body suspended over the earth. For that moment of suspension, released from the ideas that distracted and imprisoned him, he inhabits a brave new world. He has briefly glimpsed that the idea he was reading left an important matter out. The nature of things has supplied a wordless dramatization of the fact that ego, which is attachment to the idea, is limited. In a simple weightless gesture, the confinement of ego attachment gives way to a larger intelligence. The experience of my pedestrian is a slapstick bit of fun, but it shares with *The Divine Comedy* insight into the nature and the effects of attachment. With Virgil as his guide, Dante takes his reader around and around in an exhaustive and exhausting survey of the subject. Before Dante can rise to the light, his comic quest has to begin with insight into all the different kinds of holding cells. Chaucer's "The

Knight's Tale" follows a less elaborate but similar path.

Since people are instinctively attached to the idea of knowing things, there's resistance to the confusion at the heart of comedy. The action of a comic narrative tends to strip away the idea of a character, which, by extinguishing the light of the idea, leaves that character in the dark, but this action is what lights the way forward to health and happiness. Chaucer begins "The Knight's Tale" by having Duke Theseus undergo the experience. Looking back to where this introduction began, I equated a comic vision to the light of clear seeing and wisdom, but paradoxically that light only goes on when a comic protagonist finds himself in the dark. This is why Homer and other seers from ancient times such as Tiresias are depicted as blind.

Like Homer, Chaucer and Shakespeare have represented a realistic prospect for the continuing and prospering of human life, and this vision establishes a timeless form for government. Government first and foremost means self-government, and self-government derives from insight into the limited nature of ideas. The comic protagonist has to experience for himself the overwhelming greatness and the constancy of what he doesn't know. This is true whether a person is a teacher, a policeman, a mechanic, a businessman, or a senator. Like the slipup does for the pedestrian or a fall to earth does for Dante, comedy reminds us of the ground under our feet, the reality of things-as-they-are. Without an idea's enchantment—for example, the idea that we know enough to keep ourselves safe without particularly paying attention to the world as it is— we find ourselves among real people and objects and can act in accordance with them as-they-are. The ancient Hebrews used to call a circumspection about what we know "fear of the Lord." For the purpose of my text here, I am calling it "insight" and "wisdom."

The comic narratives that have come down to us from past generations outline an archetypal pattern. Chaucer recognized it as the movement of the heart and mind from attachment (*cupiditas* in Latin) to insight (*caritas* in Latin). We also learn from him that if we are going to study this path, it's best to start with reality, with things-as-they-are in the world, and not with abstract and otherworldly speculations about the goal. Because insight is an active presence of mind, not a fantasy or a program that can be learned by rote, it is difficult to transmit. If we would study this path, we need the strictness of the material world and the richness of our folly to sustain the work. Chaucer understood that ego and insight are complementary parts of the whole process so he begins his pilgrimage to Canterbury concretely with characters who are attached to material power and material things. Not only does he understand the pattern, he presents it to his reader with vivid and entertaining details that we can enjoy six hundred years later. A gifted storyteller, he portrays the essence of a character or a situation in a few incisive and timeless images. It used to surprise my students that a medieval writer, whose Christian culture would appear to be exclusively concerned with spiritual teachings about the world to come, told explicit, bawdy stories about ordinary men and women.

Because comedy points to an experience and not an abstract fact, learning the pattern is just the first step.[14] We can only enter a comic world when, like the pedestrian horizontal to the pavement, we wonder at the limit of our own idea. Comedy shows us the outward shape of wisdom as characters go through the experience, but maybe, when we take our own comic falls, as we do almost every day, we'll recognize and appreciate the pattern.

THE KNIGHT'S TALE

Chapter one:
The Way To Canterbury

Vermeer's *The Love Letter*

Framing Devices as Thematic Settings

Chaucer has used the medieval devotional practice of a pilgrimage to frame his picture of the human comedy. The verb "frame" suggests several meanings, both of which are important to my theme. In the play within a play at the end of *A Midsummer Night's Dream* Pyramus finds the bloody mantle of his Thisby in the place where they were supposed to meet. He takes the blood as proof of her death and cries out:

> *O wherefore, nature, didst thou lions frame,*
>
> *Since lion vile hath here deflowered my dear?*

William Blake emphasizes the same word in his poem "The Tyger":

> *Tyger! Tyger! burning bright*
>
> *In the forests of the night,*
>
> *What immortal hand or eye*
>
> *Dare frame thy fearful symmetry?*

In these examples the word frame means "create" as when builders frame a structural shell in the making of a house. But the word can also mean "limit"; when an artist frames his picture, the frame signals where the picture ends. Chaucer frames his picture by limiting it to the going to and the coming from Canterbury of his pilgrims. Their past and their future, except as they are suggested in "The Prologue" or in their tale, are not recorded. This limits the scope of the picture, but at the same time makes it possible for him to create it. The limitation gives it a basic structure.

As I am interpreting it here, the word frame contains within it the paradox of a constraint that resolves into freedom, and this characterization of the word links it to comedy as a way of framing or picturing human experience. Pyramus' question quoted above points to the most basic constraint of human life: if not a lion or a tyger then eventually something will limit, like a picture frame, the life we hold so dear. Because Pyramus sees no life without his Thisby, he runs a sword through his heart. Comedy puts the story of his death into a larger context. The audience has just been shown, but Pyramus has not, that his dear ran away before the lion could kill her. Because he has a limited point of view, Pyramus mistakes, for Thisby lives. The poor boy ended his life based on an assumption, but he lives on (for here I am writing about him) to serve as a wake-up call for those who take his story to heart. His story may yet save from a pointless death one who still lives.

Chaucer also frames his picture with the consciousness of a single, limited point of view. The reader can only access the tales through the mind of Chaucer's persona, a rather simple rhymester. This persona joins a cross section of English society at a London inn where they all decide to travel to Canterbury together and amuse themselves on the way by telling tales. I call this consciousness Chaucer the Pilgrim to distinguish him from Chaucer the Author. I have argued in the introduction that a comic worldview is significantly different from a tragic or a nihilistic world view. The device of a first-person narrator humanizes this concept of a worldview or point of view without having to explain itself at all. The device gives the reader direct access only to what the persona is thinking and therefore limits what the reader knows to this window on the world.[15]

As in my illustration of the pedestrian unaware of the banana peel, a point of view may leave important matters out. In other words, Chaucer's first-person narration represents or imitates the limited perception of Everyman. Despite the fact that as readers we depend entirely on the persona's point of view, a master of the device like Chaucer can make the reader aware that there is a significant blind spot in his persona's thinking. Because he's a limited point of view, Chaucer the Pilgrim sometimes misjudges the character of his fellow travelers, seeing them as they would like to see themselves rather than as they are. For example, he calls the Pardoner "a noble ecclesiast," and it would appear that he means what he says. But the evidence, unwittingly supplied by Chaucer the Pilgrim, demonstrates beyond a shadow of a doubt that the Pardoner is a fraud and a blight on the Church.[16] In Chaucer's hands, a limited point of view expresses an essential insight of comedy—no one individual can know everything.

The pilgrimage also serves to frame their stories with a purpose. The pilgrims' physical goal is Canterbury Cathedral, but they have unspoken, spiritual goals as well. Chaucer's lines about this are true for seekers of any time or place who are moved by juices percolating in the ground, in plants, in animals, and in themselves to come to life once more in the spring:

Then people long to go on pilgrimages

And palmers long to seek the stranger strands

Of far-off saints, hallowed in sundry lands,

And specially, from every shire's end

Of England, down to Canterbury they wend

To seek the holy blissful martyr, quick

To give his help to them when they were sick.[17]

We don't have to be a medieval Christian to identify with the purpose of a pilgrimage. Everyone seeks to be whole physically and mentally. A pilgrimage to make us whole is like the quest for home in *The Odyssey*; we're at home and happy when we're healthy. Some look for health in far-off places like Jerusalem, and others seek it out in a nearby town like Canterbury. Some may look in a score of city centers and rural retreats before they find that a strong will to lead a good life has been sleeping in the same bed with them in all the places they have ever been.

Chaucer's Diagnosis and Prescription

Once the frame is established and once we have read through all the pilgrims' stories, we get a better sense of Chaucer's structure. It reminds me of a great cathedral like that at Canterbury which is lofty in its overall design and is composed of precise individual parts—like stone figures of saints that frame the great doors of an entrance, gargoyles that serve as gutters for rain water, stain glass pictures that depict scenes from scripture, chapels of individual families all along the aisles and around the front, and carvings in the wooden pews of the choir. It's a building that's been put together over time out of different pieces, some fearful like a crucifixion and others comforting like a Madonna and child. There's an image from moviemaking that helps me to make my point. To show how the movie was made, the creators sometimes reveal the different "takes" on it—Take One, Take Two, Take Three, and so on. This is the overall effect of Chaucer's design. Each pilgrim provides a different "take" on the world, but the structure as a whole directs our attention to the role that the mind plays in our health for better or for worse. The many mental "hang-ups" of the characters and the storytellers lead us step by step over many stories to an appreciation for Chaucer's general conclusion about the problem: the narrowing of obsessive thought, he observes, is bad for our health.

Chaucer is not a doctor, but his conclusion may be difficult to dispute. It's a medical fact that obsession can lead not only to mental illness but to physical disorders. For example, obsessive-compulsive thought about food is driving the epidemic of obesity and all the health problems that stem from being overweight; obsessive-compulsive habits of working and playing lead to stress that puts millions at risk for high blood pressure and heart problems; people who obsess over social and political issues can fall into a constant and debilitating fight or flight response to the world; and men and women worldwide, fed with media images of power, success, beauty, and passionate relationships, suffer crippling feelings of inadequacy, isolation, and depression while involved with those pictures to which they obsessively attach.

"The Knight's Tale" develops the overall theme of health and wholeness by telling the story of two boys who have been sentenced to life imprisonment and who eventually pass their days and nights obsessing over a beautiful young woman. This plot device conveys Chaucer's insight that obsessive thought is a prison, and it ties his story directly to *The Consolation of Philosophy* which was one of his favorite books. Just as Philosophy teaches Boethius that the life of the mind is infinitely larger than his prison cell, Chaucer's tale sets up a narrative structure to show that the freedom of the two young men depends not on external factors like prison walls and an all-powerful duke but on a comic insight of mind and heart.

When I first designed the AP course in literature, I began with Chaucer largely because I wanted to start the year with shorter and more lighthearted pieces. I worried that high school students might be put off by studying an author who wrote in medieval times, but my concern turned out to be unfounded. For all the years that I taught the course, Chaucer's tales were consistently the most popular unit we did. The longer I did the course, the more I appreciated his tales as the perfect starting point for the course's overall theme—the pattern in comic literature that depicts how a character is freed from the confinement of a limited idea. To that end, I used Chaucer to introduce the literary concept of irony, for irony is a device specifically designed to reveal the limited nature of ideas.

Since I had taught junior high students for many years before getting the AP assignment, I discovered over time that less is more for young people learning how to read and write. Instead of learning many things badly, I wanted my students to learn a few basic things thoroughly, and so I focused our study of Chaucer on irony. The characters of Chaucer's tales have their ideas relentlessly exploded in plots that are built around situational and dramatic irony, and I brought these moments to the students' attention over and over until they could easily recognize the pattern themselves. The recognition of the pattern for Chaucer's characters and for those who read them is so important to the author's purpose that I liken it to the pilgrimage itself. The light that reveals the limited and illusory nature of ideas illuminates the way to Canterbury. If the goal is wholeness and health and the sickness is obsessive thought, these narratives would persuade us that a wake-up call can break an obsession and let in the real world.

A Life That Goes in a Different Direction

The opening of "The Knight's Tale" is similar to that of *The Odyssey*. In both a triumphant general sets out for home after war in a foreign land, but before they can return to their homelands, they are knocked off course. Right from the start, the story throws the meaning of victory into question by the uncertainty and confusion of their homecoming. In "The Knight's Tale" Duke Theseus traveled from Athens to Scythia with a troop of armed men. There he defeated the Amazons by force and married their queen, Hippolyta. He then sets out for home "with solemn pomp and glory... victorious and with minstrelsy." This procession is a little like the springtime pilgrimage described in "The Prologue" of *The Canterbury Tales*, which is the actual setting for all of these stories. It's a happy time for high and low, the duke and his princely party as well as all his knights and their retainers. It's a time of healing in the warmth of the south after the sickness of war in the wintery mountains of Scythia. Theseus, however, is stopped in his tracks before he can enter the town where he undoubtedly hopes to consummate his triumph. Chaucer has put the stopping here at the beginning of the first tale to serve as the archetype of a wake-up call, and it's much like the time I was stopped in the midst of the vagaries of youth by the prospect of becoming a father.[18] In both cases, the stopping led eventually to a life that went in a different direction. Here's how it happens in "The Knight's Tale":

This Duke I mentioned, ere alighting down

And on the very outskirts of the town

In all felicity and height of pride

Became aware, casting an eye aside,

That kneeling on the highway, two by two,

A company of ladies were in view

All clothed in black, each pair in proper station

Behind the other. And such lamentation

And cries they uttered, it was past conceiving

The world had ever heard such noise of grieving,

Nor did they hold their misery in check

Till they grasped bridle at his horse's neck.

"Who may you be that, at my coming, so

Perturb my festival with cries of woe?"

Said Theseus. "Do you grudge the celebration

Of these my honours with your lamentation?

Who can have injured you or who offended?

And tell me if the matter may be mended

And why it is that you are clothed in black?"

Theseus at first shows irritation that he has been stopped. The direction of his life is for Athens and for a comfortable marriage bed after the wars; these women in black pose an obstacle to that purpose. To his credit, though, Theseus quickly recognizes his anger. After he questions whether they begrudge his happiness, he openly wonders whether the significance of the situation may lie more with them than with him. This ability to question his initial idea and to consider that he might not see the whole situation is the true "stopping." It's a narrative emblem or a picture of comic wisdom and true government.

The ladies' spokeswoman boldly answers the charge:

"O Sir, whom Fortune has made glorious

In conquest and is sending home victorious,

We do not grudge your glory in our grief

But rather beg your mercy and relief.

Have pity on our sorrowful distress!

Some drop of pity, in your nobleness,

On us unhappy women let there fall!

For sure there is not one among us all

That was not once a duchess or a queen,

Though wretches now, as may be truly seen,

Thanks be to Fortune and her treacherous wheel

That suffers no estate on earth to feel

Secure, and, waiting on your presence, we,

Here at the shrine of Goddess Clemency,

Have watched a fortnight for this very hour.

Help us, my Lord, it lies within your power.

The two speeches, that of Theseus and the spokeswoman, create an ironic pattern that Chaucer employs throughout this tale and all the others. Duke Theseus initially suspects the ladies' motive for stopping him and his victorious procession. His anger slips out when he suggests that they have done it out of envy or spite. This is his idea. The narrative, however, provides a larger context that explodes or nullifies his idea with the truth of the situation. Theseus, due to a limited point of view, has formed his idea in ignorance.

The spokeswoman addresses his charge of envy or spitefulness with moving grace and dignity. Unlike the duke, she does not accuse him of any bad faith in the way he has addressed them. Instead, she acknowledges his sovereign power to think and to do as he pleases. Nevertheless, she makes it clear to him that she is negotiating with him on the basis of equality. She and all the others are of royal estate, but Fortune has brought them low. Fortune, she reminds him, has the power to make or break a person, and this fact of human existence is a great leveler. We are all the same because everyone can only have a limited point of view, and this makes us ignorant of many things including the whims of Fortune. Thus, even mighty Theseus is not secure. Before she describes the specifics of her case, the spokeswoman wins the argument by breaching the wall of separation Duke Theseus put between them in his initial response. She proves to be master of the situation because she is entirely mistress of herself. She lives within the limits of her own power, which conveys the power of a self-possessed being. The point of equilibrium she establishes between them allows his sovereignty without relinquishing her own, and it's at this point, the center of good government in any time and in any place, that she addresses him.

By showing that a character can have the presence of mind to sense the limits of the mind, Chaucer establishes the pattern and the hope whereby Everyman is relieved from the distortions and the ill effects of obsessive thinking. In addition to opening up a path to health, these speeches taken together show that good government is grounded in this most basic form of self-government. People don't see it very often, but when they do it's instantly recognizable. The widow's example instructs Theseus that good government means respect for the sovereign power of the other even as she respects her own. It isn't a law that we have to faithfully memorize and train ourselves to obey. It's a comic insight that's embodied for Theseus in the experience we have just witnessed. By seeing things clearly without the distortions of obsessive envy or spite, the widow sets the standard, and their relationship is governed accordingly.

Having established a basis for their relationship, the spokeswoman then lays out the particulars of her case:

I, wretched queen, that weep aloud my woe,

Was wife to King Capaneus long ago

That died at Thebes, accursed be the day!

And we in our disconsolate array

That make this sorrowful appeal to pity

Lost each a husband in that fatal city

During the siege, for so it came to pass.

Now old King Creon---O alas, alas!---

The Lord of Thebes, grown cruel in his age

And filled with foul iniquity and rage,

For tyranny and spite as I have said

Does outrage on the bodies of our dead,

On all our husbands, for when they were slain

Their bodies were dragged out onto the plain

Into a heap, and there, as we have learnt,

They neither may have burial nor be burnt,

But he makes dogs devour them, in scorn.

The situation is not about the widows; it's about the outrage practiced on the bodies of their husbands. The anger of Theseus is a minor lapse and short-lived. There is no evidence for spitefulness in what the ladies did. For true and unnatural spite the queen of King Capaneus offers up the story of the tyrant Creon whose treatment of the dead reveals how he regarded others when they were alive. Alive and dead he denies them their sentience, the fact that they are or had been conscious beings and not stones. In a tyrant's country everyone and everything is determined and frozen by the tyrant's ideas. Like the transformations often found in myth where people turn into trees and women with snakes in their hair turn men into stones, people become, in Creon's perception, the building materials for his ideas. But stones are used for making a megalith, not the bodies of people. By wielding the power of an idea that forever freezes them in place, Creon terrorizes his enemies or potential enemies with a keen and cold blooded intellect.

The abuse of a dead body, however, crosses a line, breaks a natural law that has been observed by ordinary people for thousands of years, and comedy is about the recognition of these laws. Human beings in any period are instinctively revolted by abuse of the living and the dead. The newspapers and news reports on TV are filled with examples of individual and state-sponsored cruelty. It's a fact of life that fills us with dread, but it awakens within most a will to resist. It's why the bunkers of petty tyrants and great dictators have a long history of eventually becoming their prisons instead of a showcase. For Hitler, the ground underneath his chancellery became a place of execution as armies closed in on him from all directions. The totalitarian regimes of the twentieth century swallowed up whole countries and continents and governed remorselessly through terror and genocide, but they failed despite the enormous power they briefly enjoyed. Too many millions died in the wars, too many innocents were shipped off by train to camps and then disappeared, too many counterrevolutionaries were executed, and too many were exterminated when they wouldn't relocate from their homelands in massive reconstructions of the social fabric. Too many people and nations were willing to fight them.

On February 25, 1956, when the truth of these matters couldn't be suppressed any longer, the men who ran the USSR had to denounce their long dead murderer-in-chief Josef Stalin. Along with other leaders of that time like Hitler and Mao and like his tyrant brother Creon, Stalin seemed determined to make the largest pile of dead bodies the world had ever seen as a tribute to his government, a megalith of death for the ages. Once Khrushchev denounced him, Stalin's successors found a new place for his embalmed remains outside the Kremlin wall. Even they showed a little respect and didn't feed his body to dogs and birds like Creon did.

I use horrific examples from the twentieth century to make the case that there's a limit to what a government can do in order to effectively govern human beings. It could be argued that this is too obvious a case. For some, to say that a totalitarian regime will fail is no more difficult than predicting that someone who falls from a fifth-story window will probably break an arm or a leg or worse. Nevertheless, these regimes came into existence, and my generation grew up in the aftermath of those slaughters. My argument employs these examples for the simple reason that, less than a hundred years ago, supposedly rational leaders of great nations thought they could rule their nations without reference to the ordering of things being discussed here. They thought they could live by the rules they made up and which were enforced by a police state. The failure of totalitarian governments may make a gross and lumbering sort of argument that there are limits to what a government can do, but they also make a gross and lumbering argument for the power of blind willfulness. This is the power that comedy would break.

Theseus somehow manages to be open in mind and heart, and this represents what a tyrant cannot or will not be. Creon's behavior makes him an outlaw, and in a comic world where people learn the limit of ideas, it's important as well to learn the limit of what can be tolerated. By his own actions Creon proves that negotiations with him are impossible. As a human being, he should get a decent burial after his death, but his grave belongs outside the wall that defines where people live.

Theseus' willingness to question his own idea is like a lamp lighting the way. It's ironic that this light is lit in his encounter with the blackness and the lamentations of the ladies. Before they seize his bridle, the brilliance of his victory illuminates his progress. He rides to Athens with his bride beside him on a wave of power, medieval pageantry, and minstrelsy. It's no wonder he recoils from that which is so unsuited to a wedding. After absorbing the blackness of the ladies and their tale of unnatural cruelty, he cannot be the conquering horseman and the blithe bridegroom that he had been moments before. Theseus thought he was a mighty conqueror, but through the ladies' eyes he sees that the world is much larger than his immediate happiness:

> *The Duke, who felt a pang of pity start*
>
> *At what they spoke, dismounted from his steed;*
>
> *He felt his heart about to break indeed,*
>
> *Seeing how piteous and disconsolate*
>
> *They were, that once had been of high estate!*
>
> *He raised them in his arms and sought to fill*
>
> *Their hearts with comfort and with kind good will,*
>
> *And swore on oath that as he was true knight,*
>
> *So far as it should lie within his might,*
>
> *He would take vengeance on this tyrant King,*
>
> *This Creon, till the land of Greece should ring*
>
> *With how he had encountered him and served*

The monster with the death he had deserved.

Instantly then and with no more delay,

He turned and with his banners in display

Made off for Thebes with all his host beside,

For not a step to Athens would he ride,

Nor take his ease so much as half a day,

But marched into the night upon his way.

The founder of a comic world, it turns out, must get off his high horse on occasion to embrace uncertainty and suffering. The comic world is not a fantasyland for pleasure. The home Theseus sought isn't a place that's fixed and secure. Home means doing what has to be done, for he can't go home until it's done. Without a moment's hesitation Theseus transforms his intention, changes his direction, and rides off to prosecute a war against the tyrant.

This opening of "The Knight's Tale" frames the argument that will be repeated over and over throughout all the tales. Even though it's a story about pagan Greece, the author is describing the way to Canterbury. For Theseus the journey takes him to the wars in Scythia, to the gates of Athens, and then away again to the fields around Thebes, yet the whole meaning of his pilgrimage is compressed into a single moment of insight. Something, a wake-up call that's the catalyst for the unearned luck that Robin refers to at the end of *A Midsummer Night's Dream*, penetrates his preconceived idea about the purpose of his journey and sets him free to see and to hear the people that make up the situation. This happens in an instant, and then the way is clear. Dismounted from his high horse and guided by the direct perception of things, Theseus no longer depends on a habitual expectation but "marched into the night upon his way."

Chapter Two:
Everyman's Story

Frontispiece from edition of *Everyman* published by
John Skot, c. 1530

The Birth of Ego

"Ego" refers to what human beings have wrestled with for thousands of years—a person's awareness of selfhood. At least from the time that the story of Adam and Eve was first told, human beings have associated this consciousness of self with the falling into a constraint and the alienation described in the Introduction. When I was growing up and going to school in the fifties and sixties, psychoanalysis and Sigmund Freud's definitions of ego were all the rage. From a child's perspective, it appeared that Freud had unearthed or invented for the first time the natural laws of the human psyche. Over forty years later the psychoanalytic craze of that time looks more like a collective swoon onto the couch or as if science personified was vigorously patting itself on the back and taking credit for what it alone could uncover. This is also just an impression.

It might be an anachronism to interpret the events and images of a medieval tale in terms of ego when this concept would not be invented for another three hundred years, but just because the concept as Freud defined it is relatively new (in Latin ego is the personal pronoun "I") doesn't mean that the phenomenon it refers to had gone unnoticed before then. Freud's definition of ego is the heart of an extremely complex theory whereas these comic texts define it less abstractly and quite simply as attachment to an idea. In comedy ego is not the reality principle. Reality is reality, and, as we see over and over in *The Canterbury Tales*, ego limits and distorts a person's perception of things-as-they are.

Chaucer begins with Theseus, for the full implications of the tale lie with him and his development. Since everyone's story properly begins with ego, Theseus is not exempt from it, but he quickly recovers from his benighted indictment of the ladies to find his way in the dark toward Thebes. The whole sequence of events is a quick introduction to what Theseus himself will later refer to as an "experience" that helps him to understand and to describe the comic realm he would establish. Just as Dante spends one-third of *The Divine Comedy* in an inferno of frustrated desire before moving on to more habitable places, Chaucer next introduces

Palamon and Arcite into the story in order to describe in detail the birth and development of ego. His method is a little like putting the subject under a microscope or filming it in slow motion long before these technologies were available.

Like the widows, Palamon and Arcite have suffered from the misconceptions of Creon, Ego's king, for he has made them fight in a losing cause. They were on his side, and as such they are his creatures. Their side lost, though, primarily because Theseus took it upon himself to deal with Creon on a chosen field outside Thebes:

> And to speak briefly of so great a thing,
>
> He conquered Creon there, the Theban king,
>
> And slew him manfully, as became a knight,
>
> In open battle...

In the aftermath of the battle pillagers had a busy night:

> And so befell among the heaps they found,
>
> Thrust through with bloody wounds upon the ground,
>
> Two pale young knights there, lying side by side,
>
> Wearing the self-same arms in blazoned pride.
>
> Of these Arcita was the name of one,
>
> That of the other was Palamon;
>
> And they were neither fully quick nor dead.
>
> By coat of arms and crest upon the head
>
> The heralds knew, for all the filth and mud,

That they were princes of the Royal Blood;

Two sisters of the House of Thebes had borne them.

Out of the heap these pillagers have torn them

And gently carried them to Theseus' tent.

The pillagers are unusual midwives, tearing out of the great heap of war these babes, the strange fruit of war and fear. The hundreds of recent murders, the grisly task, the night fog, the gore, and the torchlight of flickering impressions provide perfect atmospherics for the appearance of a ghost which, like the knights, is "neither fully quick nor dead." The characteristic of being neither fully quick nor dead also describes the nature of fear. In itself, fear is not a creature, a living thing. It's a feeling rooted in a lifeless, bodiless idea, but the feeling and the idea live in the creature who experiences it.[19]

The babes of war and fear have little to distinguish them other than different names. They are princes of the Royal Blood equally covered with mud and filth. Like newborns, the distinction of a name and title is less important than the fact that they live at all, newly brought forth from a netherworld. Without their participation in the matter, Theseus condemns them to life imprisonment; he wants to be done with the constant threat from Thebes. When the boys awaken from the blackout of neither life nor death, they are conscious of themselves in prison.

Let the world take note: we have just witnessed the birth of ego. Others might refer to it as "consciousness" or "self-consciousness." He's the little guy that a modern philosopher calls "the ghost in the machine,"[20] and images like this remind us that thinkers and writers in the West have wondered for centuries about that which animates a human body and whether the soul of a human being participates with the Holy Ghost. Palamon and Arcite have had a brush with death. As it breathes its noxious, mortal spell on them, the conscious self of each young man awakens. It has run into something external to itself that is cold, hard, and confining.

As an aside, I add that this is an experience adolescents know well. It's Everyman's story. Young people touched for the first time by an awareness of mortality lose the openness and freedom of movement they enjoyed as children and retreat to a holding cell of self. Chaucer makes a basic issue available by means of a straightforward and down-to-earth narrative. No wonder he was so popular with my students even if he wrote over six hundred years ago.

The effect of the situation on the prisoners, however, is not so happy:

And in a tower, in grief and anguish lay

Arcite and Palamon, beyond all doubt

For ever, for no gold could buy them out.

The tower looms as a primary fact, and, for the prisoners trapped inside, an obsession with the walls around them characterizes the first flush of self-consciousness. From the terms of the judgment imposed on them, it would appear that ego is a life sentence. As they do in the life of an adolescent, these walls play a leading role in Chaucer's tale and Shakespeare's play—so much so that Shakespeare has Snug the Joiner play the part of Wall in the Pyramus and Thisby production at the end of his play.

Ego and Love

The story briefly relates that "year after year went by, day after day" for Palamon and Arcite in prison, implying in this summary account that the prisoners eventually accept their separation from the world. Even if they have accepted it, what happens next proves they still crave experience of the prison space. At this point experience will manifest as powerful feelings. For Palamon to fully be Palamon and Arcite to fully be Arcite, there must be that fateful and mutual glimpse of a beautiful young woman. As with an electric jolt, the sight of her will transform the dullness of their confinement into tingling currents of passionate love. Ego with a kick to it.

Chaucer the Author constructs a tableau where the whole situation—the setting as well as the narrative action—tells the story of attachment. From the point of view of the storyteller, it begins in freedom with Emily:

Year after year went by, day after day,

Until one morning in the month of May

Young Emily, that fairer was of mien

Than is the lily on its stalk of green,

And fresher in her colouring that strove

With early roses in a May-time grove

—I know not which was fairer of the two—

Ere it was day, as she was wont to do,

Rose and arrayed her beauty as was right,

For May will have no sluggardry at night...

She is described as the spirit of May newly released from winter. Unlike those mired in routine who struggle even during the day to stay awake, she is naturally alive and alert. In contrast with the monotony of Palamon and Arcite's confinement, her movements as well as her appearance convey the spontaneity and grace of one completely at home with herself and the world:

And in the garden at the sun's arising,

Hither and thither at her own devising,

She wandered gathering flowers, white and red,

To make a subtle garland for her head,

And like an angel sang a heavenly song.

Since the rest of the story will be determined by Emily's timeless beauty, my recreation of the narrative holds its breath for a moment to wonder at her. Maybe she's a little too good to be true. Maybe she's just an idea, a picture of freedom. It may be too much of a stock image for a modern reader accustomed to realism. For the most part we see her as an object the way an admirer might, but several details bring to life her own consciousness. The narrator tells us that she wanders "at her own devising" and gathers flowers "to make a subtle garland for her head." Here she comes alive in herself and not as a picture for someone else. Self-possessed, she moves with a graceful, unaccountable purpose, and that purpose celebrates and graces the head. The making of a garland is a traditional gesture, but coming as it does in a philosophical poem of great seriousness, the gesture here emphasizes her head as the source and guardian of her grace. If that's the case, then like Philosophy coming to Boethius in his cell she represents the power of the mind to release a prisoner from mind-forged manacles and walls.

Ironically her image in the garden will have the opposite effect on the prisoners locked up in the tower, for it sparks a violent obsession in Palamon and Arcite that lasts for many years. This is just one facet of the several ironies embedded in the scene. The most important irony involves a contrast between two points of view that is carefully built into the structure. My story about the pedestrian and the banana peel illustrates how this irony works. If that sidewalk scene were part of a vaudeville show, the audience would enjoy the larger view, for it would see the banana peel lying in the way of the pedestrian reading his BlackBerry. Writers use this device to dramatize the smallness of the idea that occupies the attention of characters like the pedestrian. The idea is too small, we know, because it leaves out the banana peel. In the garden scene of "The Knight's Tale" the storyteller has the larger point of view; he observes Emily in the dark even before the sun has come up and freely conveys his observations to the reader. For him and for us it's a continuous 360-degree view. We see her getting dressed, we see her going to the garden, and then we see her at leisure wandering around picking flowers. Even though it's a walled garden, she moves with a feeling of limitless space. Breaking in on her, the narrator suddenly introduces a much smaller point of view that interrupts the grace and freedom of what we have just witnessed. This smaller consciousness is represented by the tower where the boys are kept:

The great, grim tower-keep, so thick and strong,

Principal dungeon at the castle's core

Where the two knights, of whom I spoke before

And shall again, were shut, if you recall,

Was close adjoining to the garden wall

Where Emily chose her pleasures and adornings.

The organic beauty of the woman and the natural world now exist in tension with this fixed thing, so thick headed and ignorant, that some conqueror built, and the story now belongs to the tower and the fixed idea about to overwhelm the lives of Palamon and Arcite. For many years to come we will view Emily only from the point of view of the tower where the young men are kept. Once we view her only through their desire, the freedom we have witnessed in the garden fades from view; it reappears, tempered by all that has passed, only at the moment of Arcite's death. Nevertheless, these glimpses of health and freedom at the beginning and at the end frame everything in the tale like a lover's arms around her love.[21] Eventually, the whole experience with Emily has an effect similar to Philosophy's effect on Boethius in his cell, but the men's obsession with her first has to play itself out.

What does the world look like when viewed from the cell on top of the tower? The slenderest of openings there determines the mind of Palamon for years to come:

And so it happened on this May day morn,

Through a deep window set with many bars

Of mighty iron squared with massive spars,

He chanced on Emily to cast his eye...

In Puerto Rico I once walked through an old Spanish fortress that had a window similar to the one in the tower. The walls were over ten-feet thick so looking through the window was like looking through a long stationary tube at something. The view was significantly limited. In Palamon's case the deep window is also heavily screened with a grate, and he can see Emily only when she chances momentarily into the picture. Compared to the vastness and freedom of ordinary seeing, it is the barest of glimpses, but at that moment:

...he blenched and gave a cry

As though he had been stabbed, and to the heart.

Into even so slight a vision Palamon projects a desire as great as life itself. In this way the tableau instructs us about the nature of his passion. It is rooted in a lovely but ephemeral image. The great stone tower, the distance, and the limited visual and auditory impressions separate the lover from any real knowledge of Emily and the world she inhabits. Put this way, Palamon's passion is ridiculous, something out of a fairy tale or an asylum. Nevertheless, it is an accurate representation of ego as a passionate attachment to an image. This attachment is like the tower itself, a somewhat human figure that's been frozen onto a vast landscape filled with life.

Ego and Hate

To underscore and confirm that Palamon's experience reflects the way human beings are hardwired, within moments Arcite's passions are inflamed in the same way and by the same cause. As Palamon explains to his cousin why he cried out in pain, the image of Emily once more briefly comes into view:

Now as he spoke, Arcite chanced to see

This lady as she roamed there to and fro,

And at the sight, her beauty hurt him so

That if his cousin had felt the wound before,

Arcite was hurt as much as he, or more,

And with a deep and piteous sigh he said:

"The freshness of her beauty strikes me dead,

Hers that I see, roaming in yonder place!

Unless I gain the mercy of her grace,

Unless at least I see her day by day,

I am but dead. There is no more to say."

Arcite's words, heartfelt and as true as anything he has ever said, set him on a collision course with his cousin as each would possess the woman for himself. Just as Palamon's original glimpse of Emily in the garden illustrates the character and the nature of attachment, so Arcite's chance encounter illustrates the natural corollary of attachment: it ignites a passionate hatred for any obstacle that comes between the lover and his love. At the same time that they attach themselves to Emily, their mutual declarations of love will attach them equally to the idea that they have a rival.

Palamon immediately seizes on Arcite's words as the worse sort of bad faith and betrayal:

I trust you with my secrets, make no doubt,

Yet you would treacherously go about

To love my lady, whom I love and serve

And ever shall, till death cut my heart's nerve.

No, false Arcite! That you shall never do!

I loved her first and told my grief to you

As to the brother and the friend that swore

To further me, as I have said before,

So you are bound in honour as a knight

To help me, should it lie within your might;

Else you are false, I say, your honour vain!

The feeling is so real. To be betrayed by the one to whom you have confided the pain of your heart! Instantly, a cousin and comrade-in-arms becomes an enemy, and thus begins a battle that will last for many years.

Once again dramatic irony forces the reader to see the smallness of their idea and its lack of connection to the real world. The hatred they feel for each other, much like the passion they feel for Emily, is a projection. All this within seconds of glimpsing a girl impossibly out of reach and who is now "my lady!" Neither one has any real claim to the woman. They are incarcerated forever, and, as Theseus points out later, she doesn't even know they exist. Chaucer has constructed the scene to show that the whole drama is taking place in their heads. Also, their rivalry brings out a subtle but important irony about the desire for Emily that has implications for Everyman who has ever desired anything. A person can only desire that which he doesn't have so, even without a rival to complicate things, desire by definition implies an obstacle to its fulfillment.

Thanks to the way Chaucer has designed the different perspectives, insight into limited points of view now informs the scene for the reader whereas love and hate now contend to enliven the prison space of ego for Palamon and Arcite.

Ego and Ideas

Even though Palamon and Arcite, in the current phrase, "have no life" because of their confinement, once Emily appears on the scene things perk up for them. There's a buzz, some excitement. Contrasting their situation with Emily's freedom in the garden, however, we sense that a voyeur's perch high above affords only an overly anticipated and momentary pleasure. What do they do when Emily isn't in view and the emotional buzz of love and hate begins to fade? How can they make it last?

Ego is the answer, and this time it's the thinking man's ego. Already in the first few pages of the tale, dramatic ironies create a larger intelligence around a character who suffers from obsession. Along with instances within the individual stories, Chaucer has added a series of framing devices to hammer home the effects of dramatic irony. Each story is told by a character on the pilgrimage, the character introduced in the title of the tale. That character, in turn, is observed by the one I have called Chaucer the Pilgrim, the somewhat naive and inexpert rhymester. Then there's Chaucer the Author whose hand is behind all the writing; and finally, as Chaucer the Author worries about at the end of the work, there's God the Creator who may not be pleased with what his creature has dared to create. (Chaucer the Author voices this concern in a "Retraction" at the end where "The author of this book here takes his leave.") The series of frames is a narrative device that pictures for the reader ever-expanding spheres of intelligence that may have reminded Chaucer of the celestial spheres surrounding the earth that he read about in Ptolemy.

One might assume that an awareness of dramatic irony would be a sign of intelligence. What a surprise, then, to find that both Palamon and Arcite are adept in intelligent applications of the device. But just because these lovers are benighted doesn't mean they are stupid. Quite the contrary. In the arguments that follow the sighting of Emily, we see that ego has appropriated this best vehicle for exposing the smallness of ego as a means for expanding ego's domain. This is how the young men prolong their excitement when Emily is not in view and the buzz of her image wears off. In this stage ego fixes itself and its pleasures in ideas.

They play a simple game: a character expresses an idea, his opponent then trumps that idea with a larger vision, and the larger vision wins the point.[22] This may involve one exchange, but, as in political debate, it can involve an infinite number. The game begins with Palamon's cry of pain upon seeing Emily. Arcite assumes that it's a cry of despair over his imprisonment, his helplessness in the face of planetary forces. He encourages him to take heart and bear it like a man. Palamon wins the point by explaining that his cry was prompted by the fairness of the woman he has seen. But he prefaces this assertion with an admonition to Arcite:

> Cousin, believe me, your opinion springs
>
> From ignorance and vain imaginings.

Ironically, this is how we might describe Palamon's own opinion about Emily. Palamon is aware that a mind can do this; he just isn't aware that his own mind is doing it. He scores a point with Arcite, perhaps, but he loses the point to the reader.

Then it's Arcite's turn. He, too, sees Emily, and puts words to his pain:

> Unless I gain the mercy of her grace,

Unless I see her day by day,

I am but dead. There is no more to say.

It's clear that Arcite claims Emily for himself. Palamon tries to disarm this idea with a larger vision. His prior claim, like the laws of primogeniture, puts him first in line and guarantees knightly obedience:

"It's no honour, then," he said, "to you

To prove so false, to be a traitor too

To me, that am your cousin and your brother,

Both deeply sworn and bound to one another,

Though we should die in torture for it, never

To loose the bond that only death can sever,

And when in love neither to hinder other,

Nor in what else soever, dearest brother,

But truly further me in all I do

As faithfully as I shall further you.

In a time when men lived and died for feudal bonds and the honor of their oaths, Palamon would appear to have trumped a petty, personal passion.

But before Palamon can score his point, Arcite recalls Palamon's own words to neutralize Palamon's idea. He reminds Palamon that he guesses "Emily" to be Venus herself, for Palamon had said of the figure he had seen:

"Woman or Goddess, which? I cannot say.

I guess she may be Venus---well she may!"

He fell upon his knees before the sill

And prayed: "O Venus, if it be thy will

To be transfigured in this garden thus

Before two wretched prisoners like us,

O help us to escape, O make us free!"

Palamon's claim is invalid, Arcite argues, because:

Yours is a mystical, a holy love,

And mine is love as to a human being...

Palamon can worship a goddess all he likes, but the woman belongs to Arcite. As to the feudal law that strictly governs the relations of these knights as well as Palamon's prior claim, Arcite overpowers them both with the priority of himself:

What do I care? Suppose you loved her first,

Haven't you heard the old proverbial saw

"Who ever bound a lover by a law?"

Arcite finishes by seeing their situation pragmatically. They have no hope of justice or love in prison. They are two dogs fighting over a bone:

And so it is in politics, dear brother,

Each for himself alone, there is no other.

"The Knight's Tale" derives much of its power from its frank realism. Two hundred and fifty years before Thomas Hobbes wrote *Leviathan*, Arcite argues that life in a state of nature is a war of man against man. Although Arcite's opinion was written over six hundred years ago, he sounds like a political pro advising a politician in modern times (as long as the microphone is turned off and no one is taking notes). Even though it would appear that Arcite has won the point with Palamon (he intends to love Emily to his heart's content), as with Palamon's argument earlier, he may not have won the point with the narrative itself. We have miles to go before we are done with the "other" that Arcite dismisses so easily.[23]

The game that the young men play in the tower brings the insight of the narrative frame—that ideas are limited—into the consciousness of the characters, as opposed to the consciousness of the author or reader. It's an echo of the overall structure in which the tower figures so prominently. The tower and the cell block at the top represent visually and architecturally that attachment to an idea is like a holding cell. It's a restating or an illustration for Chaucer the Author of Boethius' imprisonment, and it foreshadows as well that the prison experience can be a prelude to wisdom. Everyman's story begins with the two Thebans locked up in their obsession, and their game prefigures the intervention of a larger intelligence into their narrative. "The Knight's Tale" is moving us by degrees toward Arcite's insight into his obsession which can only come after it has run its course. Even then, the summing up and the fullest application of Arcite's insight has to wait for Theseus' speech at the end. There he creates a space that's fit for marriage and for bringing children into the world.

Chapter three:
Ego's Sold-out World Tour

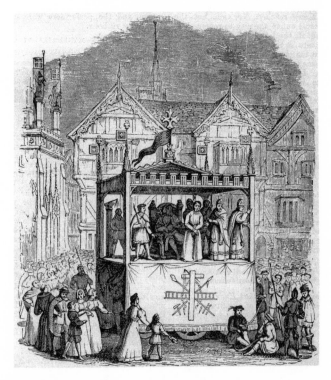

An engraved drawing from Robert Chamber's *Book of Days*, 1864

Self-Hatred

A. A One Man Show

A prison cell serves as the barest sort of stage for viewing the operations of ego. The Palamon and Arcite material in the story represents something like a clinical description of a patient's disorder. The patient "has no life," and the narrative then documents the way these patients "self-medicate" their way out of an unhappy constraint. The two subjects of our study, having practiced for many years in the confines of the tower, are now ready to take the art of ego on the road and perform with more freedom. They embark on a quest similar to that endured by writers, players, musicians, and entertainers of all kinds as they work their way up through the small pay and surly audiences of provincial clubs, theaters, and arenas to the big bucks and bright lights in the capital. Their trip, regardless of its success or failure, is all ego. Though it involves others, "Everyman's Story" is essentially a one-man show, for ego provides the setting and plays all the parts.[24]

After so many years of practice, the two young men have rehearsed to the point where the tower is no longer needed as an incubator; ego now carries those walls everywhere it goes. Whether in a cell or at large in the world, ego plays the leading man, it plays the rival that would deny ego what it desires, and Emily, of course, lovely Emily is ego's love of ego. Welcome to Arcite's world in which "there is no other." As a matter of ethics this justifies doing whatever an egotist wants. If experience is entirely subjective, no object or objective law can penetrate the sacrosanct subject. So there he sits in a self-contained cell.

The storyteller has told us that when Arcite was initially imprisoned, no gold could buy him out, but it happens that Theseus' love for Perotheus could:

A certain famous Duke, Perotheus,

Friend and companion of Duke Theseus

Since they were little children, came to spend

A holiday in Athens with his friend,

Visiting him for pleasure as of yore,

For there was no one living he loved more.

His feelings were as tenderly returned...

Now this Perotheus knew and loved Arcite

In Theban days of old for many years,

And so, at his entreaty, it appears,

Arcita was awarded his release

Without a ransom...

The loving relationship of the two dukes reminds us of the love the two cousins once had for each other. More importantly, the love of Theseus for Perotheus and the love of Perotheus for Arcite set up yet another ironic and telling contrast. The love of the dukes is free to act in the world whereas the self-love of Arcite is impotent.

B. Ego and Paranoia

Arcite is freed by the love of another for him, and his idea that he would be a captive forever ends in the time it would take for Theseus to embrace his friend. It's a gracious gesture, but Theseus places a crucial limit on Arcite's freedom telling him that:

... he could go in peace

And was left free to wander where he would

On one condition, be it understood...

And the conditions, to speak plain, went thus,

Agreed between Arcite and Theseus,

That if Arcite were ever to be found

Even for an hour, in any land or ground

Or country of Duke Theseus, day or night,

And he were caught, it would to both seem right

That he immediately should lose his head...

The condition conveys a sense that love and freedom are complex or layered. When one door opens, Arcite can walk into the next room, but he can't occupy the room he just left. He is still saddled with a basic constraint: when he goes to Thebes, he cannot see Emily; if he returns to Athens to see her, the sword of Damocles hangs constantly over his head. It's a constraint that's of critical importance in any conflict. Even with all the surveillance that technology can supply, we still can't actually be in two places at once in order to insure our safety. There will always be gaps in what the cameras see. No human being will ever be omniscient, and no government will ever spy into every corner of the world. Before the love of Perotheus returned as a factor in Arcite's life, he knew only the love of seeing Emily in the garden. Because of the choice Theseus has given him, the perfection of his self-love is now divided into conflicting camps. He wants to be free from prison, but he also wants to see Emily every day. This division undermines his confidence.

Arcite's transition from physical bondage to freedom marks a critical liftoff in the life of ego, and it signals the starting point for a tour that will take him through six distinct psychological realms or states of being. He is free to live as he likes in Thebes, and he's still as free to think as he was in prison. But these freedoms don't lend him the grace of Emily in the garden.

Instead, at Thebes his thoughts besiege him like imps run amok, for Arcite spends his days envying Palamon who can see Emily through the window of Theseus' tower. Palamon, he thinks, will win the prize (which, the reader notes, is only the reward of a vicarious pleasure), and his vulnerability fuels a jealous fear and rage.

C. Hell

When he was locked up in Athens, the play of ideas and images gave Arcite the victory in their game of Biggest Ego. He won the point by denying Palamon's otherness, but the otherness of Palamon has the upper hand once he leaves the prison. In the tower ego was a comfort, but in Thebes it reveals its nasty side. Arcite, a living organism that once was whole, is now divided into that which is prepared to mutilate itself:

> *He wept, he wailed. How piteously he cried*
>
> *And secretly he thought of suicide.*
>
> *He said, "Alas the day that gave me birth!*
>
> *Worse than my prison is the endless earth,*
>
> *Now I am doomed eternally to dwell*
>
> *Not in Purgatory, but in Hell."*

Anger once directed at the walls that confined him or at Palamon is now directed at his own life.

Arcite's world has now shrunk to a mind filled with jealousy and rage. This confinement to his own head in Thebes is far more claustrophobic than the confinement to a prison cell in Athens had ever been. Once again he sees this intelligently as a form of dramatic irony. He notices that he used to think:

That if I only could escape from prison

I should be well, in pure beatitude,

Whereas I am an exile from my good,

For since I may not see you, Emily,

I am but dead and there's no remedy.

These painful thoughts come at the end of a long discourse about Fortune and about being careful what you wish for. The same device ego used to defeat Palamon is now used to defeat himself. His own mind and what it wants have become the enemy. This is hell. It's a psychological state, but for the subject of the state, hell is real and everywhere. Here's a big problem with the subjectivity he touted earlier in the argument with Palamon. Even so, one thread of his speech hints at a way out, a real key that will remedy his suffering as opposed to the key in Athens that merely let him out of prison. In the last two lines Arcite addresses Emily as if she were actually there, and this reminds us that everything in this state depends on his attachment to her image. But the insight is available only to the reader at this point. Because his attachment completely consumes him, Arcite sees no remedy.

The narrator next describes Palamon in hell. It's a mirror image of Arcite (in reverse). There he is in the tower where Arcite now would like to be, but like Arcite he weeps and wails and cries out to the cousin who has escaped the cell:

Alas, Arcite, dear cousin! In our dispute

And rivalry God knows you have the fruit.

I see you now in Thebes, our native city,

As free as air, with never a thought of pity

For me! You, an astute, determined man

Can soon assemble all our folk and clan

For war on Athens, make a sharp advance,

And by some treaty or perhaps by chance

She may become your lady and your wife

For whom, needs must, I here shall lose my life.

The reader now knows what Arcite doesn't, that Palamon is also in despair thinking that the resourceful Arcite will use his freedom to win Emily while he languishes in prison.

This hall of mirrors proves that they carry hell in their minds. The blind spots that make tyrants paranoid stir up in these tyrant lovers a biting fear and hatred. Since both prison and freedom produce the same state of mind, we have to conclude that place has nothing to do with it. While they are locked in deep introspection, the tempting shape of a beautiful woman and the fear of a rival drive them both to despair. When Arcite wins the game in the tower by asserting that "there is no other," there is no consideration that an actual woman, her warm body pressed against him, is what feeds and satisfies the flowering of a man's passion. Once free, Arcite doesn't seek out a real woman in Thebes where, being young and well born, he could safely have a relationship; he prefers the dream world of desire.[25] The violence of his attachment to the image of Emily appears to have overwhelmed him, but it's the business of comedy to show him that it's a choice.

D. Self-Hatred

How they hate that which divides them from their love! For Arcite, the obstacle is now a lifetime exile from Athens, but he agreed to this condition on his honor as a knight to win his freedom. He himself is involved in the obstacle. Then, too, the freedom of Emily in the garden surrounds his tortured thoughts with a divine spaciousness. Thebes could be just as spacious if ego—attachment to the image of Emily—didn't hold him in thrall. If the mind intuitively knows all this, in gaps that ego cannot fill, how he must hate himself.

Hunger

A. The Eating That Makes Him Hungry

The next stop on the psychological world tour offers a little more space and opportunity than the rock-bottom despair we have witnessed thus far. Arcite lives freely at Thebes, but starved for lovers' food—the sight of his love—he acts out what his love lacks by starving the body:

Meat, drink and sleep---he lay of all bereft,

Thin as a shaft, as dry, with nothing left.

His eyes were hollow, grisly to behold,

Fallow his face, like ashes pale and cold...

Medieval anorexia. It was common with lovers back then, a stock image, but again it's an archetypal symptom associated with the disorder Chaucer would describe, the painful thoughts and behaviors that follow in the train of attachment to a deeply rooted image. The narrator even speculates the way a modern neurologist might about the roots of fantasy in "those cells that front the brain."

A great deal of modern research using machines and brain mapping is devoted to locating thought (consciousness) in the chemistry of the brain. While Chaucer may have been interested in this, he seems far more interested in the actual experiences of consciousness, which he explores through the insights of poetry. For example, if we compare desire to hunger, we see how it falls into a catch-22, or, more appropriately for a medieval example, into the traditional image of a dragon eating its own tail. A person feels hunger because he is empty; he doesn't have what he desperately wants. But as the conflict initiated in the tower is designed to show, desire has a built-in separation from the desired object; the hunger of desire, in other words, can never be satisfied. The dragon eats and eats, but the eating only nourishes the habitual desire. In a closed circle of desire feeding on itself, there's no end to the suffering.

B. The Pretending That Makes Him Hungry

A little light breaks on Arcite in the form of a dream. In sleep the god Mercury comes near, wishes him well, and tells him to return to Athens where his woe will end. Because he is now a deathlike shell of his former self, the new look effectively disguises his true identity. The hunger then assumes a different form and in fact has to do with masking and pretending. As in so many other instances in the story, it's a state of mind bound up with a tension between two pictures. Arcite is attached to a picture of himself as a true knight (his previous identity), which accounts for why he stayed in Thebes after his release for as long as he did, but he is also attached to the picture of Emily as his love (his identity since he saw her). The tension arises as soon as he accepts exile from Athens as the condition for his freedom while maintaining the attachment to Emily. A mind grounded in two irreconcilables tends to be restless, lean, and hungry to somehow paper over the differences. Mercury, the god of thieves and deception, is just the one to negotiate a peace. Arcite goes to Athens disguised as a poor laborer and obtains employment in Emily's household. Eventually, he is able to see her often while serving as her page. He continues to rise in the civil service ranks (just as Chaucer himself did) and becomes a middle class man of substance. This is all to the good. His fortunes are heading in the right direction.

It all falls apart, however, on a beautiful May morning just like the one seven years before when he first saw Emily in the garden. The day begins well:

Thinking to do observances to May

And musing on the point of his desires

He rode a courser full of flickering fires

Into the fields for pleasure and in play...

He sings a happy tune and roams into the woods with a light heart. He is almost the perfect copy of the woman he saw in the garden so many years before, but his mood suddenly changes for the worse. He is so overwhelmed that he cries out loud to the world in a bitter lament. He can no longer pretend to hide that he is from Thebes and that the royal blood of Cadmus animates him as well.

And I that share his lineage, I that spring

By right descent out of the royal stock,

Have fallen captive and am made a mock,

Slave to my mortal enemy, no higher

Than a contemptible, a menial squire!

Yet Juno does me even greater shame;

I dare no more acknowledge my own name.

Time was Arcita was my name by right;

Now I'm called Philostrate, not worth a mite!

As Philostrate, he knows that he is a fraud, not a true knight according to the terms he has agreed to with Theseus. Also, to be close to Emily he has pretended to be a lowborn servant. Although playing this role has served him well for a while, it can no longer sustain him.

Arcite can don a disguise, but he can neither suppress nor hide the nobility and the power of his own mind. For a noble mind that pretends and hides from itself, Emily begins to have a different meaning:

You kill me with your eyes, my Emily,

You are the cause that brings my death on me!

Emily's beauty is tied to that moment in the garden when he first saw her, when everything about her expressed the harmony and wholeness of her person. The continuing power of her beauty expresses the continuing power and truth of his own being. He can't hide from himself that he is living an impossible double life. Even if she is in the same room, smiling, talking, and looking at him with her bright eyes, he sees (in imagination) that she doesn't see him at all because of his low estate. More than a class distinction, it's the deepest sort of threat; he sees that he is common, not because he is a servant but because, looking at himself from Emily's point of view, he is nothing, the way in death a man is nothing.

If we put ourselves in Arcite's shoes, like him we'd find this nothing to be an impossible state of mind. There's no gravity pulling us to earth, no traction with the ground, as in a fever dream when we try to run and yet are unable to move. There must be something, not nothing. Of course, it isn't Emily's fault. She can't see Arcite as a lover because he has deliberately hidden himself, which brings him eventually to the falsity of his position and the suffering he experiences on that beautiful morning. Acting the role of the servant Philostrate, he has to constantly remember his lines and stay in character. An actor's great fear, that he will forget his lines, stems from a fact as hard (and hollow) as the stage he treads upon—the mask he wears is essentially empty. It depends on memory. Playing a part is fine as far as it goes. It can entertain for a while, but a person who has to constantly remember his lines and the role he has to play will suffer a terrible hunger for a life that isn't made up. Like the dragon earlier, it's a tableau of something alive trying to live on itself. There's no real food there.

Although he says that Emily kills him with her bright eyes, he intuits that the problem lies with the dimming of his own. He is not wholly himself. Perhaps he caught himself trying to imitate Emily, and it made him self-conscious. He is a man and a knight; he can't be Emily. Neither can he be a true knight by merely imitating Emily's grace.

C. The Memory That Makes Him Hungry

As an actor, Arcite has to remember his lines. Emily, too, is a memory for which he hungers. Even though he may have seen her often when serving as her page, the story tells us nothing about any of these face-to-face meetings. It may be that he doesn't need to "see" her after the transformational magic of that moment in the garden, but that moment is becoming an ever more distant memory. This is a common problem for people who have had a transformative spiritual experience. When the emotional high of the experience inevitably fades, there's still the memory of it to cling to as the catalyst for a new identity. It's a story one can rehearse to oneself and share with others. As in desire, though, there's a built-in frustration in this, for memory involves separation. By definition it can't be present. A memory of Emily in the garden can't sustain him even if he attaches himself to her picture with a steely will. Perhaps the Philostrate role exhausts itself because the memory has lost its force. Perhaps he has caught himself looking at a limitation like death itself, the limit or the end of ego, for ego is memory. Just as Philostrate cannot reveal his true identity on pain of death, ego cannot admit an end, for that is the death of ego. This is a big problem for someone who lives on a made-up identity[26] or an ideology.

For Arcite "Emily" is memory and ego. "Honor," too, is memory and ego; he has to remember that he was once a prince. Arcite hungers for both Emily and honor the way one hungers for food when empty, and the harder he tries to remember the more he hungers.

D. The Boxed-In Feeling That Makes Him Hunger for Great Escapes

In the woods by himself on this beautiful day in May, Arcite brings himself to a trial where he plays all the parts. Exhausted by the psychodrama, he falls into a trance. What can be next for someone so boxed in? After he awakens, the text says that "he moved apart." "From what?" we wonder. He is in the middle of nowhere, and as far as he knows he is alone. But it makes perfect sense. This is separation, the nature of ego.

Yet being in the box may satisfy, in a wretched sort of way, the hunger for a reassuring excitement just as the first sight of Emily does. The box adds tension and drama to the dullness and routine of ordinary life. Just how, Houdini-like, is he going to escape? Poor Arcite. The uniform he pulls on puts him in the vicinity of the game, but it keeps him on the sidelines. There's a beautiful world all around, but he wants to play on the A team of his dreams. How frustrating! How starved for action and attention he is, and yet he remains on the sidelines, watching the game.

Habitual Behavior

Arcite thinks he is alone in the grove as he unpacks his heart. He doesn't know that Palamon escaped the night before to that very place and is listening to every word. In speaking from the heart Arcite betrays his true identity to his enemy.

Once Arcite has exposed himself in confession to the wood, Palamon thinks he has a deadly card to play in the war for Emily so he comes out of hiding to declare that his rival is a cheater and unworthy:

Arcita! Traitor! False and wicked,

Now you are caught that love my lady so,

For whom I suffer all this pain and woe,

And of my blood---sworn friend---for so we swore

As I have told you many times before,

And you have cheated Theseus with this game,

False as you are, of a pretended name!

Palamon's explosion from the thicket and subsequent diatribe act like a splash of cold water on Arcite's trance and funky bad mood. His charges against Arcite are true and give voice to Arcite's own fears. Coming from Palamon, though, they are words guaranteed to change Arcite's subject in a hurry. Palamon's presence in the wood represents the perfect antidote to depressing mind games. Here is a real enemy again in the flesh, not some ghost of himself. Self-hatred and self-perpetuating doubt vanish the instant Arcite hears that voice, and his identity as a knight returns. As if he never left his calling:

Fierce as a lion he drew his sword...

With this practiced, habitual behavior Arcite is back. With it comes the haughty, aristocratic scorn he has had to keep under wraps while pretending to be a commoner, and so he tells Palamon:

By God that sits above,

Were you not sick, and lunatic for love,

And weaponless moreover in this place,

You never should so much as take a pace

Beyond this grove, but perish at my hand.

And I denounce all covenants that stand

Or are alleged, as between you and me.

Fool that you are, remember love is free

And I will love her! I defy your might.

Using the sword to swear by, rather than as a weapon, he sets the terms of their combat, and noble terms they are, ensuring a fair fight. Prior to their defeat in the war against Theseus, everything in their life has directed them into a knightly code. We have heard hints of it before this as when Palamon reminded Arcite, just after they saw Emily for the first time, that as knights they are:

> Both deeply sworn and bound to one another
>
> Though we should die in torture for it, never
>
> To loose the bond that only death can sever...

Arcite's soliloquy in the woods also reveals that he sees himself in his royal roots (I that spring / By right descent out of the royal stock). From the time they were but babes in arms, these two have been raised to take up arms in defense of their aristocratic liberties and the codes of their class. No wonder he is reminded out of the blue of his Theban identity.

Palamon couldn't have popped out of that thicket at a better moment. What a relief for Arcite to return to his roots and do what he has trained for all his life. Drawing the sword is so easy and so right. When they meet the next morning, the narrator compares the two combatants drawing near each other to a bear or a lion drawing near a hunter lying in wait. In each case a human being thinks:

> Here comes my mortal enemy!
>
> It's either death for him or death for me...

We aren't told what the lion or the bear thinks, and that's the point. Lions and bears just act according to their nature without thought. During the course of their mortal combat, though, both men transition into a psychological state of unselfconscious behavior that we associate with animals:

You would have thought, seeing Palamon engage,

He was a lion fighting-mad with rage,

Arcite a cruel tiger, as they beat

And smote each other, or as boars that meet

And froth as white as foam upon the flood

They fought till they were ankle-deep in blood.

For some, the quest for selfless action may end here. The disregard for loss of blood and loss of life, the courage and the strength that enable them to fight "at amazing length"—these are not the actions of ordinary self-interest. It may appear that the fighters have developed a selfless, spiritual quality, but the text grounds Arcite and Palamon at this point in the world of habitual behaviors. They act with the single-mindedness of an animal looking for food or fighting for its life. This animal never loses its instinctual focus. It follows its nose till it eats and is no longer hungry, or it fights until one or the other wins.

The "selflessness" of Palamon and Arcite is not an absolute, timeless, and pristine state; it is conditioned. Precipitated by mortal combat, their selflessness ends at the sudden appearance of Theseus at the head of his hunting party. For a time the two knights "forget" themselves. But each fights for his own picture of Emily, and soon enough a conscious sense of self comes back with a vengeance. This can be said about many experiences of a heightened consciousness. What happens when the game is over, the music stops, the painting is done, and the book has been written? Might the ex-running back's memory of happy aggression and speed point him unhappily into murdering his estranged wife and her lover? In the long hours in between the magic onstage, might the musician self-consciously try to reproduce that enchantment in a chemical high? In love with his art, maybe the painter would recreate the ecstasy of creation by bringing the frozen model to life in his arms. Or is the painting the memory of when

he came to life in the model's arms? When the writer's thoughts pour out of the thoughtless pen and wind themselves up in nice little construct, is that it? Is his mind empty now?

A conditioned behavior is a product of thought and memory whether it takes the form of instinct (genetic memory) or the gracefulness that results from long practice. Science as well as our own experience can confirm that the body, in a moment of intense activity or crisis, shuts the ego down in order to respond without a fussy middleman. This doesn't mean that ego has been eradicated or even reduced. Years of practice in the arts, in prayer, and in meditation can also produce a sense of clarity and well-being, but if there's attachment to that state of mind (the power it confers) and to the means of achieving it, then it can easily slide into what we called in the sixties an ego trip.

Arcite couldn't have known that Palamon was hiding in the grove within earshot of his soliloquy, and Palamon never could have anticipated that Arcite would end up there. Neither one could have known that Theseus' love of hunting would take him that day to that same grove. To some these coincidences might seem overly contrived and strain the realism and credibility of the tale. But in this reading, the sudden interruptions reinforce the narrative structure in which a character's idea or expectation is constantly deflated by things-as-they-are, and this is the heart of Chaucer's realism. Arcite thought he was alone and washed up as a knight, but it turns out he wasn't. They both thought that one of them would die in mortal combat that day, but Theseus turns up to stop the bloodshed. The narrative constantly reveals to its characters the limitation of their ideas.

The structure is real enough, but ego is well insulated against the thousand daily proofs that it is fallible; it exists to be proud of itself. When Theseus catches them literally red-handed in the woods, Palamon jumps in ahead of Arcite to unmask the man that Theseus knows as Philostrate and to confess what they both have done and why they are there. Even though he must know at some level that his confession means death, the speech rings with the clarion call of ego:

This is Arcite and your mortal foe,

Banished by you on forfeit of his head,

For which alone he merits to be dead.

This is the man that waited at your gate

And told you that his name was Philostrate.

This is the man that mocked you many a year

And you have made him chief equerry here.

This is the man who dare love Emily.

Now since the day of my death has come to me,

I will make a full confession and go on

To say I am that woeful Palamon

That broke out of your jail feloniously.

And it is I, your mortal enemy,

That am in love with Emily the Bright

And glad to die this moment in her sight.

And so I ask for judgement and for death;

But slay my fellow in the self-same breath...[27]

Palamon the tattle-tale! Even as he scatters to the winds his oath of loyalty to his cousin, it sounds as if he, too, has rediscovered a voice full of high-minded, aristocratic sentiment, and in the original as well as the translation, the "I" of "It is I, your mortal enemy" comes through loud and clear. In the fight with Arcite, Palamon regains his habitual pose.

Picking and Choosing

What an uncomfortable trip it has been so far, but when Theseus and all the ladies appear on the scene and welcome the boys into their set, everything changes for them. This scene has a fuller treatment in chapter five. It suffices for now to say that Theseus forgives them both, Palamon for escaping his prison and Arcite for breaking his word. Once he understands that the lovely Emily has driven the young knights to these extremes, his heart softens. Instead of an execution, he imagines a tournament as a way to resolve their differences with each other and to resolve his differences with them and their city.

Theseus himself hints at the next psychological state of our world tour in his instructions regarding the tournament:

> My will is this, to make a flat conclusion
>
> And end all counterpleading and confusion,
>
> (And you will please to take it for the best)
>
> That each shall take his freedom, east or west,
>
> And without ransom or constraint of war;
>
> And, a year later, neither less nor more,
>
> Each shall return, bringing a hundred knights,
>
> Armed for the lists...

He wants them to be free to travel, to study the world for themselves with complete freedom and security. Theseus has gone from being their mortal enemy to being the best parent imaginable. The men are young and high-spirited, and they have been cooped up for so long. Time to let it rip. Time to find themselves, learn their strengths and weaknesses. There is a big world out there, and in a year's time there will be the big battle for

Emily—a test and a gatekeeper for the life to come.

But the big battle will not be a repeat of the one-on-one combat in the woods during which neither killed the other even after hours of fighting. According to Theseus' terms, they are free, but the freedom again carries a condition that each man pick and choose the best team possible, one that suits his character and that can counter the character and the power of the other. Having been recognized by Theseus as princes of Thebes and as legitimate suitors for Emily, Palamon and Arcite find they no longer have to squeeze themselves into the cheap seats. They have more room to move about and be themselves without physical discomfort or pretense. But, to continue the metaphor from contemporary travel, they are still flying in a heavier-than-air piece of metal that stays aloft only if it moves forward at breakneck speed; they are still on an ego trip.

This stop on our world tour has a mundane feel to it. Before this we were in hell, in some ghostly otherworld, or plowing along, nose to the ground, oblivious to all but an instinctual task. In these states an Arcite could believe and behave as if "there is no other." But overall conditions have gradually been improving. Even as they rush along in ego-space, the two appear to be more "grounded." Reversing the direction of the imagery, it may feel like they have surfaced from being buried or drowned. They can breathe normally again. They are around pleasant people who are wishing them well. They have choices that give them hope for a future in which their lives can be pleasant, even beautiful.

Choices belong to the human world, a step up from the hellhounds of despair, hungry ghosts, and thoughtless animals. According to Genesis human history begins with Adam and Eve's choice to disobey. Medieval Christianity featured the device of the good angel and the bad angel giving contrary advice into the ears on opposite sides of Everyman's head; Everyman then has to choose. For a medieval Christian, a choice was a test of spirit. By locating the story in a pagan setting animated by both gods and men, Chaucer's characters also act in a theater where the everyday and the archetypal share the same time and space.[28] Choosing objects and friends and occupations in this environment has a spiritual power and meaning.

The narrator describes in detail the knights that Palamon and Arcite choose to be on their team. Not surprisingly, the opening description addresses their armor and their weapons since this is what has meaning for Palamon:

> *Some carried heavy plating, front and back,*
>
> *And some a Prussian shield to ward attack;*
>
> *Some cased their legs in armour, thigh to heel,*
>
> *Some bore an axe and some a mace of steel*
>
> *---There's never a new fashion but it's old---*
>
> *And so they armed themselves as I have been told.*
>
> *Each man according to his own opinion.*

The last line, especially, implies that each of these fighters (or the culture that he represents) has made a choice based on his idea about the best way to defend and attack. Palamon, in turn, chooses how to execute his game plan, given his own temperament and the specific skills and strengths of the talent available.

To bring Chaucer's tale into a contemporary context for my students in the eighties, I compared Palamon's champion, Lycurgus, and Arcite's champion, Emetrius, to those outrageous pro-wrestling "dudes" of the Hulk Hogan era. Lycurgus is a bear of a man:

> *Black was his beard and manly was his face.*
>
> *To see the circling eye-balls of the fellow*
>
> *Set in his head and glowing red and yellow!*

And like a gryphon he would stare and rouse

The shaggy hair upon his beetling brows.

He is King of Thrace, as wild and as strong as a bear native to the mountains there. Palamon, who thus far appears to be the more courtly and prissy of the two cousins, picks a barbarian to be his soul mate in battle.

Arcite, the budding nihilist, travels further east to select Emetrius, a warrior of exotic refinement from the Indian subcontinent:

His surcoat was in cloth of Tartary,

Studded with great white pearls; beneath its fold

A saddle of new-beaten, burnished, gold.

He had a mantle hanging from his shoulders,

Which, crammed with rubies, dazzled all beholders.

His hair was crisped in ringlets, as if spun

Of yellow gold, and glittered like the sun.

Aquiline nose and eyes with lemon light...

For all his disparagement of the law earlier Arcite picks an epitome of culture as his champion. Emetrius is but a youth and rides a horse instead of a chariot. (The reader wonders if a horse could even carry Lycurgus.) What he lacks in mass, he makes up in speed and mobility. And what do we make of that lemon light in his eyes?

In addition to the worldly choices of knights and weaponry, the combatants choose the planetary god most favorable to their cause. For Palamon it is Venus, the goddess of sexual passion. For her aid he promises to do all within his power to combat chastity, and in return he tells her exactly what he wants:

I neither beg nor borrow

Vainglorious praise, nor do I make profession

Of prowess---but would fully have possession

Of Emily, and die thy worshipper.

Earlier Arcite accused Palamon of worshipping Emily as the goddess Venus herself, calling his passion "a mystical, a holy love." Apparently this mistook Palamon's intention, for he sets the story straight in his prayer. He wants his lady "in his arms."

Arcite chooses Mars, the god of war, promising to honor Mars above all the other gods if he would "Grant victory to my sword." This is plain speaking, but Mars is a fighter and a lover. Arcite remembers the famous incident told by Homer in *The Odyssey* when Mars loved as he does:

By that same suffering and burning fire

That long ago consumed thee with desire,

Having in use the incomparable flesh

Of fair free-hearted Venus, young and fresh.

Pity me too that suffer the same smart!

These passionate lines show that both knights are fully engaged in combatting chastity. They differ only in the style of their wooing. Palamon chooses the passive approach, praying that the woman be dumped in his lap. Arcite chooses the active approach as he intends to overpower his rival and her.

In addition to being addled and aroused, Arcite admits to being ignorant and young, and what he says next proves it beyond a doubt. The problem, says Arcite, is Emily:

> *Little she thinks, in all the grief she's giving,*
>
> *Of me, or cares whether I swim or sink,*
>
> *And well I know ere she can learn to think*
>
> *Kindly of me that force must have its place,*
>
> *And well I know without thy help or grace*
>
> *The little strength I have is all too slight...*

Now here's a problem. Arcite has already shown that he can fight all day with a man in mortal combat, but it appears he requires the help of Almighty Mars to subdue a woman.

Arcite may have made a tactical mistake in asking for victory. As we will see, this gives Saturn the wiggle room he needs. Also, Arcite's martial approach goes against the courtly tradition within which Chaucer is writing where the woman is in control of her own body. Nevertheless, Arcite represents a real courtship strategy. There are young men who drug their dates and then rape them where the drug plays the role of Mars. Some marriages are loveless political or business arrangements where money plays the role of Mars. Some men win a woman's favor with a martial display of masculine skill or wit. Then again maybe women who find the courtly tradition too effete for their taste prefer a bruiser like Arcite.

Without taking sides, Chaucer turns the prayers of both into pure ego by means of a simple separating device. In between the worshipping of Venus and Mars, he has Emily worship at Diana's temple. Here the reader encounters for the first time what Emily herself thinks. In short, she thinks sex and marriage are a bad idea. End of story. This opinion separates the longings and the silly prayers of the men from their object, a real woman who belongs to no man.

Since the tale gives no indication that either young man has ever had contact with Emily as an officially recognized suitor, she remains for them what she has been from the beginning, a picture that they have projected out of themselves and which they have approved and fastened upon for themselves. They have lost their heads over her beauty. But the image of her that they project is also their way of seeing and complimenting themselves, like looking in the mirror to confirm "the fairest one of all." She represents the intelligence and good taste of the one who has chosen her for his heart's desire. This one is ego.

As all the earthly picking and choosing comes to a close the day before the tournament, a quarrel breaks out in heaven over Palamon's and Arcite's requests from their patron gods. Palamon has prayed for Emily, and Venus is happy to grant him the lady. Arcite has prayed for victory, and Mars is happy to grant him that success. Understandably, Venus objects with bitter protests. How can Mars grant victory when she has already granted the lady! For any parent who has ever settled an argument between siblings, it's a familiar sort of problem. What do you do when two headstrong children want what they want because one way or another they think it has been promised or they think they can promise it to themselves? Either the one gets Emily or the other; they can't both have her. Faced with an either/or choice like this, a parent may feel like an amateur magician who has been asked to saw the lady in half without any idea of how the trick is done. Saturn, however, isn't taken in by that which, contrived by a limited intellect, seems to hinge on a choice. The wisdom of Saturn sees the space that opens up around a headstrong definition of things-as-they-are.

Striving to Be the Best

Two more stops to go on the world tour, and the days of down-and-out dives are behind us. These are the big leagues and a very big deal. Our little band, which started out with just the two scruffy and touchy players, plus Emily's offstage part which she didn't know she was performing, has swelled to an Event-That-Involves-Everyone. Thanks to Theseus' decree that each man find 100 knights to fight with him, there are 202 players, and everyone else will be in the stands of Theseus' arena neatly stacked row by row. It's a marriage of Woodstock and the Super Bowl, a summer of love (Venus) contending in people's hearts with a winter of discontent (Mars).

What a way to finish—an ego trip to end all ego trips at the center of the universe, the darling of all eyes. On the day of the tournament the whole dukedom has been set in motion by the love of Palamon and Arcite for Emily. Everyone is up early to get ready, each doing the work of his station. While this activity is swirling around them, in the eye of the hurricane Theseus' court gathers to hear the duke's solemn decree: death will no longer determine the outcome. Instead, Theseus changes the rules into an outsized form of capture the flag with Palamon and Arcite as the flags. This decision is very popular, puts the crowd in a good humor, and wins the duke the blessings of his people.

But our story is with the two young men, and with assessing their states of mind at this crucial point. We are such a long way from Arcite's assertion that "there is no other." Others have almost entirely taken over their story. The whole world is involved, making bets on the outcome, drinking in the spectacle, living vicariously on the upcoming contest. When the two knights are brought before the duke that morning in the middle of all that ferment, how can they not feel the grip of a great power over which they have little control?

Sitting in the presence of the duke, they hear that he has banished mortality, but this doesn't change the problem the tournament represents for them. Even before the fighting starts, they are wrestling with mutability—the fact that the world consists of things in motion and that things in motion move them whether they like it or not. For months they have been enjoying the good life and all the stuff they have been amassing to feel comfortable and secure. In the business, excitement, and pageantry of the mission Theseus has given them, it would have been easy to bury the fact that, at the end of the year, they might lose Emily—the heart and soul of the whole enterprise—to another man.

So it has come to this: all the intelligent picking and choosing can't secure a positive outcome because the other guy is working just as hard to secure his own positive outcome. Intelligent picking and choosing has brought them to this point, but once they are in the throes of this wave of people and energy, it looks more and more like a throw of the dice. Mutability is a pain for ego. Ego would fix things, that is, pin them down, but mutability undercuts ego's pleasures with motion and uncertainty.

What can they do, then, but fight and strive to be the best that day. High above them in the stands they still have Emily, their picture of heaven, to spur them on to ever greater feats, especially in combat with each other:

Many a time our Thebans in the flow

Of battle met and did each other woe,

And each unhorsed the other. There could be

No tiger in the vale of Galgophy

Raging in search after a stolen cub

So cruel as Arcite with spear and club

For jealousy of heart to Palamon.

No lion is so fierce look upon

In all Benamarin, and none so savage

Being hunted, nor so hunger-mad in ravage

For blood of prey as Palamon for Arcite.

The blows upon their helmets bite and beat

And the red blood runs out on man and steed.

This state of mind is about competing for ultimate peace, a place where things stay put after you have arranged them to your liking. Because that hasn't happened yet, it is a state, "pumped" with a jealous and a ravaging heart.

The final chord of this movement belongs, as in the last stop when Venus complained to her father about Mars promising Arcite victory, to the gods watching from their perch in the heavens. Venus is outraged with the result. Her worshipper Palamon has been dragged to the stake, and she has lost face:

> *What now can lovely Venus do above?*
>
> *What is she saying, hapless Queen of Love?*
>
> *Wanting her will her eyes were filled with mists*
>
> *And shining tears fell down upon the lists.*
>
> *She cried, "I am disgraced and put to shame!"*

In her person Venus is an archetype for the attachment of Palamon and Arcite to Emily. We find in this little vignette about her the competitive drive for a goal, biting jealousy, and the fear of loss that accompany attachment. Venus and her emotions are human archetypes tied to ego.

Victory

Everyone knows what "victory" means, but for me it's more than just a goal or a concept. It has a physical force and resonance. For twenty-two years I was the boys' junior high soccer coach in our school. During the season our teams would take road trips to neighboring schools for games. Sometimes the girls' junior high soccer team would join us on the bus so we'd be riding to and from the games with three on a seat throughout, girls on one side and boys on the other. Those were rollicking afternoons, especially on the ride home if one or both teams won their game. As soon as we hit Main Street, every window in the bus would come down, and the people who lived there would hear, repeated over and over:

Naples! Naples! Hear our cry

V-I-C-T-O-R-Y!

Maybe that's why the word and even the spelling has a special power for me. From all those years of hearing it so loudly spelled out, I know the power of a word to cast a spell over the heart and mind of the sturdiest unbeliever. Oh, to be able to sing that chant and ride in glory around your town!

After Theseus proclaims him the winner, Arcite takes his victory lap in a similar state of mind:

The fierce Arcita, with no helmet on,

Riding his courser round to show his face

Cantered the whole length of the jousting-place,

Fixing his eye on Emily aloft;

And her returning gaze was sweet and soft...

It's a heaven of complete self-absorption. Nothing more needs to be done. The attachment has bloomed into everything and everyone singing and trumpeting praise. It's a perfect circle, from the first to now. The grossness and physical pain of the past is burned away as Emily and Arcite fix on each other with their eyes. Their bodies would appear to have been transformed into light, the lightness of a lover looking at a lover.

CHAPTER FOUR:
THE OPENING OF ARCITE'S HEART

Carracci's *Pieta*

As ego does, the wake-up call plays a crucial role in comic dramas. Arcite's victory lap for soaking up the praise of an adoring crowd brings Everyman's Story and its world tour to a point of perfection. What a power this image has over our imaginations! How else to explain that every four years at the Olympics we see it reenacted again and again by victorious athletes, and every four years we see it at political conventions when the presidential candidate stands in triumph before the rapturous throngs and cheers of his party. Even if only a few ever reach these heights, the image endures as ego's ideal resting place.

If only it would last. But it won't. It can't. Something is bound to change. All this energy and attention make the attachment seem so real and encompassing that even the narrator expresses surprise as:

> Out of the ground behold a fury start,
>
> By Pluto sent at the request of Saturn.
>
> Arcite's horse in terror danced a pattern
>
> And leapt aside and foundered as he leapt,
>
> And ere he was aware Arcite was swept
>
> Out of the saddle and pitched upon his head
>
> Onto the ground, and there he lay for dead;
>
> His breast was shattered by the saddle bow.
>
> As black he lay as any coal or crow
>
> For all the blood had run into his face.

For all its intensity, the lightness of Arcite's love is not insight, nor has Arcite's body been transfigured. It is still but a body of flesh and blood.

Arcite could not possibly know or anticipate what Saturn has in store for him, could not know the politics in heaven that causes what happens next, and could not know how these things would change his state. His victory lap inscribes in the dust a two-dimensional circle, and I picture him then taking his place in the middle of it and the surrounding arena. The world defined by his attachment lies inside that circle. This is what he knows. If we put ourselves in Arcite's shoes at his moment of triumph, we can appreciate how everything in his view—the thousands of common folk, the court of Theseus, the hundreds of knights on the field of play, and even the arena itself—is successfully rooted in the attachment. The fury that leaps up from below, however, now reminds us of all that lies outside or below or above that limited circle, the world beyond Arcite's powers of perception. It's a portrait of ego ultimately immersed in the greatness of what it doesn't know. In the blink of his courser's eye, Arcite's victory ends. In the same moment that his desire has been fulfilled, his heart is crushed (tenderized) by a thrust of the saddle bow. With that small movement ego's world tour suddenly stops and goes dark.

The precise details of Arcite's injury make me think that Chaucer might have seen the effects of such a wound during his long life in a time full of wars and peasant revolts. He describes a chain of cause and effect. What happens to the face follows from what happens to the heart, and that follows from what the horse and saddle bow do because of the fury's sudden motion, and so on and so on. As we trace the cause further and further back, we eventually arrive at the shock to Arcite's "heart" all those many years ago when he first glimpsed Emily from his cell in the tower. This time, like a trumpet call or a crack of thunder, the bolt from the saddle bow (as opposed to Cupid's bow) intimates to him the kiss of death.

The crushing of Arcite's heart has figurative implications, but the narrative specifies that he dies by degrees from a physical wound and infection:

Up swells Arcita's breast, the grievous sore

About his heart increases more and more;

The clotting blood, for all the doctor's skill,

Corrupts and festers in his body still,

That neither cupping, bleeding at a vein,

Or herbal drink can make him well again...

All, all was shattered and beyond repair,

Nature no longer had dominion there,

And certainly, where nature will not work,

Physic, farewell! Go, bear the man to kirk!

This passage describes the end of the heart's worldly existence, but it points at the end to its passage from a material to a spiritual state. It is time to take that broken heart to church. In his final moments, as his heart gradually shuts down as a physical organ, Arcite confesses to Emily in a last rite of love. She is no priest, but he tells her the truth. Acknowledging the painful attachment that has been described over the course of his confinement and world tour, his confession bears his own heart to church.

The speech has two movements. The first is a cry of pent-up pain and suffering:

Alas the woe! Alas the pain so strong,

That I have suffered for you, and so long!

Alas, O Death! Alas my Emily!

Alas the parting of our company!

Alas, my heart's own queen, alas my wife,

O lady of my heart that ends my life!

What is this world?

What does man ask to have?

Now with his love, now in his cold, cold grave,

Alone, alone, with none for company!

Farewell, my sweetest foe, my Emily!

The physical heart may be crushed, but these words come from the heart with a full-blooded honesty. This is Arcite's moment of truth:

Alas, O Death! Alas, my Emily!

Into these six words Chaucer distills the essence of Arcite's long and fruitless attachment to the image of Emily. He sees his desire to possess her now as one-half of a painful equation. After so many years of strife and expectation, the story concludes in the marriage of Emily to death. For the time it took to circle the arena his heart was warm and full, the goal of a lifetime. How quickly that comfort has turned cold! As his heart empties out, he glimpses the solitude of the grave which from the start has been closely tied to the solitude of his desire, the painful longing for what will always be out of reach.

But even as these words express the opening up of Arcite's heart, the equation holds within it another effect: the emptying out of "Emily" tends to empty out fear and jealousy as well. Paradoxically, his empty heart is now full to the brim with a different kind of love. The opening of his heart has opened his eyes,[29] and he calls this "wisdom" as he speaks for the last time to Emily (and as far as the story is concerned, these lines at the end of life represent the first time he has spoken to her):

O softly take me in your arms, I pray,

For love of God, and harken what I say.

I have here, with my cousin Palamon,

Had strife and rancour many a day now gone,

For love of you, and for my jealousy.

And may Jove's wisdom touch the soul in me,

To speak of love and what its service means

Through all the circumstances and the scenes

Of life, namely good faith and knightly deed,

Wisdom, humility and noble breed,

Honour and truth and openness of heart,

For, as I hope my soul may have its part

With Jove, in all the world I know of none

So worthy to be loved as Palamon,

Who serves you and will serve you all his life.

And should you ever choose to be a wife,

Forget not Palamon, that great-hearted man.

To realize his idea of possessing Emily, Arcite prayed to Mars for victory over Palamon. Worrying about the strength of Emily's resistance, he also prayed to Mars for the power to "be the man" with her. His militant desire to possess her image represents a movement of mind and heart that medieval Christians called *cupiditas*. This form of love has proven to be an illusion, and so he lets it go. The opening of Arcite's heart that we are witnessing, on the other hand, is real, and Emily receives it by opening her arms to embrace him. The tableau before us, Arcite in Emily's arms—so similar to Michelangelo's *Pieta* and to images like the one illustrating this chapter (where both figures look like the subjects of a romance, an interpretation the artist encourages by including the winged, Cupid-like putti)—represents the movement of heart and mind that a medieval Christian called *caritas*. In the game of Biggest Ego earlier, a player won a point by disarming an opponent's idea with a larger intelligence. This advances the cause of ego. Here Arcite has to play the game with his own idea about possessing Emily, and he has the virtue or the strength to see that his own idea has lost. It's a victory in defeat; a deep wisdom at the limit of his life dissolves his attachment to Emily and dissolves as well the deeply rooted fear of losing the light of his life to a rival. So we see him in the fullness of insight, neither quick nor dead, an insight and a seed of life in Emily's arms. As we will also see in good time, his words and this embrace bear fruit at the end of the tale.

Could Arcite ever have guessed that after all he had endured to gain Emily for himself, he would end by wooing her for his bitter rival? And yet this is what he does. He's a man who has been upended, and with his head on the ground and his feet in the air, all his ideas have emptied out like spare change in a pocket. What he sought, it turns out, was merely an image. Also, Arcite can see for himself now the "play" of love and war, that his love for Emily was tied to his jealousy of Palamon and that he was the source, as in a dream, of both emotions. They were projections, and the enchantment of them has vanished like waking from a dream. Firmly rooted now in the world to which he has awakened, he acknowledges the reality of those knightly virtues he learned as a child. Most importantly, in his final breath he recognizes Emily's own freedom to be and to love as she chooses. She, too, is a subject not an object, just as he is, and with all the same trials of self and perception. He sees that Emily doesn't belong to him and never did; following the example of this lesson, he may also glimpse that his own life doesn't belong to him and never did.

In this softness and openness of heart, Arcite dies.

CHAPTER FIVE:

THE GOVERNMENT OF THESEUS

Schiavone's *The Marriage of Cupid and Psyche*

Insight and the Transmission of Insight

"And then?" Narratives have this property. They are always pushing forward into new territory. With his ever-expanding spheres of intelligence Chaucer has imagined a potential for insight almost as open as modern thought, but the death of Arcite also points to the conclusion that all things are limited and have an end. Chaucer's questioning of ideas may have helped to propel those who came after him toward a modern view of the cosmos, but his tale stays within the boundaries of the system Aristotle and Ptolemy described. For the present purpose these observations lead a reader to conclude that for the characters and for the reader the story has a definite shape and a law that governs it. The story doesn't extend into infinity; it has an end and a purpose the way a sentence does. It exists, the way a sentence does, to help us make sense of the world. At the end of his life, Arcite discovers a structure and a meaning in his life that previously had been hidden, and his story, even if it is just a story, is designed to show that insight has an integral role in the great chain of being.[30]

Arcite touches on this theme in his final speech when he calls on the wisdom of Jove to help him speak to Emily. The translation reads as follows:

And may Jove's wisdom touch the soul in me,

To speak of love and what its service means...

In the original, the link between his experience and the government of a life is made more explicit. He is the link in the great chain which helps to hold it all together, and this insight allows him to see and to speak of the role he now must play in bringing the narrative to a comic conclusion:

And Jupiter so wys (wise) my soule gye (govern)

To speken of a servaunt proprely...

As in the invocations of the classical poets, Arcite prays that the wisdom of Jupiter's sphere will govern his speech,[31] emphasizing that he speaks not as a "law-giver" or a maker of laws, like a king or a duke, but as a servant to the law. Unlike those long and miserable days in a subjective holding cell, Arcite now understands that the law exists, and he aspires to be governed by it. It is noteworthy that he is no longer praying to Mars or following the advice of Mercury. In the government of a person or a state, physical strength and cunning have a role to play, but wisdom has precedence. As Arcite lies dying, these questions about the law that governs his life come to the surface, and this is why the embodiment of the law, Duke Theseus, emerges once again as a focus.

"And then?" What effect can the insight of one person have on anyone else? Everyone has been caught up Arcite's story, but wisdom can't be experienced vicariously any more than one can eat or drink to maintain the body of another. Given the context of a contest, the story of the tournament can be easily interpreted to prove that bad luck has won the game with human beings. Happiness in the world appears to always be at the mercy of those moments when, out of the blue, "fate o'errules."[32] This is certainly how the people view the case:

> *Infinite were the sorrows and the tears*
>
> *Of older folk and those of tender years*
>
> *Throughout the town, all for this Theban's death.*
>
> *Wept man and boy, and sure a wilder breath*
>
> *Of lamentation never had been heard*
>
> *Since Hector, freshly slaughtered, was interred*
>
> *In Troy. Alas to see the mourning there,*
>
> *The scrabbled faces, the dishevelled hair!*

"Must you have died?" the women wailed. "For see,

Had you not gold enough---and Emily?"

Arcite's death throws a pall of lamentation over the dukedom, reminiscent of the widows' lamentations at the beginning, that engulfs the world and all things in it. The narrator marvels that the whole nation could be brought to such distress "all for this Theban's death." Still, this is true both of an individual and of a national psyche. Even if a hundred things go right in his day, a person may fret all night over the one thing that went wrong. In a nation, too, people in a difficult time may panic and irrationally doubt the basic strengths and institutions that have made them whole and prosperous for hundreds of years. Prior to this the reader has seen Theseus at war with other realms, Hippolyta's Femeny and Creon's Thebes. Here, though, the mood of his own people poses a mortal threat to the dukedom, for a state will quickly cease to be viable if the people think that their lives are governed only by malign and arbitrary powers.

And then there is Theseus. The transformation of Arcite's heart from *cupiditas* to *caritas* instills a like transformation in Theseus. We may not be able to say why it happens, but we know for a fact that it can happen. The role that Theseus now plays has much the same role in the tale as comedy (defined as a movement of the human heart from *cupiditas* to *caritas*) has in the history of human beings. Chaucer created his Theseus in the hope that those who participate in his story might find comfort and healing. The story has two movements with the death of Arcite at the center. On either side of that critical event, the judgment of Theseus expands, and he transmits insight in the government of himself and his people.

The Opening of Theseus' Judgment

The tale begins, as we have seen, with a contrast between the judgments of Theseus and Creon. Hearing that Creon has desecrated the bodies of the dead, Theseus drops everything, even his wedding night, and instantly changes course to right this wrong. His action is like the cut of a sword—quick, sharp, and decisive.

When Palamon and Arcite are brought before him half dead from the battlefield, his judgment is just as quick and final: he condemns them to life imprisonment. Their case, however, turns out to be more difficult to judge. Unlike the tyrant Creon who had consciously defied the will of the gods, the young men are more like collateral damage especially in consideration of their age. Their life sentence settles for good the long-standing conflict Theseus has had with Thebes, but many years later he tempers his judgment of them by one-half when he releases Arcite at the request of a dear friend. This decision suggests that his original judgment may have been a matter of convenience or even arbitrary, not a true judgment as much as a quick fix. It raises a question about the nature of his justice when the scales are tipped by insider pleading. It opens the question whether his judgment is a matter of his own convenience.

Just as Theseus' judgment is tempered by conditions involving his friendship with Perotheus, Arcite's release is also conditional. He understands that, if he is ever found again in Theseus' lands, his life is forfeit. By escaping from Theseus' prison, Palamon is just as guilty of a capital crime as his cousin. After Theseus discovers the two fighting in his woods, Palamon sums up their situation as well as any prosecutor:

> *O Sir, what need of further word or breath?*
>
> *Both of us have deserved to die the death,*
>
> *Two wretched men, you captives, met in strife,*
>
> *And each of them encumbered with his life.*
>
> *If to judge righteously has been your fashion,*
>
> *Show neither of us mercy nor compassion,*
>
> *And kill me first for holy charity!*

But kill my fellow too, the same as me.

Theseus is quick to agree:

This is a short conclusion. It shall stand.

Your own confession damns you out of hand.

I shall record your sentence as it stood;

There needs no torturing to make it good.

Death you shall have, by mighty Mars the Red!

Mighty Theseus has spoken in an open-and-shut case. Palamon has confessed who they are, and the legal path to an execution is clear. Like the earlier decision, the judgment falls swiftly on their heads.

The queen, Emily, and all the ladies, however, do not move in the sphere of mighty Mars the Red; they are moved instead by tender hearts when they hear the fate of these young knights:

It seemed so very piteous to them all

That ever such misfortune should befall

For they were noblemen of great estate

And love the only cause of their debate.

They saw their bloody gashes gaping wide

And, from the greatest to the least, they cried,

"Have mercy, Lord, upon us women all!"

Down on their knees they then began to fall,

Ready to kiss his feet as there he stood.

It's the second instance where Theseus is petitioned like this. At the beginning of the tale, the widows hold up his wedding procession to put before him the rank injustice of Creon. This time the ladies of his court petition him from a possible injustice of his own making. This time it's more personal and far more serious for the man who embodies the law.

In a long soliloquy Theseus in effect "counts to ten" as the women lie prostrate before him:

Abated in the end his angry mood;

Pity runs swiftly in a noble heart.

Though he had quaked with anger at the start

He had reflected, having time to pause,

Upon their trespass and upon its cause,

And though his anger at their guilt was loth

To pardon either, reason pardoned both.

For thus he argued: almost any man

Will help himself to love if he can,

And anyone will try to break from prison;

And then compassion in his heart had risen

Seeing these ladies weeping there together,

And in his noble heart he wondered whether

He should not show his clemency, and "Fie,"

He thought, "on lords who show no mercy! why

To be a lion both in word and deed

To a penitent in fear, is not to heed

His change of heart, and equal him with one

Proudly persisting in an evil done.

A lord will lack discretion among his graces

Who does not make distinction in such cases,

But weighs humility and pride as one."

And, to be brief, his anger being done,

His eyes began to sparkle and uncloud...

The pitiful sight of the knights and the women's plea for mercy touch his judgment and throw into question his custom of acting swiftly by the book that he alone has ever read. Why does he fall into a pause, a time for reflection, this time?

To borrow an expression from modern finance and politics, he pauses because he now has more "skin in the game." Unlike the war against Creon where he gave a bit of time and soldiership, Theseus has more of himself invested. According to martial law, the two should die, but Theseus is no longer merely a soldier. For some time now he has been a married man and subject to marital law. It would be difficult for this married man to ignore a wife and all her ladies who were spreading themselves on the ground before him to urge a different policy. If he grants the ladies' suit, he may lose the respect of those who want a duke's word to be absolute and final, but if he executes the two young men, his wife might not be pleased. The unmarried Theseus may have had more freedom to be cold and impersonal; the married Theseus now must question whether it's good policy to be known as a narrow, parochial sort of judge. What if the law, like the spheres of Chaucer's universe, is multilayered?

What access Chaucer the Author has given us to the mind of this character! To give the moment a life-and-death significance, his deliberations transpire with two lives in the balance. The Knight, our storyteller, uses the word "reason" to sum up why Theseus is about to pardon the young men. The scope of his deliberation helps the reader understand what the Knight means by the word. This reason is not entirely a mental activity, like the calculations a merchant uses to make his way in commerce; there's too much blood and tears and marital politics in it for that. Nor is it entirely a matter of sensation or feeling like the lovers' passionate, aristocratic defense of their interest in Emily; he doesn't sound as though he is instinctively defending himself. Anyone who is outraged, afraid, or irrational would be hard put to look at the whole situation with such equanimity. Rather, this reason is more like perception itself, an accurate picture that's composed of people, things, mind, heart, the passage of time, and anything else that constitutes Being all in an effective balance.

The knight's use of the word reason points to the experience that's the subject of comedy. The reason to which he refers springs from the opening of the pedestrian's idea as he floats suspended above the pavement, and it springs from the opening of Arcite's heart when he sees his attachment to the image of Emily—teeny-weeny Emily at the end of tunnel vision magnified by obsession—within the context of his whole life. Stopped in his tracks by the ladies, Theseus is forced by things-as-they-are to take stock. He is accustomed to making decisions that are quick and clean, but in this situation he slipped on the prostrate ladies and lost his footing when he thought he was secure in the act of judging. His pause as he "counts to ten" is an equivalent image for what I have referred to as insight and wisdom and what the Knight calls reason.

What Is So Foolish as a Man in Love

The words Theseus then speaks out loud to express the opening up of his judgment point to the insight that will now inform his realm:

The God of Love! Ah, Benedicite!

How mighty and how great a lord is he!

No obstacles for him make any odds;

His miracles proclaim his power a God's.

Cupid can make of every heart and soul

Just what he pleases, such is his control.

Like a speech at a rehearsal dinner, his words prepare us for a wedding. To a modern ear it also sounds like a concession speech after our mighty conqueror has lost an election for the first time. There's a wistful sense of what he was before, but there's also a gracious acceptance of how things have turned out. His own judgment, ego, has lost, but as he elaborates why ego has lost and love has triumphed, there's a decided twinkle in his eye. It's time for a wedding. First, though, Theseus needs to shift the bloodshed and the suffering they see before them into a comic context. In the speech that follows his tone, like that of an accomplished MC, will skip lightly over all the serious difficulties of the courtship to prepare us for when love and comedy will finally get together and be married in the persons of our heroes:

Look at Arcita here and Palamon!

Both had escaped scot-free and could have gone

To Thebes and lived there royally; they know

That I have ever been their mortal foe;

Their lives are mine, they can make no defence;

Yet Cupid in the teeth of common sense

Has brought them here to die in melancholy!

Consider, is it not the height of folly?

What is so foolish as a man in love?

Look at them both! By God that sits above

See how they bleed! Are they not well arrayed?

Thus has their lord, the God of Love, repaid

Their services; these are his fees and wages!

In Theseus' "take" on the situation love is a comedy after all. A moment ago his government was suspended in a precarious uncertainty, but when we all consider "What is so foolish as a man in love?" all the uncertainty lands with a reassuring thump on the ground. Obviously, the duke knows what he is talking about, and his judgment is rehabilitated. A comic point of view reminds everyone that it's not such a bad thing when ego loses, and the two young knights are exhibits A and B in a comic demonstration. For Palamon and Arcite love is a depressing, tragic business. An audience at a comedy sees the blood gushing from their wounds all right, but considered as the wages for their attachment, it's a joke.

With the gross folly of Palamon and Arcite so palpable before them, the joke might be entirely on them, but comedy widens its scope to anyone who would be wise:

And yet in spite of that, they pose as sages,

These devotees of Love, as I recall.

To borrow once more an expression from modern political commentary, it turns out that the mind is "in the tank" with what the eye has chosen to love. Comedy notes that desire runs the show, and the mind must find reasons for loving and behaving absurdly. The eye of comedy enlightens them by cutting the object of these shenanigans free from all their fantasies:

But still this is the finest stroke of all,

That she, the cause of all these jolly pranks,

Has no more reason to return them thanks

Than I, and knows no more of this affair

By God, than does a cuckoo or a hare!

This is the best kind of funny stuff and much wiser than the stuff that often poses as wisdom. When set against things-as-they-are, their fantasies have no standing. With a fully realized and conscious Emily cut away from the fantasies, the dreamers might glimpse a critical consequence of their attachment: in addition to limiting perception, it has almost killed them. More generally, a larger view of the situation suggests that a knowing subject, an Emily, is not apprehended by any label or conceptual claim that a man might put on her. Theseus' demonstration serves as a cautionary tale for anyone who aspires, by achieving the mastery of a skill set like sword craft, to be master of man or woman.

Palamon and Arcite are too groggy and infatuated to understand much of anything at this point, but Theseus is awake and aware of his role as duke and governor. He is still a man of action, for that's his function in the Great Chain of Being. The experience with these knights has opened up an insight into his subjects and into his role as governor that changes his government of them, of himself, and of others who are not his subjects. Courtesy of their example, Theseus remembers that a man's fancies can make him play the fool, but he is not neutered by the fact that he may play the fool on occasion. If once again confronted with a mad dog like Creon, Theseus would still march through the night to defeat him. He has experienced quite publicly that his judgment can be tempered by reason, for he can see now that the lovers Palamon and Arcite are not Creon. They have been touched by something like a divine madness, which has done no harm except to themselves, and his judgment changes accordingly.[33]

The knights, too, are at a critical juncture. Worse than the wounds they have suffered from the thrusts of swordplay, they stand before the entire court like prisoners at the stake and suffer being the object of a joke. As far as they know, they have lost everything—their dignity, their lives, and Emily. Theseus, though, does not aim to destroy them, any more than he could possibly defeat or destroy Venus or Mars. He has already conceded that. With the warmest of hearts, he steps in and picks up those prostrate egos with a good humor and a full pardon:

> *Well, well, try anything once, come hot, come cold!*
>
> *If we're not foolish young, we're foolish old.*
>
> *I long have known myself what Love can do,*
>
> *For, in my time, I was a lover too.*
>
> *And therefore, knowing something of love's pain,*
>
> *How violently it puts a man to strain,*
>
> *As one so often caught in the same snare*
>
> *I readily forgive the whole affair...*

In addition to removing the sword poised over their heads, Theseus restores their identities as princes of the royal blood and confirms them as suitors of Emily through his plan for the tournament. To resolve the conflict over Emily without deciding it himself arbitrarily, he puts into motion an institution and a public work for justice. The tournament and the stadium to house it will broaden the basis for judgment so that it includes everyone.

His decision opens up a brave new vista for the two lovers:

> *The effect on the young men is electric:*
>
> *Who looks delighted now but Palamon?*
>
> *And who springs up rejoicing but Arcite?*

As shown in "Ego's Sold-Out World Tour," however, this is the end of only one phase in the world tour of the two young men. The government of Theseus can structure the situation for them, but he can't change their hearts. Arcite completes the narrative of his attachment only when he freely releases his claim on Emily in his final words. In addition, Theseus' speech in the woods is not the final word on what belongs to reason. The death of Arcite lies in wait to test his understanding.

A Noble Theater for True Judgment

Even though no one can change the heart of another with wise words and rules of discipline, Chaucer devotes a large part of his tale to describing the arena Theseus builds to express his insight into the pardonable folly of love. The structure has the shape of a Roman coliseum and is punctuated with a separate temple for the gods linked in the love triangle. Inside, each temple is decorated with pictures that depict stories from the god's life. Together, they comprise a scholar's warehouse, chockablock with artifacts of the archetypal mind. The stories are different just as Venus, Mars, and Diana have different natures, but Theseus' comic understanding binds them all in an appreciation for love's power. Since no obstacles make any odds for the God of Love, only a fool would deny how mighty and how great a lord he is, but the power of love, that's demonstrated in the desires of Everyman day in and day out, meets its match in Theseus' sense of humor about it:

Well, well, try anything once, come hot, come cold,

If we're not foolish young, we're foolish old.

There's something about the experience of a lover that makes him smile. A clown tripping over his own feet and falling on his face is like a man tripping over the image of a woman and falling in love; the injuries are both comically self-inflicted. Having seen the plight of lovers in this light,

Theseus then builds a theater to express what he has learned about the government of his realm and about love. He employs the architecture of the arena to show that ego and insight have a complementary relationship. You can't have one without the other.

Prior to the tournament Palamon worshiped with Venus, Emily with Diana, and Arcite with Mars to pray for the outcome they and the god would favor. These three gods cover a lot of ground: Venus represents Palamon's attachment to what he loves, Mars represents Arcite's attachment to destroying the obstacle to what he loves, and Diana represents Emily's attachment to a life that would ignore or transcend the whole messy business. The stories about them makes it clear that they are all part of a family; to be themselves, these gods need each other. The temples of Venus and Mars include a gate for entering the arena at opposite ends, east and west. Diana's temple stands between them to the north, but it affords no access to where the action will take place.

Theseus has built a stadium large enough to seat everyone, for he understands Palamon's, Arcite's, and Emily's story to be everyone's story including his own, but he and his subjects can only enter the arena through the two gates east and west. This architecture expresses his understanding that people participate in the human comedy either by loving or hating. For better or for worse, we express our humanity—we become human—in our passions. Some may pretend to be above the fray, but the structure denies them. Either they own up to their passions, or they go home to their lonely house outside the community. The pictures in Diana's temple reveal some rather bloodthirsty passions inside that oratory of whitest alabaster. Diana's passion to be chaste is still a passion. Wisdom and chastity must first enter through the gates of love and hate, carried as a seed in a passionate human being. Desire is our ticket at the gate of Venus while rage is our ticket at the gate of Mars.

The experience in the woods has been a revelation for Theseus. For the first time in the tale he keenly feels the inadequacy of his rule. Prior to that, he may have thought that his judgments were "objective" even semi-divine, but he discovers that he needs those captive knights and the ladies to stir up a passionate curiosity about the nature of justice. For justice to be justice, there must be a passion for it. It's in the spirit of this revelation that he proposes a tournament, the celebration of an active struggle, as a more reliable vehicle for judgment. Given his nature, it's no surprise that he throws himself and enormous resources into the institution of the tournament as a public work. Having had his own mind changed by powers of understanding larger than himself, he is determined to express his experience in a more active and public form of judgment.

A year later, Arcite's fall from his horse in the theater brings the government of Theseus crashing to earth as well. Arcite's fall echoes for Theseus the disappointment of that other day in the woods when his law was too small to govern situations. The arena is not just a way to settle a private quarrel. In plummeting to earth, Arcite carries with him all that Theseus has done to gain the security of the state with a royal marriage, and the enterprise has been magnified by his own efforts to bring everyone in on it. The judgment of Theseus lies there in the dust as crushed as the heart of Arcite, but the rest of the tale demonstrates that the insight undergirding his theater still holds him in his fall much as Emily later holds Arcite in her arms. Insight, it turns out, is directly proportional to how much heart a person has in the game. Theseus' enormous investment in the tournament puts him in play on the grounds of his own theater. Ego and passion get him through the gate, and the contest inside involves his heart in both winning and losing. It's only in the play of his human heart that he'll win his way to true judgment.

Chapter six:
The Government of Wisdom

Van Gogh's *Landscape With Olive Trees*

The Conduct of Theseus after the Fall

A wake-up call functions at all levels of thinking. It may be entirely material and practical, like the sound of rumble-strips that warns an inattentive driver the road is about to end; it may interpersonal, like the hurt and anger in the voice of a friend that warns someone a relationship is about to end; or it may be entirely subjective, a call to life deep from within that pulls a person out of a dangerously alienated state. Chaucer's tale begins with Theseus quickly changing course when the ladies explain why they stopped him on his way to Athens. Later, it goes on to a deeper probing of his judgment when the ladies prompt him to reverse his sentence of death on the boys by recognizing:

The God of Love! Ah, Benedicite!

How mighty and how great a lord is he!

The narrative has been building its instances to the point where now, after the death of Arcite, Theseus has to consider his most ingrained orientation toward life and death.

If we compare Chaucer's tale to a magnificent Gothic church like that at Canterbury, our passage through its structure brings us inevitably to the high altar, the place of sacrifice where life is renewed. The story takes place in pagan Greece so there is no Christian cathedral for contemplation and prayer in "The Knight's Tale," but Arcite's fall brings everyone to a place where they must pause and reflect on the nature of life. Since I have been defining comedy as a realistic vision for the continuing and prospering of human life, it's fitting that Chaucer includes our mortality as an unavoidable part of the theme. Some theorists have written rules to prevent death from making any kind of entrance in a comedy, but a realistic survey of life can't avoid including it in the picture. The sudden loss of a loved one reveals to us, the way nothing else can, the depth and power of our attachment, and for most the feelings generated by the loss cannot be ignored or suppressed. The mutability of life ensures that these losses inevitably will occur, and then there's the leftover life to live for the ones who survive.

At the height of his power Theseus had established that death would not determine the possession of Emily. What a pity that the rule of Saturn proved to be greater than his own. Death simply can't be excluded from the story. In an autocratic state this loss of control can be deadly either for the autocrat or for those who begin to question the judgment of the autocrat. The conduct of Theseus from this time forward, however, is exemplary. In himself he absorbs the mortal wound to his government, and in everything he does he continues to embody the opening up of his judgment. Constantly in motion, he is the unmoving center of the events and emotions swirling around him. As far as the text is concerned, Theseus makes no speeches for many years after Arcite's fall and funeral. Until he does finally speak, his mind expresses itself in the action of government.

For example, he instinctively maintains his composure directly after Arcite's fall:

> *Theseus, attended by his company,*
>
> *Came slowly home to Athens in full state*
>
> *Of joyous festival, no less elate*
>
> *For this misfortune, wishing not to cast*
>
> *A gloom upon them all for what had passed.*

Misfortune does not mar his conduct. To succeed this conduct cannot be a "policy" or an act as in a play. Ultimately, such a policy would fail as it would be an empty gesture, a matter of ego and memory; it succeeds because he himself is a match for misfortune.

Theseus carefully observes the bedrock value of his culture—the extension of hospitality for a guest—as he sees to the needs of all who visit his city, especially those wounded in the fight:

For such as these Duke Theseus did his best,

He comforted and honoured every guest

And ordered revelry to last the night

For foreign princes, as was right.

Duke Theseus does his best because he recognizes that the situation requires it. Mighty Jupiter himself, he knows, enforces the laws of host and guest. He is responsible not only for his own people but also for those with whose customs and characters he may not be familiar. In this context, his actions here are not merely gestures of someone conditioned to behave according to certain rules. They reflect a mind that's awake. Arcite is still alive so Theseus' attention to his guests may serve as a form of prayer for Arcite's life.

Theseus doesn't neglect the politics of the great tournament, knowing that the most dangerous time in a fight could come after the fight was supposedly over:

And therefore Theseus made proclamation

To stop all rancour, grudge and emulations,

That each side was as valorous as the other

And both as like as brother is to brother.

He gave them gifts, to each in his degree,

And for three days they held festivity.

He urges "malice toward none," but it isn't just a pretty speech. The festivities are maintained, and each combatant is individually recognized with something of Theseus as well. His courtesy to his guests carries through right to the end of the three days:

Then he conveyed the Kings in solemn state

Out of his city, far beyond the gate...

Theseus goes far beyond the usual protocols, and this conveys the character of his mind and spirit at this point. His judgment is open to that which lies beyond what might be routinely defined as a sphere of interest. For three days Theseus walks in the shadow of the valley of death where life hangs in the balance, that of Arcite and that of Athens as a viable state, and yet he does what is right.

Once Arcite dies, the people of Athens fall into deep mourning. The quote bears repeating:

Infinite were the sorrows and the tears

Of older folk and those of tender years

Throughout the town, all for this Theban's death.

Wept man and boy, and sure a wilder breath

Of lamentation never had been heard

Since Hector, freshly slaughtered, was interred

In Troy. Alas to see the mourning there,

The scrabbled faces, the dishevelled hair!

"Must you have died?" the women wailed. "For see,

Had you not gold enough---and Emily?"

The passage captures a general mood of despair that, more than any specific villain or external enemy, can threaten the health and continuity of Athens or of any nation. Theseus does not withdraw from the sorrow of his people. He himself feels the loss as much as anyone, but as far as comfort goes, the comfort-buck stops with Theseus. He is at the end of the line. The narrator tells us:

> No one could lighten Theseus of his care
>
> Except his father, old Aegeus, there.

Unfortunately for Theseus, the narrator is either disingenuous or uncharacteristically unaware, for Aegeus draws his comfort from lifeless platitudes. The narrator says of him that:

> He knew the transmutations of the world
>
> And he had seen its changes as it whirled
>
> Bliss upon sorrow, sorrow upon bliss,
>
> And gave his son instructions upon this:
>
> "Just as there never died a man," said he,
>
> "But had in life some station or degree,
>
> Just so there never lived a man," he said,
>
> "In all the world but in the end was dead.
>
> This world is but a thoroughfare of woe
>
> And we are pilgrims passing to and fro.
>
> Death is the end of every worldly sore."
>
> On top of this he said a great deal more

To this effect, with wisest exhortation,

Heartening the people in their tribulation.

If we could observe the Knight's expression as he tells this part of the story, we might see a twinkle in his eye. The advice of Aegeus falls so terribly flat that the Knight would surely have noticed. In the first four lines of his speech, Aegeus lays out an utterly pointless universe from which there is no escape. He informs us that no man ever died who didn't first have some station in life, and no man ever lived in some station who didn't die. The circularity of the thought reflects the circularity of thought, thought in love with itself. Aegeus lives in a thought bubble that has yet to be burst. Like Palamon and Arcite, Aegeus is in love, but he is in love with his own thinking. All three are examples of how desire for something—in Aegeus' case, the desire to be wise—is rooted in an insular, obsessive thought pattern.[34]

There are several reasons why Chaucer the Author may have included his advice. First, it shows that Theseus can't rely on his father for comfort. He has to host his own thoughts and feelings about Arcite's sudden fall since Aegeus' pointless wisdom is powerless to deflect or mitigate them. Painful and confusing as this may be for Theseus, it engenders a self-possession without which he cannot begin to address the needs of his people. The advice also marks for the reader what the people are accustomed to accept as wisdom from their elders. If so, Theseus has his work cut out for him when he assembles his people many years later to speak on the same subject.

We know from the experience of Creon, who ignored the dead, that Theseus has to determine the siting for a sepulcher and make preparations for the fire that will burn Arcite's body:

And in the end the place decided on

Was where Arcite first met with Palamon

In battle for their love, and there between

The branches in that very grove of green

Where he had sung his amorous desire

In sad complaint, and felt love hot as fire,

He planned a fire to make, in funeral

Observances, and so accomplish all.

Theseus observes the rites belonging to his people for the burial of the dead. With a sympathetic imagination, moreover, he determines the burial site by "observing" the mind of Arcite. Theseus will burn and bury Arcite where he cried out in despair for love, fought for it with Palamon, was sentenced to death for it in the initial judgment of Theseus, and was saved for love when the judgment was overruled by the God of Love. Arcite and Theseus have been fatefully linked in the narrative, and the minds of the two men now appear to move as one as in an archetypal pattern.

The orders go out and these places are made ready:

And after this, Theseus appointed one

To fetch a bier and had it fitly clad

In cloth-of-gold, the finest that he had.

And in the self-same cloth he clad Arcite

And on his hands white gauntlets, as was meet,

He placed, and on his head a laurel crown

And in his hand the sword of his renown.

He laid him, bare his face, upon the bier,

And wept upon him, pity was to hear.

The similarity of the two now is so close that an observer might think Arcite was his son. At this point it appears that Theseus sees himself in everyone—the wounded knights, the other guests, his own people, and, most significantly, the heir of a hated enemy. The poignancy of the scene recalls the denouement in Genesis where, after their banishment, God dresses the nakedness of Adam and Eve with his own hands. They are leaving Him for a new existence, yet they are his creation still and his care.[35]

Like everyone there we see the care and the cost of dressing Arcite for death, and then we see it all consumed in a great fire. The costly gifts of Theseus as well as his most prized possession, his justice, prove to be mortal, to have an end. The fire is fueled by every variety of wood in the world. In his telling, the narrator even includes the creatures of the wood, natural and mythological, disturbed by the felling of the trees. It's a fire that involves everyone and everything. As it burns, people add their own valuable items to it. All this is Theseus' doing and reflects his understanding. He creates a vehicle for death as inclusive as the arena, his vehicle for judgment. By acknowledging the failure of that public work in the great conflagration of the funeral, he confesses to one and all the limit of mighty Theseus' power. In such a time he relies as well on the deepest customs of his people so once again his role as leader would appear to have been burned away in the actions of the day.[36]

The Possibility of Meaning

For the reader the profound silence of Theseus concerning Arcite lasts for certain years. The text tells us that he breaks his silence, in part, because a parliament is held to deal with issues of state:

And among these they dealt with certain places

With which to form alliances abroad

To keep the Thebans fully overawed,

And noble Theseus ordered thereupon

That summons should be sent for Palamon.

Palamon comes in haste to join the meeting, and Theseus sends for Emily as well. Even after everyone has assembled, the narrative underscores the depth of Theseus' silence by extending it for a bit:

When all were seated there and hushed the place,

The noble Duke kept silent for a space

And ere he spoke the wisdom in his breast

He let his eyes fall where it pleased him best.

Then with a sober visage and the still

Sound of a sigh, he thus expressed his will:

He last spoke in the spring, the season of the year that celebrates nature's triumphant return. On that day Theseus experienced a range of moods: the excitement and high spirits of the hunt, his anger at discovering the two felons, the frustration of having his judgment countered, and his bemused recognition of Love's greatness. The meeting he has just assembled, on the other hand, takes place in a great public building like a cathedral where the occasion and Theseus himself set a mood of quiet concentration. We are no longer outdoors, and so the season is not mentioned.

In keeping with his attention to present needs that we have seen in his conduct ever since the fall of Arcite, his eyes that "fall where it pleased him best" are full of the present moment. He doesn't need a prefabricated speech; he finds it all around him as he says:

The First Great Cause and Mover of all above

When first He made that fairest chain of love,

Great was the consequence and high the intent.

He well knew why He did, and what He meant.

The people have had to wait, and the reader has waited for almost three thousand lines, to hear lines like this that resound to the rooftop and beyond. These verses are Chaucer's version of "Let there be light." When Theseus looks around, what comes to mind has a shape and a meaning; otherwise, the silence would have continued endlessly or he would have babbled incoherently. This is his "sentence," a technical word for the shape his words take as well as a word that refers to the meaning of a story for a medieval speaker and writer.[37] His speech rightly begins, therefore, with the fact that he can speak at all.

On Earth As It Is in Heaven?

Having established the possibility of meaning, a meaning made of love, which functions like the overall building in which the words reverberate, Theseus moves on to that which is held and made meaningful by this form:

For in that fairest chain of love He bound

Fire and air and water and the ground

Of earth in certain limits they may not flee.

Good government of a life and of a nation begins with a recognition that the things of this world are limited in time and space.

While Theseus doesn't name Arcite, the premature death of a young person brings out the sense of limit most vividly and painfully:

And that same Prince and Mover then, said he

'Stablished this wretched world, appointing ways,

Seasons, durations, certain length of days,

To all that is engendered here below,

Past which predestined hour none may go,

Though they have the power to abridge those days.

This passage highlights a tension present throughout the tale and throughout the life of a conscious human being. On the one hand, there's creation as it is depicted in the first four lines of his speech, so calm, stable, and full of "high intent"; and, on the other hand, there is human life as it appears on the ground, a movable brewing of all the highs and lows and in-betweens, which sloshes around until suddenly or over time it falls inert. Because life in the world is so difficult, sometimes a person may "abridge" his life by ending it himself; this is something Arcite considered when he first returned to Thebes and was so filled with self-hatred. On the ground where people live, a mixture of forces and laws would appear to have locked human beings up in an unpleasant prison, a "wretched world." Nevertheless, by virtue of the opening sentences, which affirm the greatness of creation's consequence and the height of the intent to create it, all this unpleasantness rests within the infinitely larger space and power of the Prince and Mover of all things. This world is not a prison but a chain of love. Naturally we wonder how the tension is resolved.

The Experience of Relationship

As a practical man Theseus does not aim to speculate about metaphysics even though he relates a story of creation in the opening of his speech. Most people would agree with him when he observes that life is hard and people eventually die, but this is merely the unhelpful wisdom of Aegeus, his father. Given the solemnity of the space and the occasion, surely he has more on his mind than Aegeus' abstract and depressing commentary. To ground his observations more concretely, therefore, Theseus offers himself and his own experience as the basis for the argument he is building:

> I need not quote authority or raise
>
> More proof than what experience can show,
>
> But give opinion from what I know.

In the opening lines of his speech Theseus has given himself a mighty task: he would show that the tension between the greatness of creation and the wretchedness of this world can be resolved without resorting to the authority of a blind faith. By using his own experience as evidence, he invites his people to agree or disagree with him based on their own sense of what is possible or real in this world.

What is Theseus' experience? Out of all that could be said, he emphasizes the limits that have been set on the things of this world including the limit to life itself. The "ways" of these things are appointed both in space and time, and human beings like Arcite travel those ways toward a certain end. After his initial characterization of creation as a chain, Theseus' subsequent emphasis on the limit of things allows the second half of the analogy to be overshadowed. If it's a chain of love, the interpretation needs a different emphasis, and neither the reader nor Theseus has far to look in order to discover how love has changed the nature of his experience. Earlier, Theseus killed Creon in single combat. If the text is an indication, he never gave the death of Creon a second thought, for the poem doesn't record his feelings on the subject. Yet now he is composing a magnificent speech for his entire court about the death of another from Thebes, the city that represents a mortal threat to his own. Since he's a soldier, he has probably seen and been responsible for many deaths. Perhaps, as Chaucer himself did, Theseus has witnessed something like the Black Death which could destroy an entire village or town in a matter of days. When the end of a life is common, Theseus must have wondered what was different about Arcite's death that would make him pause and reflect so deeply.

Since the tale by degrees comes to focus on Theseus' relationship with the two knights, it's reasonable to infer that his experience with them is what lies behind the change of emphasis. We have seen and Theseus must have been aware that he gradually invested more and more of himself in Arcite. Touched by his friend's love, he allowed his prisoner to return to Thebes. When Palamon and Arcite were ankle-deep in their own blood and captives once more to the hatred of an ancient enemy, the man who knew himself to be their enemy nevertheless found himself embracing them with all the power of a loving parent and sovereign; later, in deep grief he dressed the body of Arcite with his own hands the way he would care for the body of his own flesh and blood.

His speech reveals that Arcite's death has triggered within him an awareness of the mutability and the limits not just of human life but of all things, including his judgment. He may have been referring to Arcite when he observes that the ways of "all that is engendered here below" cannot live beyond a "predestined hour," but when Arcite's body and crushed heart lay in the dust of his arena with his entire realm as a witness, Theseus saw the crushed heart of his policy lying there as well. In the general conflagration at the funeral, the burning away of Arcite's body represents the limit of every object—the trees, the habitat and the livelihood of animals, and all that people hold precious including thoughts and ideas engendered in the brain. He has experienced—what he has just described as the nature of things—the limit of his judgment in relationships. After all, he is now a married man and married to a woman with whom he once was at war. Subsequently, over many months following Arcite's death, being a practical and a sensible man, he has to question: What is the reality of a relationship when he wants to kill the knights (or his future wife) one minute and embrace them the next? And what does he make of himself and the divine laws he is empowered to execute? The commission can fashion him either as an executioner or an agent of mercy.

Theseus has decided to speak to all his people about this because he sees that this is true for the relationships of Everyman: Everyman holds in his hands the power of life and death, for anyone can "abridge those days" allotted to oneself or someone else. So are we an instrument for death or for life? This puzzling between whether he is this or that brings him to the heart of what he would say about his experience. Material objects alone (which include ideas about ourselves and others) don't make up experience; there are the gaps between the objects like the gap between wanting to kill and then to embrace someone. Objects don't exist without a context; there are the spaces, the relationships, the overall ground for everything. Therefore, Theseus would depict things-as-they-are including the intangible, unknowable Prince and Prime Mover. It's why he begins his speech the way he does.

To gage by his own experience where hate is transformed to love, this same Prince and Mover, he reasons, must be present in his own heart, and if in his why not potentially present in "all that is engendered here below." This is why he requires no greater authority than experience for what he is saying and for how he conducts his life, and it's why he can call creation not just a chain but a chain of love. Theseus is a noble duke, but he sees that this insight doesn't belong just to him. Everyman is an heir to it, and he would publish the patrimony to everyone. Is this life great with consequence and noble intent or is it merely a prison? His experience suggests that the Prince and Mover who guides and gives his life a coherent shape is immanent "here below" as a seed or a root of meaning in his own heart and mind. It's an experience that bridges the gap between the greatness of creation and the corruption of life on earth. This approach also invites a reader to reason with the text as I do here six hundred years after the fact. He's a free man who reasons from his own experience to act in a way that conforms with the world as it is and that affirms life.

Perception: A Glimpse into the Garden

In the previous paragraph I employed as a part of my argument the image of a seed or the root of a perennial from the opening lines of the General Prologue. Even in translation their beauty announces the springtime of English poetry:

When in April the sweet showers fall

And pierce the drought of March to the root, and all

The veins are bathed in liquor of such power

As brings about the engendering of the flower...

The opening lines of Theseus' speech under discussion here—which lay the foundation for a comic world by establishing that the creation of all and everything is animated by a noble intent,[38] great consequence, and meaning—derive from that root. Despite the drought of March, the fact of suffering, that seed or root is ripe for renewal in a springtime of rain and wind and sun along with all the other influences of everyday life. These lines plant an image in our minds that anticipates the flourishing of life we'll read about throughout the tales. To break the silent grief into which he has fallen after the death of Arcite, Theseus depicts creation not as a root dormant in a wintry darkness but as a chain that's employed to constrain human beings in a wintry bondage. Like the root which engenders the flower, this chain, which only seems to constrain, is made of love and links us to love.

Having established the possibility of meaning that's revealed in his own experience, Theseus then turns to the second great "day" in his re-creation of creation. As his speech evolves along its linked sentences and images, he now pictures the creator as a prince like himself only a prince infinitely greater than he:

Since we discern this order, we are able

To know that Prince is infinite and stable.

Anyone but a fool knows, in his soul,

That every part derives from this great whole.

Just as a prince cannot be a proper prince without subjects to comprehend (who in turn comprehend him as their prince), the world requires sentient beings to perceive it. This is why the second act of creation introduces the all-important "we" who discern creation and who infer the relationship of its parts to the whole. In addressing us directly, these lines make us aware of ourselves as subjects, not as his subjects but as independent centers of perception. We are a vital part of the great whole as it is "we" who discern it.

Earlier in the speech Theseus offers himself and his own experience as the basis for his argument. Here again is how the translator put it:

I need not quote authority or raise

More proof than what experience can show,

But give opinion from what I know.

Chaucer's original wording ends with a term that is critical for interpreting the role "we" play in creation:

Ther nedeth noght noon auctoritee t'allegge

For it is perceived by experience

But that me lists [lusts or pleases] declaren my sentence.

Chaucer's sentence ends with the word "sentence" for which the translator has substituted "opinion," and Chaucer's word has a much larger capacity for carrying the freight of his theme. (Shakespeare certainly noticed it, for he includes an important comic commentary on sentences in the conclusion of *A Midsummer Night's Dream*.) We understand from the original wording that, instead of quoting authorities, it pleases Theseus to declare his own sentence or judgment on the matter, for it is perceived by experience. As a sentence is a unit of meaning, Theseus would declare what his experience means. The intersection of these two meanings, of judgment and of meaning, survives in modern speech when the word refers to a limitation placed on a defendant's life after a judge or jury finds against him in a legal case. For the defendant, the judge's sentence is what the defendant's action means in that context.

"Sent," the root of the word, concretely refers to someone or something projected toward someone or some place, and it still has that meaning as when a king sends a messenger to the king in another country. The physical going of someone or something to someone or someplace can easily be associated with the message itself, as in "presentiment" where the word refers to a mental message coming to consciousness. Furthermore, a person who "senses" something, the recipient of a sensory message, is in the early stages of grasping or understanding it. By the commonality of the root in these usages we are made aware that sensation is a material experience like that of a messenger entering a home.

The root of these words functions as a bridge across different usages. The bridge allows me to argue that Theseus' sentence derives directly from his "sense" of the world depicted by the whole of the tale and that the young men's glimpse of Emily in the garden is an archetype at the heart of it all. Just as Palamon and Arcite root their whole lives in that glimpse of Emily, Theseus (and Chaucer) would root us firmly in the experience of life and, more immediately, in perception; the fact that we can sense the world at all ties us to the whole, the sentience and the sentence—that is, the living order and meaning of the world—from which we derive. Order and meaning take shape in perception itself, and for a prince on earth or anyone the government of a life aims at the present and accurate perception of things-as-they-are.

But how can a limited human being perceive the whole? Theseus is a ruler, not a philosopher describing absolutes, so he doesn't try to answer the question. Instead, he uses the abstract terms of part and whole as a framing device for his argument when he asserts that:

> *Anyone but a fool knows, in his soul,*
>
> *That every part derives from this great whole.*

He is framing the issue the way an architect constructs (from different parts) a gateway or a window for the viewing of a garden that can't be entered into or glimpsed without the framing device. This brings us back to the all-important window in Theseus' tower. Theseus doesn't have to answer the question of how we can perceive the whole; he has to make us aware of the problem.

Chaucer himself has prepared us for this garden of awareness by arranging with such care that morning when Emily arises to do the rites of May and wanders into the garden next to the tower. By means of Chaucer's device, we see that, like the view of Emily in the garden from Palamon and Arcite's window at the top of the tower, any individual's discernment of the world is limited. The scene is constructed so that the tower's small window restricts their view to a fleeting glimpse of Emily. At the same time, for one aware of how small a window it is, this limitation hints strongly at the greatness of what cannot be seen. Through this frame—the fact that perception is but a series of small windows on the world—the reader is led to understand that the mind tends to see the parts in the garden—the flowers, the trees, the apples, the bugs, the snakes, and finally the people, but it is locked out from what it can't see at a glance, namely what happens when all these objects are set in motion and begin to interact in time.[39] Also, the mind cannot grasp that which is not readily present to the sense, like things hidden underground or things in another country or empty space or the past or the future. The two lines that introduce part and whole as a framing device offer a striking commentary on the mind's "natural" inclination to deal only with that which is considered in isolation. By touting what anyone but a fool knows, he has made it hard to argue against the priority of "this great whole" in the way we discern or perceive the order of this world. But in case we're tempted to disagree, he reveals next the heart of the matter in a compact couplet:

For nature cannot be supposed to start

From some particular portion or mere part.

This is the crux of Theseus' argument, and it's at the heart of my argument about comic literature.

Theseus addresses here his observation from experience that a human being tends to "suppose" or assume that reality is rooted in a part. It's a way of saying that a person can be easily distracted into thinking that the whole world revolves around "a little thing" (as when people describe a setback as "just a little thing") and consequently miss or distort the importance of everything else in the world. This condition is what I have referred to as an attachment. The little thing may be real enough, but people routinely give it a disproportional and sometimes a fantastical value. Because Theseus and Chaucer are realists, they would have noticed that it is natural for human beings to suppose that nature starts from a portion or mere part. This is what ego does, and ego is a fact of life. But it is also natural to seek out the whole the way Theseus is doing here, and we know from reading the whole of his experience that his seeking began when he could admit without reservation and could publicly demonstrate— as in the great fire at Arcite's cremation—that he doesn't know everything.

Consider also the "experiences" of Arcite where his obsessive claim to "my Emily" is rendered irrelevant finally by a larger point of view. His idea is like that tiny little Emily at the end of his tunnel vision which he supposed summed up his life, but the poet has made it obvious (to the reader) there's a whole universe, around her and around him in the tower, that isn't seen. Emily in this case isn't the universe; she "derives from" the universe. Paradoxically, Arcite gains the longed-for intimacy with her only when he freely dissolves the idea of possessing her. This whole story—the good, the bad, the ugly, and the final insight—is the garden where we as readers may have a glimpse of freedom.

The Source

Theseus calls this garden a "fairest chain of love." Even though there's a suggestion of limitation and even of imprisonment in the image, that constraint is redeemed by the beauty of the world and the noble intent behind its creation. As a demonstration of this we have seen that the ego attachments of Arcite and of Theseus directly contribute to unlocking the power of *caritas*, a fresh look at the world.

My presentation of this theme and Chaucer's development of it in "The Knight's Tale" have moved from simple to more difficult applications. The story of the pedestrian's attachment to the media world of his BlackBerry, which a banana peel brings to an end, is direct physical comedy. When we fall down, we learn to pay more attention to where we are walking, and so we may be willing to give up the Blackberry while walking or driving. Arcite's obsession with Emily, which the thrust of the saddle bow brings to an end, is a more difficult case. His attachment to her comes close to the roots of life which is why giving her up is almost unthinkable. Theseus' attachment to his judgment, which is confounded by Arcite's unforeseen death, complicates the issue, for it's not a physical attachment. It has to do with the image he has of himself as a competent ruler of men. This may be even more difficult to give up than a sword of power or a woman he fancies. Finally, Theseus' speech addresses Everyman's attachment to the way he looks at life itself which in turn determines how he governs himself in the world. The story of Adam and Eve's temptation in the garden maintains that this attachment to knowing the true nature of life and its moral laws is the cause of their deaths.

Everyman wants more than eating, sleeping, and enjoying the company of his mate. He wants to know, but this knowledge, the story warns, is linked to giving up life as we know it.

After human beings have worked on these issues for so long, Everyman still determines whether to look at life as a tragedy or a comedy, and the determination will strongly affect an individual's conduct. This attachment to our picture of life is so deeply rooted in everyday conversations with others and with ourselves that it is regarded as a given, not a choice, and it fades into the background, like points of light in the night sky. So do we think, without putting a bumper sticker on our car, that life sucks and then we die? Other ideas firmly rooted in the language and the expectations of the culture—for example, the commonly expressed and institutionally reinforced idea that knowledge is power—take shape as timeless constellations there as well. Once death steps onstage in the story of Everyman, the power of knowledge, even though the desire for it brought death into the world in the first place, serves as a comfort and a shield, a holding cell of certainty.

The idea that knowledge is power is indeed powerful; it has shaped our perception of the world. And because the mind has been conditioned to regard it not as an idea but as reality, it is much more difficult to wake from its spell. An uncritical acceptance of "knowledge is power" begs a question: Does it refer to knowledge of parts or to the whole from which the parts derive? If it's knowledge of a part, then, according to Theseus, we are fools to overvalue it. If it's knowledge of the whole, are our prospects of knowing this any better now than they were three thousand years ago?

It's an ancient problem which continues to impact anyone living in the natural world—what to do when the mind easily fixes on knowledge of objects and forgets or ignores what it cannot hold or encompass so easily, the whole from which they all derive. As a practical man Theseus somehow has to make a case for the reality of that First Great Cause and Mover which can so easily be dismissed when tagged with labels that describe it as an "abstract" or "metaphysical" or "supernatural" concept of little practical value. In the modern world especially, such labels tend to petrify the reality of Theseus' First Great Cause and Mover into a known and inanimate object on a par with all other known and quantifiable objects. Because some are satisfied with labeling it as metaphysical or supernatural, they feel justified in ignoring it, but this ignoring and suppressing may have an unhealthy effect.

Those who have little patience with or interest in metaphysical questions are known as positivists, a word that implies a clear, simple, and rational way of looking at the world and of living. Yet these same positivists may, in the course of their everyday thinking and speaking, routinely obsess over the way "time" ages the body even though this involves abstract and metaphysical concepts of time and causation. A positivist's refusal to consider metaphysical concepts still leaves that person with the problem of deciding what is a metaphysical concept and what is not. If time is accepted as a material and ultimately hostile fact in our routines and expectations, this can be a source of great suffering. Time can then materialize to play the part of a tiger or a lion or anything that mauls, defaces, and eventually kills its victims. It becomes a source of fear, an enemy to subdue or avoid. Is it any wonder that a person who lives in the same house with the grim reaper might go a little crazy? And this in spite of a rigorous positivism.

These observations provide a context for the metaphoric frame Theseus establishes within the next link of his speech. A chain of love is a static and spatial image of parts that tend to a whole and reciprocally a whole that intends its parts. To complement that picture with another that adds a temporal dimension, Theseus pictures creation in motion:

> For nature cannot be supposed to start
>
> From some particular portion or mere part,
>
> But from a whole and undisturbed perfection
>
> Descending thence to what is in subjection

To change, and will corrupt. And therefore He

In wise foreknowledge stablished the decree

That species of all things and the progression

Of seed and growth continue by succession

And not eternally. This is no lie,

As any man can see who has an eye.

We see the visible objects of this world emerge not from a part but from "a whole and undisturbed perfection," and then they move down like the water of a stream that pours forth from a spring. The descent, though, is a rough-and-tumble affair as time takes its toll. Things corrupt over time, but the Prince and First Great Cause has decreed a renewal of living things by a succession of new generations. Chaucer may have been familiar with the Greeks' speculations about time—Parmenides arguing that change was impossible, Heraclitis arguing that everything was only change, Aristotle tilting the argument strongly toward change from Plato's static forms, and Greek Theseus may have been familiar with them as well. As a ruler and teacher of restive, impressionable, and passionate people with little inclination for philosophy, however, Theseus avoids speculating past what "any man can see who has an eye" that things decline over time toward corruption and death.

To illustrate this he draws attention to how an oak slowly develops into a great spreading thing until it falls. He points out that a rock can slowly be worn away to nothing and rivers can dry up and cease to be. So it is with human life:

There is no help for it, all take the track,

For all must die and there is none comes back.

Surely it is wisdom to recognize the effects of time on a human body or on anything. We can't live well if we don't acknowledge the changes taking place in our bodies, in our environments, in our jobs, in our tools like cars and washing machines, and in our societies. Theseus' imagery and tone suggest he has adopted a Stoic outlook to deal with the incongruity between the great consequence and high intent of the First Great Cause and life as it is lived in the dust of earthly existence. Life runs on a downward slope; it is up to each of us to face that squarely with courage, with a human heart.

This is the way a soldier sees time. It's like Theseus doing battle with an outside agent like Hippolyta or Creon. It's like Palamon and Arcite fighting each other desperately and at great length. Such conflicts result from a dualistic view where ego is attached to that which it prizes, like the vitality and beauty of youth, and is at war with the world for it. Without negating the Stoic approach Theseus has just described, the next lines suggest a different way to look at time:

> Who orders this but Jupiter the King,
>
> The Prince and Cause of all and everything,
>
> Converting all things back into the source
>
> From which they were derived, to which they course?
>
> And against this no creature here alive
>
> Whatever his degree may hope to strive.

When all things are converted "back into the source / From which they were derived," there can be no dualism, and there can be no conflict that comes from dualism. When we think about time, we tend to think about it as Theseus did in the examples of the oak and the rock and the river, yet these examples are only partially true. All must die, but this is only after they have come into being. Time is also a "source," an opening into life.

Seen this way, time gives birth to an awareness and a thankfulness for life that's like a timeless and all-encompassing embrace. Also, we have seen in the case of Arcite and Theseus that individual and social processes of great consequence and high intent work themselves out in time. There's room, in time, for that glimpse of Emily in the garden to be redeemed for its true value. Finally, time (as we know it) is a human invention, a projection. We are its source, and we can convert it.

The last two lines contrast the power of any one person with the way the Prince and Cause of all and everything has made the world:

> *And against this no creature here alive*
>
> *Whatever his degree may hope to strive.*

Looked at one way, these lines could mean that no one can hope to strive against death, but that meaning depends on what "this" refers to. If it refers to time as the tiger that mauls and eventually destroys us, then "this" is a cause for grief. But if it refers to the source "of all and everything" and the greatness of its consequence and the height of its intent, then we have the basis for a comic world.[40] The lines are addressing someone who needlessly grieves and resists the fact that he was born out of this amazing source and still lives. For as long as we discern the world, "we" are willy-nilly the source that makes all one. Seen in this light, an attachment to grief is an affront to life and to things-as-they-are. Long before Einstein, a medieval poet describes time as a space that opens to bring all and everything into existence. In this understanding we can affirm time in the wholeness of all and everything and in the fact that we exist at all. In addition, if we truly feel the pull of that Prince and Cause of Everything "Converting all things back into the source / From which they were derived," the stream that was falling down reverses course. Instead of descending toward death, time ascends toward life.

To sum up, Theseus initially outlines a dualistic tension at the heart of human life: the greatness and the loftiness of creation's consequence versus the fact that all "engendered here below" are constrained to live in a limited and wretched world for only a "certain length of days." This tension, he finds, is resolved when all things are converted into the source from which they derive. The "time" that descends is an idea of time, a part, and:

> *Anyone but a fool knows, in his soul,*
>
> *That every part derives from this great whole.*

As a practical man, Theseus has confined his observations to his own experience. He doesn't claim to be a priest or an oracle of the gods. In the same spirit, I would use imagery from nature, as he does, to comment on his theme. If we study nature, we notice, as Theseus suggests, that the species of all living things carries within it seeds for the future: trees have them; flowers have them; skunks, bears, and human beings have them. The death of Arcite and the life that now stirs within Theseus have led him to conclude that every moment of our life contains within it a seed for death and a seed for life. As in a medieval morality play where a bad angel and a good angel stand at either ear of Everyman, each dispensing advice as to the nature of life and what to do, the one voice is like a seed buried deep with a hidden capacity for death. Sometimes, for reasons we can't begin to comprehend, the heart stops beating or a single cell out of the billions of which we are composed goes rogue and loses its sense of proportionality within the structure. Also, a bad idea or a freak accident may convey a mortal consequence. This capacity for death can cast a cloud over the whole imagination, and it can speak to us like a voice arguing that life is on a hopeless downward slope, a vehicle for death. There's another seed, though, and it argues that life is an upward return to the source of all and everything.

It's with the second voice that he concludes his speech in the hope that the power of his vision will lift the cloud that has darkened the imaginations of the people for so long, but this will depend on whether the people can give up the knowledge that has been their comfort and their shield from the time they first knew fear.

A Comic Conclusion

Theseus finishes on a simple and pragmatic note:

So what conclusion can I draw from this

Except that after grief there should be bliss

And praise to Jupiter for all his grace?

So, ere we make departure from this place,

I rule that of two sorrows we endeavour

to make one perfect joy, to last for ever.

He is persuaded that a situation can work itself out in time, and he has raised our deepest fear about time only to show that it, like everything else, is limited and that it's time for grief to die.

The marriage and the perfect joy of Palamon and Emily have been there all along, waiting for their cue to come on stage. Palamon has loved her since he first saw her, and Arcite blessed their marriage with his last breath. Time is also a peacemaker; it's time for the ancient war between Athens and Thebes to die. Peace is no longer an idea or a policy. It's a man and a woman coming together to have children, and the peace of this man and woman is now tied to all the normal expectations and customs that for thousands of years have been built up around the birth and the safeguarding of children. Politics is being converted back to the source of human life. This peace, too, has been waiting in the wings for as long as boys and girls have been born into the world and for as long as a Jack must have his Jill.[41] A Jack's intent to have his Jill may be a bit of low comedy compared to the high intent that made the world, but throughout the work of this great comic poet I glimpse the twinkle in Chaucer's eye that sees how they are related. In that great chain of love the Prime Mover is linked to the searing passions of hate and love that move men and women to folly and to marriage.

Theseus ends his speech with a vision where the separate strands of the narrative are knitted together to make a new life for all those involved. There's no telling where that vision "of one perfect joy" comes from or why it is that Theseus aspires to it. It's the gift of his experience. The vision may have been freely given to him, but the perfect joy of his vision will derive as well from their "endeavor," the hard work that will make the vision a reality. The creation of a comic world is more than a vision; it involves a conscious choice and the labor of realizing it. Theseus has already tasted this new life for himself. Through bitter experience, the quick sword of his law has been transformed over the course of the narrative into the great care he has taken and the many preparations he has made to set the stage for a presentation of the vision.

His conclusion contrasts starkly with that of Creon in which a tyrant's law is attached to a corpse that lies unburied and ravaged by dogs and the sun. As a man who consciously ignores the will of the gods, Creon the Tyrant would build a Kingdom of Ego, but that kingdom could not stand up to the force of Theseus' comic vision. In their passionate attachment to Emily, the two knights suffer from a similar tyranny; they build a little kingdom around an attachment to her image. They resemble today's celebrity stalkers who fall in love with pictures and create a fantasy world around projected ideas and feelings. These folks are a little crazy, and they rule in this world the way a tyrant rules in his kingdom. Naturally, though, the real world rebels. In the knights' case "the real world" ironically pushes back in the shape of a tyrant cousin who is the mirror image of himself. These two discover the hard way that playing the tyrant's role involves putting themselves into a mental and physical meat grinder. What about Theseus? He defeated Hippolyta in a war and then married her. Would she have married him if she had won? What hopes can there be for such a marriage? Chaucer was writing for a courtly audience as intimately versed in the traditions of courtly love as he, so the reader may wonder why, when so much else is included, the storyteller omits the courtship of Hippolyta. It's a small detail, but it takes on more significance as Theseus comes to the conclusion of his speech.

If absolute power corrupts absolutely, as has been said, then Theseus would be a candidate for corruption and tyranny as he looks and acts and sounds like a mighty man with total control over his people. It can also be said that in fearful times one might be tempted to give the power and freedom of deciding the architecture of one's life to a strongman. It may well be that Theseus has that effect on others, but the tale is more interested in its effect on Theseus himself. After all this display of power and wisdom, in his own mind the success or failure of his government apparently depends on someone else. That is why he turns to Emily and addresses her directly:

> Sister, he said, it has my full assent,
>
> And is confirmed by this my parliament,
>
> That gentle Palamon, your own true knight,
>
> Who loves and serves you, heart and soul and might,
>
> And always has since first he saw your face,
>
> Shall move you to feel pity, gain your grace
>
> And so become your husband and your lord.
>
> Give me your hand, for this is our award.

Here is a congruence with what he maintained earlier in his speech. The government of the world involves a recognition of limits, he said, and he recognizes that a man's sphere effectively ends around the contours of a woman's body. The whole speech has been working its way to a final test of its truth: What does Emily think about it? If Theseus is a tyrant, why would he ever allow the fate of his foreign policy and the security of his nation ride on the heart and mind of a woman? He asks for her hand, but will he get it?

Chaucer presents this scene with dramatic power. Scenes like this can be found at the end of Shakespearean comedies, and there too a director reading the text has to imagine the actions underlying the speech. So I imagine here a pause as Emily does not immediately give him her hand. This would explain why Theseus has to resort to persuasion and even the pleading of a courtly man to a lady:

> *Let us now see your womanly compassion.*
>
> *By God, he's a king's nephew! Were his fashion*
>
> *No more than that of a knight-bachelor,*
>
> *What with the years he served and suffered for*
>
> *Your love (unless his sufferings deceive me)*
>
> *He would be worth considering, believe me.*
>
> *A noble mercy should surpass a right.*

His speech perfectly balances courtly love with the laws that govern royal marriages. It also recognizes her power as an independent subject, for better or worse—a mind at the center of the universe. As he turns next and speaks to Palamon, it is safe to say that Emily has given him her hand:

> *And then he said to Palamon the knight,*
>
> *I think there needs but little sermoning*
>
> *To gain your own assent to such a thing.*
>
> *Come near, and take your lady by the hand.*

With that, this survey of human behavior and human thought comes to rest with a simple gesture by two individual parts of his tale. It's only the touch of another's hand, but in that touch there's the transmission and the generation of new life..

The narrator goes on to describe in the closing lines the new world that has risen out of the spiritual force of Arcite's insight, the power of Arcite's experience to transform the life of Theseus, and the taking of hands by Palamon and Emily:

And thus with every bliss and melody

Palamon was espoused to Emily,

And God that all this wide, wide world has wrought,

Send them his love, for it was dearly bought!

Now Palamon's in joy, amid a wealth

Of bliss and splendor, happiness and wealth.

He's tenderly beloved of Emily

And serves her with a gentle constancy,

And never a jealous word between them spoken

Or other sorrow in a love unbroken.

Thus ended Palamon and Emily,

And God save all this happy company!

Palamon expresses for Emily a gentle, constant love, likely because his marriage is inextricably linked to and made possible by the death of his virtual twin and alter ego. Along with an instinctive attraction to her, he loves with a gratitude for life itself, for he doesn't forget that his life has been spared when it could easily have ended at critical points. Then, too, all his efforts to possess Emily for himself utterly failed. These experiences have disciplined him to accept that he lives by a power greater than his own. His marriage to Emily is the gift of that power, and she stands before his eyes to continually remind him that life itself is a gift. By serving Emily in a love unbroken, he serves the source of all and everything.

So Chaucer concludes his tale, but the story doesn't really end there. A little acorn from an old oak contains within it the stirrings of new life. The "gentle constancy" of Chaucer's Palamon transports itself like a seed over a span of two hundred years and reemerges, in a slightly different form, when Hippolyta in *A Midsummer Night's Dream* glimpses a "great constancy" in the dreams of Shakespeare's lovers. In addition to reviving Chaucer's language, Shakespeare relives in his play the trials and the insights of Chaucer's characters. By means of a narrative, Chaucer has given us a purchase on that "airy nothing"—wisdom, the prosperous governing of our lives.[42] The wisdom that's Chaucer's subject cannot be taught or learned in the usual ways of instruction. It belongs to the school of hard knocks.

There's a passage in "The Knight's Tale" that describes that school's muddy curriculum, and it may have suggested to Shakespeare the setting for those middle acts that take place at night in the Athenian wood. The passage is part of Arcite's soliloquy after his release from the tower and return home to Thebes. He regrets ever having prayed for freedom since freedom now takes him away from what in prison he regarded as his home—his sporadic, little glimpses of Emily. In his reflections he concludes:

Our ways are drunkard ways---drunk as a mouse;

A drunkard knows quite well he has a house,

But how to get there puts him in a dither,

And for a drunk the way is slip and slither.[43]

Under the influence of an obsessive attachment, Shakespeare's lovers behave in the woods much the way Chaucer's drunkard does. Such a life may be "slither" like a topsy-turvy midsummer's night, but in a comedy the slithering and the hard knocks turn out to be the road to Canterbury, the way the heart grows whole.

The transmission of wisdom is not just a matter of reworking a word or a phrase, the suggestion of a scene, or an idea. Chaucer maintains, as Shakespeare does, that it requires the presence of another who loves us in the way of wisdom, and both poets summon up that presence as the sure and reassuring touch of a hand. At the end of Chaucer's poem Theseus, as the representative of government within the tale, appeals to Palamon and Emily to take hands as a sign and seal of their new life; at the end of *A Midsummer Night's Dream* Robin appeals to the audience to "give me your hands." It's a timeless gesture of acknowledging another, and like a hand outstretched it holds out the promise of friendship. For these poets, hands that touch in true friendship represent the conclusion of all that has gone before as well as a new beginning. They challenge us as readers (or listeners) of these works to hear the passion and the power of a voice that still lives in the spirit of the words. Like the touch of a friend, it's a power for life, and it's from the constancy of the vision in each poet's voice that the title of my book derives. To explain that connection more fully, I turn now to a reading of Shakespeare's play.

A

MIDSUMMER

NIGHT'S

DREAM

Chapter seven:
Athens

Rembrandt's *Aristotle with a Bust of Homer*

Introduction: Autonomy Then and Now

The Odyssey may be both the earliest and the greatest expression of a comic theme in Western literature. As a young husband and father, Odysseus leaves his island kingdom to seek in the Great War the ideal form of a hero's immortality. After an exile of twenty years that reduces him to a naked man in a vast ocean, he eventually returns to resume his place as the true king of Ithaca and ends his labors in bed with his wife Penelope for one night. When read as a whole narrative, the theme of exile and return functions as a unifying structural device for both the Hebrew and the Christian Bible. Adam and Eve begin innocently in a garden; aroused by an ideal form separate (on pain of death) from themselves, they fall from grace into a difficult exile where the naked self is exposed at every turn; but the alienation and difficulty of life in the world after the fall prove to be fortunate for those of their descendants who wake up to the true nature of desire and follow righteousness.

In "The Knight's Tale" Chaucer adapts this theme within the conventions of medieval courtly love. Here, two young cousins fall hopelessly in love with the ideal form of a young woman. As each young man would possess her for himself, the conflict that ensues alienates them from ties of blood and honor that previously had given their life meaning. Stripped of their knightly trappings, they pursue her with a naked desire. The suffering caused by the narrowing of desire eventually awakens one of the young men from his obsession. Despite the death of the main character, Chaucer's rendering of Arcite's story outlines a comic pattern for those who, after falling into a dream that works like a death wish, are redeemed from that dream by a larger intelligence.

If read as a continuous narrative, the story of Western philosophy falls into a pattern of exile and return. It begins innocently in a cosmos, a Greek word referring to a harmonious whole, with earth and man at the center. Human beings have a definite place here, especially human beings who can see the essential forms of this world. Socrates, Plato, and Aristotle had an innate confidence in the value and meaning of their colloquiums, their formal speeches, and their writings. Early Christian writers largely borrowed the classical cosmos, and they, too, conveyed the confidence of Greek philosophers about the value and the meaning of their work, heightened undoubtedly by an overriding faith in divine providence and man's special place in Creation. When read as a story of innocence and exile, though, for some time now Western philosophy and modern life have fallen from the safety and comfort of that confidence and faith into wrenching doubt about whether we can know anything about the world "out there." Blaise Pascal, a brilliant French mathematician and physicist who was born just a few years after Shakespeare died, saw what the physics of the modern world implied and wrote of it, "The silence of these infinite spaces fills me with dread."

Like the earth itself, which at the beginning of the modern era was liberated from its position as the ground of existence to become an object in space that moves around the sun, human beings realized a new autonomy to move in all directions from ancient ways of thinking about themselves and the world. Slowly but surely, this autonomy became the dominant note in our culture, and its effects can be found in all branches of the sciences and the humanities. After Copernicus, people were free to develop their knowledge of the world without the limitations of an incorrect cosmology, and the freedom to re-imagine the world eventually led to freedom from other limitations of religious doctrine. But this autonomy also has exposed human beings to a colder, more impersonal universe drained of ancient meanings.

Thanks to the influence of science in every aspect of our life, we look at the world the way science does. The stars now are lumps in space that we notice because they are (rather pointlessly) burning. The perfection of the patterns man used to study in the sky has been lost, and our previous place and purpose in existence have been lost as well. The center did not hold. Without it, traditional narratives are losing their meaning. Without our literature, language itself suffers from disrepair and confusion. Because words and sentences and stories are strictly subject to the will of an autonomous individual, it's difficult for discourse between individuals to find a common ground. This threat to our language is a threat as well to a government grounded in the rule of law.

The autonomy of modern man, a self-awareness which is the source of so much pride, has made us master of so many things. Modern man knows so much more. At the same time, this intense self-awareness and pride of human accomplishment has not resolved and may not be able to resolve a gnawing fear that so many experience even in the richest and most powerful country the world has ever known. In the past we fought Germany or Japan or Spain, or Britain, but now we are fighting a war on terror against an enemy that lurks in our blind spots. When we profess to know so much, it's difficult to acknowledge the blind spots that are vulnerable to a devastating attack. The attack, as the idea of a war on terror suggests, does not have to be material, and it doesn't have to involve a human enemy. People (who knows how many) are living lives of quiet desperation because they think, whether consciously or not, that life itself is the enemy for having set them in the middle of an alien universe, an infinity of space and of objects that exists outside the self and which, without providing a script for why this is so, at any moment threatens the self with extinction.

I put the case this way to observe that the predicaments of modern man still revolve around the problem described long ago in ancient stories like that in Genesis where desire for some thing (nowadays it's a desire for many things) awakens in the observer a strong sense of self and prompts an exile of the self into a world "out there" chocked full of objects the self doesn't possess. The pattern described earlier in Homer and in scripture includes three phases: it begins with an innocent, selfless harmony, there's a middle period of exile presided over by an overwhelming sense of self, and it concludes with a mature resolving of the self with the world. Since modern philosophy can be largely characterized by a passionate mistrust and deconstructing of grand, universal narratives like the one I have just described, it would appear that it has left us in the middle phase—starring people in a naked encounter with the world—without the recourse and the comfort of a resolution. A resolution would depend too much on an unscientific grand narrative.

When a sense of self is featured so prominently, it's not surprising that there would emerge from this conflict the idea of a Superman for setting things right. He alone, people decide, can master the autonomy of individuals and forge a new world order. In modern times the image has become a secular figure, and for the most part it works its will through the power of the state and large organizations. The social experiments of the twentieth century have proved, however, that the election of a Fuhrer may mask a deadly wish. The experiments failed, at a cost of millions of lives. It turns out that the super will of a Superman cannot replace the natural creativity and incentives that previously rescued individuals from a debilitating alienation.

When I was a child, I used to think that the historical events and people I read about were infinitely removed from me. No longer. I notice that the disarray in Ithaca after Odysseus had been away for twenty years is similar to a modern state where the rule of law is assumed to be dead; I'm moved with fear and wonder as, along with Plato and other disciples, we witness a great teacher calmly die for reasons of state; Chaucer and Shakespeare, despite all the difference of their style and idiom with our own, speak with great clarity to timeless psychological and political issues; and, compared to these more distant events, it seems like we are still caught up in the debates and battles engaged in the founding of our own country.

These stories and situations have the same common denominator; they are all concerned with the effects to the design of the whole when an autonomous self breaks away from an established state to fulfill its own will. The pattern we find in history has strong similarities with the way a child develops within a familial structure into a man or woman who can survive and prosper in the world or with the way partners in a business or a marriage negotiate their differences to create a more perfect union. The problem represented by the pattern shows no sign of being resolved once and for all. Just as every child has to go through the experience of leaving the nest and living in the world, so in every generation we debate the nature and extent of a human being's autonomy and the form of government best suited to it.

Rembrandt's painting *Aristotle with a Bust of Homer* conveys in a single compelling image a grand narrative, and it serves to refute the grand narrative of those who would argue that a grand narrative doesn't exist. The painting involves us in a series of visions: Homer looks at the world (even though he is blind) and captures his vision in timeless stories about men and gods that still resonate in the modern world; Aristotle looks through Homer's eyes at the world and "translates" the human encounters with the gods he finds there into the rational encounters with the natural world that people have every day; Rembrandt then looks at the two visionaries and sees the great respect and love that Aristotle has for the lifelike head of his teacher. In Rembrandt's eyes, Homer's head—the yellow hair and beard like spun gold—looks like the balding pate of an old friend. Even though Aristotle has his hand on the head of his teacher, the painter has suggested that he does so at some distance, given the relative sizes of the two heads. It suggests, too, that Aristotle knows he is looking at and touching a mind larger than his own.

Rembrandt's picture makes it clear that for Aristotle Homer can only be an idealized image, for his representation is severely cropped into a bust of the man. He is in fact a block of stone transformed by the sculptor's art, but we sense from Rembrandt's rendering of the scene that Aristotle has brought this idealized form of his teacher to life in his own life. This is what the invisible Rembrandt has done with his images of Homer and Aristotle. Because the subject of the painting is a linking of these three in a chain of vision, we who are looking at it in the present are made aware of our own vision. The picture exists there before us, and we exist to see it. Rembrandt has put us in a position where we are the next stage in what is and will be an endless chain of vision. The connection is suggested by the golden chain that Aristotle wears; this chain (cropped by his robe) is what we see. It also suggests the richness of life that we seek as these others have done before us, something golden and true that illuminates, like light streaming in from an unseen source, the way to good health, a comfortable home for oneself and one's family, and a decent life. Except for this, it's a dark picture. We have the freedom to look and to miss the great intent and consequence of what we are looking at, but not after these three have awakened us.

Why does Rembrandt's work, which imagines the viewer as an autonomous observer in an ordinary domestic setting, spring from such an intimate point of view? We'll never know exactly, but *A Midsummer Night's Dream* strives in every scene to show the same interplay of characters and points of view that Rembrandt's painting does. It can't be proven, but, given the religious and commercial ties England had with the low country during this period, it's not unreasonable to suppose that Shakespeare's works might be a link in Rembrandt's chain of vision.

Autonomy and Social Order

A. True Government Is Self-Government

Just as I have employed Boethius' *The Consolation of Philosophy* as an interpretive frame for "The Knight's Tale," I rely on *The Canterbury Tales* as an interpretive frame for *A Midsummer Night's Dream*. It's well established that Chaucer structured "The Knight's Tale" around themes he found in Boethius, and it's my thesis that Shakespeare borrowed not only characters and plot situations from Chaucer but also the *cupiditas* and *caritas* theme that's the basis for my interpretation of the tale. While Shakespeare constructed his story on the frame he found in "The Knight's Tale," there are differences, and his play begins with one of them.

Except for the widow of King Capaneus, in Chaucer's tale the women are largely silent. Hippolyta marries Theseus after the war between them and then returns with him to Athens. Chaucer describes nothing of their courtship or their relationship. It's a fair question why not, for she was the

Amazon queen of female warriors who lived to fight men, not marry them. Shakespeare, on the other hand, opens his play with a lively conversation between his not-yet-married Hippolyta and Theseus. Shakespeare's Hippolyta now has a voice; moreover, she makes it clear that she's a seasoned veteran in the battle of the sexes. If she has a voice, she might have learned not only to speak to but also to master a man by modeling herself after Chaucer's middle-class Wife of Bath, a woman who never met a man she couldn't wear out with her overwhelming vitality and native wit. Since my interpretation maintains that Shakespeare's opening scenes are designed to introduce the autonomy of individuals to act, speak, and see the world as they will, the Wife of Bath has a place in this reading as an archetype of an autonomous individual. Within the mansion of *The Canterbury Tales* there are many rooms for Shakespeare to rummage for comic material.

During the two hundred years between the writings of Chaucer and Shakespeare, feudal structures came under increasing pressure from the rising autonomy of ambitious, talented commoners. Chaucer was born into a middle-class family with a business in London, and, starting as a page in a royal household, he lived his entire life in the employ of nobility. Despite being a commoner he, like the Wife of Bath, found his voice and a place of respect among those with authority over him by being a gifted linguist, bureaucrat, diplomat, judge, and poet.

Shakespeare came from a middle class family in a provincial town and so was even more removed from the centers of power than Chaucer. When Shakespeare first began to make a name for himself as a writer, a rival with a university education described the largely self-taught Shakespeare as an "upstart crow" who "beautifies himself" in the feathers that properly belong to university men. That public insult hints at what may have motivated him to work as hard as he did. Will Shakespeare, a man from the middle class, will act, speak, and see the world as he will, and to that end, before Act I is done, he will have added the middle-class Athenian mechanicals to Chaucer's story about princes in love. In particular, he gives us Nick Bottom the weaver who, like the Wife of Bath, is a portrait in autonomy. In the end, it's these middle-class laborers, and especially Bottom, who enjoy a triumph as great as any of the nobility will know on a wedding night.

In our own time autonomy—the freedom to think, act, and speak as one chooses—is at the heart of our culture and political system. It's no wonder, for the Declaration of Independence enshrines it as the founding principle of our government, and the First Amendment has made freedom of speech and other freedoms that preserve individual liberties a matter of law. Shakespeare lived his whole life under a monarchy, but he had an intense awareness and appreciation for the autonomy of human beings and its implications for the social order. He was also keenly aware of English common law, and his name appears several times in court records. The autonomy of individuals, he knew from his family's history and his own ambitions, lay behind the rise of his class.

For hundreds of years prior to Shakespeare's time merchants and burghers had organized and maneuvered to wrest from aristocrats and princes a seat at the table of government, and since then it has been a movement working itself out politically and economically even in developed nations. It's a movement that some say underlies the violence taking place in those countries that are still governed by tribal or feudal structures.[44] The autonomy of women, Shakespeare knew from a wide acquaintance and observation, assured the rise of their sex in the social order. He dramatizes this in his comedies, and the autonomy of women is still changing societies all over the world, perhaps more dramatically than any other factor. Shakespeare sees the great power inherent in the forces that autonomy unleashes, but he doesn't insist on a particular form for managing these forces. He describes for us, as Chaucer did, the nature of our autonomy and its relationship to the social order.

The play begins in Athens at the court of Duke Theseus where he is busy making arrangements for his upcoming marriage to Hippolyta. He is not too busy, though, to complain to his bride-to-be about the interval between their present single lives and the consummation of their marriage:

> Now, fair Hippolyta, our nuptial hour
>
> Draws on apace; four happy days bring in
>
> Another moon. But oh, methinks how slow
>
> This old moon wanes! She lingers my desires,
>
> Like to a stepdame, or a dowager,
>
> Long withering out a young man's revenue.

Theseus expresses a man's usual frustration; he can't have what he wants. He tells Hippolyta that this interval is a waste of time, like the pointless wasting of an inheritance on an elderly person who will soon die anyway. A woman may understand and forgive her lover's impatience, especially if the attraction is mutual, but Theseus makes his point by referring to the moon as the means for measuring out the interval. When symbolized by the moon in its final phase, the interval is not just an elderly person. In the eyes of Theseus, it's a tedious old woman who is taking her time about dying.

Even though he presently is playing the role of a lover, Theseus can't help but view the situation the way a soldier would: time is an enemy that is presently keeping him from his victory. Perhaps on the periphery of his consciousness, his impatience may stem from his awareness of time as the ultimate threat to the beauty of all that he loves, to the pleasure that the strength and grace of youth afford him in himself and in others. Imagine the possibilities for a comic scene, though, if Theseus had commented on the uselessness of a stepdame or a dowager to a woman with the seasoned temperament of a Wife of Bath. To her credit Hippolyta seems not to interpret his remark as a complaint about the power a woman has over a man by insisting on the proper forms that regulate relations between the sexes. She also ignores the hint that over such a long interval she will age and lose the form that attracted him to her in the first place. Instead, she addresses the root cause: mighty Theseus would be the master, but he fears that Time has the mastery. So she describes how:

Four days will quickly steep themselves in night

Four nights will quickly dream away the time,

And then the moon, like to a silver bow

New-bent in heaven, shall behold the night

Of our solemnities.

In the gorgeous, liquid beauty of the first line every part and particle of four days dissolves into an indistinguishable state, and in exactly the same way, time itself dissolves in the second line as it does in sleep. Both actions clear the universal stage of space and time for a vision of the moon "like to a silver bow / New-bent in heaven." Through the might of her vision, where she can imagine the progress of their solemnities from that height, all the problems of her impatient lover dissolve as well. There's nothing left to be an obstacle, or at least not until he considers what that moon, like the silver bow of the huntress Diana, might mean for him when he becomes aware that it's the only thing left in his life.

To his credit, Theseus does not immediately address what the image of a youthful warrior queen, which rises before the eyes of his entire court, implies for the conduct of their marriage. Instead, he turns to Philostrate, his page, and gives instructions concerning the marriage festivities. Theseus tells him to make sure the people are in a celebratory mood, and this most likely will include entertainments for them of food, drink, and possibly a masque or a play. Like the arena that allows the entire dukedom to witness the battle for Emily in "The Knight's Tale," Theseus' wedding will involve everyone in a ritual where the combat of two warriors ends in a marriage.

After Hippolyta's striking assertion of a woman's strength and independence, his instructions to Philostrate establishes Theseus' customary place once more at the head of the table during the upcoming feast, but it also provides a space to recollect, as much as a man can, the way forward with Hippolyta. The aside with Philostrate removes from its immediate trigger the things Theseus might have felt or said after Hippolyta asserted a vision of her own power, and, having had a reflexive impulse interrupted, he now can address what she said in a measured way:

Hippolyta, I wooed thee with my sword,

And won thy love doing thee injuries;

But I will wed thee in another key,

With pomp, with triumph, and with reveling.

From Theseus' brief mention here about their relationship, we have to picture them earlier in no-holds-barred tactical maneuvers and swordplay at close range. When a person is engaged in mortal combat like this with another, there's an instinctive urge to find out the other's weaknesses as well as strengths; but if their long entanglements as enemies have led to respect for a worthy adversary, the relationship that follows the war is more likely to stand on firmer ground than that which is based on a brief or superficial impression.

Structure is important in all works of art, and this is especially true of comedy, which is about people living within a social order. Theseus' words open the play as befits his position as the ruling power of the social order. But since comedy is about that which undergirds social order, his position of absolute authority begs the question as to who or what governs him. The initial exchange with Hippolyta suggests that when all is said and done he, as an autonomous human being, must govern himself. Somehow during his battles with Hippolyta, he recognized that she was born with an autonomy the exact copy of his own. This understanding is the true basis for courtesy.

Courtesy, a few simple rules of the road that govern the social life of his court, is not merely the social niceties that people learn by rote. It's the air, the oxygen people breathe in successful social situations. Courtesy—the ceremonies, rituals, patterns of speech, and patterns of conduct at court—structures into Theseus' life the pause that allows him to gain a measure of self-control in social situations. Comedy is about those rules of the road that allow people to arrive safely and with a minimum of fuss at the goal of a decent life for themselves and their families, and that success depends largely on how the principal partners in the family govern themselves. Even an all-powerful duke needs the rules of courtesy to succeed. This is why Shakespeare begins his play, as Chaucer did, with the mom and the dad of Athens, Duke Theseus and Queen Hippolyta, and why we look and listen to what they say and do in a formal setting.

Rules of the road, moreover, provide a social context that, while it may not be perfect, allows us to gauge the behavior of others as well as our own. A few simple rules commonly understood and agreed upon are also less intrusive and expensive than having a policeman at every corner. The narrative structure in "The Knight's Tale" functions in effect like a social structure, where characters are deeply enlightened by their own misjudgments in relation to others, and this structure reinforces for them the spiritual force that underlies the whole. Whether an awareness of this force is conscious or not, the survival of the structure (and the survival of the comedies of Chaucer and Shakespeare) depends on people recognizing through their own experience that true government, as actually practiced in the conduct of a life, is self-government.

Shakespeare has built his play on the foundation he found in Chaucer, and this practice reinforces my argument that people depend on the structure of language, culture, and social custom that has enabled them to survive up to that point. The opening scene of *A Midsummer Night's Dream* structurally resembles the one with which "The Knight's Tale" begins where the spokeswoman for the ladies in mourning deftly corrects the judgment of mighty Theseus and turns the orientation of his life around. Neither scene is a cause for laughter, but they both establish a comic foundation for all that will soon follow. These scenes stand in the entryway of the poet's home, which is graced with the figure of a man who is compelled to recognize that his understanding of a situation is just an idea and not reality. Hippolyta's vision of a new moon rising awakens Theseus to the fact that he is not just earnestly planning or idly conversing before getting to the real business of a marriage. For better or worse, he is now engaged, and at all times, with the active point of view and interests of another.

B. A Flawed Social Order

From observing him in the opening scene of Shakespeare's play, those in attendance (including the audience) may be reassured by their little exchange that Theseus is competent to govern himself in a relationship on which the security of the state depends. Like children absorbing the behaviors of their parents without necessarily understanding everything, we observe the two closely and listen for signs that the relationship is secure. When we consider that Henry VIII was Elizabeth's father, Shakespeare's audience would have been acutely aware that the strength and stability of a royal marriage was a life and death matter. It would appear that Theseus and Hippolyta are well matched, but they have not done anything out of the ordinary in marrying. They are both noble and heads of state, and it was common for noble families to smooth over conflict with a marriage to unite them. The accommodations they have made as heads of state, while important, do not tell the whole story of government. We have just begun to hear that story.

The scene that immediately follows his exchanges with Hippolyta places Theseus in the middle of another family where he will have to exercise his judgment on behalf of a larger sphere of interest. Theseus may have put his own house in order where both parties are quite familiar with the rules, but like Chaucer's Theseus, he still has much to learn about guiding a ship of state. The problem is compounded when the social order depends on a rule that is judged by some to be outdated, unnecessarily cruel, or unnatural.

This test of his government comes up when Egeus presses on the duke a suit against his daughter Hermia and Lysander, the man she wishes to marry. Egeus has chosen Demetrius for her and begs from Theseus:

> *the ancient privilege of Athens,*
>
> *As she is mine, I may dispose of her—*
>
> *Which shall be either to this gentleman*
>
> *Or to her death, according to our law*
>
> *Immediately provided in that case.*

It's a case that puts the question of autonomy front and center for the entire state, and it tests the viability of the nation's laws where a life is at stake. A typical instance of a child's disobedience could have large implications for the dukedom when viewed as a legal matter in a capital case. If Hermia gets her way, the verdict may set a precedent for any worker or member of the court who disagrees with a boss, for the autonomy of every person to act as he will may set the state on the slippery slope to anarchy. If Egeus gets his way, on the other hand, a child would be sacrificed to the self-love of a father. Egeus is no Abraham called by God to the ultimate test of obedience. Rather than a deep faith, he is moved by a fixed opinion about his role in family matters. The love of that role has changed a father's deep concern for the life of his child into a righteous but mortal enmity.

Theseus could make a summary judgment and quickly move to other, more pressing matters of state. Instead, he encourages Hermia to speak:

> *What say you, Hermia? Be advised, fair maid,*
>
> *To you your father should be as a god,*

One that composed your beauties—yea, and one

To whom you are but as a form in wax

By him imprinted and within his power

To leave the figure or disfigure it.

Demetrius is a worthy gentleman.

He encourages her to speak, but the picture Theseus paints of a father's power effectively denies her the freedom to act as she will. Since long practice in Athens predisposes him to think that she does not possess that autonomy, Theseus tries to solve the problem by smoothing the way to Demetrius.

Unlike Chaucer's Emily, however, this young girl has an inclination and a voice to speak for herself so she replies:

Hermia.   *So is Lysander.*

Theseus.   *In himself he is;*

        But in this kind, wanting your father's voice,

        The other must be held the worthier.

Hermia.   *I would my father looked but with my eyes.*

Theseus.   *Rather your eyes must with his judgment look.*

In the end Theseus supports the father's authority within his own family, but he tempers the judgment with a small mercy. If Hermia decides not to wed, instead of dying the death she may choose to "abjur / forever the society of men" and live "in single blessedness" as a nun. The rest of the family's audience with Theseus is rounded out with assertions and counter-assertions by Lysander and Demetrius. For example, Lysander undermines

Demetrius' claim by pointing out to the duke that Demetrius had already made love to Helena, the daughter of Nedar, and won her heart. This argument between aristocrats that have known each other all their lives makes it clear that there is no difference between the two men's material standing as suitors. Demetrius is undoubtedly correct in claiming that he is "as well derived" as Lysander. The case comes down to whether the father or Hermia herself will decide whom she marries.

So it's about the autonomy of a young girl, and that autonomy is clearly present in Hermia. She could not wish that her father "looked but with my eyes" without being aware that there is a difference between the way he looks and the way she looks. She looks at Lysander and sees the man she wishes to marry. He looks at Lysander and sees a man unsuited to his daughter. How can one man be seen so differently if two autonomous minds aren't at the bottom of it? Theseus also officially acknowledges her autonomy by giving her a choice in the matter even if the choice she would make is not an option. In a small way Shakespeare has introduced the central problem for government in the modern era by dramatizing that a duke has to concern himself as a matter of policy with the way a young woman looks at a man. This subject of the Duke is not merely a pawn on the chessboard that can be moved at will by the master. She is a subject, a mind which thinks and perceives, the beginning and the end of an individual consciousness. Just as Hippolyta and Theseus have conflicting visions of the moon, Hermia and her father look at Lysander with different eyes. These two short dramatic scenes illustrate that this autonomy (or subjectivity) strongly impacts the relationship of man and woman, parent and child, and a duke with his people.

A Symposium on Love

A. So Quick Bright Things Do Come to Confusion

These first interactions in the play establish that different people see things differently. Reduced to its simplest form, "The Knight's Tale" is a demonstration that one person can see things differently at different times. The difference depends on whether the looking is governed by *cupiditas*, the love that would possess an object, or *caritas*, a love that sees the whole of which the object is a part. Shakespeare has borrowed "The Knight's Tale" as the frame for the story he would tell, and he uses these opening scenes to prepare for a presentation of this theme. He like Chaucer would show that the good government of Duke Theseus (and the surest foundation for self-government) derives from a thorough grounding in the difference between the two forms of looking which are also two forms of what is referred to as love.

In art and in life, love is a problem as well as a great good. Men say of women, they can't live with them and can't live without them. Children and their parents, though they deeply love, drive each other crazy. Friends who have grown up and gone to school together can quickly become bitter enemies when love enters the equation. We have already seen examples of this in the first few minutes of the play. The heartbreak of love, which we'll witness in the next scene, can make people feel that life itself has let them down and can trigger a serious depression. So why is it that love, the thing we desire with all our hearts, can be so volatile and cause so much pain? The confusion about love may arise because the word can refer to two very different states of mind. People tend to see their love solely as the ultimate good angel in their life because they associate it with the selflessness and nobility of *caritas*, but then they are blindsided by its selfish and grasping twin which goes by the same name.[45]

To clear this up, "The Knight's Tale" describes Arcite's experience of the two kinds of love with narrative details and imagery of great power and beauty. His brief glimpse of Emily's grace in the garden gives birth to a passionate, combative attachment. This represents the birth of his autonomy; he would win her by any means he can for himself. He is bound to be disappointed, however, for it's the nature of *cupiditas* that it can never be satisfied. Once his heart is literally crushed by his saddle bow, a larger context opens up around the attachment to Emily. Knowing that he will die without ever possessing her in the way he dreamed he might, he sees her and the rivalry with his cousin in a completely different light. He sees the pain to himself and others, especially his cousin, of having constricted his vision so narrowly. He sees, too, that there is an intelligence greater and stronger than the attachment of *cupiditas* that can place his passionate love and hate within a more stable order. As he lies dying in Emily's arms, he catches a glimpse, which echoes the glimpse he caught of Emily's grace in the garden so many years ago, of a completely different kind of love:

I have here, with my cousin Palamon,

Had strife and rancour many a day now gone,

For love of you, and for my jealousy.

And may Jove's wisdom touch the soul in me,

To speak of love and what its service means

Through all the circumstances and the scenes

Of life, namely good faith and knightly deed,

Wisdom, humility and noble breed,

Honour and truth and openness of heart,

For, as I hope my soul may have its part

With Jove, in all the world I know of none

So worthy to be loved as Palamon,

Who serves you and will serve you all his life.

And should you ever choose to be a wife,

Forget not Palamon, that great-hearted man.

A vision of this order prompts him to give up ownership of that which he never possessed and never can possess. Arcite's release from an obsession to possess Emily is Chaucer's vehicle for approaching the nature of *caritas*. The whole of his tale is an exemplum that one person can see things differently at different times, but look what it takes for Arcite to look in a new way. He begs for his speech to be touched by Jove's wisdom only after years of suffering and the final, catastrophic wake-up call of his fall in the arena.

This brief look at Shakespeare's source helps me to interpret a symposium on the nature of love that completes the rest of this scene. Once Theseus and his court leave the stage after the judging of her case, Hermia and Lysander remain to talk about their disappointment. Lysander begins the conversation using the language of a love sonnet:

> How now, my love! Why is your cheek so pale?
>
> How chance the roses there do fade so fast?

Together they then cite some of the social constraints that obstruct "the course of true love." By focusing on the obstacles to love, they characterize the nature of their love. They want something they don't have, and they don't have it because there's an obstacle. This is *cupiditas*, an attachment to that which can't be possessed, like the beauty of roses or the blush of color in a woman's face. Unlike Theseus and Hippolyta, who have taken each other's measure in mortal combat and stand their ground in conversation, Hermia and Lysander are swept up in a current of love talk and desire. They are in love with a pretty picture of love.

After they recite how social customs keep lovers apart, Lysander sees obstacles that are more universal than a father's objections:

> Or, if there were a sympathy in choice,
>
> War, death, or sickness did lay siege to it,

Making it momenteny as a sound,

Swift as a shadow, short as any dream;

Brief as the lightning in the collied night,

That in a spleen, unfolds both heaven and earth,

And ere a man hath power to say "Behold"

The jaws of darkness do devour it up.

So quick bright things do come to confusion.

A paterfamilias is not a lover's only obstacle. The quick, bright nature of love is strangely wedded to confusion. Like a striking picture that arrests our attention at a first glance, these lines have an immediate sensual power, and once the mind is engaged by them, the effect deepens.

The lightning at the end of the passage is chiefly what catches our attention. Everyone has experienced a night when a sudden strike tears jaggedly across the sky with a power beyond the scope of any human being. It's terrifying and humbling. The ancient Greeks saw it as an expression of Jove's power, which overawes the lesser lights of a mortal. Jove's wisdom, to which Arcite refers in his last words, can't be codified into a text or a law. It's a bolt out of the blue demanding respect for what we cannot know; "Jove's wisdom" therefore is a figure of speech for what we intuit from these displays. The Hebrew Bible refers to it as a "fear of the Lord."

Lysander begins the discussion of love with the usual analogy to something lovely and fragrant like a flower, and he continues in this vein by comparing it to a sound and a shadow and a dream. For someone in love with love, a primary obstacle to love is that it is so brief and evanescent. He ends this train of thought by associating love with a stark image of raw power. Lightning is light and brief, too, but this image gives love a completely different character. Shall we compare love to a summer's day, with its pleasant sounds, pleasing shades, and fanciful wishes?[46] Lysander begins in that key, but he ends in another. With a single, compact display of power, the lines prefigure that the love light of Lysander and Hermia may yet come to confusion. People who play with love, the way Hermia and Lysander appear to be doing, are setting themselves up for a shock that's like a brush with death. As in Chaucer's treatment of the material, there's a force above and below the enchantment of an ideal form, like the hidden powers of heaven and earth, that can suddenly strike and throw a person into confusion. Love (as *cupiditas*) has a dark side that can't be ignored, and that darkness has to penetrate to the bottom of the lovers' hearts before the comedy is complete.

Even though she argued forcefully for her own point of view earlier with Theseus, Hermia resigns herself to the judgment of her father and the Duke:

> *If then true lovers have been ever crossed*
>
> *It stands as an edict in destiny.*
>
> *Then let us teach our trial patience,*
>
> *Because it is a customary cross,*
>
> *As due to love as thoughts and dreams and sighs,*
>
> *Wishes and tears, poor fancy's followers.*

She sees the judgment of her father and Theseus as a cosmic law, but she also regards her obedience as a sacrificial offering to love, prefiguring a crucified savior who comes into the world after the time of Theseus.

Lysander sees the situation quite differently. Arguing with a father or a Duke is not like arguing with the grim reaper. Lysander can dream and sigh as well as any man, but he still has his wits about him. He has a plan of action that's just as important as his vision of an ideal love in that it will allow him to enjoy Hermia. Since the law of Athens prevents them from marrying, he will take her to the house of his dowager aunt who lives outside that law. If his aunt is anything like the dowager Wife of Bath, Lysander may have learned from her how to get what he wants despite an oppressive, patriarchal authority. Where there's a will, there's a way, especially when the characters are imagined by the puckish Will Shakespeare.

We have seen that Theseus is impatient to enjoy the pleasures of his wedding night with Hippolyta, and Lysander is just as impatient with the obstacles that prevent him from consummating his love for Hermia. They both suffer from the desire to possess that characterizes *cupiditas*. Do the women they would possess represent *caritas*, the form of love that comes into being when the school of hard knocks dislodges an obsessive attachment? Are they selfless lovers? Hermia compares her love for Lysander to a "customary cross," and she appears eager to sacrifice herself on the altar of true love. The sacrifice of an attachment is a characteristic of *caritas*, but whether Hermia is actually capable of giving up what she loves (the way Arcite did) remains to be seen. She may be just playing a part that she learned from the books she has read. Hippolyta, on the other hand, has a vision of an unearthly, timeless quiescence and beauty. It's a breathtakingly original and appropriate response to what Theseus has said to her, not a stock image. Far more than Hermia's rote recital, Hippolyta's vision captures the breadth and depth of a mind surrendering itself to a creative power infinitely greater than itself, and it, too, tenders a characteristic of *caritas*. She captures it in brilliant images, but it is Theseus who is being asked to surrender, not herself. In the world she describes, she's what she has always been, an avatar of the huntress Diana who will forever roam the heavens as white and perfect as a new moon. Her response to Theseus' complaint serves as a live demonstration before the entire court that love does not take dictation; it comes, like unearned luck, from the heart. These are stringent terms. It remains to be seen whether she or Theseus is capable of them.

B. Oh, Teach Me How You Look

As the two lovers are making plans to meet the following night and flee the law of Athens, Helena interrupts them, and Hermia acknowledges her with, "Godspeed, fair Helena! Whither away?" Helena's reply develops another variation on the conflict of visions:

Call you me fair? That fair again unsay.

Demetrius loves your fair. O happy fair!

Your eyes are lodestars, and your tongue's sweet air

More tunable than lark to shepherd's ear

When wheat is green, when hawthorn buds appear.

Sickness is catching. Oh, were favor so,

Yours would I catch, fair Hermia, before I go.

My ear should catch your voice, my eye your eye,

My tongue should catch your tongue's sweet melody.

Were the world mine, Demetrius being bated,

The rest I'd give to be to you translated.

Oh, teach me how you look, and with what art

You sway the motion of Demetrius' heart!

Hermia sees her as fair, but Helena begs to differ. We already learned in the previous scene that Demetrius recently courted her and won her heart. Now that he loves only Hermia, Helena has proof that she is not fair.

She also might be speculating why his looking changed when she, Helena, has not materially changed at all. Perhaps it was Hermia's eyes or maybe her voice. If so, then Helena would learn to "catch" the brightness of her eye or catch the sound of her voice the way one might catch a cold from another. More than that, she would be "translated" into a Hermia clone that Demetrius would love. This foolishness is merely a set up for what burns in her heart as she arrives at the punch line of the speech:

Oh, teach me how you look, and with what art

You sway the motion of Demetrius's heart.

The first half of the sentence can be paraphrased (or translated) as, "Teach me how to be a beautiful object like you," which goes along with what she has been saying. But given the context of how the word has already been used in the play, as when Hermia complained, "I would my father looked but with my eyes," and Theseus corrected her by instructing, "Rather your eyes must with his judgment look," the word "look" refers to a subject perceiving the world rather than the way an object "looks" to another person. This is why Helena's preemptory command, "Oh, teach me how you look," can be translated as "Teach me how you look at a man and play the game of love with him."

The second half of the sentence supports this way of looking at what she means by "look." Helena is wondering what Hermia is prepared to say or do to sway the motions of a man's affections that Helena, being more modest, is unwilling to entertain. It's not just Hermia's appearance that has won the day. It's her intention. Perhaps Helena would learn the way a woman can excite desire by the way she looks at a man, but she mostly burns to call Hermia out for not playing fair. This reading of "Oh, teach me how you look" emphasizes that Hermia, as an autonomous and resourceful woman, can have an intention, and Helena, who is also autonomous and resourceful, can readily observe the intention. She knows that the charms of a woman like Hermia blind the men so they cannot readily observe that she has not only an intention but a mind to boot. In a brief rebuttal, Hermia gives evidence that she doesn't entice Demetrius and offers in conclusion the strategy she and Lysander have devised as the final proof. They plan to leave Athens so Helena will henceforth have Demetrius all to herself. It's a solid defense, but it can't ultimately settle the question touching Hermia's intent. That's something she could easily mask or of which she is not conscious.

The first movement of our symposium on love opens the topic with the observation that love is involved with obstacles like fathers that cross the lovers' desire and that love has a dark side like a beautiful summer's day suddenly changed into a violent storm. The second movement looks at why a lover might not have seen that storm coming. A man looking at a woman falls in love with how she looks and may not be aware of how she looks at him. Her intention is difficult, if not impossible, to divine. What appears to be an intention to love, which shines forth in the eyes, may be but a pretense that masks an equally passionate intention to control. All this is true for a woman looking at a man as well, and it proves to be the cause of Helena's suffering. If she had glimpsed Demetrius' true intention (or the lack of it) when she fell in love with him, she might have seen him differently.

C. Love Looks, Not With the Eyes [*caritas*], but With the Mind [*cupiditas*]

With that, Hermia and Lysander leave to prepare their flight, and the heartbroken Helena is left on stage alone. Hearing about their plans and wishing a like adventure with her love as Hermia is about to have, she reflects further on the conflict of visions introduced throughout the opening of the play:

> *How happy some o're other some can be!*
>
> *Through Athens I am thought as fair as she.*
>
> *But what of that? Demetrius thinks not so,*
>
> *He will not know what all but he do know.*
>
> *And as he errs, doting on Hermia's eyes,*

So I, admiring of his qualities.

Things base and vile, holding no quantity,

Love can transpose to form and dignity.

Love looks not with the eyes, but with the mind;

And therefore is winged Cupid painted blind.

Nor hath Love's mind of any judgment taste;

Wings and no eyes, figure unheedy haste.

And therefore is Love said to be a child,

Because in choice he is so oft beguiled.

As waggish boys in game themselves forswear,

So the boy Love is perjured everywhere:

For ere Demetrius looked on Hermia's eyne,

He hailed down oaths that he was only mine;

And when this hail some heat from Hermia felt,

So he dissolved, and showers of oaths did melt.

How happy it is for some to love, she thinks. This is the way it is for Hermia, but for Helena love is a problem to solve. How is it that Demetrius does not think her fair when all others do? And why, when Demetrius cannot see her fair, does she continue to admire his qualities. The problem, it appears, has to do with the seeing, the looking that has been the subject of all the movements in the scene. She observes that the eyes of one who loves can transform a person of an average stature and intelligence and who is also a vile schemer into an ideal form, and she resolves the problem by concluding that there are two kinds of seeing. Demetrius looks at her and at Hermia "not with the eyes, but with the mind."

The mind that Helena refers to here is a creator of sorts. Both Theseus and Hippolyta are looking at the same moon, but one sees in it a present and unattractive adversary whereas the other sees its dynamic potential as a timeless, ideal form "like to a silver bow / New-bent in heaven." Hermia sees true love in Lysander, while her father sees only feigning and the willful theft of Hermia's innocence. After Theseus rules against her, Hermia sees a hopeless trial of love, and Lysander sees an opportunity for a quick overcoming of their obstacles. All of Athens knows that Helena is as fair as Hermia, but Demetrius "thinks not so."

Through these illustrations, the play has prepared the audience for Helena's summation, but she needs only the one demonstration that the mind of an autonomous subject has the creativity to interpret as it will. Unfortunately for her (but not Hermia), beauty is in the eye of the beholder. This explains why Demetrius doesn't see her beauty, but it doesn't get to the bottom of the problem. Some might be satisfied to explain people's choices and behaviors simply as a matter of taste. Today I'll love Helena; today I'll love Hermia. This over a period of two days. Helena wants to be loved, not to be the flavor of the day. To get to the bottom, it has to be established that there is a bottom, and this is what is added when Helena asserts that there is such a thing as seeing "with the eyes." If there were no bottom, no constancy as opposed to a myriad interpretations provided by the minds of limited and fallible mini-creators, then chaos is come again. Helena's formulation of human perception allows her to say that it's possible (although we don't know how at this point) to see things as they are without the distortions of a mind's conscious and unconscious bias, but this is not what happens in love. Love looks not with the eyes but with the mind.

The old stories about Cupid support her argument. Because love looks with the mind rather than the eyes, Cupid is represented as blind. This, however, is not the blindness of the seers Homer and Tieresias. Cupid transports himself on the wings of his ecstasies with no regard for where he is actually going. What matters is the feeling of flight. "The Knight's

Tale," which Shakespeare used to frame the actions and the theme of his play, provides an additional context for interpreting Helena's formulation of the problem. Cupid may be blind, but he enjoys great success shooting his bolts into the eyes (as in love at first sight) of those he would make as blind, flighty, and careless as himself. Palamon and Arcite are afflicted in this way when they see Emily's grace in the garden, and the rest of the tale reveals them to be wounded by a classic case of cupiditas, an attachment to an object that's less about the object and more an expression of self-love. They fancy that the love of the ideal they have glimpsed will give them a form and a dignity that sets them apart from others.

In her catalog of Cupid's attributes, Helena adds that Cupid is a child and so lacks the judgment that can only come from corrections that derive from the trials and errors of long life. This seasoned judgment is the closest approximation in Helena's speech to what she means by seeing "with the eyes." In Chaucer's tale it is best represented by Theseus at the end when he, like Arcite before him, has his self-understanding painfully tested and yet maintains the form and dignity of his person and position. Already Shakespeare has given us a brief glimpse of a timeless presence of mind in Hippolyta's initial speech. Also, Theseus' acknowledgement of Hippolyta's striking independence and the assertion of his own indicates that he sees their relationship realistically.

In both Chaucer and Shakespeare there is no easy path or shortcut to seeing with the eyes. This is why Chaucer constructs his arena, where Palamon and Arcite will battle for Emily's grace, in such a way that everyone, knights and spectators alike, must pass through the gates of love or hate, and it's also why the union of Theseus and Hippolyta comes after the war they have fought. People can only enter the human comedy through these passions; those who think they can avoid or transcend a passionate love or hate by being spiritually or intellectually superior are denied entrance. These authors write to show that the two kinds of love, which reflect two modes of perception, are separate, but they make it clear that it's equally important to see them as one. I have argued throughout the reading of "The Knight's Tale" that *cupiditas* and *caritas* are separate and distinct states, but I have done so only in service of the overall argument. Over time, the two interpenetrate each other in a complete understanding. The bolts of Cupid (that lead to *cupiditas*) and the bolts of Jove (that lead to *caritas*) are equal parts in the comedy that unlocks the wisdom of Everyman.

Helena's speech shows that she has glimpsed the direction in which the play is headed. She now has "intelligence" that matters to Demetrius:

I will go tell him of fair Hermia's flight.

Then to the wood will he tomorrow night

Pursue her; and for this intelligence

If I have thanks, it is a dear expense.

But herein mean I to enrich my pain,

To have his sight thither and back again.

She will give Demetrius her intelligence, and this intelligence will make him crazy to follow Hermia. Her information about the lovers' flight looks like intelligence, but it's Helena's heart, her passion for this man, that's driving her actions.

It's a crazy plan, but it's in line with the insight underlying Theseus' arena. She is going to enter that arena of love (for Demetrius) and hate (for her rival), even though it will only enrich her pain. She's going to tell Demetrius about Hermia's flight, and as he acts out his passion for Hermia in the wood (wood has the same sound in Shakespeare's language as wode, their word for crazy), she will act out her passion for him. It's in this crazy wood that the heart goes to school and the business of looking gets sorted out. Her attachment to Demetrius will have to hit bottom in darkness and confusion before the play can arrive at a comic conclusion.

In Chaucer's tale the World Tour of Palamon's and Arcite's obsession with Emily guides the reader through the many forms that the pain of love can take. Like Dante before him, Chaucer depicts this love as a primal wrestling match of the self with the world.[47] The incident when Palamon and Arcite find each other in a wood near Athens and fight almost to death will be reprised in Shakespeare's wood when Lysander and Demetrius intend a fight to the death and Hermia intends to scratch out the eyes of Helena. But Shakespeare has added his own special subplot for exploring the bottom land where *cupiditas* feeds, and to make his point more obvious he calls the star of his show Bottom.

Productions of the Wooden O

Shakespeare built his reputation as a successful playwright on the simple fact that there are good plays and bad plays. People know a good play when they see it, and Londoners came again and again to see his. So what's the secret of his success? His most precocious character states it as clearly as anyone ever has: Hamlet explains to the players about to perform *The Murder of Gonzago* that a play succeeds with an audience when it succeeds in holding a mirror up to nature.

Since he was deeply involved with playing as a business proposition, Shakespeare had a keen interest in presenting something that would please his audience with its verisimilitude. This, he understood, is a profoundly difficult task. After his company built the Globe Theatre, they opened it for business with *Henry V*, and the Chorus begins the play with a meditation on and a warning to those who dare to recreate a battle or, by extension, any part of Creation:

> But pardon, gentles all,
>
> The flat unraised spirits that have dared
>
> On this unworthy scaffold to bring forth
>
> So great an object. Can this cockpit hold

The vasty fields of France? Or may we cram

Within this wooden O the very casques

That did affright the air at Agincourt?

Oh, pardon!

Shakespeare's Chorus here raises the same problem that Chaucer wrote about in *The Canterbury Tales*: How can people know and represent the world when our perceptions and representations of it prove to be so limited?

For example, in "The Knight's Tale" Theseus builds a theater for judgment to determine who will marry Emily and to make lasting peace with Thebes, but it fails to solve the problem for which it was constructed. The advent of a fury from the ground, impossible to anticipate, foils the duke's purpose and represents a mortal setback for his government. In the same spirit, the Chorus of *Henry V* makes us aware that the "wooden O" of their theater is an unworthy scaffold for representing reality, and in *A Midsummer Night's Dream* Helena's formulation broadens and deepens the question. The Chorus points out that people can't adequately recreate or know the past, but Helena points out that we can't even know what's right in front of us when our eyes are distorted by the instrument of knowing, the wooden (meaning crazy) O of our heads.

Theseus has instructed Philostrate to "Stir up the Athenian youth to merriment," and the scene that follows Helena's soliloquy shows the effect of the duke's command. A company of amateur actors assemble to prepare a play for the duke's wedding. They would ready themselves for a competition in which they hope to be "preferred" by the duke. Philostrate's ancestry makes him the right messenger for the job since, in Chaucer's tale, he is actually Arcite, a prince of Thebes, who is playing the part of a lowly page in Theseus' household in order to serve the duke's sister-in-law Emily.

Shakespeare, who made his living from "playing" like this, was aware of its perils as well as its pleasures, and Arcite's experience with pretending to be someone he is not is a case in point. Theseus releases Arcite from prison after he agrees on his honor never to return to Athens, but Arcite evades the promise by returning as the page Philostrate in order to gain access to Emily. For a time the new identity gives him great pleasure, but his alter ego and alternative reality ultimately fail with its most important critic, Arcite himself. He comes from a royal line and can no longer pretend to be a servant. Despite the many years of successfully maintaining it, his alternative reality collapses in a matter of seconds; it doesn't reflect his true self. Modern writers may question whether there is such a thing as a true self, but Arcite's breakdown in the wood indicates a disabling disconnect in the psyche. He can't be two different people, and the strain of it causes him to fall into a catatonic state. Just as love does, playing has a dark side.

The imagining of an alter ego or an alternative reality is another demonstration of the creative power that's the subject of Helena's soliloquy. The mind has the freedom to interpret the world as it will and even, if a person is skilled, to build a virtual world, a walled pleasure garden of thought, which rivals the actual world from which it has sprung. These productions of the mind have given people great pleasure from ancient times. Building, and then living in them, however, is a risky business.

Great poetry has always been about more than an evening's entertainment. It holds a mirror up to nature to the extent that any one person or any company of creative people can, and helps us to see things-as-they-are. A poem like *The Odyssey* has been preserved for thousands of years for this reason as others are drawn to the truth they find in Homer and then write about it in the language of their own culture. Before the craze in modern times that requires an artist or writer to represent reality as if it has never been done before by anyone else, Shakespeare openly borrowed the form and content of other writers, and the culture he and Chaucer and Boethius drew on was deeply rooted in a comic vision of life, what Dante called *The Divine Comedy*. Shakespeare demonstrated a high regard for "The Knight's Tale" by using it to write not only *A Midsummer Night's Dream* but also, in collaboration with John Fletcher, *The Two Noble Kinsmen*. He borrowed Chaucer's characters and the plot, and, more importantly, he looked through Chaucer's eyes to secure a foundation for a comic outcome.

Since experiences that lead to wisdom have been written about from ancient times and are still meaningful in our own day, it's not hard to imagine that, when their own vain imaginings had locked them up in doubt and confusion, the stories these authors loved helped to confirm that which on occasion they had seen for themselves: a glimpse, like lightning in the collied night, of Creation's unimaginable depth and power, the world when seen "with the eyes." These timeless, unexpected bolts put Everyman's creative powers on a proper footing. The theater of mind is not the Creator. It's a rather flimsy, wooden affair, an unworthy scaffold, but the productions of Chaucer and Shakespeare serve a worthy goal if they help us to see the flimsiness of perception when looking "with the mind."

The Cockpit

Shakespeare's actors in this scene are just the people for constructing a play that will likely be flimsier and crazier than most. They are mechanicals, unused to this kind of work, but they have answered Philostrate's call and so appear before us. The impatient duke would have an entertainment that will "let the world slip" for himself, the duchess, and the court in the hours between the ceremony and the actual union of husband and wife on their wedding night.[48] In the words of Hippolyta's vision earlier, the play will succeed if those daylight hours "quickly steep themselves in night" as the audience dreams away the time, lost in a magic mirror held up to nature. But what sort of play is more likely to prefer them to the duke, a comedy or a tragedy? Which idea about life more successfully reflects reality so that the company can realize the reward from the duke that they seek?

Peter Quince, the director and the steadiest wit among them, has in hand his version of *The most lamentable comedy, and most cruel death of*

Pyramus and Thisby. Peter Quince is a carpenter, not a literary man. Because he doesn't see a difference between comedy and tragedy, the title indicates a hybrid that somehow bridges the two. This may seem like ignorance, but Peter Quince's ignorance proves to be divinest sense when the play is actually performed. Even in the title, his play announces that it exists in a space, like the wood that looms ahead in the narrative, outside the mind's usual categories. What seems like ignorance may be closer to seeing with the eyes in Helena's terms, for, truly, life is a strange mix of tragedy and comedy.

Peter Quince and the other mechanicals who would put on this play are the creation of another amateur, "an upstart crow" in the opinion of those who thought university men should have a monopoly on literary productions. In the end, though, all these upstarts steal the show. By the time he wrote *A Midsummer Night's Dream*, the glove-maker's son from Stratford was a widely popular author, and in the play his mechanical company succeeds in transforming the nobility's tedious interval before bedtime into an occasion for the wildest mirth. This is after one of Shakespeare's upstarts, Nick Bottom the weaver, plays the fairy queen's leading man in the primal romance of the midsummer night. The mechanicals all make the most of their opportunity by being transparently who they are even as they play at being legendary figures. They are mechanicals, but they play their parts in the creation of a timeless comic vision.

Nick Bottom, the company's star, is a transparent egotist who challenges Peter Quince for control of the play. From the start, Bottom takes over the direction: he blocks out the assigning of the parts, praises the script as a very good piece of work without knowing anything about it, and generally spreads himself around. Peter Quince assigns him the part of Pyramus, who kills himself for love. A lover is emotional, which is good, but Bottom tells him that his humor is for a larger-than-life figure like Hercules in which his swashbuckling, bombastic acting style can be given full scope. To give the company a taste of Ercles, as he calls him, he recites:

The raging rocks

And shivering shocks

Shall break the locks

Of prison gates.

And Phibbus' car

Shall shine from far,

And make and mar

The foolish Fates.

Bottom sees himself as a force that can shake the foundation of the earth and change the course of destiny. When he shakes, everything shakes; when he shines, the world is changed. Next, when Flute objects to playing the woman Pyramus loves, Bottom wants to play her as well, despite the considerable loss to verisimilitude. The one-man or one-woman play may have become somewhat popular in modern theater, but Peter Quince is adamant about traditional playing. "No, no. You must play Pyramus and Flute, you Thisby," he tells them. When Peter assures Snug the Joiner that the role of lion will not tax his memory as it is "nothing but roaring," Bottom sees a part that's made for him, and he would play it. After some further arguing, Peter finally pulls out all the stops as director and tells Bottom flatly: "You can play no part but Pyramus."

If we look at Bottom through Helena's formulation, we understand that he looks at the world with a mind saturated in self-love and sees himself everywhere. What do we get if we have a world full of actors like Bottom? The Chorus in *Henry V* compares this world to a cockpit, that little arena where a rooster single-mindedly would eliminate the "other." By asserting his role as director, Peter Quince suddenly finds himself face to face with Bottom in that cockpit. Although he may have taken his somewhat heroic stand without thinking about the consequences, he also knows (at bottom) that their best chance for success lies with a play where each actor plays his part and no more. This is the same as saying that he has an instinctive sense for comedy (which, thanks to all involved, is what the play becomes) where no actor dominates the whole. A play about a tragic hero who breaks the locks of prison gates would be out of place at a marriage celebration; after all, a marriage celebrates the contract that yokes a man and a woman to each other for their mutual benefit. The hero in a play about marriage is the company itself that survives and prospers when no one in it overreaches. Because at bottom he's a comic character, Bottom milks all the suspense he can from the company over his decision before agreeing to "undertake" the part of Pyramus.

Overreaching Don't Pay

The peaceful resolution of Peter Quince's bout with Bottom brings these opening scenes set in Athens to a close. I have interpreted them to show that they are structured by a conflict of visions and that this structure comes to a thematic climax when Helena observes that "Love looks, not with the eyes, but with the mind." Helena's formulation represents a stark contrast between two modes of perception. Either a person sees things-as-they-are with the eyes the way an omniscient narrator can, or a person looks at the world through a limited and self-interested lens the way Bottom does.

Since no human being ever has or ever will enjoy omniscience, it can only be a literary device that helps us to see the limitations of our own point of view. Despite this fact, it is also true that people can experience the wake up calls that comedy enacts. These wake up calls aren't like the revelation on Mt. Sinai; they don't dictate a set of commandments or open up the point of view of providence. They inform a person that an idea which lies at the heart of his endeavor is a distorted or perhaps an entirely false picture of reality. Because it's the nature of human beings to have ideas about the world and to employ these ideas as a ground for action, ordinary individuals, if they claim they can look at the world and act on a comprehensive and unbiased perception of it, overreach and usurp a power they don't have. If ordinary people as a general rule are stuck with ideas as the ground for the everyday activities of their life, comedy helps us to be content with a middle position between the completely conditioned mind of a mosquito and the omniscience of Mighty Jove. A person who undergoes a comic wake-up call learns to appreciate that, if he wishes to survive and prosper, some ideas are better than others.

We could say that Peter Quince fought and won an important battle, but it would be more accurate to say that he made an important sale. His idea, that no one individual can play more than one part, wins the day with an actor who willfully overreaches, and he does it by "selling" the idea with firmness and persuasion. After telling Bottom point blank that he could play no part but Pyramus, he massages Bottom's headstrong pride into a more manageable state by adding, "for Pyramus is a sweet-fac'd man; a proper man as one shall see in a summer's day; a most lovely gentlemanlike man. Therefore you must needs play Pyramus." In the interim between "You can play no part but Pyramus" and "Therefore you must needs play Pyramus" Peter Quince leaves off insisting on a fixed price and resorts instead to bargaining. He knows his bottom line, but he adds to that some effective salesmanship, and this is the way the project moves forward. Bottom agrees to undertake it, and the crisis passes. The deal costs Bottom the extra parts and forces Peter into upping the ante with flattery, but both parties in this agreement get something they want. Peter keeps control as director, and Bottom is still the star. Not playing is not an option for Bottom, and someone else playing Pyramus is not an option for Peter Quince.

Comedy forces an idea, like the thought that one is the center of the universe, out of a fortress like tower or bunker into the open where it has to defend itself in the marketplace. When he's given the opportunity to act in Peter Quince's play, for example, Bottom's ego-centrism slips out of the closet and makes a big entrance. Once on stage it's subject to a comic treatment. Since the mechanicals are tradesmen who live by selling their products and services to their neighbors, the marketplace is where they spend their days. There people can determine for themselves that some wares are better than others (for the price). In a marketplace of ideas people can determine for themselves that some ideas are better than others. Even more importantly, people can see for themselves that they are just ideas and not a monolithic absolute. This is the essential function of comedy. Once an idea has lost that mystique (of being reality), it's easier to . see which one is a better idea.

It's the business of comedy to show that people who peddle or buy into an idea without reservation claim too much for it, and when they cloak themselves in the idea, they claim too much for themselves. Mark Twain, the greatest comic writer in American literature, sums this up in a chapter of *The Adventures of Huckleberry Finn* called "Overreaching Don't Pay." It's about two con men who could have made off with a large part of another man's fortune by pretending to be someone they are not, but Huck exposes them when they try to make off with the whole thing, including the sale of slaves. "Overreaching Don't Pay" establishes in an American idiom a comic critique of ideas and suggests a marketplace as the proper place for ideas in a civil society. Hucksters and sleight of hand artists are just as eager to peddle ideas as they are everything else; sometimes, in a vulnerable time, fraudulent ideas seem almost to sell themselves without any help. Nevertheless, an open air marketplace is still the best place to survey them, for there they can be freely scrutinized, investigated, and exchanged.

Plato describes how men would get together for a symposium on love. It's clear from *Love's Labors Lost* that Shakespeare was familiar with philosophical retreats like this, but in *A Midsummer Night's Dream* it's the ladies who approach the nature of love from a philosophical point of view. Act I lays out competing ideas about love and how to cope with the pain of love. The play opens with Hippolyta prescribing patience. In patience Theseus will discover that space and time, the coordinates of his existence, are immaterial and can dissolve like a dream does upon awakening, at which point his life will be filled with a new moon of love. For Hermia, love is an otherworldly faith. In the language of sonnets, courtly love, and religious persecution, she imagines that somewhere, somehow in a better world she and Lysander will fulfill their love through present sacrifice.

The symposium ends with Helena's formulation, and she establishes a richer and more fertile ground for the growth of love than in Hippolyta's austere and abstract vision or in Hermia's childish infatuation with self-sacrifice. Helena once was happy in love, like a radiant full moon, but now that light has shrunk to almost nothing. She offers an explanation for love's changes, but it's not enough for her to rationalize simply that "Beauty is in the eye of the beholder." Without thinking all this through as a logical, step by step process, she would get to the bottom of the whole mess by throwing herself even further into it. The way love looks in the melee to come is no classical, perspective, like that of the new moon looking down on a consecrated ceremony. Nor do the lovers volunteer to sacrifice themselves on a cross, however customary that may be. Rather, in the melee to come love's point of view is that of a rangy bird in a cockpit about to fight for its life with any means at its disposal. Love here is sharp, jagged, and selfishly directed, like Jove's lightning bolt hurled across the sky.

That's where the play is headed. Nevertheless, when people stop overreaching, there's room for Hippolyta's vision. We passed through such a space, like an entryway, on our way into this remarkable building that the poet has made out of airy nothing. Love is like this taut new moon, the only object in existence, emblem of a bright and brave warrior transposing confusion into form and dignity. Also, when lovers aren't blinded by overreaching, they may unlock the courage needed in Hermia's vision, for a comic view of life has always been an act of faith in a dark time.

CHAPTER EIGHT:

NATURE

Fragonard's *Annette a l'age de vingt ans*

The View from Olympus

In the time of Socrates there were those who doubted the existence of the gods. Rather than attributing lightning to the anger of an anthropomorphic super being, they preferred naturalistic explanations for it and other events in nature. While these philosophers as well as subsequent skeptics, agnostics, and atheists may have stopped attributing phenomena on earth to the gods, those who aspire to know the world and govern it continue to love the view from Olympus, which can be gained from technologies like satellites, from intellectual heights like those of Hegel, Marx, and Freud, or from a concentration of power where all the roads and all the intelligence of a vast empire converge to raise one man into a god-like omniscience.

The old stories may have associated the gods with mountaintops for several reasons, but from the evidence in Homer the anthropomorphic gods live there because they can see so much more. The gods aren't the only ones drawn to high places; Xerxes watched the battle of Salamis from a mountain on the east side of the bay. Salamis is a cautionary tale for those who seek this kind of advantage, though, in that the badly outnumbered Greeks soundly defeated the Persians in one of the world's most significant battles. Xerxes had a great view, but the Greek view, strategically and operationally, turned out to be superior. Their smaller ships and fewer numbers proved to be more maneuverable in the crowded waters of Salamis Bay, and Greek captains at sea level were able to seize the initiative when they saw their opportunity. From his mountaintop Xerxes discovered there can be some odd twists in the nature of a superior view.

Drawing on deep traditions in mythic storytelling, Homer integrates his tales of gods and men in a coherent structure that allows the reader to identify with both perspectives. He begins *The Odyssey* by affording his reader the view from Olympus concerning Odysseus. Athena, given her superior mobility and knowledge, sets the record straight for the reader from the start; Odysseus is alive but a captive of the nymph Calypso. She loves him so much, in fact, that she offers to make him immortal.

Penelope's suitors, on the other hand, have convinced themselves that Odysseus is dead, and even his family is on the verge of giving up hope for his return. Athena's intelligence sets the rest of the story in motion and establishes a foundation for the central theme. Unlike those back home in Ithaca, the reader knows that Odysseus is alive and where he is, knows that Athena is committed to getting him home, and knows that fate and her father Zeus have determined it.

Since we possess the truth of the situation, we constantly contrast this intelligence with the ignorance of those who don't know these things. Even though Odysseus is assuredly alive, the suitors hope to advance their own interests by rising above all the uncertainty about his fate and declaring that he is dead. It may be reasonable to make that assumption since no one has seen or heard of him for ten years, but this shows the limitation of reason in the case of Odysseus. It's still just an assumption, and Odysseus' actual return will put the assumption to the test. When he does return, Homer's narrative establishes a simple but severe ethical marker for the characters who inhabit this world: the people who recognize the true king of Ithaca, in his person or in loyalty to him, will live, and those who don't will not. The reader may not want to identify with the suitors, but any rational person will recognize that their ignorance is the common inheritance of any human being. *The Odyssey* therefore serves as a warning that there's nothing easy about an ethical life.

Whether one believes in the gods or not, the stories about them set up a contrast between intelligence and ignorance, and this may be because, from ancient times, people keep discovering that there's a big difference between the two in the practical business of human affairs. Since human beings began noticing that the accuracy of a person's vision could determine whether he lived or died (as, for example, in throwing a spear or in sizing up the way a battle might develop), storytellers have made this their subject in the narratives that have come down to us, and this is an essential theme of comedy. These stories have survived because they show how people survive. If, as the stories indicate, there is a more intelligent point of view in existence, that intelligence becomes a worthy goal for a person of any capacity.

Homer pays the reader the ultimate compliment by putting him in the godlike position of knowing what the storyteller knows. We can see the whole unfolding and rest assured how it will end. Our consciousness suffuses the whole, and this coronation by the author makes us intelligent. It's a wonderful place to be, but there's a warning built into the story if we have the mind to observe it. The suitors have flattered themselves with a similar position. They think they are intelligent and can control their own and other's destinies, but because they are in fact ignorant the story ends badly for them. They base their actions on a bad idea. The suitors' ignorance is offset by the commonsense intelligence of Odysseus who manages to survive in a world that also tempts him to assume the seat of a god. Instead of rising in the world the way the suitors would, however, he falls as a nobody into the lowest possible estate, and it's from this perspective that he manages to reclaim his kingdom.

The divine powers in Shakespeare's play seem to have undergone a humbling of their estate similar to that which Odysseus endured, for the play now moves from Athens, where everyday life was overlooked from the Acropolis by Athena, to the country around the city where the magnificent gods of Greece have been translated into the little people, the fairies of English folklore. Also, as the day wears on, the light begins to fade so that Acts II, III, and IV will take place in twilight, darkness, and the half-light of dawn. The dense, natural environment and time of day frustrate anyone who seeks a superior view and the grandeur of intelligence. Instead, it's a realm ruled by passions of love and hate and by irruptions of sudden fear.

I have selected a painting by Fragonard to illustrate this chapter because, like Shakespeare, he was a master at creating a sense of drama within a carefully crafted setting. Also, Act II ends with an incident similar to the one in the picture. Fragonard's characters are youthful and passionate actors. The man finds himself alone in the country with a beautiful woman and would seize the moment by taking her hand (and the rest of her if he can). The woman is also an actor and alert to what the man desires, but the picture cannot tell us what she says or does next. It's left to nature to speak of it. The view from nature, unlike the view from Olympus, is ambiguous. Behind them, the gnarled and broken old trunk overshadows and points right at them; it looks as though they recline on a swelling in the ground created by the tilting of this dark and stricken thing. Everywhere else, there's a perfect serenity of blue sky, billowing clouds, an outline of distant trees and hills, and comfortable sheep unmoved by what the lovers are about. For the moment, the lovers inhabit a natural setting for what comes naturally. A final detail, however, hints at the way these contrasting forecasts about the weather (the whether she will or won't) will be resolved. The woman still wears a beautiful dress, which refers us back to the place where she resides, the house and village and family she left to come into the country. To this place they must eventually return, for human beings with few exceptions live with others within a social order.

On Pearls and Fool's Gold

Shakespeare's fairies are actors, too. What they lack in size, they make up in high spirits. Also, the opening dialogue of fairyland quickly establishes that their intelligence comes, not from a distant mountaintop, but from an intimate knowledge of nature that's gained by being so small. When asked by Robin Goodfellow, "Whither wander you?" a fairy describes the scope of her work as well as the speed and precision with which it must be done:

Over hill, over dale

Thorough bush, thorough brier,

Over park, over pale,

Thorough flood, thorough fire;

I do wander everywhere,

Swifter than the moon's sphere;

And I serve the fairy queen,

To dew her orbs upon the green.

The cowslips tall her pensioners be;

In their gold coats spots you see.

Those be rubies, fairy favours;

In those freckles live their savours.

I must go seek some dewdrops here,

And hang a pearl in every cowslip's ear.

The fairy loves her work, laboring lightly and with imagination. Though very little, she feels she has been given a great responsibility by a great power, the queen herself. It's not just a job. It's a life and full of the flavors and colors and the marks, like freckles, that give her work distinction and sudden pleasures. In working with such beauty, she adorns the world and herself with the wealth of numberless rubies and pearls.

This little fairy is embodied perfectly in the innocent, singsong lyric she recites to describe whither she wanders, but Robin Goodfellow sings a different tune. When he hears that both Oberon and Titania, unbeknownst to each other, have selected this very spot for the gathering of their separate entourages, he explains why the queen had best stay away:

For Oberon is passing fell and wrath

Because that she, as her attendant, hath

A lovely boy, stolen from an Indian king;

She never had so sweet a changeling.

And jealous Oberon would have the child

Knight of his train, to trace the wild;

But she perforce withholds the boy,

Crowns him with flowers, and makes him all her joy.

And now they never meet in grove or green,

By fountain clear or spangled starlight sheen,

But they do square, that all their elves, for fear,

Creep into acorn cups and hide them there.

Despite the lyrical sweetness of the fairy's life and work that she describes, all is not well in fairyland.

For the audience, the fairy's moonstruck fantasy fades when we hear about a man and woman fighting over a child. This is too much like the ordinary life of human beings, and the warfare has the usual cause. Like Palamon and Arcite battling in the wood over the beauty of Emily, Oberon and Titania have been stricken with the beauty of an exotic Indian boy (an echo perhaps of Emetrius, Arcite's champion, when the knights fought for Emily in the arena), and they obsess over possessing him for themselves. The violence of their brawls terrorizes the others in the family, but Robin seems curiously unaffected. If he were as afraid as the rest, he could hardly have noted this contrast:

And now they never meet in grove or green,

By fountain clear or spangled starlight sheen,

But they do square...

The two principals are entirely focused on their argument with each other, but Robin recreates for us the beauty surrounding the cockpit of their quarrel.

As a storyteller, he adopts here the point of view of "The Knight's Tale" narrator who provides the overall context for the moment when Palamon and Arcite first become obsessed with Emily. The knight telling the story and, of course, Chaucer himself, see so much more of her since they are omniscient. Like the fairy we have just met, Emily is a lively spirit, especially in the spring. She throws off sleep and rises in the dark to dress herself long before others. Like the fairy and like the woman in Fragonard's picture, she loves to be in the world, in nature. Therefore, to complete her wardrobe she would go to the garden where:

> She wandered gathering flowers, white and red,
>
> To make a subtle garland for her head,
>
> And like an angel sang a heavenly song.

The knight and Chaucer see all this and peek into her mind as well to note the subtle purpose that underlies her actions. She would honor her own power of youth, beauty, and consciousness by honoring the beauty of creation. For Palamon and Arcite, though, the largeness of this view is then constricted by the thick walls of their prison tower into a tight field of vision that's limited to what they desire.

Returning to Robin's point of view, we notice that he still can see the beauty of the whole—of grove and green and of starlight shining on the moving water—even as his lord and lady, engaged in their obsession over a single part of this world, have forgotten it. Robin is an inferior, but in this instance the audience might be inclined to think that he is more intelligent in that he is able to see more than the others. Selling a superior view to an audience is relatively easy; it's what people instinctively aspire to own. If only, we think, we could be as spirited, carefree, and intelligent as a spirit like Robin. Shakespeare's task, however, is much more difficult. He would show that the fall from a superior view and its intelligence is a critical ingredient of the potion he's distilling for his characters and the audience. The fall has the bitter taste of earth and darkness, but it's a liquor that makes people hardier and wiser. Chaucer describes it in the first lines of *The Canterbury Tales*:

> *When in April the sweet showers fall*
>
> *And pierce the drought of March to the root, and all*
>
> *The veins are bathed in liquor of such power*
>
> *As brings about the engendering of the flower...*

This liquor drives the action of Chaucer's tales and *A Midsummer Night's Dream*. Robin has an admirable intelligence, but comedy is more interested in those characters who drink the earthiness of that which engenders the flower.

The encounter between Robin and the fairy conveys the quickness of fairy life as we learn a great deal about them in a short interval. When the fairy suspects her interlocutor might be the knavish sprite called Robin, she then catalogues some of the pranks for which he is famous. Women are favorite targets: he likes to spook country maidens at their labors with sudden surprises; he arranges it that poor housewives huff and puff when all their churning won't cause the butter to "come". More generally, he laughs when he misleads night wanderers in the dark. Here's the other side of fairyland when magic is mixed with frustration and fear and when it's easy to suspect that the eye of an antagonist is bent on making a person's life difficult.

Robin freely acknowledges his trademark pranks, but there's no malice in what he does. He remains a comic figure. Like the fairy he addresses, he loves his work, but he has a completely different sort of job. He employs his wit to puncture the illusion of a comfort zone into which all creatures like to settle, the routines and expectations that pass for knowledge and control of a situation. The country maidens don't know what makes them suddenly jump for fear; the housewives don't know when the butter will come and why it won't; night wanderers, because of their limited vision, suddenly don't know how to find their way in the world. Instead of preserving the peace and beauty of nature, Robin prefers opening the sluice gates of pent-up passions.

Thus, he cheerfully acknowledges who he is:

Thou speakest aright;

I am that merry wanderer of the night.

I jest to Oberon and make him smile

When I a fat and bean-fed horse beguile,

Neighing in likeness of a filly foal;

And sometime lurk I in a gossip's bowl

In very likeness of a roasted crab,

And when she drinks, against her lips I bob

And on her withered dewlap pour the ale.

The wisest aunt, telling the saddest tale,

Sometime for three-foot stole mistaketh me;

Then slip I from her bum, down topples she,

And "tailor" cries, and falls into a cough;

And then the whole quire hold their hips and laugh,

And waxen in their mirth, and neeze, and swear

A merrier hour was never wasted there.

It's a recital that captures the humor as well as the deep purpose underlying comedy. Robin knows well (from the example of his master) that nature is only occasionally peaceful and rational. The peaceful surface masks a deep ocean of energy and passion. It just takes a Robin Goodfellow neighing like a filly foal to get that bean-fed horse galloping. Robin finds the inevitable weak link in the armor of those who put on airs. With a slight and deft adjustment, he can turn a lady, who prides herself on the neatness of her manners and her person, into a slovenly drinker reeking of ale. Saving the most important for last, Robin has a vision for turning the wisest aunt's "saddest tale" into an occasion for the wildest mirth. What a relief, when engulfed in the morass of her sentiment, for the audience to find their storyteller suddenly sprawled on the floor, speaking in tongues, coughing incoherently, and yet, not crazy or sick, but wholly herself. The first fairy we meet deals in rubies and pearls. Robin has a nose for fool's gold; that's his gift and his intelligence. Instead of rubies and pearls, he tempts mortals with a priceless foolishness that's fit for a king (if only he would wear it).

Human beings, whether we like it or not and whether we are aware of it or not, are lords of creation by virtue of being born into this world; for Robin Goodfellow, there's little difference between a gossip telling her tale and a Caesar running his empire. As a conscious being, Everyman surveys the world in order to deal with it, and since we are conscious of mortality from a young age, a critical part of that survey inevitably involves a choice of perceptual frames; everyone wonders at some point and at some level whether the scene before us is a tragedy or a comedy. A tragic hero—the ancients noticed that to be a tragic hero he must be a king like Oedipus—may think he enjoys a superior view and a superior intelligence, but this positioning is of no help whatsoever if he, like the boy Cupid, is actually blind. Shakespeare's *A Midsummer Night's Dream* will now demonstrate that this is as true for a king of the spirit world as it is for a strategic blunderer like Napoleon or Hitler.

Who Has the Mastery?

When these blithe spirits exit the stage, we next encounter a situation that could easily tip into tragedy. To accentuate that possibility, the narrative covered in this section includes a tragic event at the end. Having been told by Robin about their estrangement, we hear for ourselves the passion of Oberon and Titania. Oberon initiates the action with a simple but provocative greeting:

Ill met by moonlight, proud Titania.

His mock romance and scorn trigger a like response:

What, jealous Oberon? Fairy, skip hence.

I have forsworn his bed and company.

These two pretend they are sorry to see each other, but both are itching for a fight. Behind it all looms the question that ruled the dowager queen of all wives, Chaucer's Wife of Bath, namely "Who has the mastery?" If Oberon is feeling more than a little testy, Titania knows it's because she has forsworn his bed until she gets what she wants. If all politics is local, then for these two all marital politics is sexual. To heighten that sexual tension, Oberon makes explicit what he meant by "proud Titania" when he commands and asks:

Tarry, rash wanton. Am not I thy lord?

In two quick strokes, Oberon opens up the meeting for old business. What better way to provoke Titania's temper than to suggest that, as someone who proudly embraces her wantonness, she needs governing. On the surface his remark could be read as the hypothesis of an experiment. By baiting her like this, he is about to prove that a beautiful, proud woman who is also a queen still requires a husband to be her lord.

Titania is perfectly aware that success in the battle with Oberon depends on her intelligence. She must demonstrate to him that she enjoys a superior view of the battlefield. Oberon asks a simple question, but it rests on the assumption of wantonness. To disable the assumption, she points out that the question has a fatal flaw if the observer does not include his own weakness in the observation:

Then I must be thy lady; but I know

When thou hast stolen away from fairyland,

And in the shape of Corin sat all day,

Playing on pipes of corn, and versing love

To amorous Phillida. Why art thou here,

Come from the farthest steep of India,

But that, forsooth, the bouncing Amazon,

Your buskin'd mistress and our warrior love,

To Theseus must be wedded, and you come

To give their bed joy and prosperity.

This is her intelligence; she knows why he is there. She knows where he has been at other times. Oberon should concern himself with his own behavior, for he's hardly in a position to judge hers. To his pretensions of lordship she offers a mocking, scornful acquiescence. To his charge of wantonness she offers the proof of his own. This proof comes garnished with withering illustrations of his dalliances and their unworthy objects, featuring a boffo caricature of her chief rival Hippolyta. How in the world could anyone, much less a lord, be remotely interested in these absurdities?

Because her words have the power to cut Oberon down to size, they serve the same function as Robin's pranks, only on a much more important target. With her frank appraisal and sharp wit, Titania exposes the emptiness of his manly expectations. If this revelation does not unleash the natural impulses of his temper, at least she has given him a taste of her own.

A provocation like this, as we know from the many instances of domestic violence trumpeted in the media, could easily turn into tragedy, and Oberon increases the tension by responding in kind with his own intelligence and proof of Titania's rashness:

> *How canst thou thus, for shame, Titania,*
>
> *Glance at my credit with Hippolyta,*
>
> *Knowing I know thy love for Theseus?*
>
> *Didst thou not lead him through the glimmering night*
>
> *From Perigenia, whom he ravished?*
>
> *And make him with fair Aegles break his faith,*
>
> *With Ariadne, and Antiopa?*

Oberon needs only the nearness of Titania's boy toy Theseus to make his point and force Titania out of her stronghold on the moral high ground.

Oh, the adventure and the excitement of stealing Theseus from all those other women! What she has done is a cheap and a low thing to do considering her overwhelming charms and the harm it causes; but Titania's headstrong actions, the exotic names of her rivals, the ravishing evocative sound and rhythm of the adventures, and the passion of Oberon's recitation give the memory of them a glimmer of romance. Titania is the emotional focus of his life, and the retelling of these wild adventures heightens this sense of her. There would certainly be a potential for tragedy in a situation like this, but only if Oberon and Titania were not the principal actors. We sense that the two of them are old hands at this game and that their words now may be the prelude to an equally passionate reconciliation. Like Theseus and Hippolyta in the opening scene, they are too well matched and too well versed in these wars for it to spin out of control. Nevertheless, the battle over mastery ends in a stale mate, a spouse in a marriage that has stalled.

Neither one is an angel. Both are sensitive and intelligent, but they are also creatures of earth and full of the fits and feelings that follow desire. Unlike clumsy human beings blind with passion, however, Titania still has the grace of a fairy and lightly jumps over Oberon's sweeping accusations. She tells him:

> These are but the forgeries of jealousy...

And then she changes the subject. In these opening salvoes, it would appear that they have been revving themselves up as in a prelude for physical intimacy and release from sexual tension, but Titania's new subject brings up another issue that lies deep in the lives of men and women who are also parents. It's one thing for a man and woman to manage their jealousies over interests in other adults, but it's quite another to manage their jealousies over the children they have in their care. It's to this subject that Titania now turns.

The play has already established a pattern like this when the opening scene between Theseus and Hippolyta, which concerns their personal relations, gives way to a suit concerning a child brought by one of Theseus' subjects, which he must adjudicate. Titania opens up this larger subject to remind Oberon that being the queen of fairies involves more than being his consort. She enjoys playing Oberon's lady as much as he enjoys playing her man, but at this point in her life it would appear that her duties as an earth goddess have trumped that other role. Now that Titania has arrived on the scene, it reminds us that Hermia's mother does not make an appearance and is not even mentioned when Hermia's life is threatened. It's a tragic imbalance in the nature of things, which Hermia's flight into the wood may yet set right.

Titania sets out on this new subject to put Oberon on notice that he will have to accept the strong maternal instincts she is presently experiencing. She begins by arguing at length that, because of their brawls, the ecosystem has been knocked out of joint:

> *Therefore the winds, piping to us in vain,*
>
> *As in revenge, have suck'd up from the sea*
>
> *Contagious fogs...*

There's too much rain, floods kill the crops and the cattle, and the seasons alter:

> *Hoary headed frosts*
>
> *Fall in the fresh lap of the crimson rose;*
>
> *And on Hiems' thin and icy crown*
>
> *An odorous chaplet of sweet summer buds*
>
> *Is, as in mockery set. The spring, the summer*
>
> *The chiding autumn, angry winter change*
>
> *Their wonted liveries; and the mazed world,*
>
> *By their increase, now knows not which is which.*
>
> *And this same progeny of evils comes*
>
> *From our debate, from our dissension;*
>
> *We are their parents and originals.*

Even if modern parents don't think their behaviors can change the weather, it not difficult to see the implications of the imagery. Arguments about the children—about who is going to have the final say concerning discipline and underlying issues about who is more loved by parent or child—are bound to change the atmospherics in a family, and these cold, clammy moods carry some noxious effects. A frost out of season settles on the children. As Robin tells us earlier, the little ones hunker down; their motion freezes. In the previous scene the fairy describes her tender ministrations to each and every lowly cowslip, and, even though Titania and Oberon seem to have their other jealousies under a measure of control, we wonder now how they let their governance of everything else slip so badly in this matter of the child. On the other hand, if we recall the way Egeus cared for his daughter, Titania's maternal instincts stand out in sharp relief against a faceless and deadly flood.

The flood is real, and the suffering is real. In the last three lines, however, Titania shifts the nature of these things into a completely different dimension when she asserts that she and Oberon are "their parents and originals." Like a practical man of business or a soldier, Oberon presents a simple solution: all she has to do is give him the Indian boy. Playfully again, Titania seems to agree. "Set your heart at rest," she tells him, but then she dashes his hopes with a fierce declaration of independence:

The fairyland buys not the child of me.

Oberon can continue to be as restless and testy as he likes, but it will not change her determination to mother this child.

To give her determination a larger context she describes how the bond between her and the Indian boy was formed. Yet her story does more than that. Shakespeare's moving lines suggest why a great goddess of earth like Titania came to be worshipped by women whose children so often died and who carried the threat of death in their wombs:

His mother was a vot'ress of my order;

And in the spiced Indian air, by night,

Full often hath she gossip'd by my side,

And sat with me on Neptune's yellow sands,

Marking th' embarked traders on the flood;

When we have laugh'd to see the sails conceive

And grow big-bellied with the wanton wind;

Which she, with pretty and with swimming gait

Following (her womb then rich with my young squire)

Would imitate, and sail upon the land

To fetch me trifles, and return again,

As from a voyage, rich with merchandise.

Like a child in the womb, everything in the scene envelops the expecting mother in an intimacy with Titania—the thick scented air, the gossiping side by side, the softly yielding sands, the shared view of the big bellied ships so like the young mother's shape and rocking motion when walking about that she leaps up to imitate them as she brings little treasures from the shore to the Queen Mother. Titania, already filled with delight and wonder, somehow finds room for each new loving gift. It all resonates with the fullness of a mother with child, and it's a moment that defines them as women as they laugh together "to see the sails conceive / And grow big-bellied with the wanton wind." Titania and the young woman share the wonder of that day, and not long afterward Titania bears the loss of it alone and witnesses for Oberon its conclusion:

But she, being mortal, of that boy did die,

And for her sake do I rear up her boy;

And for her sake I will not part with him.

With great feeling she describes all this to her husband while also drawing a line in the sand between them. As a woman, she sees the child differently, and Oberon must accept this. Titania sees a division in the natural order that runs deep, and Oberon sees it as well. The Indian boy will be a man someday, and he needs to learn from a man how to be one. There's intelligence behind each point of view.

At the same time that the child divides a man and a woman into separate camps, the young woman's death draws a line in the sand between her and the fairy queen. Titania's day with the Indian vot'ress is as close as she can come to mortality. Mortals like ourselves might wonder why an immortal goddess would be interested and involved in the life of this woman and her baby, but she is. It's a curious relationship, almost as curious as the relationships we have seen so far between men and women. The two women share a scene that's full of longing for something imported from another shore, and if longing has a scent, its musk might be much like the spiced Indian air where the vot'ress was born and died. The young woman, so different in essence from Titania, is instinctively drawn to her and to the vast natural world that opens up when she's with her; and Titania, an immortal who is incapable of experiencing tragedy, loves the young woman's fragile beauty and would preserve some part of it.

Titania's and Oberon's quarrel over the Indian boy raises the question that inevitably comes up when autonomous individuals in relationship have radically different views of a situation: Who or what has the mastery? Who will rule when Theseus and Hippolyta marry and they can't agree on something? Does a father have mastery over his daughter as to whom she marries? Is Oberon Titania's lord? Is it Peter or is it his dramatic vision that masters the conflict with Bottom? Can intelligence master a situation? Does Titania and Oberon's intelligence about each other master the conflict between them or merely add to a flood of emotion and confusion?

In respect to the gods, even, who has the mastery? After all, some power greater than her own has compelled the great goddess Titania to work for the young Indian woman's estate as the nurse and governess of her baby. Shakespeare's play distills all these ingredients—mixing high and low, dark and light, comic and tragic, intelligent and ignorant, human and divine—into a potion, the liquor of life, which is then poured onto the eyes and into the ears of his audience. When we've drunk it all, we can judge for ourselves if, under the influence of its spell, we agree with Robin to let comedy and friendship reign.

The Intoxication of Oberon's Revenge

In a brief coda, Titania invites Oberon to join her rounds and moonlit dances, but they cannot come to terms and so part. As he watches her leave the stage, Oberon has already conceived his revenge. He tells her, even though she is out of earshot:

Well, go thy way. Thou shalt not from this grove

Till I torment thee for this injury.

To say that Oberon has conceived his revenge uses the language of Shakespeare's time to show the relationship he and others saw between the conception of a child in a woman and the conception of an idea in the mind. The imagery of conception and the swelling of the womb are already centrally placed at the heart of the play in the story of the Indian boy's pregnant mother. Because Oberon focuses his attention now on a swelling desire for mastery and revenge, all the action in the wood will revolve around the grove to which Titania and the child repair. This grove is the cockpit where the business of seeing gets sorted out. It's where Oberon's love turns to desire for mastery and revenge, where the Athenian men's love for Hermia turns in an instant to hate, where hatred of Helena turns to love, and where all their relationships are realigned by the new day's first light.

It's to this grove that the characters and the audience must repair to understand that love is a problem as well as a great good. In "The Knight's Tale" the people can only enter Theseus' arena through the gates of love or hate (it doesn't matter which because they are so closely tied together). Both emotions are evoked in the poetry with which Oberon makes manifest his plan for revenge:

> *My gentle Puck, come hither. Thou rememb'rest*
>
> *Since once I sat upon a promontory*
>
> *And heard a mermaid, on a dophin's back,*
>
> *Uttering such dulcet and harmonious breath*
>
> *That the rude sea grew civil at the song,*
>
> *And certain stars shot madly from their spheres*
>
> *to hear the sea-maid's music.*

We picture the two of them enraptured by perfect beauty. It's a timeless, frictionless state, and perhaps even we who hear of it through this poetry will, like the rude sea, pause to take in the harmonies of a deep friendship with another and with the world.

"I remember," replies Puck, as who would not. But then Oberon goes on to reveal that the music drew another "star" (and he's still a star in our mythological heaven) to it. This new one unleashed a different kind of magic:

> *That time I saw (but thou couldst not)*
>
> *Flying between the cold moon and the earth*
>
> *Cupid, all arm'd. A certain aim he took*

At a fair Vestal, throned by the West,

And loos'd his love-shaft smartly from his bow,

As it should pierce a hundred thousand hearts.

But I might see yon Cupid's fiery shaft

Quenched in the chaste beams of the wat'ry moon,

And the imperial vot'ress passed on,

In maiden meditation, fancy free.

Yet mark'd I where the bolt of Cupid fell.

It fell upon a little Western flower,

Before milk-white, now purple with love's wound,

And maidens call it love-in-idleness.

The story illustrates another kind of love, one that's closely tied to revenge. The knavish lad Cupid shoots his darts not to make people happy, comforted, and wise in love but rather to take revenge on those who refuse to acknowledge what's due to Venus.

The love that rests in the flower is idle because it missed its target. Because it missed, the flower combines in the story about it a strange mixture of passion and chastity. With both great powers, Venus and Diana, involved in its story, the flower stands for love as practiced in the lives of human beings; it's a vehicle for the suffering of love and for the good that comes from love's disappointments. This plain little flower was also called "heartsease," and modern gardeners would recognize it as the pansy. But "love-in-idleness" and "heartsease" suggest a state few human beings ever know. A pretty little flower was given these names because people sometimes wonder what it would be like if desire took a vacation, if all that burning and aching for beauty or revenge was quenched, like an arrow with its tip on fire, in a vast, bottomless ocean. It's life as it is lived on some other shore, on some other planet.

This last image brings to mind Titania's vot'ress who imitates traders setting out between the cold moon and solid ground for something they want in another land. It's easy to understand why the young expectant mother loves the strong, stable, and beautiful goddess and wants to be close to her. Titania is the guardian any mother would wish for her child and herself in a world that shifts as easily as Neptune's yellow sands. People aspire to the life of the immortal gods as they have been depicted for thousands of years, supposing that that life transcends somehow the pain of desire. The gods live in palaces with stunning vistas, they enjoy infinite leisure for pursuing whatever they wish, they nurture themselves (as if they needed anything else to live) on ambrosia—and all this never changes. Even though the gods as the Greeks depict them have their passions and their flaws, they don't suffer the consequences of them, and so their life represents an upgrade.

Why is it, then, that the immortals in general and Titania in this case are so attracted to the travails and the transitions out of life that mortals endure? Another way of looking at this question is to wonder why, in a comedy, the playwright brings the audience so close to the death of a young mother and the abandonment of her baby to the shifting sands of a changing world. The argument of these essays rests on a few simple observations about comedy as a literary form; distilled to its essence, comedy is about seeing things-as-they-are as opposed to wishful thinking. Just as Chaucer makes the death of a young and vigorous man a turning point of his narrative, Shakespeare makes the death of this young woman the catalyst for volatile actions and reactions in the wood. The presence of the fairies might lead the audience to expect a pleasant fantasy, but the issues they raise are real and universal. Comedy is about the real world, which includes the mutability of all things.

To borrow Helena's formulation, comedy is about seeing with the eyes as well as with the mind. Seeing with the mind involves having one's vision shaped or framed or chemically altered by some device or factor. Seeing with the mind is an intoxication like that brought on by "spirits," including the awful spirit of revenge. In ancient Greece comedies were performed in theaters dedicated to the worship of Dionysus and the ecstatic mind. It's a theater for drinkers. Ecstasy would appear to be the goal of the cult, but as Shakespeare represents it, it's not the final goal of comedy. The ecstasy is only part of the process. The intoxication of seeing with the mind induces the madness, and the madness is what exhausts the mind and body to a point where something gives, something lets go, something settles into a state unlike any ever driven by an idea. It's like the arrow of desire quenching itself "in the chaste beams" of a larger intelligence. As in Hippolyta's first lines of the play, the poet embeds his complex narrative vehicle with little glimpses of where the action concludes long before it actually does; the conclusion is there all along in the fabric of the play.

To give the goal of comedy a concrete form for his audience, Shakespeare's play personifies it as Queen Elizabeth since it is clear that she was the target of Cupid's arrow. He missed, though:

And the imperial vot'ress passed on,

In maiden meditation, fancy-free.

When a little island nation is being threatened by the overwhelming opposing force of a universal monarchy (the Spanish rule of Philip II), it needs a leader focused on the task at hand, a realist who also can inspire her people to gather the resources they have to best effect and to make a unified effort. Shakespeare's nod to Elizabeth is not just a formal acknowledgement of the monarch in their midst. It's an assertion that comedy is about good government and a stable social order that helps its people to survive and prosper.

To give the intoxication a concrete form for the audience, Shakespeare has his characters act it out in different forms. Demetrius and Lysander are intoxicated with Hermia; Egeus is intoxicated with his authority as a parent to the point that he would rather the child were dead than that he should be seen as having lost that authority; and Bottom is intoxicated with every inch of himself. In the stories Chaucer and Shakespeare adapted from classical literature, we find even spirits under the influence. Titania and Oberon are intoxicated with the idea of having the mastery in a marriage, and they both get high and mighty on the fumes of jealousy to the point where they ignore their primary function, the stewardship of nature. Titania is immortal so she can never know the motions of her young votress' heart, but she is enchanted by the spiced Indian air, the yellow sands washed by the sea, the boats that sail over the horizon with goods for an unseen shore, and a mortal woman who carries in her womb a mortal child full term to live in a changeable, uncertain world. Titania can't know these things the way a mortal does, but under the influence of these stimulants, she imagines her votress' life and death in most memorable poetry.

These reflections on Titania prepare for a puzzling detail in a play that delights audiences with its lighthearted fairies and moonlit magic: Oberon's revenge. If mortality presents a problem for immortals, because they can never know it, then making room for revenge in a comic world presents a problem for mortals because revenge in its true form is a narrowing, selfish, and bloodthirsty driver of emotion and action. People often kill for revenge, whole nations have gone to war for revenge, and sometimes those in despair end up hurting and even killing themselves as revenge on life itself. Oberon sets his plan into motion by telling Puck to:

Fetch me that flow'r; the herb I show'd thee once.

The juice of it on sleeping eyelids laid,

Will make or man or woman madly dote

Upon the next creature that it sees.

It may be that Titania's latest scourging of his judgment has given him the idea for his revenge. Since she made such brutal fun of him for wasting his time on an easy conquest like "amorous Phillida" and for being so captivated by the bouncing warrior queen with her whips and leather boots, he plans to shame her own judgment with a little help from the flower:

> *Having once this juice,*
>
> *I'll watch Titania when she is asleep*
>
> *And drop the liquor of it in her eyes.*
>
> *The next thing then she, waking, looks upon*
>
> *(Be it lion, bear, or wolf, or bull,*
>
> *On meddling monkey, or on busy ape)*
>
> *She shall pursue it with the soul of love.*
>
> *And ere I take this charm from off her sight*
>
> *(As I can take it with another herb)*
>
> *I'll make her render up her page to me.*

Titania may think she is immune to a lapse of this kind, but this new infatuation will level the playing field between them and will overshadow all other attachments, including that to the Indian boy.

It's their nature apparently to engage in these thrusts and counterthrusts. So what's puzzling about Oberon's revenge isn't that he wants to score a point against her, it's the way he intends to go about it. Again, it's clear that, just as she shamed him with having been intoxicated by an unworthy object, he intends to induce the same experience for her. He seems, though, to be so intoxicated with his scheme that he has forgotten that he's pimping his own wife to the first creature she happens to see upon waking in the grove. Since so many of Shakespeare's plays are laced with references to men whose wives have put horns on the heads of their husbands and since this is universally regarded as proof of the husband's shame, Oberon's plan seems as self-destructive as it is vindictive. If the play is not simply a farcical romp in the woods by cartoonish characters, which from the greatness of the poetry we have already encountered it cannot be, then Oberon's revenge is a puzzle for audiences. We wonder, once more, what it would be like if desire and jealousy could take a vacation—where love, in idleness, would have nothing to do, and the heart would find ease and content. For the answer we have to look past Oberon because, while he may not be bothered by jealousy, he is still hell-bent on revenge.

And Here Am I, and Wood within This Wood

As Chaucer did before him, Shakespeare would illustrate that the love swelling in the heart of one pierced by Cupid's arrow and the hatred swelling in Oberon's mind are as closely related as cousins in the royal line of obsession. Oberon has just sent Puck to fetch from the nature of fairyland the poet's vehicle for introducing this theme, the little Western flower that's purple with love's wound. There's love in it all right, but there's also the pain of the bolt, the blood, and the bloody-minded passions that are expressed in war. Even though Oberon doesn't have it in hand yet, this flower has taken center stage because of its power to induce both pleasure and pain:

> The juice of it, on sleeping eyelids laid,
>
> Will make or man or woman madly dote
>
> Upon the next live creature that it sees.

When love is such a crazy experience—mixing as it does extremes of light and dark, high and low—it's a fair question why human beings have always made such a fetish of it in the poems, stories, and songs that have come down to us from ancient times. People thousands of years from now will probably do the same, if the species still exists. This is just a speculation, but it's rooted in those authors who have passed on the wisdom traditions from ancient times. After all, Shakespeare's device of the flower juice argues (figuratively) that there must exist some power in the nature of human beings (and thus in nature) which can cause someone to madly dote on an image like this.

Oberon's thoughts of revenge are interrupted by the entrance of Demetrius with Helena following him. We don't know exactly how either one was first smitten, but both have appeared onstage to represent the dotage that Oberon has just described. Like the effect of the flower juice, the love of Helena for Demetrius is a projection, a subjective event with no secure root:

> Dem.   *Thou told'st me they were stol'n unto this wood;*
>
>   *And here am I, and wood within this wood*
>
>   *Because I cannot meet my Hermia.*
>
>   *Hence, get thee gone, and follow me no more!*
>
> Hel.   *You draw me, you hard-hearted adamant!*
>
>   *But yet you draw not iron, for my heart*
>
>   *Is true as steel. Leave you your power to draw,*
>
>   *And I shall have no power to follow you*
>
> Dem.   *Do I entice you? Do I speak you fair?*
>
>   *Or rather do I not in plainest truth*
>
>   *Tell you I do not nor I cannot love you?*
>
> Hel.   *And even for that do I love you the more.*

I am your spaniel; and, Demetrius,

The more you beat me, I will fawn on you.

Use me but as your spaniel—spurn me, strike me,

Neglect me, lose me; only give me leave

(Unworthy as I am) to follow you.

What worser place can I beg in you love

(And yet a place of high respect with me)

Than to be used as you use your dog?

Helena continues to assert a clinging, obsessive loyalty, and so Demetrius threatens to run away again and leave her to the mercy of wild beasts. She answers:

The wildest hath not such a heart as you.

Run when you will. The story shall be changed:

The dove pursues the griffon; the mild hind

Makes speed to catch the tiger—bootless speed,

When cowardice pursues, and valour flies!

This wood is wood; it's crazy. Everything is topsy-turvy, like liquid elements heated over fire and boiling in a beaker. Demetrius, who admits he's out of his mind for chasing after Hermia in the wood, finally gives up talking and runs away as fast as he can. He's still on the hunt for Hermia, and Helena runs after him:

I'll follow thee, and make a heaven of hell

To die upon the hand I love so well.

Oberon, who has observed the scene from behind a cloak of invisibility, must wonder as much as the audience at this beautiful young woman's absurd debasement of herself. Yet knowing that the flower juice is on its way, he sees the remedy for it:

Fare thee well, nymph. Ere he do leave this grove,

Thou shalt fly him, and he shall seek thy love.

He regards the flower juice, then, as the means for rebalancing their relationship, but the whole scene also serves as a diagnosis and description of Helena's pathology. She suffers from an obsession, an irrational attachment to an image that has been induced by something like the flower juice. The juice produces an effect like looking at the world through a fixed telescope that's always trained on the same object. Since it leaves out most of life, it's a state of mind, as Helena's final words reveal, that works as a death wish.

Oberon would relieve the suffering of Helena at once, and this response to her signals a significant change in his government of the wood. The audience has been given good reason to want this for Helena as well. Of all the Athenians in Shakespeare's play, she wins our sympathy with her forthright self-appraisals. Yet because she can see (with the eyes) the problem of looking with the mind, she experiences a kind of double vision. Alternating between the two, she finds herself in an impulsive, painful muddle made more painful because she sees the problem but can't help herself.

Our comedy is about love, and so we have young lovers running after each other in a confusing chain of attraction and rejection. But our comedy also looks at that other more intimate love—the love affair Everyman has with what he knows, and this form of love makes an appearance at the end of the scene. When Puck returns with the flower, Oberon tells him to put the juice of it on Demetrius' eyes, ensuring that he sees Helena when he awakens. It seems a simple enough task. Puck "shalt know the man / By the Athenian garments he hath on," but in this comic world even a spirit's knowledge is incomplete. Oberon is unaware that there is another man wandering about in Athenian garments, and this is how his knowledge—his attachment to knowing that there is a man with Athenian garments in the wood—works to create confusion.

Like Helena, comedy looks at the world with double vision. For thousands of years, it has represented a practical vision of a social order that allows human beings to survive and prosper despite the chaos of events. At the same time, it describes a situation where a man who has been prefigured or outlined in the mind by his Athenian garments can turn out to be the wrong man even if he is wearing Athenian garments. Comedy demonstrates that the words (and by extension the knowledge of the world the words represent) we depend on for order don't reliably fit the world; often enough they are round pegs in square holes. Chaucer and Shakespeare continually make the case that this is especially true about the word "love" which stands for two contradictory states of being. So comedy is about a Jack's love for the brightness of his Jill, but it is also about splitting the atom of a brightly lit intellectual object to briefly reveal a vast, dark, and inscrutable universe. A glimpse of this darkness provides a snapshot of what it was we thought we knew, which, like the size of a snapshot relative to the size and complexity of the world, is very little. As it is for the fairies, it's even easier for us to be wrong.

This last scene with Helena and Demetrius interrupts Oberon's thoughts of revenge. In the play's opening scene, after Hippolyta leaves that striking warrior moon hanging in the heaven for all to wonder at, Theseus gives his page Philostrate commands about the upcoming nuptials. It's state business, but it is also a break from the line of thought he and Hippolyta were pursuing. The brief pause gives him a little space before he approaches once more his one-time enemy and now his bride-to-be.

Similarly, the interlude with Helena and Demetrius allows Oberon to pause and gives him a chance to observe, as in a play, what an obsession looks and sounds like. The rest of *A Midsummer Night's Dream* will continue to illustrate the absurdities that follow from the limited, obsessive knowledge of the lovers and from the irruptions caused by Oberon's own meddling. Oberon is presently a little wode in his own wood. Since he inhabits a comedy, eventually he'll sober up from the intoxication of mastery and revenge as mishaps and his own deep feelings for Titania dictate. When he does, he'll be better positioned to agree to a sensible resolution of the quarrel; he and Titania can drop their individual claims to raise the boy and enjoy him together.

The Story Shall Be Changed

The title of this section comes from what Helena says to Demetrius in the last scene. As in the story of Apollo and Daphne, she tells him, a man is supposed to chase a woman, but in her case the story shall be changed. Daphne will now chase Apollo. Helena's speech highlights her expectation, which is a form of knowing, and so it develops the theme illustrated at the end of the last scene: Everyman's love for (or rather, attachment to) what he knows. The scenes that conclude Act II flesh out this theme and are structured around the expectations of Titania, Helena, and Hermia.

In the wood it's getting dark. The clear outlines of the day steep themselves in night. Soon, in sleep, daytime objects will cease to exist as the sleeper dreams away the time. Titania prepares for bed in a bower unsurpassed for softness, fragrance, and beauty; Oberon describes it at the end of the last scene as he pictures where she will be when he applies the flower juice:

I know a bank where the wild thyme blows,

Where oxlips and the nodding violet grows;

Quite over-canopied with luscious woodbine,

With sweet musk-roses, and with eglantine.

There sleeps Titania sometime of the night,

Lull'd in these flowers with dances and delight...

When the audience finally witnesses Titania's resting place. Oberon's earlier visual impression is represented more in sound as the fairies sing Titania to sleep. Like Hippolyta's first speech and Titania's memory of the young Indian woman on Neptune's yellow sands, the fairy song creates once more a glimpse of the goal, love-in-idleness—the resting place of comedy:

You spotted snakes with double tongue,

Thorny hedgehogs, be not seen;

Newts and blindworms, do no wrong,

Come not near our fairy queen.

Philomel, with melody

Sing in our sweet lullaby;

Lulla, lulla, lullaby; lulla, lulla, lullaby:

Never harm

Nor spell nor charm

Come our lovely lady nigh.

So good night, with lullaby.

In addition to the security she feels in the beauty of the song and of the place, Titania goes to sleep secure in the knowledge of what she achieved that day. She met with Oberon and dressed him down. Also, the source of the quarrel, the Indian boy, remains with her. Oberon has been told that the child belongs to the estate of the young mother, and Titania, as a woman, is the executor not only of the young woman's will but also of what belongs to women. It has been a good day, a good victory, and now she's ready for rest.

In "The Knight's Tale" Arcite's quest for Emily ends when he and his men drag Palamon to the stake, and he takes his victory lap around the arena, thinking he has finally achieved the resting place he had fought so hard to attain. But just as decisively as that contest ends, Saturn sends up a fury from the earth next to Arcite's horse, which rears up and crushes Arcite's heart with the saddle bow. Like Saturn displaying his mastery over the things of this world, Oberon now steps out of the shadows with the little flower to turn Titania's victory upside down. He pours the juice of it into her eyes while intoning:

What thou seest when thou dost wake,

Do it for thy true love take;

Love and languish for his sake.

Be it ounce or cat or bear,

Pard or boar with bristled hair

In thy eye that shall appear

When thou wakest, it is thy dear.

Wake when some vile thing is near.

The description of the bower proves to be just an idealized image of love-in-idleness and heartsease, the resting place of comedy, for the quarrel between the two is far from being played out. While the arena for Arcite and the bower for Titania seem to crown them with a wreath of victory, both sites turn out to be the ideal resting place not of comedy but of ego. Like the ground through which the fury can so suddenly spring or like the bower guarded by a sentry which Oberon can so easily penetrate, ego proves in the end to be haunted and insecure.

Arcite and Palamon, Theseus and Hippolyta, Hermia and her father, Lysander and Demetrius, Oberon and Titania, even Hermia and gentle Helena—all are warriors, fighting for what they desire, and desire, as Chaucer and Shakespeare painstakingly document, is synonymous with the operations of ego. Modern audiences easily recognize Arcite's victory lap; we see it in athletic competitions and political rallies, and if we were mind readers we might view a victory-lap brain wave that comes up anytime someone scores a point against someone else. Arcite's moment of triumph is a heaven of self-absorption, but it's inherently unstable. Titania's sleep will not last forever any more than Arcite's victory lap does. Eventually, like every other thing or mental state, the moment will change into something else. Titania may be sleeping, but there's a long way to go before the comedy itself can sleep. Mutability, the domain of Saturn, undermines ego which would fix things, pin them down, and then hold on to them for dear life. Given nature's volatility, including the volatility of ego, ego's mission is a losing proposition. The story of Titania's day is about to be heated up, liquefied, and distilled into something else. In ignorance she awaits a false dawn when love's arrow will shatter all former sense of heart and mind.

But before this happens, two more lovers from Athens arrive to prefigure the fairy queen's sudden change of allegiance from one ideal form to another. Athens is surely the place where young people would learn to love an ideal form since, up to the time Shakespeare was writing, academies and lyceums all over Europe had been teaching Plato's lessons about the love of beauty for almost two thousand years. So when Lysander and Hermia appear onstage, we might be inclined to breathe a sigh of relief. After the brawls of Oberon and Titania, these two lovely young

Athenians—who have been trained in love, who have sacrificed all for love by coming to this wood, and whose love is pure, without the taint of self-interest—arrive to set right the vileness that Oberon foresees for the grove.

If that's what the audience expects, it is quickly disillusioned. In the failing light, Lysander can't find the way to his dowager aunt's house, and he proposes that they bed down in the woods until dawn. Hermia agrees and imagines two separate rooms on the forest floor, one for her and one for him. This isn't what Lysander had in mind. He has a vision of them already married, and so:

> One turf shall serve as pillow for us both;
>
> One heart, one bed, two bosoms, and one troth.

They disagree, and although Lysander invents arguments for why they should sleep together, Hermia insists:

> Such separation as may well be said
>
> Becomes a virtuous bachelor and a maid,
>
> So far be distant; and good night, sweet friend.
>
> Thy love ne're alter till thy sweet life end.

Like a school boy disciplined by his teacher, Lysander stands corrected and prepares to lie where he is told:

> Amen, amen, to that fair prayer say I,
>
> And then end life when I end loyalty!
>
> Here is my bed. Sleep give thee all his rest!

She may not be ready to share her bed, but Hermia is happy to share a figure of speech right down the middle:

> With half that wish the wisher's eyes be press'd.

Much like Titania in her quarrel with Oberon, Hermia goes to sleep secure in the victory she has just won for virtue. But this time Robin, Oberon's agent, arrives with the flower juice that will change the story of her day. Robin has been told to look for the man with the Athenian garments, and he stumbles on the two of them:

> Night and silence! Who is here?
>
> Weeds of Athens he doth wear.
>
> This is he (my master said)
>
> Despised the Athenian maid;
>
> And here the maiden, sleeping sound
>
> On the dank and dirty ground.
>
> Pretty soul! she durst not lie
>
> Near this lack-love, this kill courtesy.
>
> Churl, upon thy eyes I throw
>
> All the power this charm doth owe.
>
> When thou wak'st, let love forbid
>
> Sleep his seat on thy eyelid.
>
> So awake when I am gone;
>
> For I must now to Oberon.

The audience knows, but Robin does not, that he has made a mistake. The juice was intended for Demetrius' eyes, and his eyes were to be pierced with the sight of Helena. In most people's estimation, mistakes are confusing, expensive, damaging to one's reputation, and sometimes fatal, but in a comic world they are a prerequisite for the insight by which a person survives and prospers. Since he is only a spirit, Robin can't be harmed by anything, but in keeping with the mission of his character his mistake is the perfect catalyst for mixing up the fixed ideas of the four lovers. Employing the ancient and unscientific device of personification, science teachers used to explain that nature abhors a vacuum. While it might not be a scientific conclusion, the person who observes Robin's careless meddling in human affairs might be led to conclude that nature abhors fixed ideas, for Robin's confusion in the wood proves to be an antidote to the impatience and blindness brought on by obsession. The confusion's the thing that's needed now to catch these lovers with a strong dose of ideal love run amuck.

Adding additional ingredients, the other two lovers arrive as Hermia and Lysander sleep, Demetrius first and Helena chasing him. Demetrius quickly exits and Helena remains:

O, I am out of breath in this fond chase!

The more my prayer, the lesser is my grace.

Happy is Hermia, wheresoe're she lies;

For she has blessed and attractive eyes.

How came her eyes so bright? Not with salt tears.

If so, my eyes are oft'ner wash'd than hers.

No, no! I am as ugly as a bear;

For beasts that meet me run away for fear.

Therefore no marvel though Demetrius

Do as a monster, fly my presence thus.

What wicked and dissembling glass of mine

Made me compare with Hermia's sphery eyne?

If confusion is the goal, then Helena has already arrived. Her speech is packed with antipathies. She prays for grace, and the prayer turns against her. She would be attractive and has argued that she's equally as attractive as Hermia, but she gives up imitating Hermia to declare herself ugly. As a team player in the sisterhood, she would like to be happy for Hermia's success, but everything she says about her can only be delivered with bitter sarcasm as in:

What wicked and dissembling glass of mine

Made me compare with Hermia's sphery eyne?

She just doesn't see anything special about Hermia. Most important, she loves Demetrius and even offered to be his spaniel, but the beastly way he treats her proves over and over that he is no gentleman. His unworthiness makes her doubt her own judgment.

If she is confused now, she is about to be even more so when she discovers Lysander sleeping on the ground at her feet, all primed (unbeknownst to her) for love at first sight:

But who is here? Lysander! on the ground?

Dead, or asleep? I see no blood, no wound.

Lysander, if you live, good sir, awake.

There's no blood, and she can't see any wound. He's alive, but his vision has suffered a critical injury. Henceforth, he lives as in a dream. Since the word "dream" is in the title of the play, since my reading of Chaucer and this play have made the wake-up call a critical ingredient of comedy, and since an awakening has been the goal of spiritual disciplines from ancient times, Helena's command—"Lysander, if you live, good sir, awake"—sums up a deep longing in the heart of every sleeping beauty.

The whole point of comedy can be summed up in this word "awake," and yet the situation has made it so that her command is actually the signal for Lysander to fall into the dream magically supplied by the flower juice. At any rate, awaken he does, rearing up from the ground to tell her:

> And run through fire I will for thy sweet sake.
>
> Transparent Helena! Nature shows art,
>
> That through thy bosom makes me see thy heart.

All her life Helena has wanted a man to look at her like this, to say such words, sweet and sexy in his longing, and now it's finally happening. She used to think she was attractive, but the business with Demetrius and Hermia convinces her otherwise. Just as she decides she is as ugly as a bear, along comes this. Helena prides herself on knowing the difference between seeing and hearing with the mind—that is, with wishful thinking—and seeing and hearing things with eyes and ears—that is, pragmatically. Looking at things pragmatically has taught her that she is as ugly as a bear, but now with eyes and ears she sees and hears a man who is ready to run through fire for her sweet sake.

In keeping with the volatility and instability of elements being heated by the press of events, Lysander immediately changes the subject:

> Where is Demetrius? O, how fit a word
>
> Is that vile name to perish on my sword!

As quickly as he falls in love, his mind turns to hate for his rival and to revenge for his suffering (which he has endured for less than ten seconds, the time it took for him to utter the three lines before these two). Oberon has already cut a figure or a pattern of love and revenge in the narrative. Desire by its nature means separation from that which is desired, and so love for something automatically creates an equal and opposite hatred for the obstacle to love. As the old stories tell, Venus and Mars were lovers; love (more accurately, desire) and hate go together.

When Lysander turns his thoughts to his rival, Helena is ready to forget what he said about her bosom, and fixes instead on the threat to Demetrius:

> Do not say so, Lysander; say not so.
>
> What though he love your Hermia? Lord, what though?
>
> Yet Hermia still loves you. Then be content.

Helena is mystified why either man would love Hermia. Lord, anyone who does is a very poor creature indeed and hardly deserves killing. Since Lysander is also a poor creature for loving Hermia, he should count himself lucky to have her. In fact, the two of them are well matched. Lysander, though, returns to his first subject, his love of Helena, spicing it this time with a variation that Helena has also longed long to hear, a comparison with her rival Hermia where Helena is the victor:

> Content with Hermia? No! I do repent
>
> The tedious minutes I with her have spent.
>
> Not Hermia, but Helena I love.
>
> Who will not change a raven for a dove?
>
> The will of man is by his reason sway'd;

And reason says you are the worthier maid.

Things growing are not ripe until their season;

So I, being young, till now ripe not to reason;

And touching now the point of human skill,

Reason becomes the marshal to my will

And leads me to your eyes; where I o'erlook

Love's stories written in Love's richest book.

So much of what Lysander says is so true and so beautifully put if only it weren't Lysander saying it. Comedy would teach us exactly what he says here, that reason is more a living organism than a syllogism and that our trials and errors teach through painful experience that some human skill, intelligence, or reason must overlook our story and become marshal to the will if we are going to survive and prosper. So Shakespeare has Lysander briefly summarize the gist of Theseus' speech at the end of "The Knight's Tale," but by putting this wisdom in the mouth of a crazy man, the audience has to separate what is being said from the person saying it.

The wisdom expressed has become, like the image of Helena, another ideal form to which a love-sick person can attach himself. Shakespeare makes it clear that Lysander's little speech is just the flower juice talking. Since we are forced to distance ourselves from the wisdom he describes, the speech conveys a live and graphic warning for the ages as if Lysander, who has already revealed that he may have harbored a sexual motive for luring Hermia into the wood, were actually saying: "O my people, all you who like myself have been trained to love ideal forms, beware of anyone who makes an argument by an appeal to reason. This reason is but a wolf in sheep's clothing, a supposed intelligence that hides the voracious appetite of a low creature."

Lysander's argument rings false to Helena as well even though

Lysander means it with all his heart. She responds:

> *Wherefore was I to this keen mockery born?*
>
> *When at your hands did I deserve this scorn?*
>
> *Is't not enough, is't not enough, young man,*
>
> *That I did never, no, nor never can,*
>
> *Deserve a sweet look from Demetrius' eye,*
>
> *But you must flout my insufficiency?*
>
> *Good troth, you do me wrong! good sooth, you do!*
>
> *In such disdainful manner me to woo.*

Helena falls back on her recently acquired knowledge that she is ugly; it's a safer position than believing that she might be loved since she's quite used by now to being scorned and insufficient. She is giving herself reasons for not believing Lysander, but since the writer has given the audience the advantage of seeing all that has transpired thus far, we know that Helena (despite all her reasons and good reasons they are) is wrong. She is truly loved even if it is just the flower juice talking. Nevertheless, she runs away but only after pronouncing judgment:

> *O, that a lady, of one man refus'd,*
>
> *Should by another be abus'd!*

So she retreats to preserve the dignity she enjoys from being a lady, from not getting too dirty in affairs of the heart, and from transcending his abuse by removing herself. This, too, is not a real resting place. Despite her maiden pride, she followed her heart and entered the wood. She's in it for good, whether she likes it or not, until the whole movement of mind and heart is played out.

The scene begins with Titania being sung to sleep secure in her self-possession and in the guardianship of her page. When Helena rejects Lysander's declarations as a cruel game that friends sometimes play on each other, she continues to rest secure in the knowledge that she's the victim of an ugly cosmic joke. Nearby, Hermia is sleeping secure in Lysander's love and his plans to marry her, but the audience has seen that Lysander, like the horse in Chaucer's tale, has reared up with an action that eventually will crush Hermia's heart.

Meanwhile, Lysander has completely forgotten about Hermia until after Helena flees:

> *She sees not Hermia. Hermia, sleep thou there,*
>
> *And never mayst thou come Lysander near!*

As easily as he declared love for Helena, he now declares hate for Hermia. With that he rushes off to be Helena's knight by saving her from her desperate flight. With that, too, Hermia suddenly wakes up:

> *Help me, Lysander, help me! Do thy best*
>
> *To pluck this crawling serpent from my breast!*
>
> *Ay me, for pity! What a dream was here!*
>
> *Lysander, look how I do quake with fear.*
>
> *Methought a serpent eat my heart away,*
>
> *And you sat smiling at his cruel prey.*
>
> *Lysander! What, remov'd? Lysander, lord!*

What, out of hearing? gone? No sound, no word?

Alack, where are you? Speak, an if you hear.

Speak, of all loves! I swoon almost with fear.

By being in the position of a god on the mountaintop where we see all things, it is impossible for us to feel the full impact of Hermia's cry. Given the state of their relationship when she went to sleep, she has to assume the worst, that a wild beast has grabbed Lysander and dragged him to his death. If she had found him lying dead beside her on the forest floor after she woke from her dream, the words she speaks here could easily be the same. The audience can't hear her words that way, though, because we know that Lysander is alive and well. There's an additional irony in that when she hears in Act III that Lysander's love has been changed to hate, she may secretly wish that Lysander was safely dead instead.

Comedy requires, just as tragedy does, a wake-up call like this one where the ground on which Lysander was lying and on which Hermia depended proves to be empty. She doesn't know to what extent her story has been changed, but the audience does. It would appear that the poet has given us a position of eminence, which is why most people instinctively love it, but our post has a dark side. An audience blessed with omniscience can never be wrong or in the dark. Until we are in the dark, we can't enter the comic arena, and so we are invited to identify with poor little Hermia. Swathed in easy conquests and bedecked with all the trinkets of courtly love and safely asleep in the plans she has made, she has awakened in darkness to what she cannot know. When her cries for Lysander go unanswered, she comes to herself:

No? Then I well perceive you are not nigh.

Either death or you I'll find immediately.

As she heads out into the dark wood with no idea of where she is going, clueless Hermia, like embattled Helena, is on her way to becoming a worthy comic heroine.

CHAPTER NINE:
NIGHT

Chagall's *In Philetas' Garden*

If Horses Had Hands

This reading of Shakespeare's play begins with the theme of autonomy, the power of every mind to imagine reality for itself, and holds that the opening scenes of the play outline the implications of that power in dramatic form. For example, we witness Duke Theseus and Queen Hippolyta, who used to be absolute monarchs in their respective realms, having to negotiate the terms under which they will rule together in one. Egeus then brings a suit at the court of the duke because he and his daughter look at Lysander differently. The events of Act II develop the narrative of Hermia's autonomy. When she agrees to run away with Lysander, the world opens up with new possibilities, but by nightfall her world has become smaller than ever. In the absence of the customs and comforts of her home in Athens, she has no assurance that she'll pass the night safely. Her only shield against the darkness is the shared idea that she and Lysander are in love and live for each other.

When Hermia dreams of the snake at her breast and wakes to find Lysander no longer near, she makes acquaintance with the dark side of her love and of a willful autonomy. Dreams aren't always pleasant nor are the consequences of acting on a dreamlike scheme. Without the customary forms of social life to frame her relations with what's "out there," she finds herself living in an alien place more constraining than the autocratic rule of a duke and a father. When she goes to sleep with Lysander beside her, she is confident and in control of her destiny; this confidence is a gift of Athens and her father in that, thanks to the security they provide, she's accustomed to acting as she will (as in her choice to love only Lysander) and sleeping well. Now the destiny the duke and her father once secured seems to be at the mercy of wild beasts. As prefigured in the imagery of Hippolyta's first speech, Hermia's sense of control over people and things is steeping away as the dark wood presses in on her. That loss impacts her self-possession as well; she's about to go a little crazy. It's a pattern that holds for all the Athenians over the course of their midsummer night.

Thanks to her autonomy, Hermia's world is shrinking, but a play like this one testifies as well to the power and reach of one man's autonomy. Shakespeare's dream comes to life on the stage and may even catch the attention (and the conscience) of a queen. If Shakespeare agreed with his character Hamlet that the purpose of writing and of playing is to show "the very age and body of the time his form and pressure,"[49] then perhaps the Athenians' night in the wood represents the changes of form and the pressures of his own age. Since Luther's and Calvin's reforms earlier in the century, people all over Europe were leaving the security of the Roman Church to establish religious practices based not on the sacraments and the intervention of a sacred priesthood but on direct, individual contact with God's word and a continual, solitary wrestling with one's conscience. This sea change in their spiritual life was happening at the same time that the physical world was opening up to the explorations in seagoing ships of hardy pilgrims who would live in that new world. It was a time that produced the greatest poet in our language. It was also a time of deep division over freedom of conscience in the practice of religion, and in England those divisions eventually flared into the bloody civil war of the mid-seventeenth century.

In our own time we are undergoing a similar sea-change as nineteenth-, twentieth-, and twenty-first-century thinkers, artists, musicians, activists, and eccentrics encourage their followers to plunge into ever-greater reaches of secular autonomy and self-absorption. Some claim that the trend accelerated in the nineteen sixties with the Me Generation, of which I have to admit I'm a member. Marc Chagall painted a series of scenes from Longius' *Daphne and Chloe* just as the leading edge of the Me Generation was finishing high school. The incident from Longius' romance that illustrates this chapter features an old cowherd who educates the innocent lovers in the trials of love. Prior to this, Daphne and Chloe lived a pastoral life without any cultural filter to instruct them about relations with the opposite sex. In adolescence they begin to suffer greatly from an inexplicable longing in each other's presence. The longing is like a feeling left over from a dream they can't remember. Philetas explains to them that the only cure for the pain of it is kissing. Chapall's picture reminds me, not only of flower children from the sixties who dropped out of "the system" to live and love in nature, but also of Shakespeare's lovers who leave Athens to pursue their love in the wood.

The colors, the lovers, the winged spirits, and the dark figure who appears to be conjuring it all up recall the wood governed by Oberon and Puck. We know that Chagall was aware of Shakespeare's play, for he also painted a picture of Bottom embracing Titania. Here, in Philetas' garden (as in many of his paintings), images swim weightlessly around without any sense of depth or up or down; it's the world as if it's lived underwater. Chagall's dreamscapes reflect a time whose form and pressure led many twentieth-century artists to deconstruct traditional "realism" so they could express personal, subjective visions of the world, and often enough the world expressed in their dreams is overwhelming and hopeless, like wrestling with a whirlwind or like Hermia's sudden abandonment. In the short term, this proves to be the case for Daphne and Chloe. They take Philetas' advice but discover that kissing only increases the pain of love.

So autonomy, the power to dream, is a power for pleasure and pain, for confusion and insight. In Longius's story and Shakespeare's play the pain and confusion of unsatisfied desire is only an episode in the overall comic narrative. While the alienation of unsatisfied desire is very real, especially for poor Helena and Hermia in the wood, a comic narrative reveals this state to be but an impression or a feeling that can change over time. We can't always control events or even the longing of our own hearts, but our autonomy is more deeply rooted than a dream or a passing fancy. We are born with hands and legs and motion and soon enough—without any conscious effort—with imagination to shape the things of this world into a home that's well built, comfortable, and good. By nature and by trade people have always been creators and builders. After the disappointment of dreams that don't pan out, the show must go on, even in the new world that has opened up in the absence of the dream. This is our autonomy, and the pattern realized in a comedy is one of the greatest creations of it. It continues to be a comfort and a guiding light.

Act III begins with the six mechanicals from Athens preparing to rehearse their play in the wood. They are all creators within the trades they practice; they build houses, frame doors, weave cloth, mend bellows, repair pots, and make clothes to fit. These are the people a company would need to be at home in a wilderness. They have left Athens to avoid scrutiny so that the wonder of their production at the actual performance will blaze their way into the duke's esteem. The rehearsal is about creating an effect that will produce the gold they anticipate, but before that can happen there are various problems to solve. If Pyramus draws his sword to kill himself, will it not frighten the ladies? This is resolved by explaining in a prologue that all the action they see on stage is merely playing and all those doing the action merely players. To sophisticates, those of Theseus' court and those like ourselves who are presently watching, Shakespeare's hard-handed and hardheaded workmen may seem like simpletons who suppose their playing might be taken for reality. These artisans work through the problems of playing mechanically, but if sophisticates laugh unkindly at the mote in the players' eyes, it's because they don't see the beam in their own. Intellectuals are just as quick and maybe quicker to confuse their own imaginings with reality.

The mechanicals wonder if a lion onstage might frighten the ladies. A prologue to the lion's appearance will take care of this too. Prior to roaring, Snug the joiner will speak through his costume to reassure everyone that he is not a lion but a man "as other men are." How will they bring the moonlight by which the lovers will meet into the chamber? They briefly consider opening the casement windows to let in actual moonlight, but Peter Quince's suggestion wins the day. He will have Robin Starveling the tailor present the figure of Moonshine. The remaining obstacle—a wall to separate the two lovers—turns out to be the comic focus of the show. Now that they are getting the hang of it, they find it unnecessary to bring a wall into the chamber. Instead, Tom Snout the tinker will present Wall, and he will hold out his two fingers to represent the cranny through which the lovers communicate. With that, they have their play fitted and are ready to rehearse.

These solutions to the problems of representing reality remind me of what the poet philosopher Xenophanes (c.560-c.478) observed concerning the stories about anthropomorphic gods who controlled the sun and the moon and other natural phenomena. If oxen, lions, or horses had hands, he asserted, they would undoubtedly form gods with bodies and shapes like their own. For the mechanicals all things, and not just the gods, have the shape of a human being. In their hands, the play is a notably literal translation of the world in human terms. Like the handicrafts that make their lives more pleasant and by which they make their living, it's a way of looking at the world that enables the mechanicals and their families to survive and prosper in it.

Their discussion of these matters also serves as a prologue for when Robin "translates" Bottom into an ass. If the autonomous imagination of a mortal can translate the natural world into a human being, then it must be that a human being can be translated into the natural world. There's a sweetness in this little scene about people's relationship with the world, and by extension with the gods, that you may not find in the tomes of theologians. These mechanicals intuitively imagine themselves in nature, and for people so inclined it's but a short step to see the anthropomorphic creator of nature imagining himself in us.

Robin's Alchemy

Even if he never thought he was divinely inspired, Bottom has always had great self-confidence. So the rehearsal for his star turn begins, and when Robin enters the scene, he sees an opportunity for his usual kind of fun:

What hempen homespuns have we swagg'ring here,

So near the cradle of the Fairy Queen?

What, a play toward? I'll be an auditor;

An actor too perhaps if I see cause.

It doesn't take him long to write himself into the play. Bottom leaves the stage briefly, and when he returns, Robin has changed him into an ass declaring:

If I were only fair, Thisby, I were only thine.

The meaning is somewhat blurred, but we can say with certainty that it's a fine expression of wishful thinking. The words suggest that he might be wishing, "If only I were fair, I would be beloved." From what we know of Bottom, it's more likely that he is saying with a great generosity of spirit "Even if I were the only fair in the world, I would still be thine."

Either way, Bottom expects that his Thisby will observe the script and confirm that he is both fair and beloved, but bedlam breaks out instead. His fellows are terrified by his grotesque appearance and run screaming in all directions. Robin adds to the confusion by stirring up these Athenian youths even more with his own exertions:

I'll follow you; I'll lead you about a round,

Through bog, through bush, through brake, through briar.

Sometime a horse I'll be, sometime a hound,

A hog, a headless bear, sometime a fire;

And neigh, and bark, and grunt, and roar, and burn,

Like horse, hound, hog, bear, fire, at every turn.

Peter Quince must have been running in circles because after a bit he runs headlong into Bottom once more. In fear and trembling, he exclaims:

Bless thee, Bottom! Bless thee! Thou art translated.

The motions of the players as Robin urges them on, the ingredients from the woods he adds to excite their fears and move their legs, the burning they feel of a fire in their whole being, and finally the way everything revolves around the cradle of the fairy queen—all this suggests the simmering of elements in a great pot or beaker that are being "translated" into some other form.

My discussion of Act II has already employed imagery from distilling and alchemy to describe the comic process initiated in the wood: the wood is the lab, Robin is the alchemist, and the lovers are the main elements. Now it's the mechanicals' turn to be heated with sudden surprise and liquefied into action with Bottom as the catalyst and the center of the whole experiment. All the characters in the play and the things of this world are spices and garnishes added to make the magic that will eventually spill out of the wood, even into the heart of Theseus' court. In its essence this discipline is nothing new. From ancient times human beings have sought to find for themselves, in the heat of chaotic experiences, a pearl of great price. Alchemy derives from the spiritual seeking of ancient days, but in Shakespeare's era it took a decisive turn towards a material interpretation of the quest. Not everyone sought to transcend the things of this world as the church instructed the faithful; instead, some did experiments to prove that the things of this world could be reduced to the purest, most beautiful, and most lasting of all material substances: gold.

Once they are all in involved in the process, there is no autonomy for the other players as they whirl around and are brought to a boil over Bottom's transformation, but Bottom himself achieves a self-realization through Robin's alchemy that will have a comic effect on all the other characters. He is about to be changed from an obnoxious egotist into a tractable and attractive member of a corporate body. If Bottom can be so transformed, then anyone can. Like Shakespeare, Chaucer took a keen interest in the entire spectrum of people who make up the human comedy. *The Canterbury Tales* features stories from men and women, from those in secular and sacred vocations, from the nobility and commoners, from honest folk and hypocrites, from people who are happy and those who harbor deep self-hatred. Regardless of educational development, status in society, gender, race, or material wealth, everyone is a philosopher in that everyone makes inquiry at some point, whether consciously or not, into basic questions about one's own capacities and about the nature of life. As a matter of survival people have to learn the hard way what they can get away with. This is what characters in comic literature do, but they are not knights like Sir Gawain on a quest for a great mystery. Characters in a comedy don't intend to gain the insight that comes their way; life does this for them.

We have all read stories about the breakthroughs of science made by autonomous individuals. No one can begin to list them all, and everyone alive today owes a great debt of gratitude to those throughout the ages who, through their insights and inventions, have helped people to live more comfortably and safely in this uncertain world. Whether they profited directly or not, these scientists, inventors, and creative individuals of all types hit the jackpot with their creativity. They found the pot of gold at the end of the rainbow, and if they didn't get to spend it themselves, then others enjoyed it for them. Robin's alchemy takes us on a different but no less important path. The path comes to an end where the individual discovers that the heart of his enterprise is only fool's gold. According to the rule of comedy this discovery is of infinite value. It puts a person within sight of where a pearl of great price can be found, for he gains from this vantage ("Seest thou this sweet sight?" Oberon later says of that which initiates a change of heart) a decent understanding of his own and his material's limitations.

Alchemy happens to be a case in point; despite the emptiness of the original goal, the process led people to a greater understanding of the elements and the mixing of elements. Robin's alchemy serves as a parable for a seeker who, like Bottom, would reduce the great, seething, multiplicity of the world to his intelligence of it. The parable teaches that, when looking with the mind, the intelligence with which one frames the enterprise is as much the subject of the experiment as the elements of it. For example, the reader who seeks a moral in Bottom's story might be tempted to conclude that during the course of his adventure in the wood, Bottom gains the knowledge that he's an egoist. A simple judgment like this, however, would be a short circuiting of Shakespeare's intent. For him and for Chaucer ego is not a problem that can be abstracted from experience and then solved. It's a problem that has no logical solution. No man or woman can consciously fix the problem of egocentricity when ego is still the warp and woof of the looking. To tenderize the egoist Bottom, Robin goes to the heart of the problem and completely transforms his head. After Robin's cure, Bottom doesn't know he's an ass; he is an ass. This may seem to be a distinction without a difference, but it helps to explain the very attractive picture we get of him after his transformation.

Bottom undoubtedly is not used to having tricks played on him so the behavior of his friends and its implications are novelties. To calm his doubts, he interests himself with a little song about some of the birds he may be hearing all around him in the wood:

The woosel cock so black of hue,

With orange-tawny bill,

The throstle with his note so true,

The wren with little quill,

The finch, the sparrow, and the lark,

The plain-song cuckoo grey,

Whose note full many a man doth mark,

And dares not answer nay.

By the end of the little ditty, he has regained his composure. The song and his singing of it has created a space for him to breathe normally and feel better. After cataloging the names and qualities of several birds, though, the plain-song cuckoo turns his attention to a husband who can't acknowledge or deny that his wife has made him a fool.

Since the flight of his friends has made him feel like a fool, Bottom reasons how to deal with the new reality:

> *For, indeed, who would set his wit to so foolish a bird? Who would give a bird the lie, though he cry "cuckoo" never so?*

Like the husband, apparently, he doesn't need to answer nay or give the lie to those who would discomfit him. If he's a fool, he knows very well from the constant companionship of those gaping at him that they are no wiser than he. By being an ass, Bottom has bottomed out in a profound equality with anyone. Others can cry "cuckoo" all they like, but the charge is no more threatening than the buzzing of a fly or some general hee-hawing of the herd. A bird has its own reasons for crying "cuckoo" just as Bottom does for singing a little ditty. The buzzing about him has a whole new meaning when he considers that the source is a foolish creature.

In addition to the equanimity he establishes on his own, Titania awakens in the middle of his song to exclaim:

> *What angel wakes me from my flowery bed?*

Bottom has already managed to settle himself in this new world pretty well, but he now has a world class admirer and promoter. Once he finishes his song, Titania wants more:

I pray thee, gentle mortal, sing again.

Mine ear is much enamoured of thy note;

So is mine eye enthralled to thy shape;

And thy fair virtue's force (perforce) doth move me,

On the first view, to say, to swear, I love thee.

Before looking at Bottom's reply, recall the way he behaves prior to his transformation. Even if he isn't physically big, he bullies everyone with a huge appetite for self-aggrandizement. He wants to play all the parts; he pretends to knowledge he doesn't have; and he expects the company of his friends to bow and scrape when it looks like he might be displeased. But listen to him now, once he has actually become an ass, as he replies to Titania's passionate declaration:

> *Methinks, mistress, you should have little reason for that. And yet, to say the truth, reason and love keep little company together now-a-days. The more the pity that some honest neighbors will not make them friends. Nay, I can gleek upon occasion.*

He's not inclined to see himself as anything special; this shrinking of himself, however, seems to have increased his powers of perception. He now understands that if honest neighbors can't agree to meet on the grounds that they are all fools, which is a perfectly reasonable position, it will prove difficult for them to be friends. This is Bottom's new "bottom line," and it establishes in the play the comic basis for civility.

Bottom has surely noticed that the most beautiful woman in existence has figuratively thrown herself at him with a heart-stopping intensity, and yet he receives the news with remarkable aplomb and humility. It's not just the flower juice talking when Titania observes, from what he has just said, that:

> *Thou art wise as thou art beautiful.*

Once again, he could have left her compliment at that, but instead he adds further insight as he codifies in a single sentence a great comic character's insight into autonomy and intelligence:

> *Not so neither; but if I had wit enough to get out of this wood, I have enough to serve mine own turn.*

Just a few hours earlier, Bottom aspired to a role "to make all split." People would experience in him a time when:

> *The raging rocks*
>
> *And shivering shocks*
>
> *Shall break the locks*
>
> *Of prison gates;*
>
> *And Phibbus' car*
>
> *Shall shine from far*
>
> *And make and mar*
>
> *The foolish Fates.*

This is an elemental power, not a man. Now that he is a fool Bottom is the perfect gentleman, and, for a mortal, as worthy as any to be loved by Titania. Thanks to the flower juice, his beauty is a moot question, so she makes commands about his intentions:

> *Out of this wood do not desire to go.*
>
> *Thou shalt remain here, whether thou wilt or no.*
>
> *I am a spirit of no common rate,*

The summer still doth tend upon my state;

And I do love thee. Therefore go with me.

I'll give thee fairies to attend on thee;

And they shall fetch thee jewels from the deep,

And sing while thou on pressed flowers dost sleep;

And I will purge thy mortal grossness so

That thou shalt like an airy spirit go.

If this is where he ends up, what man, like Dogberry in *Much Ado about Nothing*, would not cry out to be set down an ass?[50] As much as Oberon may have intended to play a joke on Titania and as much as the scheme is playing a joke on Bottom, it's being played on all those who would be the opposite of a stolid, dependable beast with ridiculous furry ears and who would aspire instead to ideal beauty, greatness, and power over others. People know from their own experiences with them that these desperate seekers, for all the alchemy of their exertions, will never be purged of their mortal grossness or like an airy spirit go.

Titania next invites Peaseblossom, Cobweb, Moth, and Mustardseed to be kind and courteous to Bottom, and throughout this first audience with his court Bottom is equally kind and courteous in return. Now that he's an ass, courtesy comes naturally to him. He holds court in an antechamber of perfect autosuggestion and wish fulfillment, but Titania herself is anxious to seal the deal with something more:

Come wait upon him; lead him to my bower.

The moon, methinks, looks with a wat'ry eye;

And when she weeps, weeps every little flower,

Lamenting some enforced chastity.

Tie up my love's tongue, bring him silently.

How happy some o're other some can be! Why is Bottom, of all people, so fortunate? Shakespeare has made Bottom an unlikely star of the show for the same reason that he has Falstaff take up so much room in his history plays. His enormous self-regard serves as a foundation for the play we witness. Like the arena in Chaucer which only lets in those who love or hate, the human comedy is acted out on the great stage of self-love that both Falstaff and Bottom wear so prominently on their sleeves. No cloak of altruism or sympathy for these egoists. They don't need to be baptized daily in sentiments of fellow feeling.

Bottom's ego, however, has been completely made over by Robin's alchemy. When the players first meet, Bottom equates himself with the earth itself including its volcanic core, for this is how he can put himself at the center of everyone's attention. Here we find that the most helpful aspect of that wish has been pressed upon him. Like the great globe of earth, he's our common ground for good; somehow, the egotist's intention to make all split has been mended. In his new form as a complete ass, as opposed to the half-assed variety that pretends to be something else, he is the bottom of self-proclaimed certainties or uncertainties. When people hit bottom, after their self-proclaimed certainties and uncertainties have disappointed and dumped them there, they, like him, may be fortunate as they discover for themselves their absurdly large ears (that latch on for dear life to what they hear) and fuzzy heads (that latch on for dear life to what they think). When all those who thrash about worrying big subjects to death hit bottom and consider the source, they, too, can push off from there. Instead of splitting, Bottom heals them.

A person who thinks he's somehow better than Bottom will miss the cure, so our poet has done his best to make the case for this comic experiment. The little song Bottom sings helps us to find him there in the depths. Having been born into this world and in the midst of great striving to make his way in a strange and alien environment, often enough Everyman hears out of the wilderness a little voice singing "cuckoo" at him. If Everyman would but follow Bottom's plunge to the bottom, he would no longer worry about so foolish a bird. For those of us who live by thinking and talking and frightening ourselves with cuckoo thoughts and assertions day after day, Bottom represents a way up, despite himself, as he is led away in perfect silence. Usually, writers make the case for the vaunted autonomy of intellectual intelligence. Shakespeare may be no different, but his Titania knows that silence is golden, and so she has her fairies tie up her lover's tongue.

The Messenger

The next scene opens with Oberon on stage unsure of what is happening in his wood:

I wonder if Titania be awak'd;

Then, what it was that next came in her eye,

Which she must dote on in extremity.

He is not kept in the dark long, for Robin appears onstage as if in answer to the question:

Here comes my messenger. How now, mad spirit?

What night-rule now about this haunted grove?

Evidently the fairies rule much the way people do. Like us, they depend on each other for intelligence. This meeting functions as a framing device for a series of scenes starring the four lovers that they are about to witness. We begin with Robin and Oberon, we see them watching the lovers interact, and we hear at the end what they think about everything that has happened. The play within a play is a device Shakespeare often employs that's similar to the dramatic irony in Chaucer's tales where a storyteller overlooks the actions of his characters, Chaucer the pilgrim overlooks the storyteller, Chaucer the author overlooks Chaucer the pilgrim who is a sweet man but hopelessly naive, and God overlooks all.

The rest of this little introduction features Robin's long monologue that recreates for Oberon the recent past:

My mistress with a monster is in love.

Near to her close and consecrated bower,

While she was in her dull and sleeping hour,

A crew of patches, rude mechanicals,

That work for bread upon Athenian stalls,

We're met together to rehearse a play,

Intended for great Theseus' nuptial day.

The shallowest thickskin of that barren sort,

Who Pyramus presented in their sport,

Forsook his scene and ent'red in a brake.

When I did him at this advantage take,

An ass's nole I fixed on his head.

Anon his Thisby must be answered,

And forth my mimic comes.

For a dramatic and poetic master, Shakespeare appears to have nodded off for a bit in these lines. While the verse is singsong and without interest (because the audience already knows its contents), it must also be said that it's a straightforward and accurate report in response to Oberon's question. Robin's words "mimic" what the audience has just witnessed in the previous scene, and their accuracy reveals a character who looks at those events with the eyes. He's a dependable messenger, and a skill in reporting is critical to the success of any relationship. It's especially important in the government of a state, as it is here.

The next section of his speech departs from a matter-of-fact presentation of the material:

> *When they him spy,*
>
> *As wild geese that the creeping fowler eye,*
>
> *Or russet-pated choughs, many in sort,*
>
> *Rising and cawing at the gun's report,*
>
> *Sever themselves and madly sweep the sky;*
>
> *So at his sight away his fellows fly...*

To mimic the mechanicals for Oberon, Robin compares their movements to the motion of birds after a "gun's report." It's the translation of things-as-they-are into a figure of speech. If his report was too literal, it would fail. Because it involves motion, the scene he describes must live in the listener's imagination if it is to achieve its true effect.

Finally, his speech concludes with a strong contrast between the way Robin and the mechanicals look at the world:

> *And, at our stamp, here o'er and o'er one falls;*
>
> *He murder cries and help from Athens calls.*
>
> *Their sense thus weak, lost with their fears thus strong,*
>
> *Made senseless things begin to do them wrong;*
>
> *For briars and thorns at their apparel snatch;*
>
> *Some, sleeves—some, hats; from yielders all things catch.*

We already have ample proof that Robin looks with his eyes. Since we have seen these things as well, we observe how faithfully he serves Oberon and the truth. As the mechanicals' imaginations run riot, they see what isn't there. Just as they did earlier when they humanized the lion, moon, and wall for the purpose of playing, they give a senseless thing like a thorn bush arms and hands and a conscious intent to harm or steal.

The self-love, the instinct for self-preservation, the night rule that governs the minds of the mechanicals in a passage of fear—all prompt what Helena refers to as looking with the mind. At the sound of a gun, the mind will "report" through a lens of self-love. For most people who live in a social context, self-love is a shaky proposition, something to be indulged in on the sly like a bad habit. All bets are off, though, at the gun's report, at which time self-love reports for duty; at the gun's report, it's every man for himself except for those rare individuals who are true heroes. People are not born self-conscious; we pick it up along the way. The psyche of a baby crying for a parent in the middle of the night is radically different from that of the teenager who yells at a parent to leave him alone. Those of us of a certain age know from personal experience that the birth of ego in adolescence is just the beginning of a preoccupation with the self that lasts a lifetime. It may be that some people are born heroes. I wouldn't know. Let it be said, though, that the firing of a gun and the firing up of self-love at the gun's report are included here in Shakespeare's comic survey of characters and situations.

Self-consciousness, which is intimately tied to an encounter with death (a theme developed in "The Birth of Ego," pp. 43-46), springs to life in an environment of threat along with the fear that's always lurking around the self. That fear, in turn, is projected out into the world. The foggy, ghostly, paranoid atmosphere of warlike Elsinor is Shakespeare's most vivid representation of this state, but everyone knows that fear can surface at a moment's notice in ordinary times. Robin's little pranks that the fairy told us about earlier expose the fear in ordinary life, and we have just witnessed it for ourselves in what he concocts for the other mechanicals:

I led them on in this distracted fear

And left sweet Pyramus translated there;

When Bottom's companions see a monster, their behavior is predictably stirred up by ego and fear, but Bottom's transformation defies the odds for Bottom himself. In contrast with the distracted fear that usually accompanies unpleasant surprises and sudden rejection, his self-love is translated into the sweetness of a gentle beast even before Titania awakens. It's the miracle of Robin's alchemy. A major invasion into Bottom's comfort zone like the one we have just witnessed doesn't shake the major premise of his life that he is the serene and unshakable center of it, and it's unlikely to be shaken henceforth when it's confirmed in a material way that few ever enjoy:

When in that moment (so it came to pass)

Titania wak'd, and straightway loved an ass.

Somehow Bottom transcends the fear that constantly surrounds self-love like a gravitational field. In *Hamlet* fear gets the upper hand and destroys all the major characters. In *A Midsummer Night's Dream* a fool like Bottom realizes his true nature, and nature returns the favor with the ultimate gift it can bestow.

As a messenger Robin performs the functions of Mercury, the trickster and the errand boy of the gods. He enjoys the favor of the poet, his creator, and he represents for those of us who engage with his work an affirmation of the poet's craft. Mercury and Robin are minor figures in the company of those they serve, but Zeus needs a messenger on occasion as an extension of his will. Oberon, too, can't be everywhere and needs some help with the work of government. In the same way, human beings need poets to reassure them that the language they depend on in the ordering of their lives can reflect the world-as-it-is when the speaker or the writer, who has been schooled in the way an obsessive self-love or self-hate colors perception, is free to look with the eyes.

O, the Drama of Latch'd Eyes

Oberon is pleased with Robin's work, but Titania's humiliation was not the only task he was given:

> *This falls out better than I could devise.*
>
> *But hast thou yet latch'd the Athenian's eyes*
>
> *With the love-juice, as I did bid thee do?*

When someone latches a window, that window is closed, and this is what happens to eyes that have been latch'd by the flower juice. Since the eyes will be closed to all but the object at the receiving end of an obsession, an image of latch'd eyes is another hint the poet has left as to the nature of looking with the mind. Puck replies confidently that he took care of that job, too, but when Demetrius, the target of the flower juice, appears onstage pursuing Hermia, not Helena, Puck is forced to admit that this was not the Athenian who got the treatment.

It's somewhat of a moot point when we remember that Demetrius chased Hermia into the woods on a hopeless quest to win her against her will and when we hear from his first words that she still won't accept him as a husband:

> *O, why rebuke you him that loves you so?*
>
> *Lay breath so bitter on your bitter foe.*

Demetrius has not had the flower juice put on his eyes, and yet he is behaving exactly as Lysander did in the last scene with Helena. He is besotted with Hermia's image, and, though he clearly hears her rebukes, he might as well have not heard them at all. He persists in loving. Apparently, this state of mind can have entirely natural causes, and the flower juice is merely a catalyst or a switch that controls the timing of it.

Hermia is also flower-juice free, and yet she exhibits symptoms similar to his. Like the mechanicals who imagine that senseless things are sentient beings snatching at their sleeves and hats and like Demetrius who lives by imagining Hermia loves him when it's plain as day that she doesn't, Hermia imagines a story to explain Lysander's absence and tells Demetrius:

Now I but chide; but I should use thee worse,

For thou, I fear, hast given me cause to curse.

If thou hast slain Lysander in his sleep,

Being o'er shoes in blood, plunge in the deep,

And kill me too.

This is typical of Hermia. She naturally favors a hyperbolic mode of expression, the big dramatic gesture. She fancies herself in her own little play where she is exactly the lover she described earlier to Lysander, the one for whom the course of true love never runs smooth and the one who is ready to sacrifice herself on the cross of true love. Since we know that Lysander has already left her in pursuit of Helena, as a matter of record her story has to be a love affair with her idea of love rather than an actual man.

To avoid an explanation she might not like, she loads her speech up with more poetic certainties and with impossibly large impossibilities:

The sun was not so true unto the day

As he to me. Would he have stolen away

From sleeping Hermia? I'll believe as soon

This whole earth may be bor'd, and that the moon

May through the centre creep, and so displease

Her brother's noontide with th' Antipodes.

As Hermia bores deeper and deeper into the pit of her fantasy, she snaps out of it just enough to notice poor Demetrius abjectly devouring her with his eyes:

It cannot be but thou hast murd'red him.

So should a murderer look—so dead, so grim.

One misperception, that Lysander would have left her only in death, gives birth to another, that Demetrius murdered him.

Demetrius hardly hears what she is saying at all as he absorbs the repeated stabs of her beauty directed at last, as he had always hoped, on him alone:

So should the murdered look, and so should I,

Pierced through the heart with your stern cruelty.

Yet you, the murderer, look as bright, as clear,

As yonder Venus in her glimmering sphere.

If this is the foolishness of latch'd eyes, it's also divine poetry. He has died to live in love. Here is a fullness of heart (in this case, the fullness of complete self-absorption) perfectly expressed, which matches Hermia's dramatic offer of her breast to his sword moments before, where there's no room for anything but the beauty he has assigned her. That is, until Hermia finds nothing of Lysander in his heart:

What's this to my Lysander? Where is he?

Ah, good Demetrius, wilt thou give him me?

Lysander's name, mentioned for a second time, has some effect at last, and in addition there's the absurd suggestion that he make Hermia a gift of this hated object. So Demetrius awakens from his swoon a little:

I had rather give his carcass to my hounds.

Though he speaks of giving a carcass he doesn't have to hounds not present except in a manner of speaking, Hermia takes this as all the proof she needs to explain her abandonment:

Out, dog! out, cur! Thou driv'st me past the bounds

Of maiden patience.

But in fairness, he doesn't. Hermia has no trouble driving herself there. Demetrius is not culpable for several reasons. He hasn't particularly been paying attention to what Hermia is saying, nor does he know anything about Lysander or his whereabouts. Hermia will have to work a little harder yet to wake him up to her theme:

Hast thou slain him then?

Henceforth be never numb'red among men!

O, once tell true! tell true, even for my sake!

Durst thou have look'd upon him, being awake?

And hast thou killed him sleeping? O brave touch!

Could not a worm, an adder, do so much?

An adder did it; for with doubler tongue

Than thine (thou serpent!) never adder stung.

It's a jumbled indictment. He's accused and banished, is invited to confess as an act of love for her which she knows is his weakness, hears how he managed to kill someone much better than he, has his character assassinated for cowardice and duplicity—and all for something he knows nothing about.

Love may have put him in a stupor, but at least he has the wherewithal to protest:

You spend your passion on a mispris'd mood.

I am not guilty of Lysander's blood;

Nor is he dead, for aught that I can tell.

For all that, he loves her still. When she storms off, he lets her go. He's tired of all the wrangling and would rest:

Here therefore for a while will I remain.

So sorrow's heaviness doth heavier grow

For debt that bankrout sleep doth sorrow owe;

Which now in some slight measure it will pay,

If for his tender here I make some stay.

All four lovers will discover as the night wears on that looking with latch'd eyes is exhausting work. It's the work of desire, which carries within it the heaviness of death, a life gone bankrupt. In comedy, all characters must die to live, but the death is only a profound and refreshing sleep. Demetrius wouldn't make Lysander a gift to Hermia, but he will make himself a payment (and he is legal tender in that he is so tenderhearted) to sorrow. And so he gives himself up to the forgetfulness of sleep.

Here For a While We Make Some Stay to Save the World for Comedy

As Demetrius grows heavy with the burden brought on by latch'd eyes, I make some stay to reflect on my theme prior to the play's most strenuous actions. We turn from the lovers' trials, which make up the central content of the play, and revisit once again the structure that reveals itself anytime the fairies or Duke Theseus appear onstage. We have just seen that the present scene is introduced and framed by Robin and Oberon who view it with the objectivity of an audience. It's a structure suggesting the view from Olympus that supernatural beings enjoy, and this view has been established previously in the play. For example, Oberon witnesses an earlier scene between Demetrius and Helena, after which he commands Robin to put the flower juice on Demetrius' eyes. Oberon's intervention on Helena's behalf would rebalance the space around her by filling the vacuum in Demetrius' estimation of this very attractive woman. Earlier still, when telling the fairy about the brawls of Titania and Oberon, Robin reveals that he is at leisure to see the quarrel in the context of the whole environment while the principals are completely focused on winning a point against their opponent. Viewed in this light, it's a structure that establishes the existence of a more intelligent point of view.

Helena refers to Hermia and Lysander's plan to flee the law of Athens as intelligence, and this is how the word is tossed into the magic potion of words and sentences that the poet is brewing. Since Helena is the one who articulates the play's theme for us in a single sentence, she herself clearly possesses an admirable intelligence, but her decision to follow Demetrius into the woods—after giving him her intelligence—strikes an objective observer as anything but intelligent. She is ruled instead by an irrational passion for one who no longer loves her. In Helena, therefore, we see the distinction between looking with the eyes and looking with the mind quite muddled in practice. Unwilling to remain at home coldly and chastely correct, she throws herself into a tangled and swampy relationship.

When Demetrius lies down to recoup his losses a little in sleep, Oberon has to confront a mistake in his government of the wood. A mistake, it's fair to say, involves that which is the opposite of intelligence. A fairy king or a duke or a father or a husband would not make a mistake if he were perfectly intelligent, and so any mistake, even a little one, leaves the administrator who has made it open to the charge that he is not fit to rule himself, much less anyone else. Oberon grasps immediately the seriousness of what has happened. Puck put the flower juice on the wrong man. Even though it's Puck's mistake, the world will suffer, and his administration will be blamed:

What hast thou done? Thou hast mistaken quite

And laid the love-juice on some true-love's sight.

Of thy misprision must perforce ensue

Some true-love turn'd, and not a false turn'd true.

Just as there are those who don't believe in major gods like Zeus or Athena or minor ones like the fairies of folklore, there are those who don't believe in the flower-juice experience or the existence of true-love. Oberon's concern, then, is of little consequence to them. They think the flower juice and a true love's sight are fairy toys for children. But for those who have known the power of a love relationship, whether it's love at first sight or developed over time, the mistake is potentially life threatening. Love, they feel, connects them to the roots of life. More than the existence of heavenly beings or spirits, the poet is concerned with a rootedness "As brings about the engendering of the flower," and this rootedness is organically linked to intelligence. Because a figure like Oberon represents (by default) the view from Olympus to which even unbelievers aspire, the government of intelligence within the play would appear to have suffered a setback on account of the mistake.

If that weren't clear enough already, Puck underscores the point with surprising vehemence:

> Then fate o'errules, that, one man holding troth,
>
> A million fail, confounding oath on oath.

So much for holding truth, for intelligence of any stripe! A lover who swears to love? Forget about it; it's a million to one his oath will fail. The oath will fail because the intelligence behind it is corrupt.

This confounding of oaths is a serious matter. Human beings don't only love other human beings. They love their country and swear to defend the intelligence of its laws and yet routinely bend or break them. People swear to uphold the intelligence enshrined in highest standards of their professions but complacently cut corners once comfortably established in their jobs and fly by the seat of their pants from one situation to the next. Scientists, who by definition exist as scientists to establish the intelligence of empirical truths, discover they can't fund their programs unless those empirical truths are politically acceptable to those who make the grants.

How many privately justify their actions by agreeing with Robin that fate has overruled what they have sworn? Here, we think, is the end of intelligence, and a kind of darkness and helplessness ensues. Robin's sudden declaration expresses a mortal fear that the universe may be ruled by a malign fate that delights in human suffering, or, if autonomous human beings rule themselves, by the intelligence of a petty self-interest that has no overriding coherence.

Just as suddenly as Robin cries out in despair, Oberon resolves these speculations with a decisive command:

About the wood! Go swifter than the wind,

And Helena of Athens look thou find.

All fancy-sick she is, and pale of cheer

With sighs of love, that costs the fresh blood dear.

By some illusion see thou bring her here.

I'll charm his eyes against she do appear.

With the sudden breath of Oberon's command, all comes to life once more, and Robin's judgment, which stands like a mighty obstacle to any government of the wood, simply vanishes. The world is not a fixed thing that can be precisely determined; it is movement and energy as immaterial as the air we breathe. Oberon and Robin don't need to judge the world, nor do we; we can't. We need to act before it's too late.

In an instant Oberon's intelligence regains its authority. He identifies Helena by name, even though her name is never mentioned in the wood when he or Puck is present, so no further mistakes of the previous kind will be made. She is Helena of Athens, not just an "Athenian woman" (as Puck describes Hermia earlier) now that he knows there are two. And he is rescuing, in the person of Helena, all those who have been made sick by obsession and drained into a pale and bloodless imitation of life, the virtual world of a usurping fancy. Rather than curing his patient with the sudden shock of reality—Oberon, after all, is a convenient fiction of his author and an actor on a stage—he will make judicious use of illusion to bring her (and everyone who identifies with her) "here" and, with attentive application of the love juice in Demetrius' eyes, bring her back to life. Oberon's lively, decisive voice has a similar effect on Robin as he responds:

I go, I go! Look how I go!

Swifter than arrow from the Tartar's bow.

The darkness of Robin's previous vision vanishes in new purpose and action.

Because the fairies are so light and small, it may be hard for an audience to appreciate how serious the misstep has been. Oberon's government has long been flirting with collapse, and this could have been the last straw. Like one waking from a dream, Oberon applies the flower juice to Demetrius' eyes and speaks to its purpose:

> *Flower of this purple dye,*
>
> *Hit with Cupid's archery,*
>
> *Sink in apple of his eye!*
>
> *When his love he doth espy,*
>
> *Let her shine as gloriously*
>
> *As the Venus of the sky.*
>
> *When thou wak'st, if she be by,*
>
> *Beg of her remedy.*

He would repair the damage done to Helena by Demetrius' disregard. From what we have learned of fairyland thus far, Oberon's government consists of actions and rituals that preserve life and create new life. The love and its effects described in this prayer, now that we are familiar with the mission of his government, must be critical ingredients in relationships that survive and prosper.

His rescue of Helena brings to mind the rescue of the natural world which till now he has ignored. As he prays for love to win Helena back to life again, we are reminded that the fairies' presence in the wood is prompted by the great quarrel between him and Titania, that the natural world is flooded with death and grief because of it, and that fairyland suffers from a reign of terror. The prayer he utters here has much the same structure but a completely different intent from the one he utters over the anointment of Titania's eyes. The flower juice and the words he applies to Demetrius can just as easily, and more significantly, be applied to Oberon himself and his relationship with the great queen of fairyland, for the repair of that relationship would help to restore the beauty and deep purpose of fairyland. We don't know why Oberon suddenly knows Helena's name. Like the audience, which has had sufficient opportunities to notice Helena's quality, Oberon is somehow aware of her worthiness to be loved and therefore gives commands to that effect. Surely Demetrius' rejection of Helena reminds him at some level of his separation from Titania, and Helena's worthiness to be loved at some level reminds him of what is due to his queen.

The play's structure, the framing devices represented by the governments of Theseus and Oberon, is closely tied to the universal human aspiration for intelligence, which tends to be associated with a view from Olympus. People aspire to it because it's through intelligence that they are made aware of and maintain their autonomy. As we observe the interactions of Oberon and the lovers in the woods, however, the view from Olympus, which is the position enjoyed by the audience, is being undermined by the ordinary drama of mortal lovers as directed by smaller-than-life fairies. The lovers, we think, desperately need intelligence. Like Bottom, they would be intelligent enough at this point if they could figure a way out of the mess they are making, but at the same time, they wouldn't be lovers if they could easily leave the wood. The audience would be intelligent, but it inhabits a world where, for the duration of this night, these crazy lovers and fairies represent our only hope for intelligence. Oberon and Puck show no apparent interest in saving the lovers from the wood, that is, from being driven crazy by love. The love juice is super-charging at least two of them in the opposite direction. Oberon, too, has been looking at his kingship and his family life with eyes narrowed by self-love, and his rule has significant, costly gaps.

Even so, Oberon and Titania and the fairies appear to be benevolent spirits who are guiding the lovers, albeit in a helter-skelter fashion, to a better place. Judging from these interactions of mortals and immortals, it could be said that wisdom, the overall theme of the play, is a marriage between the intelligence supposedly available to the gods and the ignorance that's the fate of mortals. Considering that it was Helena who sees and articulates the problem, it could also be said that it's a marriage between the more contingent intelligence available to mortals and the ignorance of those who live out of time in a world of eternal truths. Even the king of fairies can fall asleep on the job. He's not perfect, but Oberon still sets the standard for the reestablishment of a comic rule. When confronted by Robin that fate has o'erruled, he awakens with newfound energy to repair the relations of men and women. Oberon's intervention on Helena's behalf and the role he plays in the war with Titania provides a context for the audience to conclude that—as in the relationship of immortals and mortals—intelligence and ignorance are as interdependent as men and women in marriage.

The structure of a work is what governs it, and so this pause to consider the structure is once again about the way human beings have created through trial and error a workable social form for the creativity and autonomy of individuals. Theseus begins the play with a judgment that overrules Hermia's autonomy, but his suppression of her autonomy so exacerbates it that she runs away with her lover. It's the perennial problem parents and autocratic governments face. The fairies, on the other hand, seem more interested in fanning the flames of an individual's passion. Fairyland, it would appear, operates at a fever pitch, and so far the love juice is the weapon of choice for managing imbalances.

The opening acts of the play establish that human autonomy is a given whether a person lives in a strictly governed state or in the wood. In Athens our representative citizen Hermia defies the will of her father, and in the wood Lysander contrives under the cover of darkness to sleep with Hermia. If autonomy always will out, then government in the end can only be self-government. But how do we arrive at self-government? Like a seed in the earth, the play has planted the question, and over time it generates an answer. Self-government is the gold that emerges from all the experiments in government tried out in the play. We have a bonfire of the vanities where people are forced—by the power vested in a traditional father figure (who takes the form in other instances of a speaker with charismatic powers, an authoritarian government armed with guns, or a politically orchestrated mass hysteria)—to give up their autonomy to the state. We also have a night in the wood where individuals give their autonomy free play only to discover at great cost to themselves its intrinsic limits. There's danger on either extreme: a totalitarian state like the ones that came into being over the last century on one side and a formless anarchy on the other where Everyman's autonomy leads to a loss of freedom in mindless aggression and fearful panic. The players, all of them, are acting out the poet's answer. We arrive at self-government through the comic process that the play embodies.

This entr'acte with Oberon and Robin comes to a close when Robin returns after successfully completing his latest task:

> *Captain of our fairy band*
>
> *Helena is here at hand,*
>
> *And the youth, mistook by me,*
>
> *Pleading for a lover's fee.*
>
> *Shall we their fond pageant see?*
>
> *Lord, what fools these mortals be.*

Oberon decides that he will watch the wooing of Helena by Lysander:

> *Stand aside. The noise they make*
>
> *Will cause Demetrius to awake.*

Oberon is engaged now, but at the same time he will stand aside and not interfere more directly. Although the structure directs to some extent the natural passions of the lovers, the lovers themselves must own those passions for the cure to work. Oberon's prediction that Lysander and Helena's wrangling will cause Demetrius to "awake" is as ironic as Helena commanding Lysander to awake earlier, for, just as Lysander does, Demetrius will awaken into a new obsession brought on by the flower juice. The audience may find this amusing, but the meaning of the sentence as a whole is more significant. If we take the meaning more generally, the noise that naturally follows in the wake of obsession is what finally wakes a person out of a sleep of inattention. This proves to be true for all the lovers. In two short lines Oberon recognizes the lovers' need to sort things out for themselves and then sums up the pattern of comedy.

The fairy king is more awake to his responsibilities, but Robin stays to watch for another reason:

> *Then will two at once woo one.*
>
> *That must needs be sport alone;*
>
> *And those things do best please me*
>
> *That befall prepost'rously.*

Up to this point, Robin has been a more reliable witness, but now that Oberon has resumed carrying out the duties of his office, Robin can better enjoy the scene purely for its entertainment value. Shakespeare has created a structure that observes his lovers through the double vision of an Oberon and a Robin: to fulfill the dual mandate, his play would act responsibly on behalf of a comic vision, and it would make us laugh at human folly.

So Much For Autonomy

The resolving of an individual's autonomy within the social order has long been more than just the subject of an entertainment; the institution of marriage puts that theme at the heart of the social order. For as long as it has existed as an institution, marriage has served as an efficient means by which men and women find a balance through give and take, practical accommodations, commitment, timely actions (as in Oberon's rescue of Helena which is a first step in rescuing his relationship with Titania), and patience. Theseus, a powerful representative of male autonomy, and Hippolyta, a powerful representative of female autonomy, address the adjustments their marriage will require in their opening speeches. Theseus cannot expect to get what he wants by petulantly wishing it; Hippolyta is still too much a warrior queen for that. Nor is Theseus likely to cease being the warrior who won her with his sword. Nevertheless, they will marry mutually and publicly "with pomp, with triumph, and with reveling."

The balance these two have established after their long war is then contrasted with the imbalances between autonomous individuals that we subsequently witness—in the suit Egeus brings against his wayward daughter, in the way Bottom tries to upstage everyone else in the company, in the great quarrel between Oberon and Titania, in the changes of heart that rock the lives of the lovers in the woods, and in the sudden fragmenting of Peter Quince's company. Since Shakespeare includes the king and queen of fairyland and practical workmen of Athens in his survey, it can't be said that the imbalance is purely a result of youth and inexperience. As Chaucer did before him, Shakespeare locates the problem more specifically. The imbalances result from the volatile loves and hates of the characters involved, and this volatility is a symptom of an obsessive attachment to an image or idea. Chaucer wrote his tales to illustrate that the way to Canterbury opens up when his characters wake from an obsessive dream, and Shakespeare borrowed Chaucer's central theme for his treatment of the narrative. His play, as the title reminds us, is about this dream.

The theme of awakening can play itself out in great affairs of state as well as in more intimate affairs of the heart. Chaucer lived amid religious controversy. His initial patron, John of Gaunt, supported John Wycliffe's reforms of the church. Wycliffe opposed papal authority and translated the Bible so English men and women could read it in their own language. His ideas and the movement he led marked the beginning of a division in English Christendom that was initiated by earnest thinkers and that grew to bloody dynastic and political wars lasting for centuries. Shakespeare lived in the wake of that time when thousands in England and across Europe came to value the freedom of their own conscience in religious matters over the authority of the church. True believers on each side of the quarrel hardened their positions and fought to the death for their idea. Mary I, the Queen they called Bloody Mary because of her persecution of Protestants, died only eleven years before Shakespeare's birth.

In his own lifetime the poet lived through the threat of invasion by the great armada of the Spanish counterrevolution. He knew firsthand from friends and family who had to hide their Catholic faith from the state that religious disputes entailed a terrible cost for the children of those who quarreled so violently. As he reflected on these experiences, Shakespeare may have acquired a personal, literary, and an historical sense that the narrowness of an obsessive attachment robs an individual of autonomy. Blind Cupid's bolts afflict those he wounds with a like blindness. For example, Egeus' obsessive concern about his paternal authority overrides a father's natural impulse to protect the life of a child; Oberon and Titania's quarrel over the Indian boy overrides their care of the natural world and makes the little ones quake for fear; similarly, Lysander and Demetrius lose sight of everything around them in the heat of their quarrel over Hermia, and the larger world of neighbors and town and nation is transformed into an opaque wilderness, the wood around Athens, until the quarrel can be settled.

The relationship of obsessive thought and release from obsessive thought—that is, of *cupiditas* and *caritas*—is the frame the playwright has raised for viewing the lovers' passion play in the woods. His play may be an "unworthy scaffold to bring forth so great an object," attempting as it does to explain so much in the lives of individuals and nations, but, he begs the audience's pardon, he will attempt it. When people leave the theater and return to inhabit their own homes and negotiate relationships with parents, spouses, children, and those in authority, the three marriages that conclude Shakespeare's play will give those who witnessed them the hopeful prospect that radical differences between adversaries can be constructively resolved, but these outward shows are made possible only when the two forms of love and of looking at the world are made one flesh. Shakespeare was a master at embodying this in literature, and Chaucer was his master.

The scene about to engulf the four lovers begins with Lysander, the man who sought autonomy from Hermia's father by escaping through the wood to his dowager aunt's estate. When he wants to sleep by Hermia's side in the woods, he "reasons very prettily" to get what he wants. But now, having had his passion redirected by the flower juice, he reasons just as prettily with Helena:

> *Why should you think that I should woo in scorn?*
>
> *Scorn and derision never came in tears.*
>
> *Look, when I vow, I weep; and vows so born,*
>
> *In their nativity all truth appears.*
>
> *How can these things in me seem scorn to you,*
>
> *Bearing the badge of faith to prove them true?*

As he says this, I imagine him groveling on his knees in front of her. So much for autonomy and reason's role in it. Once again, he reasons very prettily, but all this reasoning is employed to express an abject servitude. Lysander's predicament illustrates the Achilles' heel of his independence in thought and action. Autonomy may bring Lysander into a personal relationship with his Creator; it may serve his interests in politics and in business; it's a critical ingredient in empirical investigations where separate lines of inquiry converge on a consensus; but Lysander here throws it on the ash heap of history in his role as a lover.

As it was in the last scene with Robin and Oberon, the light of intelligence is extinguished by total dependence on dark, inscrutable powers. Fate in the form of a woman overrules. There may be light in obsession, but it's unreliable. It's like a spotlight in a theater, which draws our attention away from everything else. It's like lightning in the collied night, which both lights up the land and obscures it with fear. This is the theme that the successive incidents of the scene develop, revealing one by one how each lover suffers from the condition. The lovers' capers act out a comedy for the audience, but the poet hints that the severe cropping of intelligence can have serious and even mortal consequences for real people. Like the plague, the madness of the potion is catching. After the love juice is applied to his eyes, Lysander abandons Hermia. When Lysander leaves her alone on the ground, Hermia dreams a serpent at her breast ate her heart away. These juxtapositions suggest that, whether spawned naturally by the body and mind or induced externally and placed on the eye, the flower juice keeps company with the power of a poisonous snake. Even worse, it's an invisible and insidious influence.

Helena, wise Helena, is the next exhibit in these trials of an autonomy that's supposedly based in reason. Because she is the brightest, she is the most resistant. We see this in the way she holds her own against Lysander's powers of reasoning:

You do advance your cunning more and more.

When truth kills truth, O devilish-holy fray!

Those vows are Hermia's. Will you give her o'er?

Weigh oath with oath, and you will nothing weigh.

Your vows to her and me, put in two scales,

Will even weigh; and both as light as tales.

As she has before, Helena speaks with grace and insight. Her own powers of reason are still intact, but they have a weak foundation. Helena's mind now rests on the (irrational) conclusion that she is "as ugly as a bear." It's not a boyfriend, but it's the idol she presently worships and to which she submits. It also has the advantage of keeping her chaste and single, which she may secretly prize as an advantage. This security was perhaps a little troubled by the tremors of Lysander's declarations, but his vows are far from the "shivering shocks" (as Bottom described them) needed to break up her fixed idea. After all, it is Lysander saying them, and she has not been impressed with Lysander's judgment. Intuiting this, he takes up the issue:

I had no judgment when to her I swore.

But Helena easily parries this thrust:

Nor none, in my mind, now you give her o'er.

In case Lysander needs reminding, the battle is indeed being fought in Helena's mind, and Lysander has lost the war for her affection in Helena's autonomy and perfect subjectivity. She may feel secure in that autonomy, for she is obviously a mind to be reckoned with, but Lysander now introduces her own Achilles' heel:

Demetrius loves her; and he loves not you.

It's a palpable hit, but Lysander wouldn't have touched that subject if he knew her better. Helena worships the idea that she cannot be loved, and his reminder reinforces her fixed idea. Also, he doesn't realize and probably could not admit that she has never been attracted to him.

Once Lysander has shot poor Helena through the heart with Demetrius' name, Demetrius himself can join the conversation. The noise of their arguing, as Oberon predicted, awakens him and activates the love juice resting on his eyes. As if conjured out of the ground by the mention of his name, he rises to tell her:

O Helen, goddess, nymph, perfect, divine!

To what, my love, shall I compare thine eyne?

Crystal is muddy. O, how ripe in show

Thy lips, those kissing cherries, tempting grow!

That pure congealed white, high Taurus' snow,

Fann'd with the eastern wind, turns to a crow

When thou hold'st up thy hand. O, let me kiss

This princess of pure white, this seal of bliss!

Like Lysander's tearful pleas, Demetrius' fulsome metaphors are the fumes of a mindless intoxication. So much for Demetrius' powers of reason and his autonomy.

But the real interest of these words lies in their effect on Helena. Surely when she hears them, the foundation of her fixed idea will suffer the eruption of a fury and a great shaking. Helena has stopped believing that she might hear words like this from any man, and coming from Lysander they might be tempting to believe but no great labor to shrug them off. To hear them from Demetrius must give her pause, and so I imagine her in a slight but very pregnant pause before she decisively returns to her default position:

O spite! O hell! I see you all are bent

To set against me for your merriment.

I you were civil and knew courtesy,

You would not do me thus much injury.

Can you not hate me, as I know you do,

But you must join in souls to mock me too?

Once Demetrius left her in the woods to be the prey of wild beasts, Helena decides against "falling" in love. Instead, she will maintain her uprightness and dignity. She will assume that she is unattractive and not presume anything else. This is only reasonable and gives her a safe, secure place in the universe. Demetrius' words nonetheless strike at the heart of the place she has been cultivating for herself from the start, the perfect autonomy of one who is universally disdained. Initially, the world's disdain helps to explain how happy some o'er other some can be, for nothing about her materially or intellectually does. Later, she loses even the hope of her attractiveness when Demetrius' pointed rejection forces her to conclude that she has been made as ugly as a bear. To maintain that identity and place of security, she must convince herself that the two men's declarations of love are merely further proof of what she *knows* to be true: rather than love, she knows they mock her. She doesn't give in to despair but takes their insults with her head held high.

This may seem like looking at the world with autonomy and intelligence, but the audience has been shown that she is looking with the mind. We know both men truly love her. The situation may be absurd, but her powers of reason and perception, which are such critical features of her maiden pride, can't see that the men speak true. Helena may be brilliant, but she ends up in the same mind-forged, flower-juiced straightjacket that binds Lysander and Demetrius: she is hopelessly attached to her idea. Even as she resists what Demetrius is saying with all the resources of her autonomy, she is far from being out of the woods. Her whole scheme of passing on the intelligence about Hermia's flight and of following Demetrius into the woods is crazy from the start, and it's only getting crazier. She hasn't hit bottom. That can only happen when Hermia completes the charmed circle and undoes her.

Just as the noise of Helena and Lysander arguing awakens Demetrius, the noise of the two men arguing over Helena opens up a path for Hermia to Lysander:

Thou art not by mine eye, Lysander, found;

Mine ear, I thank it, brought me to thy sound.

But why unkindly didst thou leave me so?

The travails of Lysander and Demetrius are much more literal and uninteresting when compared to those of Hermia and Helena. The ladies, unlike the men, do not change their affections, and this constancy gives them more substance. They are made of firmer stuff and are more apt to suffer than the men. First the men argued over Hermia, and now they argue over Helena. The constant for them is the arguing, not the woman. Their wake-up calls mark only a seamless transition from one obsession to another. Since she woke up to find Lysander gone, Hermia is becoming something more than a mouthpiece for idle fancies and literary love stories. As when she finds herself alone in the wood, the last line she speaks here has a real feeling behind it. The ladies' wake-up calls are personal, and because they are flesh and blood and not merely a shadow or a spirit, they know the suffering of flesh and blood.

Lysander suavely answers Hermia with his own cryptic question:

Why should he stay whom love doth press to go?

It's the cruelest kind of inside joke. He knows what love presses him to go, but she doesn't. Lysander's enigmatic words invite Hermia to further inquiry:

What love could press Lysander from my side?

By delicious degrees Lysander reveals a little more:

Lysander's love, that would not let him bide—

Yet another step into the mystery of Lysander. So Hermia's uncertainty grows, which begins when she wakes up alone with a serpent at her breast. More mercifully at last, though, Lysander strikes at her with an explanation that both misses and hits Hermia with a bull's eye as he looks at Helena and says:

Fair Helena; who more engilds the night

Than all you fiery oes and eyes of light.

Whereupon he looks at Hermia to ask and declare:

Why seekest thou me; Could not this make thee know,

The hate I bare thee make me leave thee so?

This is plainer speaking. His words violently thrust at what she enjoyed with Lysander only a few hours earlier, the perfect autonomy of one who is universally loved. Like Helena before her, who enjoys the autonomy of one who is universally disdained, Hermia would maintain the security of her former place:

You speak not as you think. It cannot be.

Before Lysander can clarify the situation further, Helena erupts with her own agenda. In her mind it's clear now that Hermia is in league with the men's mockery, and may have organized all of it since the men are so easily led by her. She can understand being hurt by the men; it's to be expected. It's quite another thing to be betrayed by a friend. Almost to herself she exclaims:

Lo, she is one of this confederacy!

Now I perceive they have conjoined all three

To fashion this false sport in spite of me.

And then she takes Hermia somewhat apart from the men to lay out her case that Hermia has abused the sisterhood. Always insightful and persuasive, Helena finds new heights of eloquence as she describes the full horror of Hermia's behavior:

Injurious Hermia! most ungrateful maid!

Have you conspir'd, have you with these contriv'd

To bait me with their foul derision?

Is all the counsel that we two have shar'd,

The sister's vows, the hours that we have spent

When we have chid the hasty-footed time

For parting us—O, is all forgot?

All schooldays friendship, childhood innocence?

We, Hermia, like two artificial gods,

Have with our needles created both one flower,

Both on one sampler, sitting on one cushion,

Both warbling of one song, both in one key;

As if our hands, our sides, voices, and minds

Had been incorporate. So we grew together,

Like to a double cherry, seeming parted,

But yet an union in partition—

Two lovely berries moulded on one stem;

So with two seeming bodies, but one heart;

Two of the first, like coats in heraldry,

Due but to one, and crowned with one crest.

What a picture she builds up here, remembered detail after detail and poetic image after poetic image describing, not a confederacy, but a federal union, e pluribus unum. But all this is only a prologue to her passionate conclusion:

And will you rent our ancient love asunder,

To join with men in scorning you poor friend?

Our sex, as well as I, may chide you for it,

Though I alone do feel the injury.

Helena clearly cultivates a refined behavior. She may be fighting mad at Hermia, but she contains her rage in a masterpiece of rhetoric that combines a reasoned and heartfelt appeal to fellow feeling along with a civilized but brutal indictment of a Judas.

Up to this point, Helena has maintained the ladylike pose that is the final refuge of her autonomy. No matter what the men do or even what the fellow traveler Hermia may pretend in the way of friendship, Helena still has her dignity, her maiden pride, and her independence from those who have sunk so low. The pose might have succeeded if Hermia hadn't quite honestly replied:

> *I am amazed at your passionate words.*
>
> *I scorn you not. It seems that you scorn me.*

Hermia speaks true, but Helena now looks with the mind and judges everything in accordance with her idea that the whole thing is a plot. Since Hermia insists on playing dumb, which in Helena's opinion would not be hard for Hermia to do, Helena will have to lay it all out for her:

> *Have you not set Lysander, as in scorn,*
>
> *To follow me and praise my eyes and face?*
>
> *And made your other love, Demetrius*
>
> *(Who even but now did spurn me with his foot),*
>
> *To call me goddess, nymph, divine, and rare,*
>
> *Precious, celestial? Wherefore speaks he this*
>
> *To her he hates? And wherefore doth Lysander*
>
> *Deny your love (so rich within his soul)*
>
> *And tender me (forsooth) affection,*
>
> *But by your setting on, by your consent?*

What though I be not so in grace as you,

So hung upon with love, so fortunate;

But miserable most, to love unlov'd?

This you should pity rather than despise.

We can only guess the secret pleasure Helena takes in describing piquant details of the men's courtship. This turnabout, even if she believes that they sport in spite of her, unleashes a freedom to express what a lady might want to keep from view—her burning scorn for those made happy by fortune and not by any special merit. Oh, the pleasure it gives to ask Hermia why Lysander would "deny your love / And tender me (forsooth) affection." That "forsooth" announces victory as clearly as any trumpet call. As if the men meant what they were saying, she would give Hermia a little taste of the crow she and her boyfriends had been feeding her these many months. Helena's manners are starting to crack, and this, even more than Demetrius' rejection, represents a lowering of herself in the world. As a victim full of self-pity, she is becoming petty, vindictive, shrewish, common. So much for Helena's autonomy.

Finally, it's little Hermia's turn to lose what she values most. When Helena announces that she will leave them at their sport, an argument between the two men breaks out. They would have Helena stay, and they struggle with each other to be the one that makes her stay. Lysander then challenges Demetrius to withdraw and fight a duel in order to decide the issue, and Hermia latches on to Lysander's leg. Where Helena behaves like the old gossips with whom Robin amuses himself, Hermia acts out a dumb show of her attachment. She cherishes the idea that she draws Lysander like a magnet to her, and now she is reduced to representing that attraction by holding on to him for dear life with her hands. It's hard to say which woman suffers more for her idea. The dissolving of Helena's idea—that she is a lady—is more subtle. She can't help behaving like a fishmonger. The dissolving of Hermia's idea—that she has a power over men—is acted out literally as the release of Lysander's leg, but it takes many brutal shots from Lysander to get the job done. Here's a sampling of what he says to her:

Away, you Ethiope!

Hang off, thou cat, thou burr! Vile thing, let loose,

Or I will shake thee from me like a serpent!

Out, tawny Tartar, out!

Out, loathed med'cine! O hated potion, hence!

These artillery rounds soften up Hermia's position to a point where she finally asks Lysander point-blank whether he left her that night in earnest, and he is ready with the coup de grace that puts her out of her misery:

Aye, by my life!

And never did desire to see thee more.

Therefore, be out of hope, of question, doubt;

Be certain! Nothing truer. 'Tis no jest

That I do hate thee, and love Helena.

If Hermia can't fall any further, it won't be for lack of trying on Lysander's part. So much for the power of Hermia's autonomy.

Hermia, though, isn't done, but instead of lashing out at Lysander, she turns on Helena:

O me! you juggler! you canker blossom!

You thief of love! What, have you come by night

And stol'n my love's heart from him?

A most excellent and comic catfight ensues with Hermia trying to scratch Helena's eyes out, and Helena hiding behind the men while brazenly provoking the apple of their eye, Little Miss Hermia, with comments like these:

What, will you tear

Impatient answers from my gentle tongue?

Fie, fie! you counterfeit, you puppet you!

I pray you, though you mock me, gentlemen,

Let her not hurt me. I was never curst;

I have no gift at all in shrewishness;

I am a right maid for my cowardice.

Let her not strike me. You perhaps may think,

Because she is something lower than myself,

That I can match her.

O, when she is angry, she is keen and shrewd!

She was a vixen when she went to school;

And though she be but little, she is fierce.

Her gentle tongue? Never curst? No gift in shrewishness? A right maid?

Not fierce like Hermia? It's only natural for people to desire the life that the gods enjoy on top of Olympus: Hermia, who has been on top of the world like this for some time, suddenly finds herself thrown into the cockpit to scratch out her existence. Helena's superior height gives her a tactical advantage. She has been less fortunate in love, but in her own estimation she has enjoyed a great sense of superiority over little Hermia despite Hermia's success with men. That was Helena's privilege and her comfort. For a woman of her quality, success with men is no great distinction, and yet here she is thrown into the cockpit to scratch out her existence with little Hermia. When threatened, Hermia leaps for the eyes of her rival, but Helena doesn't trust Hermia or herself in a fight and so runs away with her long legs.

These are not responses to life that they reasoned out. So much for a reasoned autonomy when you find yourself in the cockpit fighting for your life.

The Great Sleep and the First Light of Comedy

Even when it takes the form of invective, this writer treats us to poetry of the highest order. After the lunges and the barbed remarks of the ladies, the conflict shifts to the men as they prepare to fight each other. Before they do, Oberon comments to Robin on the disorder he has just witnessed, accounting for it with the easiest kind of excuse—he blames someone else:

> *This is thy negligence. Still thou mistak'st,*
>
> *Or else committ'st thy knaveries wilfully.*

Since Oberon knows Robin's character, his indictment could easily be true. Robin, who is quick about everything, quickly pleads his innocence:

> *Believe me, king of shadows, I mistook.*

> *Did not you tell me I should know the man*
>
> *By the Athenian garments he had on?*
>
> *And so far blameless proves my enterprise*
>
> *That I have 'nointed an Athenian's eyes;*
>
> *And so far am I glad it so did sort*
>
> *As this their jangling I esteem a sport.*

This frank exchange of views does more than sort out the source of the confusion; it presents two faces of comedy. One belongs to the Puckish Robin who loves nothing better than the confusion that ensues when pretensions take a fall, and the other belongs to Oberon who must give the fall and confusion a safe place to bottom out.

In keeping with his new resolve to be more involved in the government of the wood, Oberon ceases to blame and gives commands that limit the disorder:

> *Thou seest these lovers seek a place to fight.*
>
> *Hie therefore, Robin, overcast the night.*
>
> *The starry welkin cover thou anon*
>
> *With drooping fog as black as Acheron,*
>
> *And lead these testy rivals so astray*
>
> *As one come not within another's way.*
>
> *Like to Lysander sometime frame thy tongue,*
>
> *Then stir Demetrius up with bitter wrong;*
>
> *And sometime rail thou like Demetrius.*

And from each other look thou lead them thus

Till o'er their brows death-counterfeiting sleep

With leaden legs and batty wings doth creep.

Then crush this herb into Lysander's eye;

Whose liquor hath this virtuous property,

To take from thence all error with his might

And make his eyeballs roll with wonted sight.

When they next wake, all this derision

Shall seem a dream and fruitless vision;

And back to Athens shall the lovers wend

With league whose date till death shall never end.

Earlier, Robin entertained his master with a factual report about Titania's eyes being latch'd with the love juice, a scene the audience had just witnessed. Here, Oberon gives an account of what we are about to witness. Together, the speeches demonstrate that poetry can accurately recreate the past and imagine a future. These enterprises in true speech are making the author's case that poetry, when grounded in a vision of things-as-they-are, can be counted on to supply a floor under the falls and confusion that occupy the mind of Everyman every day.

Robin and Oberon are the two faces of comedy, and in this speech Oberon narrates the two essential phases of comedy. In the first phase, a fierce pride and a sense of bitter wrong will send Demetrius and Lysander chasing round and round in the pointless circling of a fever dream for something always out of reach. Completely disoriented and worn out by flitting impressions of this and that, the bats in a belfry, they will fall at last into a second phase, the great sleep of comedy. This is no ordinary sleep.

It's a release from obsession so that the eyeballs will then roll "with wonted sight."

In addition, Oberon imagines the end of the feverish quarrel with Titania that has rocked the foundations of fairyland and the natural world:

> Whiles I in this affair do thee employ
>
> I'll to my queen and beg her Indian boy;
>
> And then I will her charmed eye release
>
> From monster's view, and all things shall be peace.

Oberon has a vision, as in a view from Olympus, that all will soon be peace between them. He will "beg" the Indian boy of her, which implies his poverty and recognizes her pride of place, even if we know that her sense, the basis for that pride, has been wildly altered by the love juice. Then he will release her eye from the previous treatment, which charmed her into loving a monster. Given what Oberon has done, Titania has loved more than one monster. It's true that Robin's magic has put an ass's ears on Bottom's head, but Oberon's vengeance has put horns on his own. The great sleep of comedy is like the herb he now holds in his hand (which he quite mysteriously introduces, like a magician pulling a rabbit out of a hat), for it has the marvelous property "to take from hence all error." It's the antidote for the afflictions of the other herb. And when Titania's sight is released from monster's view, Oberon's monstrous revenge will also turn to peace.

Robin points out, though, that Oberon doesn't have much time to complete the work:

> My fairy lord, this must be done with haste,
>
> For night's swift dragons cut the clouds full fast,
>
> And yonder shines Aurora's harbinger;

At whose approach ghosts, wand'ring here and there,

Troop home to churchyards; damned spirits all,

That in crossways and floods have burial,

Already to their wormy beds are gone.

For fear lest day should look their shames upon,

They wilfully themselves exile from light,

And must for aye consort with black-brow'd night.

Like these ghosts and spirits, Oberon and Robin are active at night. It's a time for fantasy and dreams that act out the desires and fears of mortals. In a comedy these desires and fears have to play themselves out before a character can find a bottom in the dreamless sleep of comedy. They are the things people won't or can't look at consciously since they are selfish and shameful. Ego, the wolf of self-love, cleverly puts on the sheepskin of virtue, compassion, and public service to disguise its true intent. Just as Robin serves his master with great speed, ego can be just as quick about its business of preserving an image of selflessness. A comic spirit like Robin, however, knows ego's sleight of hand very well and willfully unleashes in his little pranks that which ego would ignore.

Where Robin specializes in exposing and puncturing mortals' pretensions, Oberon now supplies the healing balm of sleep and celebrates the new day that will come in yet one more burst of magnificent poetry. It is true that he and Robin are largely nocturnal:

But we are spirits of another sort.

I with the Morning's love have oft made sport;

And, like a forester, the groves may tread

Even till the eastern gate, all fiery red,

Opening on Neptune, with fair blessed beams

Turns into yellow gold his salt green streams.

Make no doubt about it, Oberon is a lover, a creature of night, and so he knows the passion and the darkness of a lover. In this, he's like an ordinary man, but he has also been granted the freedom of a king who, after lovemaking, treads the wood at dawn refreshed and awake. In this capacity, he's a poet who can imagine the sun penetrating the green wood as if its beams were transmuting salt green streams of ocean into yellow gold. Having seen this, who would not walk resolutely in the direction of a life-giving power that turns the bitter and turbulent salt of experience into a timeless and priceless gift.

Oberon's vision here reminds me of Homer's passage from *The Odyssey* with which I began my book:

> *When dawn came, fresh and rosy-fingered, Nestor the Gerenian charioteer got up from his bed, went out, and seated himself on a smooth white bench which stood, gleaming and polished, in front of his lofty doors. Here his father Neleus used to sit and give counsel as wise as the god's; but he had long since died and gone to Hades' Halls. So now Nestor of Gerenia sat there in his turn, sceptre in hand, a Warden of the Achaean race.*

Everything in *The Odyssey* is surrounded and sometimes immersed in the salt green streams of Neptune, but set in the liquid, green expanse of this wasteland there's a great treasure—the smooth white bench of true judgment. These images, in turn, recall the line from *Richard II* where John of Gaunt on his deathbed describes England as "this precious stone set in a silver sea."[51]

The watery, formless realm of Neptune is like the crazy wood in which these Athenians have been immersed on a midsummer's eve. Just as it did for Odysseus, the lovers' experience of frustrated desire and confusion poses the question as to how human beings can live in such a world. Nestor's place on that smooth white bench represents the judgment that derives from the trials and errors of experience, for these trials and errors have given the buildings, the furniture, and the placement of things in time and space a concrete shape and function that endures over many generations. The speeches of Robin and Oberon recall as well the insight Chaucer embeds in "The Knight's Tale" that the salt green streams of bitter experience and the yellow gold of insight are two sides of the same coin. You can't have one without the other. Because he and others who came before him found a way to represent it, they help us to see that the two together add up to the wisdom we strive to comprehend and write about in our own day. Throughout Western literature—from the time of Homer, Chaucer, and the modern era so richly documented by Shakespeare—there's a great constancy about the coin of wisdom's realm and the art by which human beings survive to live another day.

The Fairyland Address over the Fallen

Oberon has described for us the pattern by which people arrive at a seat of true judgment, and the audience then sees it enacted before their eyes. Robin leads Lysander on by pretending to be Demetrius and leads Demetrius on by pretending to be Lysander. After hours of pointlessly threatening the empty air, they have gone as far as their desire can take them. First, Lysander appears on stage to complain that the object of his desire (to kill) is always out of reach:

He goes before me and still dares me on;

When I come where he calls, then he is gone.

The villain is much lighter-heel'd than I.

I followed fast, but faster he did fly

That fallen am I in dark uneven way,

And here will rest me. (Lie down.) Come thou gentle day!

For if but once thou show me thy grey light,

I'll find Demetrius and revenge this spite.

As in the compactness of poetry, fairyland has packed into one night the object lesson, which can take a lifetime to learn, about the longing for some thing. There's an unbridgeable gap between Lysander and what he desires. We see this relationship played out as he follows the spirit voice of Robin throughout the wood. This does not mean that a man like Lysander could never run his sword through another man like Demetrius or that a man like Lysander could never meet and desire and finally marry a woman like Hermia or Helena. It means desire is essentially something else; it exists in a different realm the way we believe the fairies exist in a different realm. For all its apparent power, desire has the consistency of a dream. Dreams are real up to the point when we wake up from them. Comedy doesn't condemn or applaud these dreams. They exist, and a person has to deal with them the way he has to deal with hunger and a need for sleep. For a nation or a person or a marriage to thrive, poor mortals, who are chasing spirits day and night, must find a respite at some point. Most of us sleep much of the night for these reasons, but the great dreamless sleep Lysander now enjoys finds him a respite at the bottom of things.

Next, Robin brings Demetrius out of the shadows and onstage by mimicking Lysander's voice. He accuses Demetrius with cowardice and taunts him with, "Come hither. I am here," which he is, but only in a manner of speaking. Demetrius, though, is starting to get the message about these mysterious tweaks of desire:

Nay then, thou mock'st me. Thou shalt buy this dear

If ever I thy face by daylight see.

Now go thy way. Faintness constraineth me

To measure out my length on this cold bed.

By day's approach look to be visited.

In the natural world all things have an end. Much as he would like to kill Lysander, Demetrius can do no more and therefore lets Lysander go. Of course, Robin makes sure he will never have Lysander in the first place; instead, Lysander and the desire to kill him are steeped away in darkness and sleep.

The men desire to fight each other, and Helena desires to escape the wrath of Hermia. Running for her life is also better than the craziness of what she has just been through—the violent shows of love from both men, the violent show of Hermia's fingernails, and, more degrading than these, the coarseness and commonness of her own behavior:

O weary night, O long and tedious night,

Abate thy hours! Shine comfort from the East,

That I may back to Athens by daylight

From these that my poor company detest;

And sleep, that sometimes shuts up sorrow's eye,

Steal me awhile from my own company.

She runs in the end to steal herself from herself. She would preserve the maiden pride that her childhood in Athens has nurtured, and to Athens she would return. She would put daylight between herself and those that detest her company, but now she wonders what kind of company she makes. Her maiden pride made her out to be a dignified lady, but she has been behaving like a fishmonger in the marketplace. She prays that sleep will steal her away from the fishmonger she has recently become and relieve her from the sorrow of that revelation. Even as she dreams of Athens and the clarity of her maiden pride, she is given up to utter exhaustion and fancies only an abatement of her self.

The men desire to fight, Helena desires to forget a sudden breakout of shrewishness, and Hermia desires once more to find Lysander in the wood:

> Never so weary, never so in woe;
>
> Bedabbled with the dew, and torn with briers;
>
> I can no further crawl, no further go;
>
> My legs can keep no pace with my desires.
>
> Here will I rest me till the break of day.
>
> Heavens shield Lysander, if they mean a fray.

Before she sleeps, Hermia sums up, as the others have done, why desire must eventually end: the body and mind simply wear out trying to keep up with it. For all that, though, there's a charming constancy in Hermia that may redeem her in the eyes of the audience from Helena's "low" opinion of her. Her final thought is for Lysander's safety.

If Hermia shows signs of love in the midst of her distress, Robin now shows signs of Oberon's concern for the mending of their perturbed spirits as he blesses the four fallen lovers where they lie:

> On the ground
>
> Sleep sound.
>
> I'll apply
>
> To your eye,
>
> Gentle lover, remedy.
>
> [Squeezes the herb on Lysander's eyelids.]
>
> When thou wak'st

Thou tak'st

True delight

In the sight

Of thy former lady's eye;

And the country proverb known,

That everyman should take his own

In your waking shall be shown:

Jack shall have Jill;

Naught shall go ill;

The man shall have his mare again, and all shall be well.

Various intervals throughout the play allow little glimpses of comedy's final resting place. More than a vision, the grove where the lovers now sleep has the solidity and the gravitas of a ground consecrated to those who have fallen in love's wars. In solemn commemoration Robin blesses the fallen with a country proverb he conned from the rites of fairyland. The ground is sacred, too, in that it is medicinal like a wondrous herb or a relic, the cure of comedy. It's the ground where, even if for just a moment, the mind empties out in a profound rest. It's where the lovers have gotten to the bottom of desire and can go no further, where sleep is sound because untroubled by ghosts.

At the dawn of a new age when autonomous human beings will be driven to explore the far reaches of the globe, probe the heavens, dissect the body, and split matter itself into ever smaller and smaller constituent parts, this poet ends Act III with an older sense that desire can take a person only so far and that there is no real autonomy in desire. This is especially a problem for those who, since they live in a culture that worships autonomy, desire to be free.

CHAPTER TEN:
DANCING IN TIME TO ROCK THE GROUND WHEREON THESE SLEEPERS LIE

Lancret's *La Camargo Dancing*

Lapdogs and Their Large Fair Ears

At the beginning of Act IV there's an important stage direction that the lovers remain asleep where they lay at the end of Act III. Titania then enters nearby with all her train including Bottom, and Oberon follows "behind" and out of Titania's view. We last saw Bottom being led away to where love could be consummated. We have already noticed how quickly Bottom adjusts to his new state so let us count the ways in this scene that Bottom is at home in an ass's noodle. Naturally, we begin with Titania taking him in, body and soul:

> *Come, sit thee down upon this flow'ry bed,*
>
> *While I thy amiable cheeks do coy,*
>
> *And stick musk-roses in thy sleek, smooth head,*
>
> *And kiss thy fair large ears, my gentle joy.*

Titania treats him with all the loving care a great-hearted lady would bestow on an innocent lapdog. The furry head and ears of a little dog are nice to pet, and Bottom's head and ears give her that much more pleasure being so much larger and longer.

In addition, the delightful fairies are at his beck and call. For example, he sends Cobweb to bring him the honey-bag of a bumblebee. When Titania asks if he is hungry, Bottom orders up a meal of dry oats and a bottle of hay. Titania, mistress of her table, suggests the new nuts of a squirrel's hoard as a side dish, but Bottom declines them in favor of "a handful or two of dried peas." It's too delicious a picture of perfect domestic felicity, all the good things of the earth offered to him by busy and attractive servants. There is one little cloud on Bottom's horizon, though; in his first command he makes use of his new powers to have Peaseblossom "scratch my head." It has penetrated through all these newfound comforts that he is "marvellous hairy about the face; and I am such a tender ass, if my hair do but tickle me, I must scratch." Bottom earlier saw himself wise enough if he could find his way out of the wood. Now that Titania has overruled that idea, he is content to stay if his head will be scratched when it itches. It's the life of a donkey in the field, eating his provender, swishing his tail at flies, and, when he's had enough, lying down for a nap.

As it happens, despite having just ordered a meal, he is suddenly taken "with an exposition of sleep." The four lovers fall into the great sleep of comedy when the complications and frustrations of desire have drained their bodies and minds of all motion. Bottom enters the great sleep from the opposite direction, for the perfection of his state drains his body and mind of any motions of desire. When sated like this, Bottom is at home at the bottom. Just as Robin delivers a commemorative address over the fallen lovers who will at last sleep sound after their nightmare of a night, Titania now blesses him with a similar assurance:

> Sleep thou, and I will wind thee in my arms.
>
> Fairies, be gone, and be all ways away.

All distractions scatter, and all that's left is Titania herself, the source and the sustainer of all things, enfolding him. Once they are alone, she entertains for him a vision of how a man and a woman can be one in nature:

> So doth the woodbine the sweet honeysuckle
>
> Gently entwist; the female ivy so
>
> Enrings the barky fingers of the elm.
>
> O, how I love thee! How I dote on thee.

The picture she paints, the passion with which she embraces her lover, and the great tide of emotion that spills over Bottom might move any man, however brilliant or powerful, to wonder if in his lifetime he will ever hear a woman with even a little of Titania's greatness voice her whole heart over him like that.

This Hateful Imperfection

A stage direction indicates that Robin enters right after Titania speaks these lines, and this gives Oberon the opportunity to speak to him of what he has just seen and heard. Of course, Oberon himself created the conditions that put Titania in the position he now finds her. Now that he has found her, can he survey his creation and say of it that it is good, very good? Bottom is easily discounted as a rival, but surely Oberon feels the warmth of Titania's embrace and her words. Wouldn't he like her to hold him and speak to him like that, especially when banished for so long from her bed and company?

We know that Oberon is capable of feelings, for in their first scene together Titania calls him "jealous Oberon" after he has called her "proud Titania" and "rash wanton." When he questions, "Am not I thy lord," she replies sarcastically, "Then I must be thy lady," and to justify her freedom from his lordship, she reminds him of his own free-lancing when he courted "amorous Phillida" and his "warrior love" Hippolyta. This exchange is part of an on-going war, but it also reveals to us Oberon's nature. He is not just a spirit; he's a passionate spirit. Knowing his nature, Titania has learned to read him like a book; she knew he would come to see the wedding of Hippolyta to Theseus.

Stung by words that downgrade the objects of his attention and that mock his judgment, Oberon defends himself by attacking Titania's own freedom. He reminds her that she is there because of her love for Theseus, and he rehearses for her those times she stole him away from her rivals Perigenia, Aegles, Ariadne, and Antiopa. These memories serve as fuel for jealous fires, those glimmering nights that ravished Titania's heart. In the motion of his speech, which builds to an alliterative climax, we sense that

Titania has finally goaded him into expressing his own carefully guarded jealousy. (See pages 197-200.)

With this history in mind we might be surprised that as Oberon surveys the sleeping lovers, he keeps his feelings, if he has any, largely to himself.

> *Welcome, good Robin. Seest thou this sweet sight?*
>
> *Her dotage now I do begin to pity;*
>
> *For, meeting her of late behind the wood,*
>
> *Seeking sweet favours for this hateful fool,*
>
> *I did upbraid her and fall out with her.*
>
> *For she his hairy temples then had rounded*
>
> *With coronet of fresh and fragrant flowers;*
>
> *And that same dew which sometime on the buds*
>
> *Was wont to swell like round and orient pearls*
>
> *Stood now within the pretty fouriets' eyes,*
>
> *Like tears that did their own disgrace bewail.*

Pity? When she's lying with another man? Is Oberon so cold? For the audience, especially an Elizabethan audience which feared the note of the plain-song cuckoo grey as the ultimate insult that could be hurled at a man, this would seem to set Oberon apart. He is not mortal flesh and blood but something else, and so he is. Nevertheless, the rest of the passage is full of emotion. Oberon does not cry out or weep over what he has done to Titania and himself, although he acts as if he's upset when he meets with her. Instead, his narrative of the event delegates the shame and the disgrace to the fouriets' eyes.

Somehow Oberon avoids getting upset about what he sees. It's a strange detail in a play full of the supernatural. In contrast to this response, I have recalled Oberon and Titania's initial confrontation which reveals their jealous natures. Nevertheless, the two of them, instead of flying to the opposite ends of the universe where they could live without the aggravation of a spouse, have come together to sort out their situation in the wood around Athens. At the end of her indictment earlier Titania acknowledges that Oberon has come there to give the bed of Theseus and Hippolyta "joy and prosperity." Any member of a wedding party might wonder how the presence of a former lover in the pews might ensure the joy and prosperity of the newlyweds, but like the remarkable poet who invented them (and who, it is believed, wrote the play for a royal wedding), Oberon and Titania are not shy about inserting themselves as critical ingredients. Whatever their motivations, their presence in the wood strongly impacts all those who come there from Athens.

The fact that Hippolyta was once his love and that he would now bless her wedding is all the evidence we have about Oberon's relationship with her. We don't know Oberon's motivations for attending Hippolyta's wedding, but he probably brought his train to the wood as another strategic move in the war between him and Titania which has raged throughout the wet and miserable spring, a move she alertly counters. While we can't pinpoint his motivations for coming to Athens, we are now material witnesses to the fact that Oberon no longer looks at Titania as an enemy. Titania may have said that he came to give the bed of Theseus and Hippolyta joy and prosperity with dripping sarcasm, but the situation that might have moved her to irony is changing. The fires of jealousy and revenge which fueled the recent conflict, have, on Oberon's part, been judiciously banked. In the rescue of Helena, Oberon is relearning what he forgot in the heat of combat: as the guardian of nature, the king of fairies does not casually interfere with a "true-love's sight." (See page 258.)

But what is a true love's sight? It must be that Oberon knows it when he sees it. He must have seen it in Helena of Athens, for he has gone to some trouble on her behalf. Along with all the qualities he might admire, he recognizes in her, more than in the others, the pain of love:

> All fancy-sick she is, and pale of cheer
>
> With sighs of love, that costs the fresh blood dear.

For some reason, Helena's suffering in love has touched within him a deep wellspring of compassion.[52] Something moves him to open Demetrius' heart so that Helena will "shine as gloriously / As Venus in the sky" the next time he sees her, and something about his care of Helena has now opened his own heart at the sight of Titania embracing a fool. He calls it "sweet," but his rescue of Helena undercuts that assessment. If he was looking at Titania as an enemy, his vengeance would be "sweet," but vengeance is no longer his object. These essays have argued throughout that a true love's sight encompasses all the good, bad, and ugly episodes that lovers inevitably experience. As he recalls for Robin Titania's tender devotion to that which is unworthy of her love, the true love's sight of Oberon perceives the part he has played in creating the scene. Now that he overlooks the whole sorry episode, he is forced to see, as in a magic mirror, Titania embracing his own fool's head. The joke he played on her, the bitterness of its sweetness, rebounds on him, the lord of nature. How else do we explain the tears in the Floriet's eyes?

Even the king of fairies requires periodic instruction in the nature of love. To frame the question the way Chaucer did in "The Knight's Tale," a true love's sight does not desire to possess that which cannot be possessed. The quarrel over the Indian boy dramatizes the distinction between love that desires to possess and love that doesn't. The problems in the natural world arise not because Oberon and Titania love the boy but because they want to possess him for themselves. They each want to protect and discipline the child according to their own judgment of the good, the bad, and the ugly, but this can easily become a love affair with their own judgment rather than a true love's sight. The child will always be something more than a scheme for raising him up.

It's difficult enough for parents raising up their children to see this distinction between the two loves, but it's just as significant and possibly more difficult for the same parents in the raising up of a marriage. If Oberon followed the traditional form of the vow, he agreed to "take" Titania as his lawful wedded wife, a vow that ever since has been a work in progress even for the mighty king of the fairies. He and Titania have been married since time began, and Oberon has already told us that marriage is a "league whose date till death shall never end." These are the boundaries within which the game is played; this is the crucible for finding out what it means to "take" another for a spouse. As a practical matter of the heart everything in his life has something to do with his queen. In taking Titania as a wife, he is taken up as well. This insight requires a measure of discipline to maintain in good order. If he would avoid being consumed by insecurity and jealousy concerning his wife's freedom to think and act as she will, Oberon must learn the self-possession that will safeguard his happiness more than anything he might possess of a woman.

Theseus is right to point out that Titania has also come to the wood outside Athens because she's a passionate spirit. After all, it is she who infers Theseus' intent. Now that we have watched these two playing the game of love together, we can't help but notice, for all their differences, that they are indeed playing the same game and against an opponent with the same quality and intensity. As a practical matter of the heart, everything in her life has something to do with him. In taking Oberon as her husband, she is taken up as well. The two of them have drunk deeply of the same draught.

All this is more ado to explain why, when Oberon looks at Bottom intertwined with Titania, he sees her embracing his own fool's head, but it may still be difficult to understand how he can calmly observe his wife winding her arms around another. By giving the fairies a prominent role in it, the play has a built-in answer for poor mortals. This dream of a play stars jealous lovers who are lured to a better place by the illusions of fairyland. One by one Oberon, Titania, and all the lovers follow the script. Helena is brought "here" by some illusion, and Hermia is lured to the other three by the noise of Oberon's magic. Act III ends with Demetrius and Lysander diving into the woods with a desire to murder each other, but through the magic of the wood, which is actually the magic of Shakespeare's poetry, they are moved afterwards by the spirit Robin, rather than anything material. As mentioned before, even though Robin prevents one from killing the other, in reality men kill other men every day of this life. Shakespeare's device simply points out that the desiring and the actual killing exist in two different realms. In the rush of events, it may appear that the two are inevitably and causally linked, but the poem separates them. One is spiritual, the other material. A crazed jealousy is not inevitably and causally tied to murder.

In the same way, Oberon knows that Titania's desire is not directly tied to the thing she embraces, for there's the puckish spirit of the flower juice that separates them. Since he himself put the flower juice on her eyes and prayed she would open them "when some vile thing is near," he knows the source of her feelings and can hardly blame her for them. A desire to cry out and make a scene, therefore, is not necessarily tied to the "sweet sight" before his eyes; this untying opens up the potential for a pause, the time it takes to count to ten they used to say, where the supposed motive for passionate action is arrested, even if only for an instant. Just as the two grand dames—the one who spilled the ale all over herself and the other who missed the stool and ended up sprawled in a heap on the floor—can pin their clumsy missteps on the puckish Robin, Oberon can be reconciled to seeing Titania with her arms wrapped around a fool when he pins it on the puckish flower juice.

Unlike rationalizations like this, life in fairyland is an emotional rollercoaster full of oaths, accusations, jealous attachments, and bitter loneliness, yet it all seems to be winding down, right before first light, with lovers sleeping sound on the ground of a comic foundation. This is the way comedy works. More effectively than analysis, the pain and the weariness of these things is the sharpest and most thorough teacher. In Oberon's case, he and Titania, the immortal king and queen of fairyland, have been carrying on like this forever, and yet they are still devoted to each other and to the proper government of their realm. Since life in fairyland is often enough a soap opera, both suffer occasionally from an obsessive limiting of their vision. This has flared up over their jealous attachment to the Indian boy, and, according to Titania's assessment, the conflict has led to an unseasonably cold spring, the withering of crops, the death of farm animals, and great suffering for those who depend on these things for life. From that moment of crisis—from seeing the government of things slipping away from him, from seeing Helena all fancy sick and pale of cheer, and, more intimately, from seeing Titania in the arms of an ass and the tears in the fouriets' eyes—Oberon has looked with new eyes.

To appreciate the change in his way of looking at Titania, recall the way he greeted "proud Titania" when they first met in the woods. This is how a general would greet his equally proud enemy under the white flag of a temporary truce in a long and bitter war. In the passage under discussion where he observes the pearls in the fouriet's eyes, his words are rooted in a completely different understanding. Oberon imagines that the buds of the coronet weep at being forced to solemnize Titania's infatuation, and he compares their tears to round and orient pearls. This echoes the imagery we heard from Titania's fairy when she describes her work to Robin:

> *And I serve the Fairy Queen,*
>
> *To dew her orbs upon the green.*
>
> *The cowslips tall her pensioners be;*
>
> *In their gold coats spots you see.*
>
> *Those be rubies, fairy favours;*

In those freckles live their savours.

I must go seek some dewdrops here,

And hang a pearl in every cowslip's ear.

As he looks at Titania, Bottom, the coronet and the flowers, Oberon is looking at the world for a moment through the eyes of the fairy and her queen. It's a beautiful but delicate, fragile world. Beauty is as fleeting as the effect of a red ruby on a gold coat or of moonlight shimmering in a dewdrop. Because beauty is so light and fleeting, the fairy must work all night to produce the effect and then do it all over again the following night. Like the fairy looking at the delightful fruits of her labor, Oberon looks at the beauty of Titania, so vulnerable to the conditions for which he himself is responsible, holding on for dear life to a misshapen fool. The incongruity between her beauty and his vengeance makes the flowers cry, and it almost seems as if he would cry, too, if they weren't doing it for him.

Having looked in this way, he returns once more to the overall campaign of which the flower juice was but a part:

When I had at my pleasure taunted her,

And she in mild terms begg'd my patience,

I then did ask of her her changeling child;

Which straight she gave me, and her fairy sent

To bear him to my bower in fairyland.

And now I have the boy, I will undo

This hateful imperfection of her eyes.

And gentle Puck, take this transformed scalp

From off the head of this Athenian swain;

That, he awaking when the other do,

May all the Athens back again repair,

And think no more of this night's accidents

But as the fierce vexation of a dream.

He has the boy at last, which was the object of their whole quarrel, but, the victorious general, as in a war, has to observe the bodies lying about the battlefield. At his feet, Oberon sees fairyland divided into two camps, his and hers, the four lovers sprawled on the ground, and, worse of all, Titania twining her arms around an ass, who, through the miracle of projection, might as well be himself.

Luckily, it's a comic battlefield, and those on the ground do but sleep. Oberon is not an angel or a saint; like those on the ground he is subject to fits of *cupiditas*. While not perfect, he is still the critical ingredient in the liquor of love that Chaucer refers to in the opening of *The Canterbury Tales*—the murky juice that gets everything going in the spring—because he has knowledge of a pretty little flower. As a lord of nature, he has learned from experience that the juice of that flower produces a "hateful imperfection" of the eyes. Under its influence, the eyes would possess for the mind's exclusive enjoyment a pretty little thing which, the eyes must learn, belongs only to the whole. Victorious, as Arcite was the day he dragged Palamon to the stake, Oberon has the boy, but his own eyes are undercutting him and his autonomy. He must feel, as anyone does who actually looks at the world, a great compassion for the delicacy and the beauty of things that live but a moment. The ground of his autonomy is falling away as his own eyes are teaching him what it means to "take" Titania as his wife. To live in this world, to save it from overwhelming floods and unseasonable frosts, he sees that, for as long as he is king of fairies, everything in it will be orphaned without his careful attention, and so he needs to remove this hateful imperfection.

The Autonomy of Wisdom

To remove the hateful imperfection from Titania's eyes, he has the juice of the herb that Robin already used on Lysander. This time Oberon himself applies the antidote, and, as before with the other charms, he aligns its chemical power with the power of speech:

> *Be as thou wast wont to be;*
>
> *See as thou wast wont to see.*
>
> *Dian's bud o'er Cupid's flower*
>
> *Hath such force and blessed power.*

Maybe yet all things shall be peace. The actors arrive at this peace, however, by passing through an interval of night rule. Oberon sums up the process here by associating the respective phases of night rule and peace with the two flowers he has deployed from his arsenal this night. Shakespeare agreed with Chaucer that those who would attend the main stage of the human comedy, where the wisdom of Everyman is unlocked, must buy their tickets at the gate with the great passions of love and hate that are unleashed by Cupid's flower, and their characters arrive at a peace only after those passions have driven them into something like the lovers' present state of complete exhaustion. Earlier, Oberon describes the herb he now puts on Titania's eyes as having the virtuous property to "take from thence all error with his might," and this is as far as he goes to characterize it. Just as the flower that triggers an obsessive attachment is a representation of *cupiditas*, the flower he now uses to neutralize that charm—so that love now looks with the eyes at things-as-they-are—is a representation of *caritas*. Here, though, he calls it "Dian's bud" and makes it the overlord of the other flower.

In Chaucer's arena Diana's place stands between the warring powers of Mars and Venus, but she has no gate by which people may enter the arena. At the end of the tale when Theseus persuades her to wed Palamon, Emily gives up her chastity and single life to live with a man. Chaucer's tale, in other words, gives Diana a somewhat reduced role. In the beginning of Shakespeare's play Theseus, much as he did in Chaucer's tale, warns a young woman against a life in service to chastity by emphasizing its austerity. She needs to consider what it would be like:

For aye to be in shady cloister mew'd,

To live a barren sister all your life,

Chanting faint hymns to the cold fruitless moon.

Thrice blessed they that master so their blood

To undergo such maiden pilgrimage;

But earthlier happy is the rose distill'd

Than that which, withering on the virgin thorn,

Grows, lives, and dies in single blessedness.

He addresses these words to Hermia, but in practice Helena is the one who truly struggles with the choice. Having lost Demetrius' love, she is sorely tempted to live a life of single blessedness. This was surely her intent, if she could get out of the wood. More than an intent, it became her passion to escape those that hate her and to escape the disturbing implications of her own behavior. The passions of love and hate, despite her ambition to rise above them, still governed her life, and so there she lies in the wood with the rest.

Oberon has just affirmed that Dian's bud has the power to master the blood, the passion aroused by the flower they call love-in-idleness, and this can be a passion for a life of single blessedness as well as a man. Even though Helena failed to achieve a state where love is in idleness, Dian's bud represents for us that the state exists. Oberon's remembrance of it reminds us of the history of that other flower. Love-in-idleness came into being when Cupid's bolt failed to hit the great queen of a Western nation, an imperial votress of Diana, who continued to rule her nation "in maiden meditation, fancy free." This is no small matter. Here's a self-possessed woman who maintains a clarity of vision, and by the time Shakespeare was writing the play, a cult had grown up around her virginity. Maybe, people thought, it was a good thing that Elizabeth was married to England. Her successful reign was a symbol for the wisdom and the power that a chaste (and a chastened) autonomy embodies.

The politics of royal marriage aside and despite what Theseus argues against chastity, the action of the play provides a commentary on a life that grows, lives, and dies in the worldly, obsessive pursuit of an object. Ironically, the play's action demonstrates that the lovers are the ones who lock themselves up, whose world shrinks to the cloister of their obsession. The confinement of their isolation cell, though, is the necessary precondition for their release. In *The Consolation of Philosophy* Boethius imagines for himself and the reader that the cell where he is imprisoned is ignorance (a state of mind that ignores the whole in favor of a part and then suffers the ups and downs of Fortune), and he describes his release from ignorance when Philosophy appears to him in his cell. Chaucer borrows the imagery and the insight of Boethius for "The Knight's Tale," and now Shakespeare is employing them here. The two states of imprisonment and release are intimately related. Together the two parts or sides of the coin "tender" a whole, and, especially, in preparation for those who bring children into the world or who have the care of others in their government, the two together tender to us the autonomy a person gains from a wholly realized experience. The obsessive pursuit of an image may look like autonomy, but it's merely the first stage in the action of comedy where a character's heart and mind are tenderized through fair means and foul, and the illusory autonomy of obsession ripens into the actual autonomy of wisdom.

A phrase like "the autonomy of wisdom" is easily said and just as easily forgotten along with all the other phrases a person hears. The rest of the play must therefore give it a more memorable shape than four words supplied by an analysis. What better place to begin than with Oberon's loving appeal over his wife's lifeless body after applying the antidote:

Now, my Titania! Wake you, my sweet queen.

In some of Shakespeare's tragedies, a lover makes an appeal like this and gets no response, but since this is a comedy, Titania awakes and replies in kind:

My Oberon, what visions I have seen!

She lives. It's the wonder of comedy. Instinctively, in the first light of it, they take full possession of what they love: she is his and he is hers. They bring each other to life. This is what has changed, and everything else will follow from it. This is a deep, abiding recognition of oneself in another, not *cupiditas*. It's also a moment of truth for both of them as regards the past. After recognizing her husband and declaring the wonder of her vision, she begins to recall its specifics:

Methought I was enamour'd of an ass.

Titania, who like Helena prizes her own judgment so much that she's been willing to go to war in its defense, has had a most unpleasant dream. Oberon points out that it was no dream:

There lies your love.

Looking at Bottom, her bedfellow for the night, Titania hits bottom. She can only wonder:

How came these things to pass?

O, how mine eyes do loathe his visage now!

Titania takes the point, as there's no evading: her bedfellow is a monster. Her question, however, now forces the point on Oberon. She doesn't know yet how these things came to pass, but Oberon knows very well that his jealous rage for vengeance was behind it. His vanity brought her to this pass and brought him along with her. Bottom is merely an extension of his will, and Oberon has confirmed himself not only an ass but a cuckold as well. Like water sliding down a hillside, comedy seeks the lowest possible place where it can rest from falling. By making himself such a fool, Oberon, like all the mortals around him on the ground, has hit bottom.

For all that, though, the two are reconciled. Oberon may have slid to a new low, but he is quickly redeemed by the sense that fairyland is larger than the two of them. No time to waste on what is past. There's work yet to be done so he moves quickly to secure a comic basis for all on the stage. The point is not to judge but to act:

> *Silence awhile. Robin, take off this head.*
>
> *Titania, music call; and strike more dead*
>
> *Than common sleep of all these five the sense.*

Titania complies with a command of her own:

> *Music, ho, music! such as charmeth sleep!*

Robin obeys and advises the still sleeping Bottom:

Now, when thou wak'st, with thine own fool's eyes peep.

How quickly Oberon and Titania regain their balance in a few deft but necessary strokes. As if their long quarrel were but a dream now that they are awake, the work is mutually and willingly accomplished, the music sounds, and Oberon seals the end of division by asking Titania to dance:

Come, my queen, take hands with me.

And rock the ground whereon these sleepers be.

They join in a dance that will rock the lovers into a dreamless sleep deeper than any they have ever known.[53]

The rocking of the lovers by dancing fairies recalls Bottom's first scene with Peter Quince and the rest of the company. He is ready to play a lover, but he would have preferred something grander where:

The raging rocks

And shivering shocks

Shall break the locks

Of prison gates;

And Phibbus' car

Shall shine from far

And make and mar

The foolish Fates.

Prior to his transformation, Bottom sees himself in a role that is larger than life—as a prating volcano or earthquake or atomic bomb that violently divides humanity from earthly constraints and as a blazing sun that illuminates and defeats "the foolish fates."

The fairies are a far cry from being tragic heroes, but they have, with the humble means at their disposal, fulfilled the program that Bottom outlines here. Like Odysseus in the stern of the Phaeacians' ship, Bottom and the others are carried sound asleep by the dance of the fairies home to the source of all life, the molten core at the heart of all things. The despair (when Fate overrules) that Oberon and Robin momentarily entertained has dissolved in the first light of Phibbus' car, and the lives of all the sleepers are being transformed, for the better as we shall see. By acting in time, that is, in harmony with the rhythm of things, the fairies have righted the government of fairyland. Compared to the play's comic action, the Fates are foolish because they believe in their own strictures and take themselves too seriously; a tragic hero would have the entire world dance to the tune of an apocalypse. The music we hear now is more in keeping with a nuptial ceremony, and "new in amity," Oberon and Titania move freely together to express the autonomy of wisdom.

CHAPTER ELEVEN:
THE GREAT CALL

Galloche's *Diana and Actaeon*

Actaeon: Blood Sport at a Nuptial

When the fairies hear the morning lark, they trip after night's shade and exit. The theater then fills with the sound of Theseus' horn; it signals that we have arrived at the boundary between the realm ruled by the fairies and the state ruled by Duke Theseus. As in any significant border crossing, the forward movement of our narrative must come to a stop.

The wake-up call plays a critical role in comedy, and Shakespeare has given it a formal entrance here. I have called this chapter "The Great Call" as the poet intends the sounding of Theseus' horn to represent a moment that's more than an ordinary stumble or screw up. In scripture, Paul writes that the dead will rise at the last trumpet.[54] It's the great call to life: death has been vanquished; time has passed away. There are other places in Shakespeare's plays where time seems to stop, most notably the scene when Prince Hamlet commands a player to recite a passage about the death of Priam and the grief of Hecuba; the business of the court then comes to a halt as the player obliges the prince. As he recites, the court of Elsinore and the audience find themselves in the midst of a maelstrom, for the Greeks have set the fabled, impregnable city of Troy on fire. On fire with revenge, Pyrrhus seeks all over the city for the father of the man who killed his father and finally discovers him, alive and armed but hopelessly feeble. The old man falls, but when Pyrrhus raises his sword over Priam's prostrate body, time freezes for a spell at the sound of an apocalyptic thunder as the blazing walls and buildings of Troy fall to the ground all at once.[55]

Since a trumpet call, like the thunder of Troy's destruction, resonates so deeply, I pause to discuss the implications of it from the perspective of the eternal without losing sight of it as an ordinary, worldly sound. Even though a trumpet call suggests a world that's utterly changed "in the twinkling of an eye," when associated with the twinkling of an eye it has links with the things of this world like the twinkling in the eye of Chaucer's Theseus when he decides to pardon the lovers fighting in the wood. It's the twinkling in the eye of a human being, not a god, but out of this pardon a whole new world comes into being.[56] In London town those crossing the river to see a play would know at the sound of the trumpet that a play was about to begin. Once the play begins and until it ends, the audience inhabits a new world. In the field a horn is used for hunting, and the object of the hunt is sustenance and renewed life. So the call makes its entrance here along with Theseus, Hippolyta, and many lords and ladies as it coordinates hunters spread far and wide.

Theseus and Hippolyta have gotten up early to observe the rites of May. That done, he would have them climb the mountain where they can hear the sound of Oberon's hunting hounds echoing in the Western valley. This is a music Hippolyta loves as well, and she tells Theseus of a time she visited Crete with Cadmus and Hercules who brought with him hounds of Sparta for hunting:

> Never did I hear
>
> Such gallant chiding; for, besides the groves,
>
> The skies, the fountains, every region near
>
> Seemed all one mutual cry. I never heard
>
> So musical a discord, such sweet thunder.

It's the sound of hunting and it echoes, the way the Western valley will, what we have heard this night in the woods. For the audience, the chiding of the lovers creates just such a discord and fills the air with the lightning and sweet thunder of both love and fear. These lovers cry for what they want; put them all together and you have something like the music Theseus proposes they listen to on the mountain top. Their perch there will be a variation on the view from Olympus that the gods enjoy; only this time it's more like the comfortable seats above the pit that the gentry could afford at a play in the Globe Theater. It's a pleasure to hear such music at a distance sitting in a secure place. Given the uncertainties introduced by the opening speeches of the play, though, it's a fair question whether Theseus and Hippolyta have transcended the brawling and the baying of desire that we have witnessed in the wood.

What a coincidence! Theseus is pleased to tell her, "My hounds are bred out of the Spartan kind," so he has heard that music many times; the symphony she heard with Cadmus and Hercules will be played once more for her enjoyment. Like those she heard, his players are:

> *matched in mouth like bells,*
>
> *Each under each. A cry more tunable*
>
> *Was never hooloa'd to nor cheer'd with horn*
>
> *In Crete, in Sparta, nor in Thessaly.*

The sound of bells peeling through the hills and valleys is perfectly suited to celebrate a marriage, but the poet who wrote *Venus and Adonis* is suggesting a darker color as well, a discord that runs through the midst of a successful hunt. Adonis wasn't cheered with a horn; he died when a mighty boar gored him with it. The horn that introduces the scene and appears again here in this passage also brings to mind the perennial joke about the horns on the head of a cuckold that should make an appearance after Titania's night with Bottom. Rather than bringing good cheer, horns usually drive a husband into a mad, murderous jealousy as they did for *Othello*. In these cases the call of the horn is the great call of revenge and death.

The hounds of Cadmus add another dark story into the substream of their conversation. Elizabethan readers and audiences were familiar with the hounds of Acteon, a grandson of Cadmus. Shakespeare read a version of his story in Book III of Ovid's *The Metamorphosis* translated in English by Arthur Golding, and Ovid's work was also a source for his *Venus and Adonis*. The famous hunter Actaeon happened to see Diana naked in a stream. For his trespass Diana transformed him into a stag, and his own hounds then hunted him down, shredded him into pieces, and devoured him. Because the subject was a favorite of renaissance painters, in the galleries of his aristocratic patrons Shakespeare may have seen a painting of Actaeon surprising the naked Diana.

The poet of *A Midsummer Night's Dream* who turns Bottom into an ass must have noted in Golding's translation the physical force of Diana's rage and the physicality of the transformation she wrought on Actaeon:

> So raught she water in hir hande and for to wreake the spight
>
> Besprinckled all the heade and face of this unluckie knight,
>
> And thus forespake the heavie lot that should upon him light:
>
> Now make thy vaunt among thy Mates, thou sawste Diana bare.
>
> Tell if thou can: I give thee leave: tell hardily: doe not spare.
>
> This done she makes no further threates, but by and by doth spread
>
> A payre of lively olde Harts hornes upon his sprinckled head.
>
> She sharpes his ears, she makes his necke both slender, long and lanke.
>
> She turnes his fingers into feet, his armes to spindle shanke.
>
> She wrappes him in a hairie hyde beset with speckled spottes,
>
> And planteth in him ferarefulnesse. And so away he trottes...[57]

After glimpsing the naked form of Diana, Actaeon ends badly. Bottom, on the other hand, who undergoes a transformation similar to the one that kills Acteon, inhabits the wood of a comedy and lives on to have good fortune even after he has glimpsed the primal form of the fairy queen.

Of course, these are just fantastic stories. In Golding's telling of it, however, Diana's passion and her desire for revenge are palpably real, and the play has already dramatized the realistic, passionate one-upmanship of

Titania and Oberon. While there are elements of fantasy in it, the story touches on the great call for a man of a woman's nakedness and the great intent and consequences of the call—a timeless plotline that mirrors the lives of men and women. This poet ranges widely all over the known world to pour these stories into his poem about passion. He would show that passion is a liquor that mixes all the elements—of earth that grows magnificent trees, of skies that are filled with the sounds of gallant and musical chiding, of fire like sudden lightning, of water that rushes forth from a source hidden in darkness—the way the Western valley does. Passion is a composition of sweet thunder, a mixing of light and dark.

Theseus and Hippolyta have agreed to go hunting on the day of their wedding. The hunt allows them both to explore, as a dream does, the way love and hate are bound to each other and the way a comedy can come close to being a tragedy (and vice versa). Shakespeare might also have noted in Golding's passage that he links "raught" and "wreake" in a single gesture, for the gathering of the water ("So raught she water") in her hand is what allows her to put in motion the wrecking of poor Actaeon. Although entirely different in meaning, the two words are similar in sound, and this closeness reflects Shakespeare's understanding of comedy and tragedy. The cries of the hunters "cheer'd with horn" inextricably mixes a celebratory music, like those in Theseus' description of the hunt in the Western valley, with the cries of a man being torn to shreds, like those we hear if the image is considered in the light of Actaeon's story. Normally, the cries signal a triumph, but Actaeon has suffered a terrible reversal. The hunter has now become the hunted.

Hearing this story about Diana, a man might well wonder if, when he catches a glimpse of divine beauty like this, the female gods will then trumpet their supremacy with a fanfare of violence. Stocked as it is with these associations swimming around inside of it, the second dialogue between Theseus and Hippolyta is as remarkable as the first for how it reveals, basic undercurrents of feeling and thought. Even a confident woman like Hippolyta, a former votress of Diana, may be wondering how she will react when Theseus sees her bare later that day. Even a confident man like Theseus might wonder what lies in store for him now that he is about to take as wife a queen of the Amazons.

Comedy and tragedy tell stories about characters who confront the same basic problem: they make mistakes because they are not omniscient. Actaeon, who had sent his companions home after a day of hunting, ended up in the wrong place at the wrong time on his way out of the wood. Tragedy and comedy share this observation about the limits of human perception, but the outcomes are different. A tragic hero like Actaeon dies whereas a comic character like Bottom will live to peep another day with his fool's eyes. Tragedy gathers together the little handkerchiefs and the insinuations that end up wrecking a character's life (as they do for *Othello*). Comedy wrecks a character's old life but then gathers together a new one. The audience, on the other hand, gets up at the end of either a comedy or a tragedy chastened and humbled, as when lightning strikes very near, by the power of life and death that's present in any moment. Despite all our efforts to make it predictable with all the devices and fail-safes of the intellect and civilization, life is still full of mystery, sudden haps, and reversals, and these are the currents that swirl and bubble in the straits of a wedding day.

The sudden return of Theseus and Hippolyta to the play is both reassuring and unsettling. He represents the rule of law in Athens, but it's a rule of law that demands the life of Hermia unless she submits to her father's will. Theseus-the-hunter in this scene reminds us that Hermia is being hounded by Athenian law. The sport in which Theseus and Hippolyta take such delight masks in ceremony the death of that which they hunt; behind the mask, there's the suggestion that the marriage of a man and a woman is a blood sport. In Act V Theseus has to choose from a list of options an entertainment for the evening, and he eliminates one of them as inappropriate for a nuptial. Since the playwright is aware that some entertainments are suited to a wedding and some are not, it raises the question as to why he has included a hunt on the day that Theseus and Hippolyta will marry. Of course, a hunt is what aristocrats do to amuse themselves whether they are getting married or not, but the play is too rich in symbolic content for a strictly mundane explanation. Furthermore, the poet goes out of his way to suggest the well-known story of Actaeon, for he could easily have given Hippolyta another host for that previous hunt.

Comedy celebrates marriage as a form that puts the conduct of men and women under the rule of law, and the entertainment of men and women in the play reveals the need for it. Not so long ago Theseus and Hippolyta were trying to kill each other; after making love to her, Demetrius subsequently abused Helena with a blunt disdain, and Hermia turned tables on him by refusing his love; Helena mocked and discounted the desperate love of both men; and Lysander topped it all off with a point-blank rejection of Hermia. Questions remain, though, whether a law governing relationships can do anything about this. Would an arranged marriage somehow calm or suppress the passions of a man or a woman once they were legally married? Does marriage between those who have chosen for themselves necessarily keep conflicts, especially over children, from supercharging emotions?

For a marriage to work as a foundation for the health and well-being of the social order, the rule of law by itself is not enough. For the institution to be meaningful and for the meaning of it to last, men and women must undergo a comic initiation like the one we have witnessed this midsummer night whenever the need for it arises. A passage of night-rule doesn't teach a commandment or even a golden rule. Instead, the celebrants discover in the muscles, in the bones, and in the brain how pointless and exhausting it is to chase, the way people do because they are not omniscient, a phantom like Robin's voice in the night or any other idea that's false or incomplete. The trumpet call of a comic fall is the only hope for relationship.

Dionysus: the Twice-Born God of Tragedy and Comedy

Ovid ends Book III with another story about the shredding of a man which involves another grandson of Cadmus, the unfortunate Pentheus, King of Thebes. This time, though, the shredding of Pentheus is linked with the worship of Dionysus, the Greek god of wine that the Romans called Bacchus. Pentheus, like Theseus at the beginning of the play, is a stickler for the rule of law. Because he doesn't believe Bacchus is a son of Zeus, Pentheus decrees that the stranger cannot enter his town. He would govern Thebes rationally, and a rational man has to think that an unwed mother made up a story about her baby's father in order to avoid the shame of illegitimacy. Also, the followers of Bacchus behave irrationally; they give full scope to their emotions, singing and dancing in the woods. Women in particular are instinctively drawn to the man and his whirling ways. Pentheus is amazed that so many would forsake the proud martial heritage of Thebes, for he has seen the stranger's followers throw down the weapons needed to defend the city from invaders and wear wreaths of flowers and perfume in their hair instead.

Actaeon and Pentheus have the shredding in common, but their characters are different. With innocent eyes unclouded by any intention, Actaeon recognizes Diana the moment he sees her whereas Pentheus won't recognize Dionysus as a god on principle even when his grandsire Cadmus, Tiresias, and other elders advise him otherwise. When a chief companion of Dionysus, Acestis, is captured and brought before him, Pentheus refuses to believe the story about the miracle the god performed which Acestis himself witnessed. Instead, the king orders him to be tortured and killed. Pentheus' own story contains a profound but bitter irony; he follows the bent of his reason to the point where he behaves irrationally. Unlike blind Tireseas, who has recognized Dionysus, the king can't see the hand of a god behind the strange disruptions that threaten control of his kingdom, for his vision is blinded by worldly pride. He would be king, not the uninvited stranger. This is the entire focus of his rule, and so he ignores the actual government of himself and his state.

Even though he refuses to recognize Bacchus as a god, Pentheus is tempted by the sound of revelry to see for himself how the women of

Thebes worship him, and so he goes to a "goodly plaine" surrounded by wooded hills to catch them in a crime. The hunter Pentheus, however, comes so close to spy on the women that they catch sight of him; he failed to see how his plan could go wrong. Bacchus doesn't have to change Pentheus' shape the way Diana changed that of Actaeon. The women's "looking" does that for him. Aroused by Bacchus and a life lived in the open, their perception is impaired. They have left the town, which keeps them cooped up and subservient, and they range intoxicated with a new freedom. In the wood among wild beasts, their thoughts turn to hunting, and the thought of a wild boar, like the one that killed Adonis, excites their imagination. When they find Pentheus spying on them from the woods, these meek creatures are changed; instead of being hunted, the harmless and gentle dears that men are always chasing, they become hunters. Like the hounds of Actaeon, they surround their former master and tear him to shreds. They think he is a great boar rooting in their midst, and even Pentheus' own mother, the leader of the pack, doesn't recognize him until it's too late. Here is Shakespeare's theme, the vexing tension in human perception between looking with the mind (seeing a deadly boar, the most feared beast in the wild) and looking with the eyes (the mother waking up to see the mutilated body of her son) played out as a tragedy.

Though Shakespeare may not have known, as we now do, that Greek tragedy and comedy originated in the festivals celebrating the twice born god, he would have read in Book III, a little after Actaeon's mutilation, the reason why Bacchus is called twice-born. His mortal mother, Semele, foolishly asks Jupiter to show himself to her in their lovemaking as he would to Juno. Since he has already promised to do whatever she requested, Jupiter has to follow through, and Semele is burnt to a crisp. Jupiter rescues the boy in her womb, however, and plants him in his own thigh "Where byding out the mother's tyme it did to ripenesse grow." And grow he did into his present position as a world power.

Shakespeare may not have known, as scholars now tell us, that Dionysus and Adonis were vegetation gods who had cults all over the ancient world, but he was instinctively drawn to Ovid's depiction of the natural world in *The Metamorphosis*. It's a fluid dreamscape where people magically change their shapes, and it's full of gods propelled by intense desire. The gods love the beauty of mortals perhaps because, unlike themselves, that beauty is so transient and precious. Mortals like Ovid and worshippers of Dionysus, on the other hand, in dreams and in their worship instinctively desire the promise of life after life. Figures like Adonis and Dionysus, who suffer death and dismemberment (the severe pruning of the vines at the end of every season in the case of Dionysus) and then are reborn in the spring, serve as a bridge for those human dreamers who would realize their mystery. It's a mystery, they sense, that comes out of the ground.

Shakespeare's poetry contains evidence throughout that he was a country boy. As a young student he studied Ovid in the classroom, and when he wrote about nature as a man, he recreated for everyone who was once a child of nature that feeling of movement through an open field, of changes in the wind, of secrets buried in the earth, of light and shadow in a deep wood. Everything in this world is fluid; it moves and changes its shape the way water does. Ovid's collection is like an ocean surging with powerful currents where in the depths we encounter figures who are human but unlike the people we meet every day. They are archetypes who spring to life in every generation. They are perfect, blood-red anemones that are reborn every spring, and that perfection is shaped and tended to individually by the powers of nature. In addition to their own fragile beauty, in the first light of dawn nature endows these flowers of imagination with a pearl of great price; in times of trouble, too, a tiny enclosure of petals serves as a refuge for little ones affrighted by the brawls of great ones. Though fleeting to the sense, they are a locus of meaning, a pattern, something beautiful that shines out in the endless flux.

Given the transience of all things as illustrated by the tragedy of Adonis, it's no wonder that people sought a refuge in the worship of one who is twice-born. The wine of Dionysus is a spirit that tastes of all the elements—the sun's fire, the air the leaves breathe, the minerals the roots absorb once water mixes them—all blended into a sweet liquor of great power, for in wine the ancients made a great discovery: the world changes when the person looking at the world is changed—by wine, by a love juice on the eyes, or by the return from death of those figures we hear about in stories and in scripture. Ovid absorbed that spirit of wine and love as much as any poet who ever lived, and Shakespeare studied Ovid the way he studied the fields and woods around Stratford where he worked and played as a boy. The country was his natural home, the ground of his thought and poetry.

He may not have known, as we do now, that poets competing for the prize at the festival of Dionysus were required to write three tragedies and then conclude the cycle with a comedy. If these proportions and the ordering is correct, the odds are stacked in favor of tragedy, but comedy has the last word. This is a pattern that Shakespeare thoroughly understood and which he put at the heart of his stories and poems. The linking of tragedy and comedy tells the story of one who is twice-born: in a tragedy, circumstances of character and accidents of fortune dictate that the hero must die; in a comedy, as Leonato's brother tells Hero in *Much Ado about Nothing*, a hero, in this case Hero herself, must die to live. In a comedy eyes that know only tragedy are changed by the spirit of Dionysus to look in a new way.

Chaucer: The Father of English Comedy

Shakespeare admired Ovid enough to refer to his stories again and again in his poetry, he studied and may have performed the comedies of Terrence and Plautus as a part of his Latin education, and his father might have taken him to a nearby town where Herod strut his stuff on one of the pageant wagons that make up a mystery cycle. There were other influences as well, but *A Midsummer Night's Dream* is dedicated to Chaucer. Shakespeare doesn't acknowledge him explicitly; he honors him, instead, by stealing his characters, the basic structure for his plot, and his theme.

Above all Shakespeare celebrates in his comedy ordinary people who live and work in town and country, the way Chaucer celebrates them. Great folks are the subject of tragedy, ordinary folks the subject of comedy. The hero of a tragedy confronts unanswerable questions about life and death. The characters of a comedy learn how to survive and prosper in a social context, and this holds true for the English pilgrims that Chaucer assembled in his collection of stories. It may be hard not to draw on Chaucer if you would be a great comic poet, for, as John Dryden wrote concerning *The Canterbury Tales*, "Here is God's plenty."

The opening lines of "The Prologue" describe the ground and the season out of which Chaucer's poetry springs:

When in April the sweet showers fall

And pierce the drought of March to the root, and all

The veins are bathed in liquor of such power

As brings about the engendering of the flower,

When also Zephyrus with his sweet breath

Exhales an air in everygrove and heath

Upon the tender shoots, and the young sun

His half-course in the sign of the Ram has run,

And the small fowl are making melody

That sleep away the night with open eye

(So nature pricks them and their heart engages)

Then people long to go on pilgrimages

And palmers long to seek the stranger strands

Of far off saints, hallowed in sundry lands,

And specially, from every shires end

Of England, down to Canterbury they wend

To seek the holy blissful martyr, quick

To give them help when they were sick.

As in the worship of Dionysus, his poetry is inspired by a liquor of such power that it inducts ordinary people into a timeless presence. Like the flower being engendered, Chaucer's subject is deeply rooted in the soil of his native land. His poetry begins underground in darkness absorbing all the natural influences there, but it rises with spiritual force to breathe the air by which we all live and to bask in the heat of the sun. It's the blessing of that which unfolds in time. A living thing grows toward light and warmth in a world where even the sun has a specific place in a larger intent. So his poetry seeks it out, but in Chaucer it's a comic business. He and his work remind him of the small fowl that long for something (the poem doesn't say what but it can only be one thing) when "nature pricks them and their heart engages." This poet is not about to get ahead of himself by ignoring his root.

This longing is the keynote of the passage. It drives the engendering of the flower, it keeps small fowl up all night, and it sends pilgrims out into the unknown. Because a longing for the things of this world touches on a longing for that which gives life to everything (as it's all interconnected), Chaucer's miniature of creation ends with seekers who gather together in little currents and streams of movement and who then empty into a great mystery, at Canterbury, the death of a man and his rebirth as a saint.

Chaucer's opening lines serve as the universal stage on which the subsequent tales of the pilgrims and their characters will act. Even though the stage has been made with great consequence and high intent, the pilgrims who fill it with themselves and their stories are native to England and not notably consequential. Their destination is a local English shrine, not Jerusalem. They are types who represent different classes and professions, and Chaucer shows them interacting to give us the sense of the social order that frames their speech and actions. Since comedy, as I have been defining it, has to do with human beings surviving and prospering in a social context and since relations between men and women are critical to social order, Chaucer devotes some of his finest tales to this subject.

He begins the collection with "The Knight's Tale," which treats the marriage theme in a high, philosophical style; the Miller then breaks in to tell a bawdy tale about a clerk who cuckolds a carpenter. The Reeve, whom the Miller knows was once a carpenter, objects to any tale by the low-minded Miller, but there's no stopping him. Right from the start Chaucer puts us on notice that we can't expect everyone in the human comedy to maintain the knight's high style. If "The Knight's Tale" sets a standard for depth and nobility of thought about love as a spiritual force and if "The Miller's Tale" and "The Merchant's Tale" set the standard for representing love as a bodily function, "The Wife of Bath's Prologue" sets the standard for a frank discussion of the question that pricks and engages the hearts and minds of men and women as to who has the mastery in marriage. The Wife explains at great length to her fellow pilgrims her techniques for teaching husbands that mastery properly belongs to the wife. There's a simple formula nowadays that summarizes her lengthy sermon: happy wife, happy life.

In "The Knight's Tale" Chaucer ignores the courtship of Theseus and Hippolyta, those veterans in the war of the sexes, and focuses his attention on the infatuation of young lovers. Shakespeare may have found a model for the domestic battles of a married husband and wife, however, in the Wife of Bath's relationship with her fifth and last husband, handsome Johnny. Unlike her other husbands, who were old, unlearned, and virtually impotent, Johnny is younger than the Wife and more than able, being educated at Oxford, to hold his own in an argument. By marrying him, she meets her match at last physically and intellectually at a time when she is past her prime. Nevertheless she triumphs. Her natural vitality and mother wit win the mastery from a determined opponent.

Considered as a whole, the sheer length and power of the Wife's speech overpowers every other speech in the entire collection of tales. Theseus' speech at the end of "The Knight's Tale" conveys the quiet strength and comfort of wisdom, but the Wife's boisterous voice goes on and on, outlasting obstacles with an irrepressible life force. Like the length of her prologue, there's a largeness about her similar to that of Falstaff, Shakespeare's most beloved character. As Theseus' arena does in "The Knight's Tale," the Wife contains the forces of both Venus and Mars. Her coarse wit and middle-class displays of wealth show that she is common, yet she entertains the other pilgrims better than any other storyteller. Her brawling, Dionysian vitality gets people's attention. It's hard not to be caught up in some good gossip about the battles of husbands and wives, and her listeners catch the heartiness of her outlook. If she is common, well then life is common, and Chaucer's comedy celebrates it.

Shakespeare puts the stamp of English domestic life on the better part of *A Midsummer Night's Dream* by inhabiting it with the little people of English folklore. His fairies don't intersect with the lives of great ones (except in the closing moments of the play). They live in the countryside with those who make their living from the land and in small towns; Robin moves the stool of an old countrywoman, not the ambition of a king like Macbeth. The fairy king himself descends from his heights, such as they are, to involve himself in a messy, domestic brawl with his wife the way a paterfamilias in Roman comedy does. Helena, a sweet lady and wiser than most, eventually falls from the lofty standards for gentility she has set for herself into vicious bickering and backstabbing. Comedy makes the case that everyone, without exception, is subject to this commonness as surely as our life owes a death. And the commonality of foolishness and death is where our comedy has left the five human characters who have sought out the wood on a midsummer's eve. The four lovers lie on the ground dead to the world along with Bottom, that great exemplar of egocentric blindness. Thanks to the night rule of this midsummer eve, though, these five have been gathered together in an uncommon, dreamless sleep. It's a sea that has no bottom, and the sleepers are rocked and carried by the currents of this vast ocean, like the sleeping Odysseus returning home sound asleep in the stern of the Phaeacians' ship, back to the source that gave them life, the source "of all and everything."

Triton's Horn

It's a sleep laid on them in anticipation of a new life. For lovers of Ovid's poetry, Theseus' horns recall the sounding of Triton's horn from Book One of *The Metamorphoses*. The incident takes place in the Age of Iron when piety, faith, love, and truth turn to evil. In anger, Jove washes the earth clean of violence with a great flood in which all things and all creatures are drowned except for Deucalion and Pyrrha, who stand together on the ledge of a mountain. Like Noah in the Biblical story, they alone were devoted to each other and to the gods. With human life lodged so precariously, Jove finally relents, and at Neptune's call Triton rises from the sea:

Like a tower of sea-green beard, sea creatures,

Sea shells, grey waters sliding from his green shoulders

To sound his horn, to wind the gliding rivers

Back to their sources, back to rills and streams.

At Neptune's order Triton lifted up

His curved sea shell, a trumpet at his lips

Which in the underworld of deepest seas

Sounds Triton's music to the distant shores

Behind the morning and the evening suns;

And as his voice was heard through land and ocean

The floods and rivers moved at his command.

Over all earth the shores of lakes appeared

Hillsides and river banks, wet fields and meadow,

As floods receded and quays came into view:

A cliff, then a plateau, a hill, a meadow,

As from a tomb a forest rose and then

One saw trees with lean seaweeds tangled

Among their glittering leaves and wave-tossed boughs.

It was a world reborn...[58]

Triton's horn signals the advent of a powerful current that draws all that water back to its sources, and life is renewed. These ancient themes may derive from cultures like that in Egypt which depended every year first on the springtime flooding of the Nile to fertilize the ground and then on the receding of the flood so people could work the land. It's a story about the creativity of that which must be drowned to live again.

If Theseus' horn, which ends a long night of emotional outbursts, resonates with Triton's horn, which ends earth's long night of flood, it prompts us to recall that the world in Shakespeare's play suffers from excessive rain and flooding as well. It's a topsy-turvy time when the old distinctions are blurred. Like Ovid's description of trees with seaweed tangled among the leaves, Titania reminds Oberon that, along with the banks of rivers overwhelmed with flood, the seasons have lost their definition so that "Hoary-headed frosts / Fall in the fresh lap of the crimson rose." She concludes by making the connection between the disruptions in the world and the dissensions of Oberon and herself. The two of them, she argues, are their "parents and original."

Shakespeare is making the connection more generally between the flooding and the obsessions that plague the life of Everyman. With Oberon and Titania fixated only on possessing the Indian boy, the rest of the world drowns in neglect. If obsession is the problem, as it is here and in "The Knight's Tale," the world will change when their minds change, and so Oberon advises her, "Do you amend it then; it lies with you." At that point he thinks only of getting what he wants, for he explains, "I do but beg a little changeling boy / To be my henchman." Changing her mind means giving in to his. If she does, all will be well. Since for Titania the boy is non-negotiable, though, they come to an impasse.

In Ovid everything drowns in the flood except for Deucalion and Pyrrha. Because they respect the power of the gods that caused the flood in the first place and because they are devoted to each other, they represent the last best hope for humankind. These two—a respect for overwhelming, natural forces and the love they have for each other—are intimately related; Deucalion and Pyrrha gain added respect and gratitude from the precariousness of their position. Perched on their little ledge, they can see how quickly the whole world can change, and just as suddenly they find a new value and comfort in the one who stands there with them.

Oberon has had much the same experience. He has been forced to confront the fact that the world he rules is suffering from too much water, drowned crops, and drowned cattle; he was constrained to amend the mistakes he made when he meddled in the lovers' affairs; and he had to face the consequences to himself and Titania of his clever plan to get what he wanted from her. Like Deucalion, he overlooked a world drowning in a bitter sea. It was frustrating and humbling for the king of fairies to survey that which appears to be ruled, not by him, but by outside forces and accidents. This is the world from the point of view of obsession, but it's also what sets the stage for the change of heart that's represented by the rescue of Helena. Once he takes up the work of preserving a true love's sight, he eventually takes possession of the boy, but he still must confront what he might lose as a result of his scheme: the free expression of Titania's love. Without that, his kingship is on the brink. He thought he wanted the Indian boy, but the night rule of his own wood engulfs this wanting with the call of the woman he misses by his side. The night rule of his own wood brings him to that moment when Titania opens her eyes, calls him "My Oberon," and the world is reborn.

Because he was a highly imaginative and sympathetic reader, I picture Shakespeare reading Ovid's story and then putting himself on the ledge along with Deucalion. There he sees a world drowning in transience and feels within himself the life force, the sounding of Triton's horn, that makes it live again. It's the perspective of timeless stories that come to us from prehistory. Chaucer's poetry comes from the same source, but it has been domesticated by fourteen hundred years of Catholic culture, the establishment of modern European states, and the rise in large northern towns of a middle-class with families like the one into which Chaucer himself was born. From reading Chaucer's tales, Shakespeare looks with the freshness of Chaucer's persona at God's plenty as it came to be in England. The myths of Ovid and the tales of Chaucer have continued to bear new fruit, and Shakespeare's poetry, with a root back to each older poet, bears this out.

He absorbs from Chaucer's comedy the continual reminder that no one person knows everything despite that person's illusions to the contrary. Even if a mighty king or queen could somehow organize a government that, like Argus, had eyes everywhere for the gathering of intelligence, there would still be fatal gaps and blind spots. He absorbs from the fluidity of nature in Ovid's poetry that the world is too slippery an object and too complex for anyone to say with pinpoint accuracy that this is what the world has been, what it is, and what it will be. The old stories from myth and from which Ovid and Chaucer borrowed suggest a form for surviving and prospering in the midst of transience that has taken the name of comedy. Within the constant shifting, comic poets like Homer observed the presence of certain patterns—of death and rebirth, of exile and return—that endure, and they observed as well that, given the uncertainties of life, things go better with a loving companion beside you on the ledge to share the uncertainties. It took twenty years, but Odysseus finally enjoys a night of love with his wife Penelope. Twenty years earlier he built a bed for a night like this, and at last he lies in it. The ancients saw that this arrangement—the careful preparations for a night of love and the anticipation of it made stronger by a painful exile—is the surest and deepest root for social order.

The God of Love:
How Mighty and How Great a Lord

This chapter about the winding of Theseus' horn has left undisturbed up till now the five Athenians who lie on the ground dead to the world. It's time to wake them up because Theseus has noticed the four lovers lying at his feet and breaks off the praising of his hounds:

But, soft! What nymphs are these?

Theseus the hunter thought to find a different sort of game in the wood. Even though he just spoke to Hermia the previous day, he doesn't recognize her now. These are small ironies to reveal that mighty Theseus has a limited understanding and memory. Egeus, Hermia's father, is there with Theseus and identifies all four, but he adds after naming them for Theseus:

I wonder of their being here together.

This is the usual case for a paterfamilias in a comedy; he thinks he has the situation under control while their autonomous children are busy about their business.

As governments do when confronted with even a small mystery like this one, Theseus relieves Egeus of his wonder with a reasonable explanation:

No doubt they rose up early to observe

The rite of May; and, hearing our intent,

Came here in grace of our solemnity.

But speak, Egeus. Is not this the day

That Hermia should give answer of her choice?

Since the audience knows exactly why they are there, we notice that Theseus' explanation revolves entirely around himself and his big day. It does not occur to him at first that they are individuals with their own agendas and motivations. To his credit, he remembers as an afterthought how the day concerns Hermia. When Egeus confirms that this is the day of her choice, Theseus commands:

Go, bid the huntsmen wake them with their horns.

So we come to the second call for the world to be reborn. This time it's pointed directly at the lovers, and "they all start up" as the stage directions indicate. The call reprises the first, but the wording of Theseus' command also serves to wake up themes that swim in the currents of a wedding day. Initially, Theseus remarks on the ladies lying on the ground, but now he would have his huntsmen wake them all including Demetrius and Lysander "with their horns." We don't know if Theseus intends the joke, but it surely wasn't lost on Shakespeare's audience. In addition to a limited understanding and memory, Theseus hints at the dark side of his understanding. Unlike the audience, he can only guess at what has happened in the wood. The contrast between our intelligence and his ignorance outlines a major difficulty for those, like a paterfamilias, who would govern the lives of others. In touching on the age-old joke that's played on husbands whose wives are unfaithful, Theseus expresses the ancient fear that, in relationship with a woman, a man will eventually wake up to find she has played him for a fool. Theseus is unaware of the facts in this case, but it happens to some extent to be true. Lysander and Demetrius lose their heads over a woman not just once but twice, first over Hermia and then over Helena, and each man passionately woos the woman intended for the other. Are they enticed? Hermia puts on a great show of being put off by Demetrius' attention, but Helena divines the secret pleasure Hermia enjoys from it. When the men declare their love for Helena in such thrilling terms, Helena makes a great show of interpreting it as mockery, but we still suspect it is the sweetest mockery she has ever heard. She is quick enough, when the tide turns in her favor, to take advantage of the men's devotion in the skirmish with Hermia. In any case, whether the women intend it or not, the men have certainly played the fool.

Now they all are caught sleeping together. Because Theseus is something more than a father in that he wields the power of the state to preserve its good order, the situation is fraught with more than a father's stern lecture. Theseus may not know the particulars of what happened, but he's a worldly man who can see a church by daylight. He, too, is a lover. Instead of moral outrage, Shakespeare's Theseus is touched with the same benevolent amusement that Chaucer's Theseus feels when, after he discovers the felons Palamon and Arcite hacking at each other with their swords in the woods and after all his ladies petition him for their lives, he begins his sentence on them by recognizing what reduced them to that bloody mess:

> *The God of Love! Ah, Benedicite!*
>
> *How mighty and how great a lord is he!*
>
> *No obstacles for him make any odds;*
>
> *His miracles proclaim his power a God's.*
>
> *Cupid can make of every heart and soul*

Just what he pleases, such is his control.

Shakespeare borrows the twinkle he found in the eye of Chaucer's Theseus and has his own Theseus tease the lovers for following their natural inclinations in the wood:

> *Good morrow, friends. St Valentine is past.*
>
> *Begin these wood-birds but to couple now?*

In his analogy, they are wood-birds, crazy little things,[59] that are apt for love but so mixed up that they are getting down to business a few months late. His tone suggests that Theseus knows enough about the God of Love to make an educated guess about what went on in the woods that night. In his voice we hear a largeness of spirit and finally a glimpse into his own life that's missing in the first scene with Hermia and her father. It's this same spirit that has moved the lovers this night in the woods, and after a passage of death counterfeiting sleep, it's what moves them now to acknowledge a law that's larger than their individual inclinations.

Lysander, who initiated the plan to escape the Athenian law and who has the most to lose, speaks for them all by saying:

> *Pardon, my lord.*

With that, the stage directions indicate that all the lovers kneel. Theseus has acknowledged Cupid's lordship by playfully recalling the passions of St. Valentine's Day. Even if they don't laugh at his little joke, the lovers hear the kindliness in his voice and are quick to acknowledge the duke's lordship. Perhaps they sense a kinship with one who knows how mighty and great a lord Cupid is in matters of this kind. As they kneel, Theseus' government, which Lysander and Hermia defied earlier, is reinstated.

Theseus in turn recognizes them as equals under the lordship of love:

I pray you all, stand up.

I know you two are rival enemies.

How comes this gentle concord in the world

That hatred is so far from jealousy

To sleep by hate and fear no enmity?

He recognizes as well that something has transformed the enmity of the previous day. The question he asks is one that anyone responsible for the social order of a family, a business, a city, or a nation needs to investigate with all his heart and mind, and the close parallels between Chaucer's tale and Shakespeare's play at this point suggest that insight into this question will involve the great and mighty God of Love.

With the candor of one who is not fully conscious, Lysander confesses:

And now I do bethink me, so it is—

I came with Hermia hither. Our intent

Was to be gone from Athens, where we might,

Without the peril of the Athenian law—

In the middle of this confession, Egeus breaks in to beg the Athenian law upon Lysander's head and then turns to Demetrius fully expecting that he will prosecute Lysander as well.

Overnight, however, with a little help from the fairies, Demetrius has been reborn, and this is his confession:

My lord, fair Helen told me of their stealth,

Of this their purpose hither, to this wood;

And I in fury hither followed them,

Fair Helena in fancy following me.

But, my good lord, I wot not by what power

(But by some power it is) my love to Hermia,

Melted as the snow, seems to me now

As the remembrance of an idle gaud

Which in my childhood I did dote upon;

And all the faith, the virtue of my heart,

The object and the pleasure of mine eye,

Is only Helena. To her, my lord,

Was I betroth'd ere I saw Hermia;

But, like a sickness, did I loathe this food;

But, as in health, come to my natural taste,

Now I do wish it, love it, long for it,

And will for evermore be true to it.

This speech, like many images and speeches in the play, outlines the arc of love that Shakespeare found in Ovid and Chaucer. The love that derives from Cupid's archery can heat a man or a woman into a fury. It's what happens to Apollo when Cupid hits him with a golden arrow (another story from Ovid that Hermia refers to in Act One) and sends him hurtling in chase after Daphne. But his speech is about the way this love can change its object. To explain these shifts of his love, he employs analogies from the natural world and from everyday experiences that depict changes with which everyone is familiar. An enormous snowdrift exposed to the heat and the rain of spring will eventually melt into nothing. Young adults no longer play with toys that were much loved when they were children. It's perfectly natural for Demetrius' love to change. Change, as Ovid shows in *The Metamorphoses*, is an essential characteristic of nature. The sudden change of affection from Hermia to Helena reminds Demetrius of that other change when his original love for Helena suffered a physical rejection. It's a violence with which the appetite is acquainted. Under the influence of an illness, for example, a favorite sweet may upset the stomach.

Demetrius admits that he doesn't know what power lies behind the changes, but the poet has structured his play to help us with our own understanding. There's the flower juice, and when the flower juice isn't applied there's something afoot within the body and mind of a lover that brings about the effect. To supercharge the changes, the poet multiplies the one man times two and has them obsessing over the same two women. He then throws everyone involved into the same bubbling pot where the once stable characters of four people—with family names and family honors and civic duties to uphold—act and react until they are reduced to raw, volatile, and reactive emotions. These emotions work on them until they fall finally like dead things on the ground. Since they inhabit a comedy, though, the infatuation—the phantom they chase—dies instead. The lovers themselves do but sleep, and Demetrius awakens to find himself in a new world. It's the metamorphosis of comedy. Like the old stories of Dionysus, Adonis, and Deucalion it's a story about adaptation and renewal. As for what happens when the infatuation, the phantom they chase, never dies, you can read about that in other kinds of writing—in books about history, psychology, economics, politics, and crime.

The Lines of Force between Freedom and Constraint

The enlightenment signaled by the second call of the huntsmen's horns has begun with the confessions of the two men. Just as Oberon relies on the accuracy of Robin's reports in his government of the woods, Theseus relies on the accuracy of Lysander's and Demetrius' confessions to render true judgment. Because the audience was present to witness what the two lovers have just described and because their words accurately recreate it, the audience grows in confidence that a person can speak truly and that our human speech, flawed and abused as it often is in communication, nevertheless remains a viable instrument for presenting evidence and rendering judgment. As much as comedy affirms life for human beings that are born into it, it also affirms itself and the language that expresses it as a reliable form for the survival and prospering of human beings within a social order.

Having heard their confessions, Theseus responds:

> *Fair lovers, you are fortunately met.*
>
> *Of this discourse we more will hear anon.*
>
> *Egeus, I will overbear your will;*
>
> *For in the temple, by-and-by, with us,*
>
> *These couples shall eternally be knit;*
>
> *And for the morning now is something worn,*
>
> *Our purpos'd hunting shall be set aside.*
>
> *Away, with us to Athens! Three and three,*
>
> *We'll hold a feast in great solemnity.*
>
> *Come, Hippolyta.*

Theseus has seen enough to know that his government will not be well served by force in a matter of love. He is a soldier and therefore understands the use of force. Here, though, on the great day of his wedding when he and Hippolyta will put up their swords to be contracted to each other, Theseus overbears the will of a father who would rather see his daughter die than give up his idea of paternal authority.

Instead, Egeus' idea dies within Theseus' authority as the supreme court of Athenian law. By crossing the will of Egeus, Theseus runs the risk of alienating an important figure in his dukedom. Nevertheless, he must assume the risks are much greater the other way. Though risky, the decision sets an important precedent in the lives of those who are present, for it establishes the principle that love by nature is free. To be well and truly married, Hermia must freely choose to marry. Here, too, as when Theseus teases the lovers about being a little late for the coupling of St. Valentine's day and quickly forgives them, his judgment echoes that of Chaucer's Theseus who woos Emily on Palamon's behalf at the end of the tale. Chaucer's Theseus is a powerful advocate and his foreign policy is tied to what happens, but he acknowledges Emily's autonomy and her freedom to choose.

It's not enough to say, however, that love is free. In marriage, individuals freely engage themselves to fulfill a contract. Love is free, but the form of comedy maintains that once the trials of courtship are over love flourishes more fully when it is constrained in a formal acknowledgement. Like anything in a world that's constantly changing, the nature of love is difficult to pin down. Is it free or constrained? The question may not have a logical answer. Science has shown us that the invisible lines of force between magnetic poles can be mechanically channeled with generators without which our present civilization would come to a standstill, but this is not the same as mechanically formalizing once and for all the intellectual tension between freedom and constraint or the generation of life between a man and a woman.

Other Polarities When Everything Seems Double

Having made his sentence, Theseus exits the stage with all his court, and only the four lovers (with Bottom still asleep in Titania's bower) remain. For the time being, the tension between freedom and constraint in Hermia's relationships has been resolved, but this is only after it became a life and death matter. By highlighting the tension between freedom and constraint, which also supplies energy and creativity in the marriage of Oberon and Titania, the poet has set the stage for a presentation of other polarities that are strikingly conveyed in what each of the lovers has to say once they are alone together. Demetrius begins by remarking:

These things seem small and undistinguishable,

Like far-off mountains turned into clouds.

Mountains are mountains, and clouds are clouds. Yet in Demetrius' vision the solidity of an enormous material object has melted into an airy nothing. How can this be? How can something that loomed so large become small and undistinguishable? It may seem to be an idle, dreamy sort of curiosity, but subsequent discoveries that objects at a subatomic level turn out to be virtually insubstantial prove that there are latent lines of force surrounding the question wherein lies a power to move mountains. Also, we wonder what "things" he's talking about.

Hermia is next to weigh in, but unlike Demetrius she begins with an awareness of herself in relation to these things:

Methinks I see these things with parted eye,

When everything seems double.

Does the phrase "these things" refer to what she sees right now, the three of them together with her this morning? Does it refer to the rocky ups and downs of the midsummer night? Or does it refer to the sudden appearance of Theseus and his court, which just as suddenly has passed out of sight? Hermia sheds no light on any of this. Instead, she appears to be looking at perception itself and observes that when the eyes are not focused on a particular object, each eye is free to look for itself, and everything seems double. It's one thing when two individuals see the same object differently; it's quite another when one person is seeing double. The discovery may be disconcerting, but it's a kind of game that plays with our powers of perception.

Helena, who early in the play wants desperately to be Hermia's double and whose wish comes true with the help of the fairies, agrees with something that Hermia has said:

> *So methinks;*
>
> *And I have found Demetrius like a jewel,*
>
> *Mine own, and not mine own.*

Unlike Demetrius and Hermia, Helena frames what they have said about seeing or perception with an awareness of herself in relation to a specific object in the world. In sequence with the other two, Helena's comment reflects a dawning clarity. She preserves the self-awareness in Hermia's comment and changes the rather vague and subjective "these things" of the other two into Demetrius. But there's still an indeterminacy, a doubleness, about him and their relationship.

For so long she has seen and heard and felt only that the man she loves does not belong to her, and yet, unless her memory fails her, she has just heard Demetrius confess his love for her to the entire court and heard the duke himself proclaim that they would be wed this day. Memory can play tricks. He loves her, he loves her not, he loves her...Where are they in the cycle? She does well to wonder, the play suggests, because, as Ovid has it, the world is constant only in that it is constantly changing. This wondering may keep her from confusing the love they feel for each other now, which is the free gift of life, with a pride of ownership, which is forced on relationship by *cupiditas*, the desire to possess. As these essays argue, apprehending and then thoroughly comprehending the lines of force between these two loves is what animates a comic outcome.

Finally, there are the polarities of dreaming and waking. When our lovers are still suspended between the two, when "things" come up so quickly and pass out of view, when a word is spoken and is lost again in a vast silence, they have to question what is real and can be relied on for guidance, and so Demetrius asks:

> *Are you sure*
>
> *That we are awake? It seems to me*
>
> *That yet we sleep, we dream. Do not you think*
>
> *The Duke was here, and bid us follow him?*

Demetrius, an autonomous individual, has a sense of what has happened, but he can't say for sure. The others, therefore, chime in to establish the fact:

> *Her.*   *Yea, and my father.*
>
> *Hel.*   *And Hippolyta.*
>
> *Lys.*   *And he did bid us follow to the temple.*
>
> *Dem.*   *Why then, we are awake. Let's follow him,*
>
>   *And by the way let us recount our dreams.*

This little convocation may be a parliament of fools, but the audience knows that the lovers, for all the uncertainty they are experiencing, have managed in a small way to make a reasonable appraisal of the truth and to move on from there.

They have arrived at a comic conclusion despite the constraint that what any one person can know is limited. Their convocation is a small matter in the scheme of things when contrasted with the government of a nation or of the whole of nature, but their experience in the wood, the things they say to each other there, the confessions of Lysander and Demetrius to Theseus, and their searching for the truth about all of it just now—every word the poet has had them say is a model of true speech, for it's grounded in a vision of "these things," the whole of their experience. It's a comic vision because the actions they now take offer a reasonable prospect for the peace and prosperity of the social order.

The Play's the Thing

What dreams will the lovers recount? Oberon tells Robin earlier (pages 282-283) that they will consist of the adventures they had when they were fully awake in the wood:

> *When next they wake, all this derision*
>
> *Shall seem a dream and fruitless vision...*

Because the poet has added a backstory which features fairies running about in fairyland, for the audience these adventures have a dreamlike quality as suggested by Oberon in the quote and by the play's title. Shakespeare, though, is playing a little trick on us by encouraging this interpretation, and the trick reverses the charm that Oberon has put on the lovers' understanding. If we value our own sanity, we have to believe that what we have seen is not a dream. We are awake, we see the fairies running about, and we see them putting on and taking off the love juice. We overhear Oberon setting the lovers up to think that it was all a dream, but we have seen that "these things" actually happened.

Because we have a larger understanding than the lovers, the poet has put us in the position of knowing that the fairies are real, or, as Coleridge wrote, he has put us in a position where we willingly suspend our disbelief concerning these influences in our lives. This is the particular beauty, Shakespeare discovered, in live drama. Everyone knows it's make-believe.

The audience has come to see and hear make-believe, and the actors know it's make believe. They're actors. It's a funny thing, though, about acting. For the performance to succeed, those in an audience must forget they are watching a play to fully experience the drama taking place before their eyes. People are especially susceptible to this in live drama when real people are playing the parts. Even actors can forget they are playing a part. Our minds are so sensitive and open to language that the words themselves and a plausible reason for saying them can create a world.

Shakespeare's drama exists in a twilight zone much like that of the lovers in this last scene, and his play only half succeeds when those in the audience forget they are watching a play. This part of the play is about waking up characters who have drowned themselves in a dream, and it's also directed at waking up the audience. We in the audience know that the fairies are a literary device and that they are not like the great earthshaking gods of Greece and Rome. Despite this, the fairies represent a vision of the world that's magnetically attractive; we can't help but notice that they are working in the world and in the characters' lives for the good. If the acting and the staging of the play are particularly good, we inhabit this world while events onstage live in our eyes. When the play ends, though, instinctually we will leave the theater and return from whence we came. The ending of the play ensures that we will wake, and all we have witnessed "Shall seem a dream and fruitless vision."

In a world where everything seems double, dreams can seem both unreal and real. By calling the dream "fruitless," Oberon underestimates its power in our lives. After all, he's a fairy, not a human being. Shakespeare understood dreams better, and the continuing popularity of his play proves it. When we wake at the end to return from whence we came, if we have understood the play as he intended, the play may more accurately reflect the reality of the comic universe from whence we derive than the place we left in order to hear his play. The play's the thing that recalls us to that source of all and everything.

Bottom's Dream in Which There Is No Bottom

The recounting of dreams and a questioning of them serves as a prologue for Bottom's awakening, the sleepers' last call. Before his transformation he was in a play, waiting offstage for his next cue. He has been biding his time in a big way, and apparently the first two calls of Theseus' horns failed to penetrate. In keeping with his character, he wakes himself after the lovers' departure and says:

When my cue comes, call me, and I will answer.

He's awake, sort of, but it's a sleepy bit of nonsense. The cue, we all know, is the call, but no matter. Then again, to whom is he speaking? Is he talking to his director, Peter Quince? Does he think that, like a pampered actor, he'll have a nap in the brake before his next entrance and expects Peter Quince to have him ready to go at the proper time? Since he has just spent the night with the fairy queen, considering the cosmic implications of her love, is he, with a practiced wave of his hand, talking to the Stage Manager of the World with whom he is now on such good terms? If so, he is a willing actor. If called, he will answer. If this is so, then he and the world he inhabits is good, maybe even very good, for he is ready to play his part in it. What more could a creator ask of his creatures.

As he wakes more fully, the specifics of his situation begin to return:

My next is "Most fair Pyramus."

Bottom is likely to remember these words because they are the perfect cue for reminding a man like himself to make an entrance, but having remembered to his satisfaction his prominence within the company, he wakes more fully to find that he is completely alone:

Hey-ho! Peter Quince! Flute the bellows-maker! Snout the tinker! Starvling! God's my life! Stol'n hence, and left me asleep!

God's my life! Who would have thought we'd ever hear a confession like that from Bottom. It's a small miracle; Bottom is waking up from more than an ordinary sleep. Once awakened, the situation presents him with an existential question, without him having to formulate or articulate it as such. With everyone having stolen hence, he is forced to ponder his existence as an actor. For a moment, Bottom stands on a ledge of his own little mountaintop and looks out over a world with nothing in it except himself. At least Deucalion had Pyrrha beside him for comfort, and the world was made new around their devotion to each other.

In the instant of taking in how alone he is in the world, Bottom brushes against some small inkling of the bedfellow who lay that night beside him in the grove, and he, too, is suddenly made new:

> *I have had a most rare vision. I have had a dream, past the wit of man to say what dream it was. Man is but an ass if he go about to expound this dream. Methought I was—there is no man can tell what. Methought I was, and methought I had—But man is but a patch'd fool if he will offer to say what methought I had. The eye of man hath not heard, the ear of man hath not seen, man's hand is not able to taste, his tongue to conceive, nor his heart to report what my dream was.*

He awakens to exclaim a vision (to no one in particular) just as Titania did earlier to Oberon. Bottom has had a vision which renews his life, but the truth and the strength of it will go on as well to revive the fortunes of his company and cheer the entire court of Theseus with a comic entertainment. This from a man who has literally been an ass for a night and who has figuratively been an ass his entire life. The audience once again has the advantage of knowing more than he so we watch him testing his memory as he touches his head and his ears with wonder and relief. Because the audience knows more than he about his egocentricity and the joke Robin played on him, we see him struggling with those large furry ears that play such a prominent part in his "dream." Once he establishes that he is indeed himself and that he need not make an ass of himself expounding his dream, he reassures himself with what he maintains at the beginning, that this dream is past the wit not just of himself but of humankind to say what it is.

Again, though, the joke would be on the audience if we look down our noses at a man who wrestles with the fact that he's a fool. If we see the large furry ears as a big problem, we are distorting the record, for this is what Titania said to him in her bower:

> Come, sit thee down upon this flowery bed,
>
> While I thy amiable cheeks do coy,
>
> And stick musk-roses in thy sleek smooth head,
>
> And kiss thy fair large ears, my gentle joy.

Bottom's ears, which we would avoid like the plague, are what Titania chiefly loves. If we regard Bottom as a poor fool who would try to forget or cover up or say that it's past the wit of man to express that's he's a fool, then we choose to play down the fact that this fool has spent the night entwined with the fairy queen. We choose to overlook it at our peril, for it preserves a foolish sense of our own wit and ignores the poverty of our own experience.

Despite at first asserting that his dream is beyond comprehension in human speech, perhaps with the touch of Titania more prominent in his mind than those other things, he reverses himself decisively:

> I will get Peter Quince to write a ballet of this dream. It shall be call'd "Bottom's dream," because it hath no bottom; and I will sing it in the latter end of our play, before the Duke. Peradventure, to make it the more gracious, I shall sing it at her death.

With that he exits the stage to find his fellows. Peter Quince must not have wanted to insert the ballet into their performance because the play we see in Act V doesn't include it. Clowns are notorious for ad-libbing and upsetting the balance of a scene with cheap effects. Still, it shows that Bottom has fully integrated the experience into his character, on- and offstage. He justifies calling the ballad "Bottom's dream" because it has no bottom, and on its surface this is a formulation that lacks a firm foundation in sense. Without a precise, literal meaning, it's open to interpretation.

Perhaps he's saying that since it's all just a dream, it's an airy nothing. As in a dream, things lack a solid floor, a bottom. Images swim in and out of view weightlessly without the gravity of a clear and present cause. It's a world that's endlessly in all ways subjective. On the other hand, he may be saying that, since he doesn't recognize as himself the creature with long ears in his dream, then his dream has no Bottom. (The fact that the second "bottom" is not capitalized does not factor for a word that is spoken in live theater.) Bottom has disappeared. This second interpretation is reinforced by the fact that the "shivering shocks" of finding himself alone in the wood has rocked the foundation of his life. It turns out that he depends for his very existence on those other hard-handed men of Athens. Without them, there is no Bottom, the one everyone knows and loves including himself. It's a world that's endlessly and in all ways objective. For Bottom, a world in which there is no Bottom, while not quite unthinkable, could only be a dream.

The ballet he would have Peter Quince write for him (which Shakespeare has in fact accomplished in the form of the entire play rather than a ballet) will have to outline the lines of force stretched between these polarities. The lines of force radiate out around a core of question about human autonomy. At some point in our history, human beings realized that they were subjective creators of a whole world, and literature has tried to account for the great consequence of this insight. These poets would demonstrate that the world depends on even so foolish a man as Bottom being born into it, sensing it, and bringing it to life in his awareness.

Perhaps people first saw this in their dreams; for a dream cannot exist without a dreamer, and everything in the dream is a projection of the dreamer. From the subjectivity of dreams, it's a small but significant step to conclude that the conscious mind has roughly the same power. It can shape what it sees with an interpretive frame and give it a meaning that's like the power of a creator. It compels Helena to say of everyone that, "Love looks, not with the eyes, but with the mind."

The power of mind is a great power; but as people have known since ancient days, it's a sorcerer's power which can lead to all the tools and conveniences that allow us to shape the world in our own image and do our work for us but which, in the hands of an apprentice, can also precipitate a great flood. Our autonomy and creativity may be what was alluded to when scripture tells us we were made in the Creator's image, but our autonomy also exposes us to the sense that we are isolated and cut off, that our consciousness is but a tiny, drowned, flyspeck in the scheme of things. We wake up, as Bottom did, to find ourselves completely alone in the wood, or to find that we stand on a ledge of a mountain or on the deck of a small boat looking out over a world that's been drowned.

So let's relive that moment when Bottom wakes up to find himself talking to the emptiness of the wood. When he realizes that's what he's doing, it's a terrible shock. The world is no longer a predictable audience of friends and admirers. Instead, it's a place of bottomless wonder, of shifting currents of light and shade, sounds and silence, that come and go without any rhyme or reason; time, which depends on the chiming of church bells and all the ritualized movements of a day lived in a social context, ceases to exist in a limitless, bottomless present. The wonder, though, can quickly turn to fear. When his friends centrifugally whirl away from him into the void, he wakes up in the grip of an undomesticated, objective power and cries out without thinking, "God's my life."

Characters in a comedy are swept up, like a swimmer caught in the vortex of a whirlpool, and separated from the people and the things that compose their world. Bottom is separated from his companions; Oberon is separated from Titania; Demetrius separates himself from Helena, and then Hermia separates herself from him; Lysander pries open Hermia's grip on him; Oberon and Titania ignore their normal duties; and the Athenians leave their town to come into the wood. Yet the piece is constructed in such a way that individual characters can't exist without the other players or their everyday routines for very long. Social contact is the air we breathe. Bottom lingers there, underwater in the whirlpool, for a matter of milliseconds; rather than drown, he would live. In comedy, there are no geniuses who soar above the trials of ordinary life and come down with a final solution for social order. Comedy itself is king, and it speaks to us in the experiences of ordinary life. When Bottom, Oberon, Titania, and the four lovers fall into the free flow and interdependence of all things, they push off from there in time for a comic conclusion.

Bottom is an ass, but his dream may be the best we can do. In his dream he senses a world without a solid bottom (Bottom) because it consists of elements that come unglued and take other shapes, but that experience has shocked him into an appreciation for the power of the whole. His dream lays the foundation for the social order he now longs to rejoin.

The Hero's Return

Bottom's friends long for his return as much as he longs to resume his position among them. They think he is forever transported away from them, but they are not at all concerned about the shape he took. They still believe "he hath simply the best wit of any any handicraft man in Athens." More materially, they have heard about the duke's plans for three marriages. Without Bottom they have no play, and with him, "we had all been made men." These handicraft men may lack the agile wits of their betters, but they understand, perhaps better than wealthy and autonomous aristocrats, that they depend on each other for their mutual prosperity. The loss prompts Flute to exclaim:

O sweet bully Bottom! Thus hath he lost sixpence a day during his life.
He could not have scaped sixpence a day. An the Duke had not given
him sixpence a day for playing Pyramus, I'll be hanged! He would have
deserved it. Sixpence a day in Pyramus, or nothing!

Flute mourns, not his own loss, but that of the one he feels is most deserving. His generosity matches or goes beyond what the duke would give Bottom for playing Pyramus. The night is darkest right before the dawn, however, for just as Flute finishes his lament, Bottom appears in their midst greeting them joyfully, "Where are these lads? Where are these hearts?"

Even Peter Quince is glad to see him. This is an entrance to be savored, and so Bottom tempts them with the story of his adventure in the wood:

Masters, I am to discourse wonders; but ask me not what. For if I tell you,
I am not true Athenian.

He's apparently more comfortable with leaving it a wonder and a mystery than with talking about it in the light of day. Perhaps a true Athenian speaks only about that which can be verified in the light of day. To make matters even more cryptic and confusing, in the next breath he seems to change his mind and assures them, "I will tell you everything, right as it fell out." It happens that "right as it fell out" touches on how the bottom fell out of a world that a rational Athenian would recognize. Perhaps this is why, when Peter Quince presses him, "Let us hear, sweet Bottom," he replies, as if there were no Bottom in his story, "Not a word of me." Notwithstanding these puzzling non sequiturs, he follows them up with the straightforward intelligence that the duke has dined and their play is preferred. With that and some final instructions, he sends them on their way to prepare for their performance.

A Midsummer Night's Dream is a treasure trove for insight into the nature of Shakespeare's comedy. In contrast with Robin, who is so small and light, Bottom adds a worldly weight and heft to our understanding. In the end, like everything in the world, he is hard to pin down. He's a fool, and yet his fellows revere and follow him. He bullies them in the beginning, and yet he now joins them with a hearty friendship and a hopeful prospect for success. Before his transformation he was simply Bottom the Weaver, but now there's a strangeness and a mystery about him. He's the hero who has gone where none of them has ever gone before, and he has come back to make them all men. It's a narrative suitable for a romance, but Bottom is the unlikeliest of heroes. Comedy, after all, is about the everyday. They will be made men by the duke's pension, which puts their whole quest in the wood on a business footing. If Bottom can discourse wonders, it must mean that these wonders are available to everyone regardless of their birth or capacity. By a strange fluke of nature, Bottom has spent a night in the wood with the fairy queen, but the wonders that will endure for him are nestled like little pearls in the everyday labors of craftsmen and countrymen and in their fellowship.

CHAPTER TWELVE:
THE GOVERNMENT OF THESEUS

W. Homer's *Rowing Home*

The Ark of Comedy

In Act IV the lovers' exile ends, and they return home. After the flood of thought and feeling into which they sank in the wood, they are drawn back, like the swollen waters flooding the world that Triton calls back to their sources, to Athens and the law of Athens. Overnight the seat of that law subtly changes from the throne only Theseus could occupy into a structure that's more like the comedy we are witnessing. As the lovers do, almost instinctively Theseus heads for the wood to enjoy the open air, the excitement, and the beauty of the hunt. When he finds the lovers and observes the influence on them of the night rule that presides there, he overrules Athenian law far from his palace in a natural setting. Like the play itself, the seat of judgment has been established in the everyday experiences of ordinary men and women, which include the countrymen and women that are the objects of Robin's sport, the workingmen who ply their trades in the town, and the men and women who lose their heads and follow their hearts.

With that last in mind, Theseus' law and his court have been baby-proofed into a place suitable for bringing children into the world. From the beginning human beings from all parts of the globe have discovered with each generation that to live a decent life in a social context, both children and adults need a structure, a language with which they can negotiate their way with each other and with which they can shape the natural world into an environment for human life. As the opening incident with Hermia illustrates, parents quickly learn that children will test the reality of that structure, so as a practical matter it must reflect, as best it can, the world as it is. It has to have, like an ark in the midst of a great flood, a bottom the way ships have bottoms on which creatures like ourselves can stand and move and breathe the sweet air, but this bottom can't be merely a fantasy. It requires the experience of all those who have sailed those waters as they venture far from shore to explore new lands. We have seen ships like this sailing on the deep in Titania's narrative about the mother who gave birth to the Indian boy she would raise up. Those ships suggest as well the wooden ark of the theater in which people watching the play find themselves. Filing into the Shakespeare's theater, they have come one by one, two by two, or in any combination they like to be transported, like Odysseus in the stern of the Phaeacians' ship, through perilous waters to the safety of "the source / From which they were derived, to which they course."

Some ships are built with bad ideas. My wife and I visited a museum in Stockholm for the Vasa, a great warship from the seventeenth century loaded with cannon. Because it was designed more to suit the whims of the king than to suit the waters in which it would sail, the resulting design was so top heavy that it keeled over on its maiden voyage and sank before it even left the harbor. Despite the loss, this beautiful vessel—decked with elaborate carvings, decorative flags, lines of rigging running everywhere, and a huge arsenal for trumpeting the power of the Swedish state—stood on display in a grand museum after a wealthy modern government salvaged it and restored it to its former glory. It's a curious homage to a failed experiment. The Vasa sank a few years after Shakespeare's death, but for centuries before that people had frequently observed that some ships sailed the ocean blue better than others, and some captains ran those ships better than other captains. English ships and English captains that opposed the armada proved this decisively when they out maneuvered Spanish ships in the critical early sea battles of the invasion. It was a victory reminiscent of Salamis where the smaller ships and better timing of the Greeks defeated a larger and more heavily armed enemy.

If the great victory over the armada proved empirically that the ideas about ships and the strategy of one force can triumph over the ideas and the strategy of another, as Englishmen of Shakespeare's day thought that it did, then it's just a short step to affirm that some ideas about government are more successful in the way they conduct the essential business of a state than other ideas. The threat of invasion by Spanish Catholic forces awoke in English men and women a national will to defend their warrior queen, their institutions like Parliament for preserving English liberties that had been established out of previous conflicts with authoritarian rulers, and their land itself—"this precious stone set in the silver sea." The military success of English Sea Dogs sanctioned the right of Elizabeth to remain on her throne and rule her nation. The Spanish armada and Elizabeth's bravery in the face of it transformed the Protestant revolution, which began with her father as a way to solve a dynastic problem, into a way of defining England as a nation united under one government. It was a revolution much like our own in that the English now ruled themselves without interference from Rome. Just as some ships do better in rough seas, some nations do better in an interdependent but choppy modern world when the government of the state is defined by clear lines of authority, an authority that's close to the people.

To govern themselves well, though, the people cannot busy themselves merely with parochial concerns. If we read Homer's stories and the histories of the Hebrew Bible, we learn from them that the world has always been a vast network of interconnected nations and peoples. As explorers from Portugal, Spain, the Netherlands, and England opened up sea lanes of commerce both to the East and to the West, Europe was being transformed from a patchwork of feudal holdings into well-organized nation states that competed for maximum advantage and extended their influence as far as they possibly could. This kind of competition has been around from the time people began to gather into larger social units, and dominant cities created the fabled Eastern empires of ancient times. But in Shakespeare's day the locus of empire was in the process of a profound shift from those Eastern lands to northern European countries bordering the Atlantic. That shift westward has continued into the present. It must be said, however, that no single power center has ever gathered unto itself the reins of government for the entire world, though not for lack of trying on the part of those who would be an emperor of everything.

A comic worldview gives us a rational explanation for why this is so. Because human beings are by their nature radically limited, it simply can't be done. No ruling power, whether it's a single person or a politburo or an international body, can ever have sufficient knowledge of how everything works in order to govern the whole. Our play implies that the same can be said for power centers within an individual state. Absolute rulers like Theseus will always be caught in incidents like the one at the beginning of the play where a subordinate insists on killing someone (even a daughter) who will not submit to his authority. Theseus makes the best of a bad situation, but the imposition of his and Egeus' will on the body of a young girl doesn't inspire confidence. Multiply Hermia's case by millions and spread them across a nation, and this early scene in the play explains why absolute authority and the empire it seeks must ultimately fail because they cannot and will not satisfy the life force, the animal spirits of autonomous individuals.

The play also shows that a ruler like Theseus depends not on his own will but on the little people, the animal spirits of which he may not be aware, to do the real business of government. The fairies are the ones who bring the lovers to a settlement during the midsummer night before Hermia has to make her choice, and they get Theseus out of the jam into which his authority and his limited, unjust options put him. Even as this reading broadens the issue to make the case that an authoritarian juggernaut can't effectively govern its people, it's not making the case for anarchy. If true government is self-government, then the government that governs best governs least, but Jefferson's famous stricture implies the active presence of an intelligent and deeply rooted culture that teaches and celebrates in its families, in its schools, and in its laws the virtues of self-government. Given the prominent role they have had within the culture, the works of Chaucer and Shakespeare have taught these virtues in the most pleasing and persuasive way possible; they have absorbed the attention of the people with a magic mirror that reflects them both as they are and as they would wish to be—as autonomous, self-governing members of a social order.

The people of Shakespeare's time knew from the history of kings like Richard II that a government with a bunker mentality cannot successfully govern, and they learned from bitter experience that even an island like England can't withdraw from the rest of the world. The Spanish invasion made them aware (the way 911 has in our recent history) that no country exists in isolation, not when a hostile power can come calling to knock down your house without your permission. Every country, whether it likes it or not, is going to conduct its business not just in the tight confines of a homogeneous, traditional, and commonly accepted culture that's an island unto itself but also in the push and pull, the shouting and the sales pitches in many different languages, of a noisy marketplace where competition can sometimes escalate into a fight.

Shakespeare wrote extensively about the progress of English government through its history and about England's relations with foreign powers, but the image of a marketplace brings us back to one of Shakespeare's primary concerns as an actor, a playwright, a poet (who would make a name for himself through the relatively new media of publishing), and owner of a theater in a town with other theaters that competed with it for audiences. Because he was a businessman and a savvy competitor, he and his company had to convince the court of public opinion that some plays are better than other plays. He didn't live to appreciate it, but people all over the world who have attended and studied his works now for over four hundred years have conclusively proven his point. Why, then, has Shakespeare succeeded and others failed? This reading of his play argues that his great strength as a writer is rooted in the depth and accuracy of his vision, which accounts as well for the creativity he employs for conveying it. He writes from a secure source that offers the world's riches like a horn of plenty.

A large part of what he sees consists in an awareness, to which he was helped by God's plenty that he found in Chaucer, of what he doesn't see. As Chaucer did, he sees people motivated by love. It's our life force and governs our behaviors. Also like Chaucer he eventually came to understand from bitter experience that a life entirely motivated by an object of desire can effectively imprison the lover from the world as a whole. While an obsessive attachment to something beautiful, like a pleasing apple in a tree that doesn't belong to him, may excite a lover with a desire for the dignity and beauty of its form (even if it's just a mental object), the government of his life will suffer from big and little mistakes in the obsessive attempt to possess it. He fails, as the king of Sweden did, for he has looked primarily at the object rather than the whole of which it is a part. When an object of desire is so bright, pleasing, and obvious, the dark background from which it shines forth hardly registers. Because everything within a lover's field of vision intrinsically has a relationship with the lover, the lover himself is the darkness out of which the object emerges. Comedy makes the case that, for a lover who would sail through the storms of life with some safety and security, the way he looks must involve an appreciation for the narrow (but life-saving) perch from which the world is observed. If the king had realized his limitations as a shipbuilder better, he would have designed a better ship. He didn't see what he didn't see.

It's a vision like the sight of a blind man, and it guides Shakespeare's writing. Throughout his works, in different forms and with a different emphasis, he also sees that the way love looks is closely linked to the lover's conduct in the world. If love consists of desire frustrated by obstacles, then the lover unilaterally declares war on the world and fights tooth and nail for satisfaction of the Will. (Shakespeare sometimes made little jokes with his first name like this, especially in the sonnets. One legendary story has him proclaiming himself William the Conqueror after a sexual conquest.[60]) If love consists of a piercing insight, like that of Chaucer's Arcite on his deathbed, which empties out all forms of love and hate in the glimpse of a larger intelligence, then the lover and the world are no longer estranged. Then comedy is king, and like a good matchmaker it arranges a marriage between the two.

Because Shakespeare sees that love and government are informed by the quality of a person's vision, the heart of his own vision can be summarized as the first two words in Helena's formulation that "Love looks." This abridgment of her sentence emphasizes that love isn't a specific emotion which proves that we love and for which we search high and low in our emotional register. It's not hidden away like buried treasure in another person, in a perfect house or garden, in a religious or political doctrine that's the object of a lifelong quest. It's not tied to any specific outcome we wish for in the world; even in a moment, in the twinkling of an eye, the world by which we gauged that outcome is changing its shape into something else.

Like looking, love is action, not an object. Like looking is for those with eyes to see, love is what we do and can't be "helped" or suppressed. While immaterial, the way a ghost or a fairy is immaterial, love is as obvious as the nose on our face in between the two eyes, but it must be admitted that looking at our own nose takes a little imagination. It's as common as breathing and as looking at the world, but it can look either with the eyes (which in ancient tradition blind seers like Homer or Teiresias do better than sighted observers) or with the mind. Shakespeare's stories illustrate that the way love looks in the end governs whether the person's story will conclude as a comedy or a tragedy. Shakespeare has written the greatest tragedies in the language, but the vision underlying them is steadfastly comic. With great compassion, his plays act out on a rickety scaffold the anguish of a tragic vision, but they keep in mind that that vision is being played out within a much larger vehicle, something strong and seaworthy, an ark that transports those within safely through a deluge of sorrow into a world for which they have new eyes. It's a comic vision and a constant theme in the literature of mankind. The urgency with which people have sought out a comic master like Shakespeare reminds me of the passion with which Helena says to Hermia, "Oh, teach me how you look."

These observations set the stage for the conclusion of *A Midsummer Night's Dream*. The necessary action of the play is done: the war between Theseus and Hippolyta had ended even before the play began, the lovers' affairs have been sorted out so that the law of Athens can be harmlessly overruled, Titania and Oberon are new in amity, and the play of Pyramus and Thisby has been preferred by the duke. Now that the world-as-it-is has pronounced its sentence on the lovers, what's needed is only the period at the end to punctuate it, the little 0 after which all is silence. Or so it would seem. The opening scene of Act V, however, returns to that strain with which the play begins, the dark undercurrent in the relations of Theseus and Hippolyta. The little O at the end has to wait until the government of Theseus addresses it.

The Voice of Reason

And so at the beginning of Act V, Theseus takes center stage as the most important figure in the court of Athens to which the play has returned. Chaucer's Theseus brings "The Knight's Tale" to a comic conclusion with a magnificent and very long final speech, and Hippolyta gives Shakespeare's Theseus a similar opening for a thoughtful summing up when she observes:

> 'Tis strange, my Theseus, that these lovers speak of.

She doesn't specify of what they have been speaking. Most likely they were describing the adventures of the lovers' midsummer eve, so once again the play specifically raises the issue of how they will remember "these things." Oberon has commanded that they will recall them only as a dream while Hippolyta's statement implies that the things of which they speak actually happened. There's nothing strange about a dream being strange.

Theseus replies positively:

> More strange than true. I never may believe
>
> These antique fables nor these fairy toys.

Even though we don't know exactly what fairy toys he means, it would seem that the lovers have been talking about the craziness of their midsummer night. Demetrius has already told Theseus that overnight his love for Hermia melted away, and his love for Helena returned full force. In itself, this is not strange as people often enough fall in and out of love. Hippolyta must have been struck with a sense of strangeness when the other lovers elaborated on Demetrius' brief outline of events. Perhaps, they told the court that Lysander, too, broke faith with Hermia and followed Helena; that the two men then quarreled over Helena at night as bitterly as they had quarreled over Hermia in the afternoon; and that in the morning, Lysander's love for Helena having melted away while he slept, his love for Hermia returned. Perhaps they included other details, like getting lost as they each rushed to satisfy their own inclinations, and yet, when roused by Theseus' horn, woke up lying like lovers on the ground together. Hippolyta finds these stories strange, but for a seasoned man of the world like Theseus, they are too strange to be true. And fairies certainly have nothing to do with them.

When Theseus and his court discover the four lovers lying together in the wood and Egeus wonders of their being there together, Theseus takes control of the strangeness and uncertainty by giving a rational explanation for their presence. They came, he says, to honor the rites of May, which is more or less an accurate statement, and to honor Hippolyta and himself on their wedding day, which the audience knows is wildly inaccurate. Hippolyta's comment on the strangeness of the lovers' stories gives Theseus the same opportunity to take control of the strangeness and uncertainty with a reasoned argument:

> Lovers and madmen have such seething brains,
>
> Such shaping fantasies, that apprehend
>
> More than cool reason ever comprehends.

Our lovers, Theseus declares, are under the influence of love and have been engaged in a kind of dreaming. Taken at face value, though, Theseus' opening sentence affirms the power of imagination to sense more than reason can grasp. The poet who wrote these words for him undoubtedly agrees that there's a power that apprehends more than cool reason can ever comprehend. After all, Shakespeare has apprehended a fairyland—which includes all the shenanigans of Oberon, Titania, Robin, and the juice of the two flowers—in order to dramatize a comprehensive dynamism (impossible to quantify) between a love that looks with the mind and a love that looks with the eyes.

Theseus parts company with his creator, though, as he goes on to explain what he finds so troubling about the seething brains of imaginative men:

The lunatic, the lover, and the poet

Are of imagination all compact.

Like a Polonius warning his son Laertes about the dangers awaiting him when he leaves home for his first semester at college,[61] Theseus is advising Hippolyta and all the lords and ladies of his court that the lovers among them had best beware of the company they keep. His description of the lunatic sets an overall tone of disapproval:

One sees more devils than vast hell can hold:

That is the madman. The lover, all as frantic,

Sees Helen's beauty in a brow of Egypt.

The imagination drives the lunatic crazy, and it drives the lover to see in the world what isn't there, which may eventually drive him crazy.

So far in his quarrel with imagination, Theseus' reason has knocked two straw men out of the ring. When he squares off against the poet, however, his argument takes on a life of its own, and once again he appears to be arguing from the other side:

> *The poet's eye, in a fine frenzy rolling,*
>
> *Doth glance from heaven to earth, from earth to heaven;*
>
> *And as the imagination bodies forth*
>
> *The forms of things unknown, the poet's pen*
>
> *Turns to shapes, and gives to airy nothing*
>
> *A local habitation and a name.*

How quickly Theseus dispatches his first two opponents and with what dispatch his own imagination overthrows his reason to utter a timeless credo for poetry.

The rest of his little speech rallies a bit on reason's behalf:

> *Such tricks hath strong imagination*
>
> *That, if it would but apprehend some joy,*
>
> *It comprehends some bringer of that joy;*
>
> *Or in the night, imagining some fear,*
>
> *How easy is a bush supposed a bear!*

First he makes the quite reasonable argument that imagination tempts gullible people with pleasing but imaginary outcomes, and he then concludes with a folksy, homespun example of another perceptual trick. Because imagination is unstable and overactive, it tends to suppose a harmless bush to be a bear and causes panic. Since the panic of even one person can quickly infect others, a duke must fear and guard against it in the people he rules.

Unwittingly, though, once again he makes the case not only for imagination but for comedy as well. Theseus closes by indicting imagination as a cause of fear, but in the previous lines he has just imagined a way of looking at the world whereby an imaginative observer, which is Everyman, apprehends some joy despite the fear that generally rules his life. Everyone's panic, in the end, is rooted in a tragic view of life that's the product of imagination. That view of life is confirmed when something rears up to shred us into pieces. We panic, but until an actual bear tears us into pieces, the "bear" we imagine will always be only a bush. This is a fact, but it takes a strong imagination to deliver this message when the need for it strikes, and the need is always great. The power of the imagination to apprehend some joy and comprehend a bringer of that joy counterbalances the fear induced by a tragic view of life. As the basis for steadfastness and intelligent action, the power of imagination is called upon to reason with fear.

Poor Theseus. He would be the voice of reason, but his own words speak with a voice of their own against his reasons. His argument here in favor of reason is sensible and wise, and yet the play tends to undercut it. Lysander gives a speech about reason earlier when he explains to Helena, after the flower juice has been poured on his eyes, that "The will of man is by his reason swayed." He also makes perfect sense and speaks wisely when he observes that "Things growing are not ripe until their season." While he's correct to say that reason must ripen with experience, he incorrectly assumes that his own reason has reached that point. Lysander thinks he is the voice of reason, but the audience knows that it's just the flower juice talking. Theseus is far more experienced in the ways of the world than Lysander, but his reason, we are led to believe, may be as limited and as captive to subconscious motives as Lysander's. The final and most obvious nail in the coffin of Theseus' argument is supplied by the audience as it was in Lysander's case, for the narrative structure of the play itself conspires against him. When Theseus rejects the lovers' stories as more strange than true, he contradicts what we have seen with our own eyes. If we have suspended our disbelief in order to fully engage with the play acted out before us, then we know that these things, though strange, are true.

A Marriage of Reason and Imagination

As the mind plays with this fairy toy that Shakespeare has made, our interaction with it makes us more aware of what lies on the other side of reason's frontier. A reasonable man like Theseus likes to characterize that which is beyond his ken as a fairy toy, an old wives' tale a grandmother tells the children from her corner seat by the fireplace. A reasonable man's authority depends on what can be proved. Since those things beyond reason's frontier can't be proved, he, quite reasonably, discounts or ignores them. What a man doesn't know, however, can easily enough make an entrance that changes the course of his life, like a horse suddenly rearing up (over nothing) and crushing his heart with the saddle bow. For example, Theseus didn't know, when he looked at the moon and saw a stepdame or a dowager, that he might offend the sensibilities of his future wife, and the image of mighty Theseus may have suffered when Hippolyta has to inform him that he would find that moon to be a vibrant, warrior queen.

Rational thinkers have scoffed for centuries at those who believe in fairy toys and other supernatural and paranormal phenomena, and with his fairy toy of a play Shakespeare indulges their fancy. The play illustrates, though, that these thinkers are largely missing the point. The problem is not with silly ideas about the supernatural but with ignorance and with judgments that fail to properly take ignorance into account. The mind that reasons the way Theseus does here makes assumptions about life from what it knows. Reason does very well categorizing and systematizing what it knows, but all this proves to be beside the point when it has to deal with what it doesn't know. From the opening lines of the play, Hippolyta, as a woman and a representative of the moon goddess, represents what Theseus, as an autonomous subject, cannot know. He proves his ignorance when he makes it clear that he doesn't know how she looks at the moon; more to the point for their upcoming marriage, he doesn't know how she looks at him.

Theseus' speech about reason and imagination is often quoted. He probably thought it was pretty good, too, or he wouldn't have troubled himself with it. But Hippolyta's response, even without the benefit of a view from the mountain top like that of the audience, comes closer than her husband to the truth:

> But all the story of the night told over,
>
> And all their minds transfigur'd so together,
>
> More witnesseth than fancy's images
>
> And grows to something of great constancy;
>
> But howsoever, strange and admirable.

Her judgment reprises the four lovers' delightful scene when Theseus and his court suddenly left them alone, and they conducted their little parliament of fools to make sure that what each one thought happened actually happened. They needed to establish this before moving on to Athens.

Like them, Hippolyta resolves her doubts when she observes that each lover's dream confirms the dreams of the others, and taken together they grow from mere fancy to a witness of something constant and true. Moments earlier, Theseus describes in a few lines of great power the work of a poet, and what Hippolyta says here describes the great work of comedy. Like the speech that Chaucer's Theseus gives, comedy depicts a way of looking at the world that relies on experience. A small child employs no logic in learning to walk or ride a bike. The setbacks in these experiences establish a recognizable pattern derived from sensing a "something" that is constant. Unlike her husband, Hippolyta and the lovers are inclined to credit an experience, bizarre though it may be, in which they realize their love. The midsummer night of love may be a kind of madness, but in the end they all sense something that allows them to move ahead with their lives.

Because the one is a man and the other a woman, Oberon and Titania make different claims for the beautiful Indian boy. Oberon would raise the boy up to be a man whereas Titania strongly identifies with the woman who grew the child in her womb and who would have nurtured him once he was born if she had lived. Theseus and Hippolyta also make different claims for the truth (and beauty) of their respective visions. Theseus is like the noonday sun. He's hot-blooded; he puts the things of this world in a positive light and is not distracted by shadows that have no substance; and like the sun, he moves steadily forward without changing his shape. Hippolyta is like the moon. She reflects her husband, bouncing what he says back to him and out into the world with an indirect illumination; in this reflected light, objects and their shadows are harder to distinguish. Instead of inexorably moving in one direction the way a syllogism does, the moon moves forward (from east to west) and backward (rising in the sky a little later each night) at the same time, and her shape waxes and wanes, wanes and waxes. Like an old moon strangely blooming into a new moon full of promise and beauty, Hippolyta has the wondrous capacity of an autonomous subject for surprising depth and fresh insight.

Both are lovers, but they look at the world with different minds. Trained by Greek thought, Theseus looks by daylight at a world illuminated by ideal forms that reason uncovers out of dark matter. For example, to clear out the clutter of experience and clarify his vision of things, he would make a distinction between evidence that stands to reason and inferences that are too strange and improbable to be believed. For the most part, the modern world wants a leader to proceed like this as long as the leader can admit to making a mistake. Shakespeare's Theseus qualifies as a reasonable man in this way, for he reverses his judgment in Hermia's case when the evidence to support a new judgment outweighs the support for the old one. He shows an awareness that his own understanding might be limited, as in the case with Hermia, but his actions indicate that his concern is primarily with the law and its enforcement. Hippolyta allows more for the autonomy of others. She lives in a less defined world where the lesser lights of the beholder illuminate truth and beauty. She doesn't dismiss the dreams of individuals out of hand; before rendering a judgment, she waits and observes the way those individual dreams grow to something of great constancy.

Because these leaders have an awareness of themselves as a locus of perception, which they sense intuitively or learned by experience when their perceptions proved painfully inadequate, they can acknowledge that a subject like Hermia looks at the world with her own eyes just as they do. She's a subject, meaning she has a mind of her own that moves her—unlike a pawn that's moved by the master on a chessboard. They can also see that their subjects are not merely subjective, like a lunatic who sees devils everywhere or a lover who is hopelessly blinded by love; they have sense and reason enough to guide them.

It's likely, however, that Theseus would more strongly advocate for a limit to that autonomy. Because it's the nature of the law to set limits to behavior, government by nature is coercive; but when the law is aligned with that which is constant in our nature and in the world, it's easier for people to see themselves in the law. If people don't see themselves in a law—like the followers of Dionysus whose king tells them that their god will not be admitted into his town or the friends of a young girl whose father would kill her because she would not marry a man of his choosing, they may rebel and shred the social fabric. Theseus and Hippolyta are no different in the way they raise these issues with each other than ordinary parents trying their best to guide their children or than anyone who lives in close contact with others in a social context. Theseus and Hippolyta look at the world differently, but their marriage bodes well for the security and prosperity of their children and the state.

To a baseline of common sense that Theseus and Hippolyta possess, the play adds the insight that Everyman, including Theseus, is a poet in that Everyman doesn't just live in a world of material fact. To live well and to keep one's spirits up, the imagination of Everyman will give a local habitation and a name to that in life which is good. There are many names for this—like truth, beauty, justice—and one of them is comedy.

A Choice of Abridgment

A. A Written Brief in Favor of Tragedy for Abridging the Time

The marriage of Theseus and Hippolyta has a hopeful prospect because the one's autonomous point of view serves as a comic reality check on the other's. Along with consistently presenting specific instances of this autonomy, the play also makes the case that autonomous human beings have a choice about the way they look more generally at any given situation: it can viewed either as an incident in a tragedy or a comedy. For example, Theseus could impulsively dismiss Hippolyta's judgment, bait her temper with an assertion of his authority, and reignite a war between them that ends in tragedy. He could, but he doesn't.

If Theseus is put off by Hippolyta once more begging to differ with his assessment of a situation, once again in front of the lords and ladies and attendants of the court, he doesn't show it, perhaps because the conversation is interrupted by the entrance onstage of the four newly married lovers in the flesh. Theseus greets them with delight:

> Here come the lovers, full of joy and mirth.
>
> Joy, gentle friends, joy and fresh days of love
>
> Accompany your hearts.

Not for the first time he chooses to ignore a sticking point with Hippolyta;

instead, he turns everyone's attention to the appearance of these attractive young adults. Because his words are so hearty and direct, it may be that, in Theseus' eyes, the debate about them pales in comparison with their actual presence. Lysander, the ringleader of his and Hermia's little rebellion, gratefully replies:

> *More than to us*
>
> *Wait in your royal walks, your board, your bed!*

Lysander may be young, but he can be gracious with a dash of manly worldliness. He speaks deferentially but with a hint that everyone, including Theseus, shares those things which are satisfied in their walks, their mealtimes, and their beds.

Whatever the reason, Theseus takes Hippolyta's self-assertion in stride. After these greetings he directs their attention to the problem the three couples have in common. Now that the walking and the eating have been looked to, that leaves only the bed still waiting:

> *Come now, what masques, what dances shall we have,*
>
> *To wear away this long age of three hours*
>
> *Between our after-supper and bedtime?*
>
> *Where is our usual manager of mirth?*
>
> *What revels are in hand? Is there no play*
>
> *To ease the anguish of a torturing hour?*
>
> *Call Philostrate.*

Lo and behold, Theseus has returned to square one, complaining yet again about the many hours that separate him from what he chiefly wants. The time has been reduced from four days to three hours, but the gap between after-supper and bedtime would appear to be just as painful an interval, perhaps more so. He's surely exaggerating for effect, but his unsatisfied desire is exhibit A in the play of that which has grown to something of great constancy.

As quickly as ever Robin served Oberon's commands, Philostrate answers, "Here, mighty Theseus," and so Theseus asks his manager of mirth directly:

Say, what abridgment have you for this evening?

What masque? What music? How shall we beguile

The lazy time, if not with some delight?

Since he has to wait three more hours before he can release his anguish in the way he might like, he seeks from Philostrate an abridgment of the gap that divides him from his object.

A long age of three hours strikes him as an impenetrable barrier, but only if he is conscious of it. If he were asleep, like Odysseus when the Phaeacians brought him home in the stern of their ship, then the gap would disappear along with consciousness. He can't just take his leave for a nap, though. He's the duke, the bridegroom at a wedding feast as well as the host of his fellow celebrants and many guests. To solve the problem, he turns, as he did in Act I when he took that shot from Hippolyta's moon "New bent in heaven," to his manager of mirth.

Poor Theseus. People call him mighty, and like his servant Philostrate, our poet appears to agree. He deserves his reputation as a soldier, a leader of his people, and a lover, for he's an attractive, charismatic figure. Shakespeare further endows him with an understanding that goes beyond material and mundane matters. He's a mighty conqueror, but he cannot consciously defeat those three long hours. His complaint, while it takes the shine off his mightiness, sets him down as a man among other men and makes him apt for comedy.

The call for his manager of mirth is recognition by even one so great as Theseus that comedy is king. The pain he suffers from unfulfilled desire is not a personal problem. Rather, according to this reading of Chaucer and Shakespeare, it's at the heart of the human condition. Chaucer calls it *cupiditas*, and his tales present different forms of it. The prominence that Shakespeare gives the problem of desire at the beginning of the play and again at the end suggests that it's a chronic condition, an underlying and ever-present motive force common to Everyman.

A duke like Theseus may think that he can direct the passions of others in a way that's convenient for him, but his attempt to do that in Hermia's case is overruled by motive forces greater than his own. Shakespeare can imagine a magical story in which an arrow of desire is quenched in the chaste beams of the watery moon, but Oberon's telling of it suggests that the dousing of that fire is easier aimed at than effected. Instead, the burning arrow misses its target and reposes somewhere else, in a little western flower now rich with Cupid's spell. Despite Theseus' confidence that he can quench the burning of Hermia's heart, his authority fails in the attempt, and on top of that he's having trouble managing the burning of his own. The play as a whole shows that desire is not personal, but this scene with Philostrate makes the case that the way Everyman deals with it is a choice.

Philostrate has framed the answer to Theseus' question with a program he carefully prepared:

> *There is a brief how many sports are ripe.*
>
> *Make choice of which your Highness will see first.*

From the list Philostrate gives him, Theseus can choose his abridgment. Our manager of mirth calls that little piece of paper a "brief," and this is a word with important associations. First, as a noun it's a legal term. A brief is presented at a trial to resolve a disputed point of evidence, and so the word reminds us of what we have just witnessed in the dialogue between Theseus and Hippolyta. The lovers' stories about their midsummer night is the evidence, and both Theseus and Hippolyta have filed their briefs with the court concerning it. More important, the word alerts the audience that the poet, who is the real manager of mirth, is approaching the court to present his own brief about desire, the pain of desire, and how the wound of desire can be touched with understanding.

Brief as an adjective suggests the balm that Philostrate would apply to the torturing age of three hours. Unlike that obstacle, his little program is brief. It abridges the hours it would take to present the actual entertainments by summarizing them quickly, and so, since he is in an expansive mood, Theseus reads it out loud to the entire court:

> "The battle with the Centaurs, to be sung
>
> By an Athenian eunuch to the harp."

Surely Philostrate has inserted this as a joke on his boss, and it's a very good one. Theseus doesn't disappoint:

> We'll none of that. That have I told my love
>
> In glory of my kinsman Hercules.

Does he not want to bore her with a story she has already heard, or does he not want to introduce an Athenian eunuch into the festivities?

We can only guess, but not for long as Theseus moves on to the next choice:

> "The riot of the tipsy Bacchanals,
>
> Tearing the Thracian singer in their rage."

If the audience never noticed or has forgotten about the ripping and shredding of a creature earlier in the play when Theseus and Hippolyta were out hunting, it shows up here again on Philostrate's program. Since comedy derived from ancient fertility rites, a riot of drunken men and women might advance the original purpose of these entertainments, but the Bacchanalia of this work ends so badly. Our manager of mirth seems to be stuck on stories that one way or another involve a man being cut. Theseus rules this one out as well:

> That is an old device; and it was play'd
>
> When I from Thebes came last a conqueror.

Does he not want to bore himself with story he has already heard, or would a groom on his wedding night prefer not to see a fellow ripped to shreds?

Again, we can only guess as he moves on to the next choice:

> "The thrice three Muses mourning for the death
>
> Of Learning, late deceas'd in beggary."

This one's an allegory so at least it's moving away from the realism of the first two. In the first offering, the sole actor is a man—whose manhood was neutered by someone's knife—telling the story of a bloody battle. In the second, we'll hear about a man who is cut into pieces. Now in this one, it's only the idea of Learning that dies, not an actual man. Still, the vehicle follows the arc (ark) of tragedy. Philostrate's brief doesn't include any cutting in this entertainment, but Theseus finds it anyway:

> That is some satire, keen and critical,
>
> Not sorting with a nuptial ceremony.

We note that the shedding of blood in a great battle or the shredding of a Thracian singer isn't the reason he gives for scratching the first two from the list. He disqualifies them because they are old news. This last offering describes what we would call a current event, but it is disqualified because it is keen and cuts like a knife. If he is right and it's a satire, then possibly it will be aimed at cutting him. This one also cuts a little too close to home.

If what has been presented up to now is the evidence that's being considered in his brief, it appears that Philostrate is arguing, before the high court of the land, in favor of tragedy as the literary form that most nearly mirrors life. Just as people instinctively rubberneck at car crashes (ironically, they add life to the routine of a daily commute), Philostrate supposes that, in the acting out of a death or in the character assassination of a satire, time will slip away—the effect Theseus chiefly desires.

Before Theseus makes his choice as to what will successfully produce the slipping, let's present the evidence for the phenomena itself. The poet proposes that, like all the other things of this world, time itself is subject to its own dynamic; it changes its shape. It's a subject to which Shakespeare continually returns. Already in this play, Hippolyta has had a vision in which:

> Four days will quickly steep themselves in night;
>
> Four nights will quickly dream away the time...

The four days and nights dissolve in the greatness of night and time as if they don't exist as individual entities. Later in the play, the horns of Theseus announce a break in time like a biblical last trump. In keeping with the ancient Greek setting of the play, they signal the presence of timeless archetypes in their midst like a sudden glimpse of Diana bare or the sound of an apocalyptic thunder. These outbreaks show that sometimes time slips away, as it does in Hippolyta's vision, and sometimes it freezes, as in the freezes that line the walls in the temples of Mars, Diana, and

Venus in "The Knight's Tale" or when in *Hamlet* Pyrrhus raises his sword over Priam's head.

Everyone has these experiences. Time slips away in sleep, in kisses, and in any concentrated activity. On Christmas morning, long before the time set by their parents, time hardly moves at all for the children who wait to find what's buried in their stocking. When people undergo a tragic shock, it's hard to say (in retrospect) whether time freezes, like that pause in the instant of Priam's death, or whether it slips away as in moments of great concentration. After the assassination of President Kennedy November 22, 1963, for three days until the funeral the following Monday, our national life stopped; we passed it as in a dream completely absorbed with the story as it unfolded on TV.

Having established that time can change its shape, let's return to the question how best to abridge the time that separates us from what is desired. Philostrate's brief has made its argument three times in different forms, but Theseus, the chief judge in the case, has yet to agree with any of them. This is where the case stands when we come to Peter Quince's play on the list.

B. Oral Arguments over the Pyramus and Thisby Play

The thing Theseus seeks is, as always, in the last place he looks:

"A tedious brief scene of young Pyramus

And his love Thisby; very tragical mirth."

Merry and tragical? tedious and brief?

That is hot ice and wondrous strange snow.

How shall we find the concord of this discord?

Finally, something that gets his attention. Since he's a soldier who deals in death, those other stories are dull and predictable. A man is born, he lives for a bit, and then he dies. Stories like this may be true enough, but it may be that he is satiated with them, like the sweet that made Lysander sick when he ate too much of it. The brief of Peter Quince's play argues instead for a mystery, something he doesn't know, as opposed to stories with which he's all too familiar. If time slips way in rapt attention, a puzzle or a mystery may concentrate the mind more than a stock narrative. Departing from a simple reading of the prepared text, Theseus asks Philostrate to explain the puzzle.

Philostrate may be a trickster. If he likes ironic jokes, like so many modern comedians, he may have enjoyed inserting a eunuch into a program celebrating a marriage just to see how Theseus would react. At the same time, he has created a program that over and over favors a tragic world view regardless of the occasion. Like those who require constant injections of tragedy, which can be satisfied nowadays by watching news shows that are available twenty-four hours of the day, Philostrate considers himself a realist, and realism to him means mirroring life as a tragedy. Continuing the overall tenor of his written brief, he answers the chief justice's question with an oral argument against a play that's an unrealistic mix of tragical mirth:

> *A play there is, my lord, some ten words long,*
>
> *Which is as brief as I have known a play;*
>
> *But by ten words, my lord, it is too long,*
>
> *Which makes it tedious; for in all the play*
>
> *There is not one word apt, one player fitted.*
>
> *And tragical, my noble lord, it is;*
>
> *For Pyramus therein doth kill himself.*
>
> *Which when I saw rehears'd, I must confess,*

Made mine eyes water; but more merry tears

The passion of loud laughter never shed.

The chief justice continues to probe with another question, "What are they that play it?" He would like to know why these ten words are so inapt. Philostrate then makes a curious claim about Peter Quince's company:

Hard-handed men that work in Athens here,

Which never labor'd in their minds till now;

And now have toil'd their unbreathed memories

With this same play, against your nuptial.

Philostrate's answer reveals a basic assumption underlying his brief of this play. To him, people who work with their hands don't work with their minds, for the mind cannot breathe, cannot live unless it is properly stocked with memory.

The mechanicals may be vaguely familiar with the tragedies of ancient Greece and Rome, but Philostrate is arguing that they lack the literary training to understand them. In addition to their lack of learning, the enterprise is doomed from the start because the mechanicals are unaware of an essential qualification: they are not fit for tragedy; tragedy is for great men. If Philostrate looks at the world the way his betters do through the frame of a tragic worldview, a worldview enshrined in the literature aristocrats like to read since they themselves are the heroes of them, then he is laughing at these players, not with them, for attempting to be great. They, unlike his lord, are common and cannot act with tragic nobility.

But Philostrate's case is built on a weak foundation. According to his answer to the duke's first set of questions, the Pyramus story is tragic specifically because he kills himself. As a kind of thought experiment, let's suppose there's someone in the theater who hasn't the leisure and the education to transform suicide into the culminating rite of a cult or literary fad. If this person works at a trade, like grave digging, and isn't required to maintain a tragic view of life in order to serve his betters in their evening entertainments, he might be amused that Philostrate links suicide with a nobility. He also might be amused that by downgrading a commoner's ability to act out a death, Philostrate is confusing a rehearsal for death with the real thing. Everyone knows, especially a grave digger, that commoners can die with the best of them. If this is so, which it surely is, then it's the rehearsal for death (to which he refers in his answer to Theseus) that somehow makes a difference for Philostrate. For this reason, our grave digger might be inclined to turn the tables on Philostrate and laugh at him. He has been gulled by a show of nobility to overvalue that which is common, for anyone can end his own life if he puts his mind to it. If the grave digger laughs at him for seeing the foolish mote in the mechanicals' eyes without seeing the foolish beam in his own, Philostrate may be a better manager of mirth than he knows.

He's not a better advocate for his brief, however. Theseus is intrigued with Peter Quince's play, and tells him "we will hear it." If Philostrate assembled the program based on a memory of his boss's inclinations, then the joke is publicly on him even without my imaginary grave digger. It may be that Theseus has changed now that he's a married man, and Philostrate will have to assemble a catalogue of new memories in order to keep up. Until then he's in the dark which, in a comedy, is a good thing; it's better than thinking you have your boss figured out and misfire in your duty.

C. Desire and the Fruit of Desire

While on the subject of memory and of being in the dark, let's imagine attending the funeral for Pyramus. Every funeral we attend or remember attending will be exactly like the one we imagine for Pyramus in one important respect: not one of them, real or imagined, can tell us what it is to die. Every death we witness or imagine, a special kind of dumb show, can only be a rehearsal for the actual event when we are made the hero of our own tragedy. The dumb show tells us nothing about the mind after death.

Throughout this midsummer night we have seen how difficult it is for an intelligent man like Theseus to read with accuracy the mind and heart of Hippolyta; Demetrius is a complete mystery to Helena; and Hermia is blindsided by her old friend Helena's scorn for her temper and her stature. Here's evidence of people who can't look into the minds of the living very successfully. As for the dead, we're all even more in the dark. For human beings who thrive on knowing, the silence of death, not knowing what happens next, is an insurmountable vexation, that is, when we happen to think about it. Because we thrive on knowing, penetrating that silence can become an obsession, and so an audience for tragedy is born. There, in play after play, we listen to grieving actors knocking again and again on that closed door, the ultimate monolithic fact.

In his brief Philostrate would have us witness a series of deaths and in conclusion two suicides. In *his* brief, which is the play, Shakespeare introduces on the program the double suicide of a young boy and young girl to describe the nature of obsession. The essence of Ovid's story is well known to modern audiences, for Shakespeare retells it in *Romeo and Juliet*. Both stories prominently feature a parental wall that separates a boy and a girl from greater intimacy. Walls exist, but children are experts in finding ways around, over, or through them. Like all children, Pyramus and Thisby are driven to explore a world without walls. They long to touch and to hold each other, to know what has been hidden and forbidden. They also long to know the world beyond the walls of their house and the famous walls of their city, Babylon. When they finally decide to break out of their parents' confinement to begin this adventure, they choose to meet in a graveyard outside the town as if they could explore what lies beyond life itself. They fall, however, into a tragic misunderstanding. Instead of embracing the live body of a lover, they choose separately and in succession to embrace the mystery of death.

When we glimpse the narrative arc of the lovers in "The Knight's Tale" and *A Midsummer Night's Dream* in light of the Pyramus and Thisby story, Chaucer and Shakespeare are suggesting that desire—for a woman, a man, a beautiful object, or even a beautiful ideal—ultimately masks a darker need to possess that which is fatal in desire. It's an impulse and a story as old as the one about the forbidden fruit in Genesis. In tragedy the fruit of desire is death; in comedy the fruit of desire is death and rebirth. The one fruit is bitter and barren; the other is bitter but carries the seed of new life. A person who experiences firsthand that his perception is dangerously and even fatally limited has learned he can be painfully wrong. Conversely, a person who has been wrong has learned that the way he looks at the world is painfully limited. Either way, because he's aware of these things, he is now aware that the way he looks at the world is a choice based on limited or incorrect knowledge rather than a monolithic fact. Ignorance of this can constitute a dangerous and even fatal inattention. Given the fact that our perception and knowledge are intrinsically limited, do we look at life as a tragedy or a comedy? These reflections recall Philostrate's words (even if they don't reflect what he intended) when he invites Theseus to "make choice" of what he will see.

Great storytellers and writers have left us a legacy that transforms this subtle and complex theme into simple, physical comedy. Consider once more our pedestrian who slips on a banana peel because he's busy texting on his BlackBerry. He could have looked where he was going but chose not to. It's a joke that never loses its currency and still exists as a warning to those who are in danger of being turned upside down by inattention. In comedy the thinker slips up on inattention and lands on something solid, a sensible floor on which our pedestrian can consider the dream in which he was lost and the steps he can take to rejoin what he loves. If he's sensible enough to recognize that he's lying on a sensible floor, he will have learned that he loves life itself, not a dream.

D. Devouring Time, Played by Snug the Joiner

Earlier, the sounding of Theseus' horns in the wood awoke not only the lovers but also many themes related to the great call of life and death. The themes awakened in this scene have come to consciousness at Theseus' call for his manager of mirth, and they resonate with the word "abridgment." When Theseus asks Philostrate, "Say, what abridgment have you for this evening?" he wants to know how the long age of three hours can be abridged, how time can slip away in the entertainment. He uses abridgment in place of "entertainment" because he views its chief function as shortening the time from now to bedtime. Borrowing Helena's formulation, this scene with Philostrate highlights the way a lover looks at time. For the most part, characters in the play have been looking with different minds at physical objects and specific ideas. Theseus and Hippolyta look at the moon differently, Hermia and her father look at Lysander differently, Hermia and Lysander draw different conclusions about the duke's judgment, Oberon and Titania see the needs of the Indian boy differently, Peter Quince and Bottom have a different view of Bottom's proper role in the play, and so on throughout. Here, though, and in Hippolyta's first speech in the play, the poet moves the looking into a new dimension. The other points of dispute are objects in the space-time matrix, but when the poet looks at time differently and transforms the solidity of time itself into the substance of a dream, that matrix, which serves as a map to locate everything in our life including ourselves, dissolves as well.

In a play that would guide human beings to the great sleep of comedy by laying to rest all the bats in the belfry that might disturb it, Shakespeare aims at silencing the bat that squeaks the loudest, the tick-tock of that which measures out the length of our hours. It's a mighty task, for human beings have long looked at time as a thing, or, as it is in the modern world, a monolith. For example, Theseus complains in his opening speech of the play that time, as it moves with painful slowness for the lover who cannot be with his love until an appointed hour, has become the obstacle to his desire. It's a wall of separation which appears to be impregnable, but Hippolyta then ripostes with a vision in which time simply vanishes. The play opens with the opening up of time as an object, and, as the play is drawing to a close, the hunters' trumpet call in the wood suggests the end of time.

Like Chaucer before him, Shakespeare includes in his story the timeless world of immortals to contrast with the time-bound vision of human lovers. Robin's character, in particular, conveys a life lived without a sense of time; though obedient to Oberon, he is quick, alive and free to act, for he is unburdened by time. No wonder, when told by Oberon to return with the little Western flower before "the Leviathan can swim a league," he can answer, "I'll put a girdle round the earth / in forty minutes." That forty minutes is just a measure of convenience for an immortal like himself. Since he has been asked to deal with a human problem, he playfully adopts their language of time which, ironically contributes to many human problems because it's so closely related to a consciousness of mortality. Therefore, in addition to turning time into a wall of separation, human beings have dressed it up like a lion that shreds a person and eats him up. Shakespeare wrote a sonnet on the subject that begins "Devouring Time..." In the Pyramus and Thisby version of it, Pyramus thinks his Thisby has been shredded by a lion, but this story telescopes in a violent attack what a person fears that time (over time) will do to his love (either for oneself or for someone else) as it disfigures the grace and beauty of a youthful body and eventually kills it.

To relieve Theseus' suffering at its deepest level, Shakespeare has created a play in which that devouring lion is just a human device, and he has made it a device fit for comedy. At Peter Quince's direction, the lion is performed by Snug the Joiner, not Destitute the Divider. Here's how Snug introduces his character to his audience:

> You, ladies, you, whose gentle hearts do fear
>
> The smallest monstrous mouse that creeps on floor,

May now perchance both quake and tremble here,

When lion rough in wildest rage doth roar.

Having roared, he then reveals himself from behind the costume to comfort and reassure them:

Then know that I as Snug the joiner am,

A lion fell, nor else no lion's dam;

For, if I should as lion come in strife

Into this place, 'twere pity on my life.

Despite a hint of confusion whether the creature who speaks to us is a lion playing Snug the Joiner or the other way around and the confusion concerning whether a man like Snug needs to fear the beast that he himself is, his protestations are comforting and reassuring enough for Theseus to declare that he's "a very gentle beast, and of a good conscience." If his lion stands for time, then within the space of our comedy time has been transformed into a friend of man.[62]

E. A Lifeline

When Philostrate hands Theseus the program from which he can choose his abridgment, he describes the list of entertainments as a brief. In addition to its legal associations, the word brief signals that each little description is a brief or abridged version of the thing itself. This also has a place in a complex web of meaning. Any work of literature—whether a song, a history, a myth from ancient times, or a satire of current events—is an abridgment of life itself. Since human beings almost without exception learn a language, interpret the world with it, and use it to communicate with others about what has happened to them or what they are thinking and feeling, anything we say or write is a brief summary of our whole experience of life. We are limited in our understanding and can't actually recreate the whole (nor would we want to) so we speak or write to present the gist or essence of it.

Everyone has had one's understanding—about oneself and others and one's reason for being—sorely tested at times by life itself, so one would think that everyone would eventually appreciate the difficulty of making these summaries. This is not the case, however, for many who put pen to paper, and so our poet made his living by demonstrating in play after play and throughout his writing career that the symbolizations of some do a better job of holding up a mirror to nature than others. When Philostrate mocks the mechanicals' skill in writing and acting, we see that he shares this opinion, but he is an amateur in the business compared to Shakespeare himself.

Shakespeare's comedies as well as his tragedies do a better job in this attempt than many other kinds of writing because they don't lose sight of what human beings don't know. Since the unknown dwarfs in sheer size, volume, and importance the known, then a mirror that includes what we don't know within its frame will be a more realistic mirror. If we borrow the root of abridgment, we can say that the symbolizations of great literature serve as a bridge or a lifeline for connecting the little we suppose we know with the greatness of what we don't.

F. A Reason for Being

This section has thus far reviewed the evidence for two different meanings of abridgment. Theseus uses the word to refer to an entertainment that will shorten or dissolve altogether the "torturing hour" between after-supper and bedtime. An abridgment is also a shorter version of a longer work; because an abridgment means that certain parts have been left out, it suggests that any representation of the original, even while serving an important function, is inherently limited. A passage from Chaucer's "The Knight's Tale" provides a third meaning which I have already mentioned in passing. The word "abridge" appears in the opening paragraph of Theseus' great speech or sentence at the end of the tale. A "sentence" is a legal term that sums up or finalizes the proceedings of a court, but a medieval speaker or writer also referred to the meaning of a story as its sentence. To borrow Shakespeare's usage, Theseus' speech is his brief to the court concerning his relationship with the Theban Arcite, which he presents in furtherance of the marriage he proposes at the end.

Chaucer's Theseus opens his speech by emphasizing that he has learned to appreciate the greatness of creation in contrast with his own limitations:

> "The First Great Cause and Mover of all above
>
> When first He made that fairest chain of love,
>
> Great was the consequence and high the intent.
>
> He well knew why He did, and what He meant.

There is something constant in creation—he calls it a chain of love, something as great as the Creator. Although the Creator knows it very well, it's difficult for us to know it or the intent behind it or the consequence of it the way we think we know the people and everyday objects and activities that come and go in a busy life. Nevertheless, Theseus affirms (from experience he says later) that the something, the intent, and the consequence are all as great as He. He then goes on to explain why it's hard for us to know them:

> For in that fairest chain of love He bound
>
> Fire and air and water and the ground
>
> Of earth in certain limits they may not flee.
>
> And that same Prince and Mover then, said he,

'Stablished this wretched world, appointing ways,

Seasons, durations, certain length of days,

To all that is engendered here below,

Past which predestined hour none may go,

Though they have the power to abridge those days.

This passage develops the difficulty of living as a link in a chain of love. Love is light and fair, but it's also constraining and weighs the lover down into the darkness of earth from which everything here below is engendered and to which it returns. We are links in a chain of love, but it's a heavy chain. People have legs to flee from danger, but over time the legs haven't the strength even to walk or keep the body upright. Either suddenly or by degrees, the body is pulled to earth as if it were chained to it.

The juxtaposition of a chain with love is striking, and it captures the confusion about love that has been Chaucer's and Shakespeare's subject. The passage as a whole also describes the initial movement of the lovers' stories. Arcite and the lovers from Shakespeare's play all are overwhelmed and come to earth. Even though Chaucer's Theseus refers to "all that is engendered here below," he is speaking not to worms or insects or the animals of the field but to his people, and so when he observes that none may go past a predestined hour, he qualifies this doom with the observation that, unlike other animals, conscious human beings have the power "to abridge those days."

This abridgment is another word for suicide. Here's an idea to end all ideas, the quickest fix to desire and the confusion of love. Even though our play is a comedy, ever since Theseus spoke those lines in "The Knight's Tale," suicide has cast a long shadow over it. Puck notices that shadow in the play of light and shade at dawn when:

...night's swift dragons cut the clouds full fast

And yonder shines Aurora's harbinger;

At whose approach ghosts, wand'ring here and there,

Troop home to churchyards; damned spirits all,

That in crossways and floods have burial,

Already to their wormy beds are gone.

For fear lest day should look their shames upon,

They wilfully themselves exiled from light,

And must for aye consort with black-browed night.

Those who willfully exiled themselves from light were buried at the crossroads, not in a churchyard. Suicide is a fact of life. More explicitly than any story or sermon, it conveys to anyone who attends the funeral of a suicide or who hears about it some other way that life itself is a choice that derives from the way a person looks at life.

Chaucer and Shakespeare have narrowed the issue to show that the essential character or quality of our life is intimately involved with the way we look at love, and the way we look at love becomes a choice only when we're made aware in the school of hard knocks that there is a choice. When love looks with the mind, the lover loves because the object of his love is an ideal form come magically to life as it did for Narcissus in a pool of water. This is *cupiditas*, the desire to possess a projection. It's an abridgment, a short-circuiting of vision. The lover, through a magic like that of a sun looking at a moon made of mirrored light, has fallen in love with himself, but this is not the whole story for him and all those who look as Narcissus did in the pool. Like Narcissus, Chaucer's and Shakespeare's lovers fall into the death-like trance of self-love and sheer exhaustion but in the end they are brought to their senses by the great call of comedy. The call wakes them to a new clarity and purpose so that joy and fresh days of love now accompany their hearts even if, as in Arcite's case, it's the joy and the love that's carried on in someone else's heart. This is *caritas*, a sunlit state of being that springs from the shadow of *cupiditas*. The two forms of love together represent a pattern of behavior writ large in our lives, and comedy exists to make us aware of it.

Chaucer begins *The Canterbury Tales* by telling a little story about a plant in spring, and this plant introduces the theme. Its roots are revived in darkness as the strong liquor of spring rains inspires it to break free from earth and to ripen under the influence of Zephyrus and the sun. In itself the plant marries the two phases of a striving in confusion and a flowering in the light. The tales of Chaucer and Shakespeare feature narratives about human beings that observe the same pattern. If we are a lover of life who looks up and sees only an old moon waning towards death, and with such painful slowness, comedy reminds us that this is a phase of love. There's another, just as real as the suffering of the first, if we have the patience to keep looking. Patience understands this about love, and so it gives us a reason for being.

G. Some Disclaimers

Finally, it would be prudent to add a disclaimer about this reading of Philostrate. Since Shakespeare never comments directly on his characters (in a drama the writer has no narrative voice), some may interpret Philostrate not as a time server like the courtier Osric in *Hamlet*, who toadies up to the king and arranges the king's entertainments to the king's liking, but as a clown-savant like the grave digger in *Hamlet*, who maintains a perfect independence from all pretenses of power. If Philostrate is a clown, then everything he says is merely tongue in cheek, and a clown like that may have "managed" all the choices so that the duke would pick Peter Quince's absurd tragicomedy. I'm not convinced, though, that he's a clown who has delved as deep as the grave digger. Shakespeare's great clowns show themselves without deception, the way Bottom does. The brighter ones play with their master's heads, but everyone knows at the time that that's what they are doing.

Also, the arguments about time discussed in this section would appear to conclude that it both exists, as surely as a plant grows out of darkness to flower in the light, and it doesn't exist, as surely a dream dissolves into nothing once we wake. Therefore it is prudent to add a disclaimer about denoting time truly. It would appear that time, along with everything else, seems double when we look at it with the mind. So how to look at time with the eyes? The play has an answer of sorts in the music that makes its appearance throughout the play, in the poetry of their speech, and in the fairies' entertainments. The fairies don't see time; they keep it in timely action, in singing, and in dancing. By means of Shakespeare's play, we can hear it, too, as a drumbeat that rocks a lover deeper and deeper into an earthy darkness, the source of all and everything.

The Reformation of Theseus

A. The Reviving of a Dead Interval (and the Duke)

Theseus has already told Philostrate that he and the others will hear the play, but our manager of mirth tries to talk him out of it:

> *No, my noble lord;*
>
> *It is not for you. I have heard it over,*
>
> *And it is nothing, nothing in the world;*
>
> *Unless you find sport in their intents,*
>
> *Extremely stretch'd and conn'd with cruel pain,*
>
> *To do you service.*

Philostrate unwittingly suggests that there's a mystery in the play's tragical mirth that's like nothing in the world, and this is just what Theseus wants for the interval between after-supper and bedtime. The world he knows well enough; to abridge the three hours, he'll have the nothing. Trying to talk Theseus out of it, he succeeds only in talking him into it.

In addition to this consideration, the picture that Philostrate paints of the men laboring to do him service gives Theseus another reason for preferring it:

I will hear that play;

For never anything can be amiss

When simpleness and duty tender it.

Go bring them in; and take your places, ladies.

More decisively this time Theseus overrules Philostrate's judgment and, with a short thrust at Philostrate's character, explains that he prefers the simpleness and duty of the hard-handed men. Philostrate's little portrait of the actors may have acted like a glass through which Theseus can see himself, even if only for a moment, mirrored in their service. It's a portrait of a man and a leader he might find attractive.

When wily, well-versed people give him something, it's hard to know its value. The mechanicals, on the other hand, are offering legal "tender" for good faith. They serve Theseus as best they can and undoubtedly hope to be rewarded, but as practical men (as mechanicals) they will expect no more than payment in proportion to the work they have done. When Theseus hears from Philostrate that free subjects rather than paid professionals have organized themselves to grace his and Hippolyta's solemnities, the time between after supper and bedtime is revived from a dead interval separating himself from his desire to a space for expressions of loyalty and love. Earlier Oberon had to be awakened to the way he and Titania let the government of the natural world slip when they were both entirely focused on their personal stake in the little boy, and Theseus is starting to wake up a little here to his role, which never sleeps, as an example to his people. Since they serve him in good faith, he's in their debt to serve them as well.

Just as the Reformation in England and throughout Europe was as much about politics as it was about religion, the reformation of Theseus in progress now that he's a married man may be as much about politics as an insight of heart and mind. Shakespeare has made it as difficult to penetrate the mind and motives of Theseus as those of Oberon. From the evidence we have, though, it's hard to believe that Theseus has experienced a significant upheaval of heart and mind because he doesn't undergo a deep crisis in his government like the death of Arcite for Chaucer's Theseus, the flooding and famine that threatens Oberon's realm, or the comic deaths into which the lovers and Bottom are initiated.

Theseus shows good judgment in the wood when he overrules Egeus and here at court in the choice of abridgment, but his judgment is often questioned. Hippolyta's opening speech, for example, subjects it to a critique. The play itself critiques him when the audience sees the inaccuracies in his explanations and rationalizations. He's a good man, we think, and an effective leader, but the play of which he is but a part is larger than he is. The audience knows this to be the case because we have seen the fairies at work, and he denies their existence. Thus he can't possibly know the true meaning of the situation or find words that get to the bottom of it. Also, he may not fully grasp the meaning of what he does say.

Like those oes and eyes dotting the night sky that fall on occasion into constellations and that act out the unending drama of the human mind, Shakespeare's creation consists of words and sentences that light up our own minds. There's the constellation of Oberon and there's Titania, there's Lysander, and there's Theseus. We put them together out of these points of light, but the points of light, the words that represent them, have a life of their own. This is also true for the words they say about love as when Lysander tells Hermia it's:

...momentany as a sound,

Swift as a shadow, short as any dream,

Brief as the lightning in the collied night,

That, in a spleen, unfolds both heaven and earth,

And ere a man hath power to say "Behold!"

The jaws of darkness do devour it up:

So quick bright things come to confusion.

It sounds almost as if he were saying these words to himself rather than Hermia, but for those of us who hear these lines his lightning flashes throughout the rest of the play and beyond as far as light can travel.

Lysander speaks these words, but he doesn't own them. In the end they belong to a universe of timeless poetry. When Helena says to Hermia, "Oh, teach me how you look," she may have intended one thing, but the words themselves speak of a longing that literature for thousands of years tries to satisfy. Those who love literature would look with the eyes of these masters, and so we read and imagine the world they have made for us. When Bottom tells Titania in their first little tete-a-tete that "reason and love keep little company together now-a-days. The more the pity that some honest neighbors will not make them friends," the wisdom of what he says can't be attributed to him because he's an ass. The words come out of his mouth, but they belong to the ages. He got lucky, we think (which is what he thinks as well, "Nay, I can gleek, upon occasion," with an explanation that neighs and squeaks like a donkey), just as he's about to get lucky with Titania!

Like the opening speeches of the play that reveal a latent uncertainty in the relationship of Theseus and Hippolyta, Lysander's words insert an uncertainty about love itself into relationships. There's love, but there's also the jaws of darkness that swallow it up. Concern about this is magnified when the security of the state depends on a love relationship. The marriage of Theseus and Hippolyta has gone forward, but from the start Shakespeare has given Hippolyta a voice that doesn't mind informing Theseus and the court that she sees things differently. Moments before he calls for Philostrate, Theseus is once again complaining about that long age of three hours that keeps him from resolving the tension in their relationship. It seems to be what chiefly occupies him, and we sense from it much that is unresolved.

It's not the first time that Theseus has tended to be somewhat self-absorbed. This comes up in an early scene when Lysander points out that, prior to courting Hermia's father for her hand, Demetrius was engaged to Helena but broke the contract. Lysander implies that the duke should have Demetrius honor that commitment instead of enforcing Demetrius' contract with Hermia's father. Theseus defends himself, rather sheepishly, by admitting:

> *I must confess that I have heard so much,*
>
> *And with Demetrius thought to have spoke thereof;*
>
> *But, being over-filled of self-affairs,*
>
> *My mind did lose it.*

Up to now we have had only hints of unresolved issues that lie in wait for the newly married duke, but he's a sensitive man who is surely aware of them. Therefore, given his characterization as thoroughly practical and political, the reformation of Theseus now in progress is as much about politics as a deep insight of heart and mind. Philostrate's little story about the mechanicals briefly opens up a larger world than the one that's over-filled with Hippolyta, and so he chooses to stand as duke in the light of their example.

B. An Impressive Comic Doctrine

He'll have to explain his choice, however, to Hippolyta who tells him:

I love not to see wretchedness o'er-charged,

And duty in his service perishing.

As she did in the opening discussion about the lovers' night in the wood, Hippolyta disagrees in open court with how he sees the situation, and this time Theseus directly confronts her objections:

Why, gentle sweet, you shall see no such thing.

Previously when her critiques arise, Theseus diverts the court's attention to other matters and so deflects the need for an immediate public comment on what she has said. The reformation of Theseus, therefore, also involves a willingness to risk contradicting his wife. Luckily, he chooses to disagree with her over something that hasn't yet happened; there's nothing so contentious as when two people who live intimately together remember the same event differently.

In reply, Hippolyta takes up Philostrate's argument:

He says they can do nothing in this kind.

Theseus, in turn, is inspired to lay out a Comic Doctrine for getting along with people in general and in particular people with whom one disagrees. The doctrine consists of three related but quite different statements. The first is the least serious:

The kinder we, to give them thanks for nothing.

If a person can do nothing in this kind, there is nothing there to take hold of or be upset about. A nothing that gives no offense is certainly better than a something that does.

It's a clever return of the nothing she served up to him but lacks real substance, and so he elaborates:

Our sport shall be to take what they mistake.

This, too, is part of Philostrate's argument, for he tells the duke that the play was nothing "Unless you find sport in their intents." Philostrate sees mechanicals unpracticed in dramatic arts who intend an imitation of life for an audience accustomed to sophisticated and polished works. For Philostrate, the only sport in such a show would be to laugh at the grossness and the failure of the imitation. Theseus accepts Philostrate's basic argument as the actual production of the play proves. The nobility turns the viewing of it into a contest to see who can make the wittiest, most satiric comment on it. Because Theseus sees the good faith (the intents) of subjects who loyally serve him and because the mechanicals are oblivious to the nobility's intent, the raillery for him is innocent sport.

The statement, "Our sport shall be to take what they mistake," is another example of words that take on a life of their own within the poem. For starters, Theseus' observation touches on the essence of his character as Shakespeare has rendered him. He is sometimes off the mark in what he says, and when he's on the mark we're not sure whether he fully comprehends what he apprehends, even though he's the one who makes the distinction in his speech earlier. In this instance, he is unaware that his own words describe the joke that is being played on him by the events in his realm; because he denies the existence of the fairies, it's the audience's sport to take what he mistakes.

So the second sentence backfires on the one who utters it, but it also establishes, less flippantly than in the line before it, a more general Comic Doctrine for getting along with people and in particular people with whom one disagrees. It sums up the sport for those who have a view from the mountaintop. For Philostrate, it's a view that generates condescension. Because he knows so much more than the mechanicals about dramatic representations, he takes ironic pleasure in seeing the mistakes they make in putting on a play. He's the bystander watching an inattentive pedestrian slip on a banana peel. Shakespeare has given the audience that same pride of place for watching his comedy. Because we are present for every scene and know more than any character on stage, we have a better view than even Theseus or Oberon into the reality of the situation, and we have had this demonstrated on a number of occasions. Initially, we have to laugh at the follies of those who know less than we do. We laugh at poor Lysander and Demetrius, who have their affections violently changed from Hermia to Helena and who run around the woods like homicidal madmen afterwards to ease their raging heart; at poor Hermia who is suddenly bereft of her power to charm the men; and at poor Helena who rages so intelligently in her solitude even as the men declare their passions. These scenes are great sport for us. The contrast between our knowledge and their ignorance would cause anyone to blurt out along with Robin "Lord, what fools these mortals be."

The view from the mountaintop generates the sport, but a great comedy like this one doesn't end with the audience looking at the characters with condescension. We can't maintain the condescension because Shakespeare has made his characters too lifelike to be just fools; they are too much like ourselves to be beneath us. All the main characters may act foolishly at some point, but the pain of separation from what they love, even if what they love has been artificially induced, is too much like our own for us not to recognize ourselves in it. This is truer for the women's suffering than that of the men; the presence of the fairies and their interference with the men's eyes prevent us from taking their suffering as seriously. Their love is more of a joke as the flower juice leavens it with a blithe puckishness. Put the men and women in each other's vicinity, and you have a drama that's enlivened by these polarities. We in the audience inhabit the drama's gravitational field, and it gives us a comic gravitas. Along with Robin we can say, "Lord, what fools these mortals be," at the same time that we are being forced into a recognition that "There, but for the grace of God, go I."

The condescension cannot withstand the play's powerful dynamic. Once we have identified with the suffering the characters endure because of desire, we wish along with them for the pain to be relieved, and, as we know a comedy will, the play comes through for them and us. Our sport, our pleasure in a comedy, is to take assurance that a person can make terrible, foolish mistakes and survive the experience intact. It's what we would wish for ourselves, and in a sporting spirit we may learn to take with a grain of salt other's as well as our own mistakes. Philostrate is a fool because he can only laugh at the mechanicals; something there is that prevents him, at least at this point, from seeing himself in them and laughing with them. His condescension clearly is a mistake. We don't know for sure whether consciously or instinctively Theseus sees this about Philostrate, but it doesn't really matter what Theseus thinks. He has spoken the words, and they make a significant constellation in the play's night sky. Regardless of anyone's motives, Theseus' choice of the play and its success will help Philostrate to survive his mistake intact. At least he had the play on his list.

The decision to hear the play marks a turning point for Theseus as well. It matches that moment in the wood when Oberon's government appears to be sinking into randomness, and Robin says of it:

The fate o'errules, that, one man holding troth,

A million fail, confounding oath on oath.

Oberon doesn't argue; instead, he commands:

About the wood! Go swifter than the wind,

And Helena of Athens look thou find.

All fancy-sick she is, and pale of cheer

With sighs of love, that cost the fresh blood dear.

By some illusion see thou bring her here.

"Here," as we now have seen, is where Helena and the others are relieved of their suffering, but they are brought here, meaning on the stage of our theater, by means of illusion or mistaking.

Since Oberon's words and actions apply to all those who are fancy sick and pale of cheer, Theseus words, interpreted within the much larger theater of the human comedy, convey something similar for anyone acting in or observing the play of Pyramus and Thisby. Perhaps we all, too, will be brought "here" to this place to be mended (which, of course, for the audience is the same stage as the lovers shared when they slept side by side in the wood) as we follow the illusion of a double suicide acted out by mechanicals. Our sport will be to take what Pyramus and Thisby mistake, for they have been seduced by a foolish illusion concerning the good they seek in love. It turns out to be a mortal mistake for them, but for the audience, in particular an aristocratic court that tends to take stories like this to heart, it's not too late to see the foolishness that's at the heart of the story.

From the beginning of the play Shakespeare has raised the issue of autonomy, different people who look at the world differently and who can't look into the mind of another. An individual's autonomy continues to be a defining characteristic of the modern world in politics, in the economy, in art, and in literature. For all that, though, people are social animals, and when that basic need—to be part of a company like the little civic organization that Bottom and his friends have put together to create an entertainment for the duke—is not met, when an individual for whatever reason cannot identify with his fellows, that person can fall quite ill and become a danger to himself and to others. This is a fact that we find acted out too often in brutal cases of domestic violence and in terrible acts of random violence designed to make a bloody splash in the national news. Shakespeare's play is as concerned as the legal framework of a government with how an autonomous individual can live in civil harmony with other autonomous individuals. It's the problem that any married couple faces, and more generally it's the problem everyone has to work through in order to live in a social context. When we watch any kind of human drama, real or imagined, our sport is to take what the actors in it mistake, but our work is to take what they mistake as a sensible representation of our own ignorance.

To clarify his Comic Doctrine for civil peace further, Theseus adds another sentence to it:

> *And what poor duty cannot do, noble respect*
>
> *Takes it in might, not merit.*

The first clause is clear enough, but the second is somewhat cryptic. The mechanicals would show their loyalty to the duke, but they lack the capacity to act in a tragedy. The good faith of the duke's open mind, like the moon reflecting the light of the sun without resistance, "takes" what they cannot do, which is reflected in his sentence by the pronoun "it," and reflects it back to them with the noble respect with which it was taken. The second clause moves the comic resolution along by describing what lies behind the noble respect, which can take people as they are without wishing they were otherwise. This respect, it says, takes (or looks at) what they can't do "in might." Since this "might" would appear to be the foundation for the reformation of Theseus' government, it's important to understand what he sees in it.

Philostrate has just called him "mighty Theseus" (see page 372) using an adjective that suggests Theseus' reputation for heroic deeds. The story Theseus tells to illustrate his statement about taking "in might" builds on that impression:

Where I have come, great clerks have purposed

To greet me with premeditated welcomes;

Where I have seen them shiver and look pale,

Make periods in the midst of sentences,

Throttle their practis'd accent in their fears,

And, in conclusion, dumbly have broke off,

Not paying me a welcome. Trust me, sweet,

Out of this silence yet I pick'd a welcome;

And in the modesty of a fearful duty

I read as much as from the rattling tongue

Of saucy and audacious eloquence.

Love, therefore, and tongue-tied simplicity

In least speak most, to my capacity.

In the shape of this great clerk shaking before him, mighty Theseus sheds light on what he means by "might": it is, he suggests, that which overawes even an accomplished man like the great clerk. Our Theseus may see himself as representing that might. His account puts himself in that position and gives him an opportunity to make himself clear on several points. A story about preferring tongue-tied simplicity over saucy and audacious eloquence explains in more detail why he rejects Philostrate's argument. The tongue-tied simplicity of the great clerk also gives Hippolyta a vivid picture of the way he is regarded by others. Perhaps his "gentle sweet" will take the hint, and she'll remember with whom she is dealing.

After the war they fought and the subsequent courtship, though, she is probably quite aware that his capacity, to which he just refers, is limited and self-interested, and as a consequence she is unlikely to be as overawed as the clerk. The play has been designed so that the audience is also unlikely to be overawed, for we have seen more than either Theseus or Hippolyta how the three marriages and the present feast have come to pass. Dukes, kings, prime ministers, and presidents as a rule tend to take far more credit than they "merit" (a word that refers in Theseus' Comic Doctrine to what they deserve) for what happens on their watch. Egeus' suit at the beginning of the play is the only major question Theseus has to adjudicate. He makes his decision, but just as quickly as he makes it, Lysander and Hermia try to undo it. By the dawn of the following day, however, the affections of the four lovers have been realigned and stabilized. Given this new reality, Theseus overrules Egeus; the stability and happiness of the four outweigh the legal rights of a father ready to sacrifice the life of his own daughter. If this is justice, then Theseus makes the right decision, but, as the audience knows, he has nothing to do with the conditions that actually bring about the decision.

Here at the wedding feast Theseus presides in might over a peaceful resolution to the fighting that precedes all three marriages. The second case he adjudicates—the one we have just witnessed concerning the evening's entertainment—has given him another opportunity to make a judgment in might, and once again, as when he reverses himself about Hermia, he shows good sense in overruling Philostrate. The play calls his might into question primarily in respect to Hippolyta. During the course of the narrative they appear three times together at court, and each time they create in their conversation an atmosphere of unresolved tension. When they appear together in the woods, there is no debate, but there are strong suggestions that the interaction of a man and a woman at a primal level is a blood sport and not one that sorts with a nuptial ceremony. Theseus is called upon to determine what sort of "might" is required when the stage on which he and Hippolyta find themselves is not a battlefield but a marriage bed.

C. The Source of a Noble Respect

Despite any doubts he or Hippolyta may be having, a great current toward a comic resolution is now swirling around the two principal characters. We have witnessed the movement and the power of it in what happens to the Athenians in the wood and in the reconciliation, after much discord and disruption, of Oberon and Titania. Not only do Oberon and Titania hear the great call of comedy in their relations with each other, they are the great call for all the lovers. Now it's Theseus and Hippolyta's turn to hear it. Like Bottom promising to answer when called, Theseus and Hippolyta are prompted in marriage to make the transition from antagonists to loving partners.

Just as the noble respect works both ways in the case of the mechanicals, where Theseus sees the good faith with which they regard him and is inspired to look at them in the same way, there's an opening for Theseus to see that Hippolyta reflects his autonomy by maintaining her own. This way of looking at her depends entirely on those experiences when he bumps up against what he "cannot do" even if she appears to have been subdued in battle or in argument: he cannot possess her as she will always be an autonomous free agent. A husband who thinks he merits a different kind of respect "might" take offense at this, but a husband who maintains his own autonomy without trying to suppress that of his wife—that is, who sees what he can and cannot do—might not. If her autonomy gives him offense, what might-have-been, a healthy royal marriage and a stable government of the dukedom, will suffer. This is an equal opportunity observation. The same could be said of Hippolyta, but the burden of it rests with Theseus as the duke. Like the "if" that plays such an important role in Robin's speech at the end of the play, this "might" points to what is possible even if Theseus aspires to another form of it.[63]

Comedy's greatness comes from the way it continually points out what a character cannot know and consequently what he cannot do. Theseus is struggling to realize that the "might" of which he speaks, which is the greatness of what human beings don't know and which is represented in the play by the works of fairyland, is infinitely mightier than he, but it's hard to say to what extent he succeeds. Lysander has blazed the trail of one who fails in this. Under the influence of the flower juice, he praises the power of his reason which has ripened through experience into true judgment, but a man may say something true even if it isn't true in his case. Early in the play Lysander describes to Hermia how "quick bright things come to confusion." What he says is true and beautifully put, but it doesn't tell how quickly the quick bright love he has for Hermia will fizzle out.

The poet has put an image of lightning before our eyes and ears to serve as a demonstration of great power and a reminder of sudden death. When lightning strikes and dissipates so quickly, it forces the observer in an instant to do what he normally doesn't or cannot do—that is, to experience directly the life of a moment and the end of it, life without light, and life without life. It's a power of life and death that anyone experiences in a moment like this, and these experiences are common to Everyman. Since everyone stands equally exposed to them, it takes no special talent to have them. They move us with a power like the voice of the whirlwind that, because it was present when the world was made, knows its depth, its breadth, and the basis for its laws. As the whirlwind did for Job, these sudden strikes stop people short with surprise and wonder.[64]

Lysander's lightning instructs us in the nature of the "might" that's at the heart of Theseus' reformation. Might is the direct experience of what we cannot know—it is wisdom. Although we cannot know it, we can learn from it a noble respect. When present in a human being, this respect can "take" differences with other people and adversity with equanimity. Even though we have the example of Job, we tend to be like Philostrate. We mitigate the full force of doubt with irony, cynicism, and a world-weary presumption of wisdom, but this is only a holding cell that hovers over despair. Philostrate describes his situation well. He relies on a limited memory for judgment, and he mistakes the might of his memory for the real thing, which is life itself. Theseus touches on this critique when he contrasts might, which he would make the foundation for his rule, with merit. Merit is fine as far as it goes, but in the way of the world merit is a limited and socially conditioned source of power. The might of seeing with eyes is a far greater power than the merit apportioned to an idea fixed in the mind. A man may rise in society, the way Philostrate rises (primarily in his own opinion) because he advises the duke, but the merit badge of his position is still an unreliable measure of his true worth. A man of true worth, the duke implies, can see what a man cannot do (including what he himself cannot do), take him to heart, and make him a part of the day's festivities.[65]

Can Theseus take his own advice about the mechanicals and do the same for Hippolyta? We don't get an answer yet, for Philostrate interrupts their conversation to announce that the play is ready to begin. A comedy like this one succeeds only in outlining the conditions for a happy ending where people's conflicts are resolved, couples marry, and the situation is ripe for the survival and the prosperity of the characters and their families. The conditions are there, but it's still up to the individuals to find their way by the lights, such as they are, of these comic experiences. Therefore, to put a period at the end of their midsummer night and the day after, Shakespeare has prepared a play of very tragical mirth that will, as if by magic, transform a human being's deepest fears and darkest impulses into an occasion that will cause the whole audience to:

...hold their hips and laugh,

And waxen in their mirth, and neeze, and swear

A merrier hour was never wasted there.

Theseus can take some credit for having seen this opportunity; his choice reflects a slight but significant opening of his heart and mind. The title of this section, "The Reformation of Theseus," refers to the reformation within the duke and within his dukedom, but it says nothing about what lies behind his reformation. It may appear to be a reformation that he has instituted. Politicians enjoy naming public benefits after themselves, and Everyman would like to be credited with what he merits. The mechanicals, however, like the fairies in the wood, set the stage for the reformation sweeping through the court of Theseus. Like infectious laughter, this effect is what we are about to witness as Philostrate announces:

> So please your Grace, the Prologue is address'd.

> And Theseus replies, "Let him approach."

Chapter thirteen:
The Government of Comedy

Michelangelo's *Pieta*

A Prologue for the "O" at the End

A. A Perfect, Empty "O" at the End of a Sentence

We have been warned that Peter Quince's production is nothing in the world, and already the tenses of Philostrate's announcement make the time sense uncertain. If the prologue is addressed, is it ongoing or finished? Philostrate may be saying that the Prologue, in the person of Peter Quince, is ready; the need for a Prologue is addressed in the appearance of this actor. This is a practical way to read it, but it also can be said that the play is born out of a mysterious time sense in which a prologue about to be spoken is already addressed. Everything that has gone before has prepared us for this moment. There's an uncanny *readiness* for what we are about to see.[66]

The locus for social order is also losing its focus (as in seeing double) even within the heart of Theseus' court. Now that all three couples have traced the scent of a comic action to its proper conclusion, the duke's role as the ruling power of the play is reduced, and the court will be governed for the duration first by the tragical mirth of Peter Quince's play and then by the fairies. As Theseus and his guests let the time slip between after-supper and bedtime by watching a play, they like the audience give themselves over to its entertainment.[67] Because the players are now so well known to the audience—especially when it comes to Bottom their star—and because the mechanicals' gentle audience keep inserting themselves into the play they are watching, it's hard to distinguish where Ovid's intent leaves off and Shakespeare's begins. The separate stories become one as Ovid's tragedy is wed to Shakespeare's comedy, but Shakespeare's comic vision predominates.

At the end of the Pyramus and Thisby story, after both have killed themselves for love, Bottom springs up from his role as dead Pyramus to ask if Theseus would like to see the epilogue. It's a dramatic gesture that expresses the essence of comedy. Maybe some would like to "see" the epilogue of one who is dead performed by the man himself, but Theseus declines it in favor of a dance by the whole company. There have been explanations and excuses enough, he says. His ruling, however, doesn't keep Robin, Oberon, Titania, and all the fairy train from making an appearance in the palace in order to have the final word, and they speak and dance the epilogue (for the audience) that Theseus declines (for himself and the court). The fairies are not governed by mighty Theseus; they stand upon something other than Athenian law.

The law they stand on and represent as its agents closely resembles the law of comedy that's the subject of these essays. If the fairies watch Peter Quince's play along with Theseus and all his guests, no doubt they would approve its depiction of human folly, and they would laugh as heartily at its performance as the mortals in the audience do. After all it's a play and rather like their own existence in that no one actually dies. Unlike Theseus' Comic Doctrine, which is an admirable but strained essay, the mechanicals' production is comedy itself, and everything else in the play has set the stage for it.

Based on my own experience of working for nearly two decades on student productions of it in the classroom, I stake a claim that the mechanicals' rendering of the Pyramus and Thisby story is comic gold. I scheduled the reading of A Midsummer Night's Dream in the curriculum so that it fell right before Christmas vacation. For four months we had been working hard, lots of reading and tests and a paper on each important literary work. Instead of writing a paper on Shakespeare's play, though, in a holiday spirit I had them enact scenes from the play as their final project. There are a number of good ones for small ensembles in Acts II and III, but Peter Quince's production worked like a charm every year we performed it. Anyone can act these parts, and my amateurs hammed it up like pros.

Because our play within a play has a prologue, a body, and an epilogue, it suggests a completed work. Hippolyta says while viewing it, "This is the silliest stuff that ever I heard," and any critic would readily agree. It's as perfect and as empty as the little "o" that comes at the end of a sentence. The reader is permitted to call a point, like that at the end of a sentence, an "o" by no less an authority than Shakespeare himself. Earlier in the play, Lysander gestures toward the points of light in the sky and tells Hermia that Helena "more engilds the night / Than all yon fiery oes and eyes of light." A point that appears at the end of a sentence has no content, and yet in context with other sentences, it gives autonomy and meaning to the sentence it punctuates and to the whole work.

Like that little "o" at the end of a sentence, Peter Quince's play stands with autonomy and authority at the end of the play, and the advent of its autonomy and authority represents a significant break in the poem, similar to that in the wood at the sounding of the hunting horns. Peter Quince's "approach" cues an entry from another world that has the "capacity" (even Theseus has to qualify his sentence or judgment on the case at hand with a reference to "my capacity," which implies that it is a limited capacity) to content us with the time between after-supper and the end of our play. Peter Quince's creation, like Mighty Jove himself disguised as a beggar coming into Theseus' house to share a meal with mortals, represents the presence of a timeless archetype.

To link it with the archetypes that accompany Theseus and Hippolyta on their hunt that morning, Peter Quince's approach is accompanied by a flourish of trumpets. Along with the Prologue and the compacting of time into a single sentence, they announce the poet's sentence (in the sense of a judgment) on the world his poetry has created, and hundreds of years after he penned it audiences still overlook his creation and find it to be very good. The comic world of Peter Quince's play, therefore, has the same function in Shakespeare's play as Theseus' great speech at the end of "The Knight's Tale." With great care and patience both authors create the conditions, the way a gardener cultivates the ground of his garden, for the engendering and the flourishing of that which they have planted: in the earth, the wind, the rain, and the sun of our earthly life, we find ourselves linked to a world that fosters life.

B. To Be or Not To Be Content with Knowing All We Are Like to Know

Chaucer's Theseus begins his speech by comparing creation to a chain of love. It's a strange, paradoxical image. How can a chain, associated with the slings and arrows and the restraints and stops that keep a person from what he loves, be made of love? Shakespeare's brief on this question begins with Peter Quince's sentence or judgment on his own play. Here, the problem of restraint, of coming to a stop, is translated into a precious, funny, illogical expression of good will with sentences that strain at every point to say exactly the opposite:

> *If we offend, it is with our good will.*
>
> *That you should think, we come not to offend,*
>
> *But with good will. To show our simple skill,*
>
> *That is the true beginning of our end.*
>
> *Consider then, we come but in despite.*
>
> *We do not come, as minding to content you,*
>
> *Our true intent is. All for your delight,*
>
> *We are not here. That you should here repent you,*
>
> *The actors are at hand: and, by their show,*
>
> *You shall know all, that you are like to know.*

The problem is not that a sentence is injured by having to stop at some point. The problem is that a sentence has to stop at the right place. As they say about golfers when they miss an easy putt in a big tournament, Peter Quince has "choked" at the worst time in his big moment before the duke. With a little effort, the duke and those in the audience can imagine that which has been hidden by performance anxieties. When the restraint is properly applied, the pairings of Peter's words express his true intent:

If we offend, it is with our good will

That you should think we come not to offend

But with good will. To show our simple skill,

That is the true beginning of our end,

Consider then we come. But in despite

We do not come, as minding to content you,

Our true intent is all for your delight.

We are not here that you should repent you,

The actors are at hand: and by their show,

You shall know all that you are like to know.

Whether punctuated like this or not, the sweetness of Peter Quince's character shines through an innocent unlearnedness. Because the verses proceed in such a muddle of clauses largely suspended and connected to the sense by the slenderest of threads, it's no wonder he has trouble remembering the stops.

For all the apparent confusion, most of the final couplet escapes intact in both versions, and it sums up the thematic point of the prologue. Since everyone has been told that the play is about a suicide, it will feature a character who seeks to penetrate with his weapon the mystery of death, the "O" at the end of life. Peter Quince and his company, on the other hand, are firmly rooted in a comedy, and his final couplet expresses his "take" on Pyramus's tragic quest. When the show is over, he tells us, we will know what the show can show us. As the sentence appears to be somewhat tautological, the nobility in the audience might mistake this as an innocent acknowledgment that, given the company's skill, they are not likely to know very much.

Peter Quince's words nevertheless establish the ideal vantage point for a viewing of the show. It's another of those lines where a character says something, and his intent is almost beside the point. Through a comic miracle his words now outline the perfect equality—regardless of class, age, sex, or intelligence—of what anyone is like to know about the mystery Pryamus seeks to penetrate: at any moment of this life, Everyman will know all that he is like to know about this or anything. On account of the great seriousness and anxieties surrounding the subject of his play, Peter Quince is on hand to convey a wonderful simplicity and content about it, and his words are like the hand of a friend that steadies us, like the comfort Deucalion felt when, overlooking a vast emptiness, he sensed the presence of Pyrrha there on the ledge with him. The sweetness of Peter Quince's character works to lighten and redeem the confusion of the prologue, and it defines the nature of his rule.

C. Choral Responses to Peter Quince's Performance

Undoubtedly, Theseus discerns Peter Quince's intent, but the nobility as a group is quick to point out his mistakes. In this they resemble those of us who enjoy talking back to the TV in our living room. It's a sport we can play in the comfort of our home that's taboo in a movie theater. Like a great symphony which reminds its listeners of melodies and rhythms the composer has treated earlier as he works toward his finale, each remark touches on a theme that has been developed during the course of the play.

Theseus comments on one of the most important by observing that "This fellow doth not stand upon points." His point is that Peter Quince has run through those places in his sentence where he should stop, but he also paints a picture of a man trying to stand on points. If we take it literally, Theseus is expecting Peter Quince to do the impossible. A man cannot stand on points, for a point is a geometric abstraction or the sharp end of something like a knife. Nevertheless, the play provides examples of those who manage to stand where there's little or nothing to hold them up.

It prominently features Bottom, after the trap door of his life has been sprung from under him, who finds a bottom against which he can find his feet and regain initiative. He manages somehow to stand on something. He's a silly ass, but that's a small consideration when contrasted with the fact that he's a silly ass who is beloved of the fairy queen. The two together add up to a secure bottom. When Oberon looks into the possibility that fate has usurped his government of the woods, he too acts without any visible support to regain the initiative.

In addition, if we consider the nature of argument and the way one person may strive to make a point in a contest with another, the example of a clown who does not stand upon points and who does no harm to himself or others stands in stark contrast with normal people who do stand on their points and who often do great harm to themselves and others. Pyramus and Thisby are about to model for us two young people who don't just stand on points; they intentionally fall on the point (of a sword) and run it right through them. This fixes them forever!

No one can blame Peter Quince for not standing on points. Like Peter Quince among great ones, though, Shakespeare must have taken assurance from his own mind and heart to stand on the airy nothing of his poetry before his countrymen both great and small. He would express a longing to serve that which is beautiful and good, and he would call forth with his words a power that carries the day into a comic conclusion. The image of a man standing on almost nothing suggests once more the trial of Deucalion on that little ledge overlooking the flood, a flood like the one that has afflicted the land around Athens. In Deucalion's case, it's from that precarious little ledge and from the longing that springs out of the emptiness of the view that the entire world is reborn. The fairies, too, are so small that human eyes can't see them, and yet the comic conclusion of the play maintains its uprightness, its form and dignity, on the airy nothing of fairyland. It may not be much of a foundation, but for better or worse it's *something*.

The imagery and this theme can be found in "The Knight's Tale" as well. From the one window in their room on top of Theseus' keep, Palamon and Arcite glimpse, like looking at an object through a long tube, a beautiful woman in the garden below them. She may be just an image, as I have maintained throughout the reading of Chaucer's tale, but we now know that the little "0" at the end of that tube with the empty image of Emily in the middle of it is the foundation and the motive force for the rest of the tale. Because it represents "the true beginning of our end"—for it represents the beginning of a lifelong quest for meaning and purpose— listen once more to Palamon's cry:

> And so it happened on this May morn,
>
> Through a deep window set with many bars
>
> Of mighty iron squared with massive spars,
>
> He chanced on Emily to cast his eye
>
> And, as he did, he blenched and gave a cry
>
> As though he had been stabbed, and to the heart.

This stabbing of a knife's point to the heart is a kind of death, but it also gives birth to a new life, one that eventually ends in marriage to Emily. Although Chaucer doesn't specify, I hear Palamon crying "O" with sudden surprise. From the vantage point that Shakespeare has given us of looking through the long tube of a sentence (in a work like this one, it's a long series of tubes), that empty "O" at the end of what we know *is* our life. It may not be much of a foundation, but for better or worse it's *something*.

After an opening for deep thoughts, the poet offers up Lysander's "take" on the point of the Prologue's mistakes for comic relief:

> He hath rid his prologue like a rough colt; he knows not the stop. A good moral, my lord: it is not enough to speak, but to speak true.

This moral of the story, coming from Lysander, may remind a listener of the one about the pot calling the kettle black. This is the Lysander who speaks truly and with all his heart but whose words leave in their wake a great disorder. He is also the one who can speak so wisely of reason while completely intoxicated with the flower juice. If there's a rough colt in the play who runs about bucking and kicking, we'd be hard-pressed to find a better one than Lysander. Along with other examples of looking with parted eye and seeing double, there's a double meaning of "rid" so Lysander could be saying that his prologue has thrown Peter Quince off like a runaway colt throws off a rider, or that Peter Quince has tossed off (spoken) the prologue inexpertly like a rough colt would throw off a rider. If Lysander's judgment of Peter Quince is backfiring on him and if Lysander is the rider, then far more than ever the prologue "rid" itself of Peter Quince (threw him off into confusion) life has thrown Lysander for a loop.

After this bit of helter-skelter, Hippolyta has a more sober assessment:

> Indeed he hath play'd on his prologue like a child on a recorder—a sound,
> but not in government.

She, like the entire play, reflects a concern about the government of our life. Her image puts that government squarely in our own hands and in the modulations of our own breath. This holds true not just for a child but for anyone at any moment.

While their comments are unique to their characters, the three in the chorus speak with one voice on the need for self-government. Theseus judges that, even though it's a balancing act, a man must learn to stop at the right places; Lysander moralizes that a man must learn to control the rough colt of mind and body; Hippolyta observes that, if we would make our life a sweet melody, we must manage the stops of our instrument and our breath.

D. A Chain of Love

Theseus then closes this little chorus on the Prologue with an analogy derived from his ancestor in "The Knight's Tale:

> *His speech was like a tangled chain; nothing impaired, but all disordered. Who is next?*

It's a tangled chain, but Theseus knows from his assessment of Peter Quince and his company that it's a chain of love. In Theseus' eyes and ears, nothing impairs his impression of that love, but the speech that conveys the love is all disordered. The links of the speech are not "impaired." The words are paired up well enough, but the stops (to borrow Lysander's word) magically change the meaning from what the words were intended to say.

Peter Quince's Prologue and the nobility's view of him and his speech make yet another tableau where different people look at something differently. Lysander pictures a rider whose horse has gotten "rid" of him. A rough colt that "knows not the stop" could cause, as it did for Arcite, a mortal fall. Hippolyta imagines the sound an unskillful child makes on an instrument. These two have judged Peter Quince according to the standards of the court where facile speech is a prerequisite for a courtier. They both love highly specialized skills that are valued by aristocrats. Since it's the means by which he makes his way in the world, Lysander is attached to a reputation as a skilled horseman. Hippolyta loves the beautiful music of an instrument like the recorder that softens the stone interiors of a palace with melody. To return once more to Helena's formulation, they look at Peter Quince with minds that love skillful riding, music making, and courtly speaking.

Theseus, on the other hand, views Peter Quince's speech as a tangled chain, but with "nothing impaired." Unlike the other two, Theseus looks with the eyes, which is a way of saying that, like the blind seers Teiresias and Homer, he "sees" what eyes and ears can't see or hear. There is much that Theseus doesn't know about Peter Quince. We know from the dramatis personae that he is a builder. Theseus has been told he's a workman, but he can't possibly know everything he does in Athens for the people of the town to make it a more livable place. If he is a wise ruler, though, he'll have the sense to value a hard-handed man like Peter for the good work he renders his neighbors and for the value he adds to the city's capital stock. A sensible duke will "see" that there's more to him than someone who has a narrow focus like Lysander or Philostrate.

From this perspective Theseus represents the comic vision or wisdom that's the theme of the poem. A person will more likely arrive at a comic resolution of what one is hearing, words and stops and all, if one senses the motive force of poorly executed or even self-serving gestures. This sense develops in experiences like those we have witnessed during the course of the play. Twice in the play Theseus overrules men who argue for the status quo with an ill will, first a tyrant father and then a preening and overweening impresario; these actions show good sense. In relation to Hippolyta, though, this sense prevails on him to sometimes pause and take a breath when she's not meeting an expectation. He doesn't do this because he's learning to be wise. He does it because Hippolyta is such a formidable partner that there's no other possible course of action. His experiences with her have been the school of hard knocks that civilizes an impulse the way a rough colt civilizes after painful falls the rider's rough colt, his own mind and heart, into a more intelligent and stable state. Old habits die hard. Theseus may be used to controlling others with an impressive display of arms and rhetorical flourishes like his Comic Doctrine. Now that he's married to Hippolyta, he may be more concerned than he ever has been to sense and restrain the motive force of his own poorly executed and self-serving gestures.

The audience is also being asked to take the poet's point about seeing what we can't see more broadly. Like Theseus judging the performance of Peter Quince, everyone has the autonomy to judge the world that's passing into our eyes and ears. We have that autonomy, but we are also only links in a vast interconnected chain. It's impossible to know exactly the value of everything in the chain or of everything that happens within a chain of events. A comic fall, an echo of the voice out of the whirlwind, forces us to briefly confront what we are like *not* to know. Do we know the structure of the universe, the voice asks, its height, depth, and breadth? Do we know why we are born into it? And since the prologue is about the good will that motivates Peter Quince and his company, do we know the motive power behind all things? When Peter Quince tells us that by the show of things we shall know what we are like to know, what we are like to know appears to us out of a dark background of what we are not like to know. Even though we don't know it, it exists. It's the ground of everything, a life-giving darkness, and as such it's our subject.

In a comedy like this one, we are shown enough to know that the motive power is love, and its structure is like a chain of love. We see as well that people are moved by two very different kinds of love, *cupiditas* and *caritas*. The one is narrow and selfish, and the other is open and selfless. The play also shows that these two kinds of love are as intimately related as a man and a woman in a love relationship. They are in reality two sides of the same coin or two phases in the state of a plant or a human being or two links in a chain of love. They are both forms of love, but they are separate the way a man and a woman are separate. They are separate states, but how is it that one state changes into the other? How does a person come to see with the eyes, not with the mind? What's the catalyst?

E. Theaters for Comedy

The central drama of comedy is like the wrestling match of two combatants—a man versus the world out there—and the match concludes when the man takes a fall into the dust of the arena. In comedy the loser turns out to be the winner, for he is forced to look anew at the world and, if he is determined enough, to inventory his faults. This is the pattern we have seen throughout the two works. Like the arena where Palamon and Arcite come to grips with the idea of possessing Emily, the open air of the wood around Athens is where the business of looking is sorted out in Shakespeare's play. Comedy does its work in public. It's live speech and counter-speech, ideas tested in an open-air marketplace, but its effect still relies on the insight of an autonomous individual—the one who is alive to feel the great intent and consequences of it all.

Once the play moves back to Athens, Theseus' court serves as the arena where ideas are openly tested just as it did in the beginning. Now, though, it's more like a theater for merriments rather than a court for a capital crime. It's also a time to celebrate the arena or the theater that is at the heart of the social order. Theseus' reference to that which is "nothing impaired" brings to mind the three couples paired together who have so recently gone two by two into the ark of marriage and who are ready to embark to whatever far shores that marriage will take them. Like words put together that are not impaired by being put together, the priest has married them. They are nothing impaired in being so, and yet, from Peter Quince's example as well as the examples of Titania and Oberon and all the other couples who quarrel in the play, there's also a great potential for disorder. The prospect of a comic conclusion depends on where to put the stops and begin again, and comedy makes the case that this is a skill most people learn in the school of hard knocks. Theseus and the others may find that marriage is a school like that just as their courtship has been. According to Helena's formulation, though, what they learn is less a skill and more the way a lover looks when, mastered by a larger intelligence, the mind is quiet and love looks with the eyes.

"Who is next?" Theseus asks, to fall into speech that's like a tangled chain, nothing impaired but all disordered. Why, that would be whichever of the three couples has their first quarrel as man and wife.

Pieta

A. A World That's Closed and Open

Chaucer's Theseus describes creation as a chain of love, and

Shakespeare has now added his take on the image into the text of his play. They have employed the image to suggest that our life in this world is a strange marriage of constraint and freedom, and their comic narratives act out the linking of the two states. These routines are still the staple of comedy. When the pedestrian chained to his BlackBerry slips on a banana peel, the text is vacated, and he finds himself lying (and relying) instead on something more real. It's a priceless opening to the world that's worth the weight of a man in comic gold. A person who is watching this can cash in on it too if he sees it's but a short step from an old burlesque routine to the routines of his daily life. Without any effort at all anyone can slip into an obsessive attachment like Robin's gossip when—in the throes of telling her story—she misses her stool and lands in a graceless heap. Her story constrains her attention, but her mistake unleashes a torrent of comic energy and enjoyment.

Due to the addictive power of attachment, even after the crash a remnant of ego may refuse to accept that it has landed on that which is infinitely mightier than the preoccupation which led to the fall. It takes Arcite three days after his fall for the attachment that led him down that dark cul de sac to get lost in the shuffle. In his last moments, he asks Emily to hold him in her arms, and there he confesses to her the nature of his love, his *cupiditas*. Since he is slipping away from life, he asks her then to remember Palamon, "that great hearted man." He can let her go, for the loss of Emily is made whole by the gain of a larger intelligence. This is *caritas*. Arcite's fall is a tragedy and the gossip's fall a comedy, but they are both telling the same story. It's the story comedy is always telling about people waking from what they wish was true to look at the world as it is. A hundred years after the writing of "The Knight's Tale" and about a hundred years before the writing of *A Midsummer Night's Dream*, Michelangelo created his *Pieta* so that anyone who looked could see the whole story in an instant of recognition. A mother holds her son, a body fully grown to manhood, with one hand while with the other she lets him go. She has to, for it's clear that life has slipped from his body even as his dead weight is slipping down her lap. It's the most sublime representation in the Western world of *caritas*, the acknowledgment and the letting go of a deep attachment.

Shakespeare has conveyed the grasping hand throughout his play in the way characters hold on to an obsessive idea. Egeus adamantly holds on to the idea that he can determine the course of Hermia's life, and the idea is so fixed that he is willing to end her life rather than give his idea up; later in the wood Hermia desperately holds on to the idea that Lysander loves her—despite his open declaration of love for Helena—by physically grabbing him and refusing to let him go; Titania and Oberon cling to the idea of possessing the little Indian boy for the honor of their respective sexes; and Helena holds on just as fiercely to the idea that she's as ugly as a bear and only suited for single life.

These characters eventually give their ideas up but not without a fight. After Egeus successfully makes his case against his daughter before the highest court of the land, the next day Theseus bluntly overrules him and his own previous judgment without excuse or comment; Hermia finally lets Lysander go but only after Lysander tells her point blank that he doesn't love her; despite months of bitter warfare, Oberon and Titania reconcile to raise up the child jointly; after fighting all night to preserve the dignity and honor of one who would remain single, Helena wakes at the sound of the hunting horns to find Demetrius "mine own," but she still has the good sense to add "and not mine own." Helena comes close to one who, like the mother in Pieta, embodies both gestures, but Bottom wins the prize for most integrated character. He begins with a desperate hold on the idea that he is the center of the universe. During the dislocations and confusions attendant on his transformation he may have sensed, as he touched those fair large ears, that he was an ass for thinking so, but the love of Titania also gives him proof enough of his intrinsic importance. Thankfully, he no longer has to be so obnoxious about it.

Shakespeare has placed the little empty "O" of Peter Quince's production at the end of his play where it enjoys the autonomy of its own little life. Like a sentence with a point at the end, it's a cosmos with a meaningful shape which speaks to us of our life. The mother of Pieta, who comprehends in her own body the need to hold on and to let go, symbolizes a deep compassion—for her son, herself, and all life, but she also represents, in a sort of allegory, the world human beings inhabit. Just as she owns both gestures, she lives in and reflects a cosmos that is like a hand that constrains and a hand that opens up; this is the world that Shakespeare has created in his final tableau.

He constructs it around a narrative that has strong parallels with the love stories in "The Knight's Tale" and *A Midsummer Night's Dream*. The fathers of Pyramus and Thisby have shut them up from the world. To emphasize the importance of the wall that separates them, the story takes place in Ninus' city of Babylon, which was famous for the walls that closed it in from the outside world. Once they wake up to their imprisonment, Pyramus and Thisby also enliven their prison space by falling in love just as Palamon and Arcite do and just as Hermia does in defiance of her father.

Like Theseus' tower and Egeus' will, the wall that separates Pyramus and Thisby is the equal and opposite obstacle to the lovers' desire. Peter Quince gives Tom Snout the tinker a little speech to introduce himself and his all important part to the audience:

> *In this same interlude it doth befall*
>
> *That I, Snout by name, present a wall;*
>
> *And such a wall, as I would have you think,*
>
> *That had in it a crannied hole or chink;*
>
> *Through which the lovers, Pyramus and Thisby,*
>
> *Did whisper often, very secretly.*
>
> *This loam, this roughcast, and this stone doth show*
>
> *That I am that same wall. The truth is so.*

That said, he holds out his hand, spreading the index and middle fingers wide to explain:

And this the cranny is, right and sinister,

Through which the fearful lovers are to whisper.

Walls and prisons represent the limiting of a space, and those who live closed in by them will be limited in what they can know of the world. Like everything else in the world, however, that which would limit the human mind is also limited; there will always be a window or a chink or a cranny. We live in a world that is closed and open.

The crannied chink plays a paradoxical role. It's the opening that gives birth to obsessive attachments, as suggested by the passion of Pyramus:

Pyr.   *O kiss me through the hole of this vile wall!*

But it also kick-starts, like the strong liquor that bathes a root in the spring, a motion towards greater freedom:

This.   *I kiss the wall's hole, not your lips at all.*

Pyr.   *Wilt thou at Ninny's tomb meet me straightway?*

This.   *Tide life, tide death, I come without delay.*

Something has to give. The little chink through which they whisper excites them to taste more fully what their parents forbid. In their separate houses they can only hear the ghostly voice of their love (and in Ovid's narrative they sense the sweetness of the other's breath), but this little taste ignites a passion that burns up every other thing in the world including parental law. Once parental law has been burned away, it's through the chink that they make plans to meet outside. Here at last, the wall is down and the world lies open before them.

Or so it would seem. The lovers in Chaucer's tale, Shakespeare's play, and Ovid's little story all begin in prison, a closed world. Palamon and Arcite are locked up for life in Theseus' keep, Hermia is condemned to be locked up in a nunnery or in a marriage with a man she doesn't love, Helena is imprisoned in a negative self-image, and Pyramus and Thisby are kept like prisoners in their homes. In all the stories the lovers escape to the open where their love can freely manifest itself. The lovers from Athens escape to the wood around the city, and Pyramus and Thisby meet, more ominously, in a graveyard. The Athenian's freedom proves for a time to be even more problematic than the confinement imposed on them by a duke or a parent, but they enjoy a freedom to fall from their own choices into a painful correction. This is their opening for a comic ending.

The Babylonians, on the other hand, gain their freedom only to end it forever. Pyramus mistakes a bloody mantle for proof that Thisby is dead. Because he cannot let her go without him, he joins her in death. Put that way, his story is not even a tragedy but a sad and bitter joke, for Thisby lives. When she finds Pyramus all bloody from his sword and unresponsive to her calls to life, she cannot let him go without her, and so she joins him in death. Her passion, at least, is grounded in an actual, as opposed to an imagined, death, but the suicides of these lovers are haunted by human error.

The root of error for all the lovers is *cupiditas*, the passionate desire for an object and a radical narrowing of their vision.[68] Characters can suffer from *cupiditas* as easily in the open air as they suffer it in the confinement of a prison cell. The mind, not the environment, is the heart of the matter. The root for freedom is *caritas*, an opening to a larger intelligence and a letting go of what was thought. Pyramus and Thisby may have cut their story short, but this gives the play a reason for being. The audience must wake themselves up for them as a remembrance and save them from the utter pointlessness of their suicides. More than a remembrance, it's a precious legacy of what was lost.

B. Thisby's Lament and Silence

The pointless suicide of young lovers is an odd way to end a comedy; it must be that the poet regarded the bitterness of their story as essential to the overall comic effect. This effect is the opening we all seek. First and foremost, by turning the production into a farce, he has made it impossible to take the mechanicals' production seriously. In addition, in case someone was affected by the tragedy, he has Bottom suddenly spring up, after running himself through with a sword, to disagree with something Demetrius has said. It's proof for the audience that Bottom is an actor, and the play in which he lives and dies is like a dream from which we awaken when he rises. This comes closer to the play's point in that it has to do with the power of the mind to shape the things of this world in its own image as a dreaming mind does. If the mind can only dream in the language of tragedy, then the world it creates will be tragic. It's the cul de sac from which the eyes would awaken, and Bottom's resurrection breaks the spell.

In the previous paragraph I discount the possibility that the audience will be taken in by the mechanicals' farcical production. But because we all are so sensitive to language, because we tend to take at face value that which has been framed for us in an intelligible sentence even if it's a palpable invention, because we essentially live (vicariously) in a world of language, and because we tend to look at the world through the lens of tragedy, the audience may also be touched at some level by the enactment of these suicides. The poet is playing a double game. He would save his play for comedy, but for the true comic effect, the audience must suspend its disbelief and enter into the lives and the deaths of Pyramus and Thisby, despite the grossness of the mechanicals' representations. We must experience once more how the mind can get lost in a production of mind. The mind can get lost in it (and lose the time between after-supper and bedtime), but from now until doomsday its productions can only be a haphazard rehearsal and hazy guess about the death it represents, *which is unknowable*. This last is what Thisby confronts as she holds the body of Pyramus in her arms—like the mother in *Pieta* holding the one she loves—to question, to grieve, and to relinquish what she cannot possess.

Only a great poet can write bad poetry that's transcendently good. Even as she lulls the audience with the childish doggerel and comic exaggerations of the poet's verses, Thisby's lament moves us with pity and penetrating insight:

Asleep, my love?

What, dead, my dove?

O Pyramus, arise!

Speak, speak! Quite dumb?

Dead, dead? A tomb

Must cover thy sweet eyes.

These lily lips,

This cherry nose,

These yellow cowslip cheeks,

Are gone, are gone.

Lovers, make moan!

His eyes were green as leeks.

O Sisters Three,

Come, come to me,

With hands as pale as milk;

Lay them in gore,

Since you have shore

With shears his thread of silk.

Tongue, not a word!

Come, trusty sword;

Come, blade, my breast imbrue!

Her words poke and probe at the surface of this death. It's like sleep, but, no, that's not it. The body just lies there and can't get up. She speaks to it, but it doesn't answer. It's as silent as a tomb, which, she remembers, is where he'll now live. Lastly, she takes in his lips, nose, cheeks, and eyes and notices that they are losing their color. These lines may be set like humorous verse, but Thisby's sudden cry—which seems to have forced itself on her when it was left out of the catalogue of his face—that "His eyes were green as leeks" speaks of loss as poignantly as anything this poet ever wrote. She has much to say, but all these words merely catalogue her state of mind as she looks at the body and notes the changes. The body itself, she observes, is quite dumb as to its own mind. The contrast of its silence with her moaning is too much for Thisby to continue speech, and so she advises herself to follow the body's example with, "Tongue, not a word!"

The poet's jangling couplets, a poetic form so basic to every child's development as a human and a social being, reminds every listener of that love affair with language which begins in a child's earliest months and years. A love, like Thisby's for Pyramus, is easier to grasp, for the love of language is less concrete and requires an imagination to see it at all and then to plumb its depths. Still, it's a deep and abiding love. In her grief Thisby holds on to her love by speaking of it, massaging into life what lies before her with words, but when the words all fail she lets them go. This is her opening in an endless cycle of grief. Just as her grief moves her to speak of it, her grief brings her to this silence, the source from which all things engendered here below are derived and to which they course. As she did for Pyramus, let us lament this young girl who, in her brief span of life, uncovered the silence but mistook it for death.

The twentieth century poet W.B. Yeats has written that "Words alone are certain good." On most days Thisby would agree, but she now can add that, when words come to the end of what they can do, silence alone is certain good. Those of us who love the works of Chaucer and Shakespeare are grateful that they, having glimpsed the infinite power of the silence that lies behind all speech, have found a way to speak to us of that power without usurping the silence. Even though the mind and the language it employs is limited to a surface like that in Thisby's lament, these poets would show that the mind is still capable of more than the language that defines it as "mind." The mind can clutch at things and hold on for dear life with words and sentences, but it can also let it all go. In the silent contemplation of the Pieta, it's all one.

C. The Greatness of What the Mind Doesn't Know

A love of language is intimately tied to a passion for knowing. Quite apart from the mechanicals' version of it, Ovid's story of Pyramus and Thisby illustrates that the love of what we know, which blinds us to what we don't know, can lead us down a mortal cul de sac. Because Pyramus knows that Thisby is dead (from the evidence of her bloody mantle), this knowing blinds him to the fact that she isn't. He acts, with an overweening confidence, on a bad idea. We get stories like this in the news every day, and too often we see these cul de sacs manifested as car wrecks on the highway. I have in mind an accident that took the life of a student. She was in a car that was following a truck heading north on the highway. Right at the point where her driver needed to turn left, the road ahead bent somewhat to the right. Before her driver reached the turn, he looked and saw no car coming in the opposite direction. He didn't see, because the truck ahead blocked his vision in the instant that he looked, the vehicle heading south that was hidden in the blind spot behind the truck he was following. He turned left, and the vehicle heading south struck his car full force. Because the driver looked and saw no vehicle coming south, he knew that the way was clear to turn, and this blinded him to the fact that it wasn't.

People have accidents because they don't see what they don't see. This formulation may seem like a literary paradox, but it's a practical matter that we encounter every day and which only imagination can unravel. It's a vision of situations that, by "looking" into blind spots, serves and protects. Instead of merely dismissing ignorance as someone else's problem, the way Philostrate does, the Pyramus and Thisby story compels a grieving witness to wonder at the greatness of what the mind doesn't know.

D. Silence and Live Speech

In the end, the mechanicals' presentation is a triumph, but no one actor can claim it for himself. That prize is reserved for the stage itself, the place to which all have been drawn by illusion to receive the blessing of comedy. One by one Peter Quince's company clear the stage. First Wall "away doth go"; Lion tears Thisby's mantle and exits; at Pyramus' command, moon takes flight; and Pyramus and Thisby perish. With Thisby's final "adieu" the stage falls silent. After so much speech and action on this stage, it all has come to this. Though empty, it's the silent stage's moment of triumph. For those of us who are flesh and blood, a death even in a play leaves a gap, asks a question, sparks a yearning. Into the silence, into a gap momentany as a sound, Theseus is first to speak. He observes that:

Moonshine and Lion are left to bury the dead.

Perhaps he feels he should say something, and so he brings us back, away from the silence of the dead, to those who remain to carry on with the business at hand. As in response to the silence and as an expression of a deep longing, life and the speech of live people pours out again.

Perhaps to say something as well, to hear his own voice, and to add his own memory of the show to silence the silence, Demetrius reminds them: "Aye, and Wall too." As if on cue, these words spur Bottom into renewed speech and action. He "starts up" with a surprising announcement:

> No, I assure you; the wall is down that parted their fathers.

Moonshine and Lion may be out there still, but the wall is down. Bottom's sudden speech may not make his audience laugh, but it too is comic gold. Somehow, bully Bottom has gotten to the bottom of Ovid's text (Did someone tell him about the rest of the story? Did he just "know" that the story would end like that?), and it's such an important theme that Shakespeare himself treats it more fully in *Romeo and Juliet*.

If Bottom speaks for the poet here, then as Shakespeare's comedy draws to a close, we have been told that for now the old walls that tragically divide people from each other and from their own nature are down. Life instinctively speaks against the pointless waste just witnessed. The ancient fears, the doubts about life are down; people are resolved to live in the open. Those ancient fears and doubts may come back to hem them in, but that's another story.

E. A Noble Respect for Fairy Time

Once on his feet, Bottom offers Theseus an epilogue (he would love to prolong the magic), but the duke declines it in favor of a dance. The Bergomask done, Theseus judges that (finally) it's time for bed:

> The iron tongue of midnight hath told twelve.
>
> Lovers, to bed; 'tis almost fairy time.

In keeping with the theme developed throughout these final scenes, it's a judgment that sees time as a barrier that both closes and opens. The bell tolls midnight, and it tolls for them all. It's an ironclad law that the day, Everyman's day, must end. In the next breath, though, with "Lovers, to bed; 'tis almost fairy time," Theseus shifts into a different way of looking at the present hour.

The iron tongue of midnight speaks of a constraint like the iron links of a chain, and yet from where he stands, as a newly married man, Theseus now commands a prospect of love and of imagination in love, and so he sees these things as with parted eye when everything seems double. At first he says:

> *I fear we shall outsleep the coming morn*
>
> *As much as we this night have overwatched.*

This is the Theseus who lives by daylight as a soldier and a sober judge. As a soldier he knows that a dead man stays dead, and as a judge he knows that a Hermia cannot be married to both Demetrius and Lysander. He knows as well as Solomon did that Egeus' child can't be cut in half to satisfy both parties. She's a limited resource, and a proper judge must determine how this limitation can be resolved within a legal framework.

But Theseus is no longer just a soldier and a judge of what he knows to be the law. He's a married man, and during the course of the play his better half consistently probes at his own limitations and makes him aware of that dark side of the moon—all that he doesn't know and can't know of a woman. For this he needs the help of a poet who gives "to airy nothing / A local habitation and a name" the way Hippolyta has in her lively replies. As we listen to the rest of Theseus' final speech, the two ways of looking— as a martial judge and as a married man—would appear to have come into balance. He fears dreaming too long, for this can only take away from the coming morn when his wakeful attention to practical affairs of state will be required, but he acknowledges a noble respect for fairy time:

This palpable gross play hath well beguil'd

The heavy gait of night. Sweet friends, to bed.

A fortnight hold we this solemnity

In nightly revels and new jollity.

The iron tongue of midnight has spoken to close up the day, but it also opens up for the lovers a fortnight of fairy time, a stronghold of nights for love and for comedy. In Shakespeare's play, heavy hours locked up in a tower of unfulfilled desire have been transformed into "nightly revels and new jollity."

If Peter Quince's play has "beguiled" the time as Theseus says it has, then the play has made one what time divided. Just as Oberon echoes the speech of the little fairy at his moment of reconciliation with Titania, Theseus now echoes Hippolyta's speech at the opening of the play, for it is she who imagines an end to the suffering of those whose love looks with the mind:

Four days will quickly steep themselves in night

Four nights will quickly dream away the time;

And then the new moon, like to a silver bow

New bent in heaven, shall behold the night

Of our solemnities.

Peter Quince's play has realized Hippolyta's vision of their "solemnities." Hippolyta had the vision, but it's the mechanicals who make it a reality for the long age between after-supper and bedtime. The moon new bent in heaven looks with the eyes of one who has passed away and come back to life, and this is what the dancing mechanicals represent as well. These are eyes and these are dancers with "a most rare vision," a comic view of life. They have done their job and set the stage for love; this is their cue for the lovers to act.

Overlooking Love's Stories

The government of Shakespeare's play is about to change again. Theseus has retired, the mechanicals have done their job, and now it's fairy time. To celebrate their inauguration, my reading of the play stops again to overlook, as inaugurals do, the state of the realm. Because the play has established important polarities that strongly influence its overall health, the reading pauses to overlook the state of these unions.

We can begin with the polarities of man and woman. As the happy couples have gone to bed, nothing more needs to be said about that. The play touched on the polarities of being and not being, and Peter Quince has put that question to bed by showing us all that we are like to know about it. His play has also, almost by magic, united the polarities of comedy and tragedy. If we turn to the business at hand, the transition into fairy time, we are made aware of the force field between dreaming and not dreaming. The two settings of Shakespeare's play serve as his magnetic North and South poles, and his characters are animated by the creative tension that exists between the fairies' night rule in the wood and Theseus' government in Athens. This polarity expresses as well the creative tension within every individual between an autonomous individual's desire and the need for order within a social context. As we approach the next transition from fairy time to when we leave the theater to peep at the world with our own fool's eyes, we overlook the state that's a union of dreaming and waking.

The autonomy (and subjectivity) that's become the dominant note in our culture is best exemplified in a dream, and dreams are essentially about love. If you consult the dream visions of popular music, for example, your ears will be filled with love, love, and more love. Here's what Rogers and Hammerstein have contributed to the annals about love at first sight:

Some enchanted evening

When you find your true love,

When you feel her call you

Across a crowded room,

Then fly to her side,

And make her your own

Or all through your life you

May dream all alone.

A character who dreams all alone lives as an exile. Since we live in a culture that has made a fetish of dreaming and of dreams, since desire can never be satisfied by the possession of an object, and since it's impossible to materially possess anything in this world except in a manner of speaking, millions of people in comfortable situations suffer from the exile prompted by desire. This alienation may be a pronounced characteristic of our own time, but it's nothing new. It's part and parcel of the human condition as described in our literature for thousands of years.

For all the pain and frustration we suffer from desire brought on by social situations, human beings still are social animals. Without the warmth and sustenance of social contact, people wither in isolation. Unlike the dreamscapes that prompt desire, comedy would show that a glimpse of someone across a crowded room is only the first movement in the work of relationship. In addition to studying the psychology of love as *cupiditas* and its alienating side effects, therefore, these comic narratives outline the way human beings are restored to their true birthright as organic links in the social order. The desire of the individual and the stewardship of the law are intimately related, and in their interaction the essential functions of both are fulfilled. They mend each other.

A dream, like Bottom's, is inalienably subjective. What happens to him in his dream must be more than just an idle fancy, however, in that it transforms him and enhances his fortunes at the court of Duke Theseus. This is why he is right to call it "a most rare vision." Despite the dream's personal and revealing nature, Bottom's first impulse is to share it with his fellows, and so he runs to town to have Peter Quince write a ballet of it and make it public. Perhaps this is the epilogue that he wants to perform for the duke. But the duke declines the offer, and the company treats him to a Bergomask instead. Even though the court doesn't hear the story of Bottom's dream, his inspiration, his drive and initiative after the dream carry the project forward when it appears that all is lost, and his buoyant character have now become the possession of everyone. Bottom is a case study of an autonomous self breaking away from an established state to fulfill its own will and then, on its return, impacting the design of the whole. Bottom, it so happens, impacts the design for good; other autonomous actors, like Iago in *Othello*, impact the design for evil. This is the burden of autonomy.

Of what exactly does his dream, the one that initiates a comic conclusion, consist? Here's what Bottom says of it at the time:

> *I have had a dream, past the wit of man to say what dream it was. Man is but an ass if he go about to expound this dream.*

Commentators beware. The man who just spent the night with the fairy queen has concluded that his experience can't be expounded; those of us who have not spent a night with the fairy queen are in no position to expound it for him. He may have enjoyed the fairy queen, but we all now know that his "fair large ears" played a large role in winning her affection.

For those of us who pride ourselves above all on our intelligence and not our foolishness, this is a difficult, maybe even an insurmountable, barrier. Bottom also wrestles with this part of his experience:

> *Methought I was—there is no man can tell what. Methought I was, and*

methought I had—But man is but a patch'd fool if he will offer to say what methought I had.

There is no man who can say what Bottom was. He's right for several reasons. If it was a dream, no man in the world, apart from himself, is privy to it. What he was is also past, and the past is as lost to one presently alive as a dream is hidden from an outside observer. In addition, his transformation has tangibly proved that the world and all things in it are constantly changing their shapes. An experience like this tends to put a man's certainty about things, including himself, in doubt. Because everything is subject to these changes, man (in general) would be a fool to say what Bottom or any man possesses whether it's a feature or characteristic he thinks sets him apart from others, like beauty or ugliness, or anything he thinks he owns, like Titania as a partner in bed. Along with those other attributes which he touches his head to find, Titania is no more.

Bottom's words about his dream and what he thought he had echo Helena's uncertainty when she wakes up to find Demetrius "mine own, and not mine own." Any more than Helena's questioning of an expectation, Bottom's jumbled exclamations may not seem like much of a foundation on which to stand and create a new world, but something behind his assertions establishes a little ledge or a lifeline for him to conclude with a positive flourish:

> *The eye of man hath not heard, the ear of man hath not seen, man's hand is not able to taste, his tongue to conceive, nor his heart to report what my dream was.*

It's a positive conclusion, for his dream, we know, has a positive effect for him and everyone. He is transformed for the good, but of the dream itself it is supremely difficult to speak. It doesn't belong to the world of looking, listening, touching, tasting, imagining, feeling, or reporting. So what is the reality of that which, though it seems not to be of this world, nevertheless has the power to change this world for the better?

The speech that Chaucer's Theseus gives at the end of "The Knight's Tale" wrestles with this same question; to set the stage for a comic conclusion, he has to make the intangible "First Great Cause and Mover of all above" as real to his listeners as a loved object like Emily for those who would possess her. The desire to possess a mere part of the whole, Theseus argues, is an understandable but a misplaced love, for "Anyone but a fool knows, in his soul, / That every part derives from this great whole." By all means, love Emily and the things of this world, but remember the source of all and everything.

Along with all the usual poetic devices for giving an airy nothing a tangible reality, Shakespeare also employs the make-believe of theater and specifically the make-believe of fairyland to convey the reality of a comic intelligence that overlooks the drama of our life. Lysander has already spoken of this overlooking when praising Helena's beauty:

> Things growing are not ripe until their season;
>
> So I, being young, till now ripe not to reason;
>
> And touching now the point of human skill,
>
> Reason becomes the marshal to my will
>
> And leads me to your eyes; where I o'erlook
>
> Love's stories, written in love's richest book.

He describes here reason's true function. Reason that has been ripened or seasoned has developed a quality of vision that, despite all the temptations to do otherwise, has been marshaled by experience to see what needs to be seen and to do what must be done. Even though Lysander is far from actually seeing this way, he imagines most memorably looking from a point of view where one can intelligently and compassionately read love's stories in love's richest books.

For as long as there have been cynics, there have been those who discount that anyone can look like this, that is, with an unimpeded love of life. Shakespeare's theater, however, has put a doubter like Theseus in a position where he becomes the subject of the play's alchemy. By degrees, through the incidents of the play, he is led to believe that a power to look in this way is as real as the fairies who are about to make their way onstage once more to overlook the affairs of Athenians.

For those of us who live to respond to him, an unimpeded love of life is as real as the Puck who reclaims the stage now that the human actors have vacated it.

Fairyland Dances "A Chain of Love"

Puck comes to announce the fairy time that Theseus foretold; with a broom in hand, he speaks of this time and his reason for being there:

> Now the hungry lion roars,
>
> And the hungry wolf behowls the moon;

It's a time when desire, somewhat contained and controlled by the busyness of the day, cries out. For some, though, the busyness of the day has already exhausted them, and they can only sleep:

> Whilst the heavy ploughman snores,
>
> All with weary task fordone.

This may be a blessing, considering the pain of desire, but human beings are not just donkeys in the traces of a greater power who sleep their life away even when awake. Like any human being, the heavy ploughman fordone with labor will sometimes have the sleepless nights of a hungry lion or moonstruck wolf. So Puck describes his thoughts as he lies awake in bed:

Now the wasted brands do glow,

Whilst the screech owl, screeching loud,

Puts the wretch that lies in woe

In remembrance of a shroud.

It might be easier to live without a human brain that can remember and think about so much, but even the heavy ploughman can't do it.

These screech owl thoughts come out at night in the fairy time whether we like it or not, and in imagination our thoughts go wandering like departed spirits:

Now is the time of night

That the graves, all gaping wide,

Every one lets forth his sprite,

In the churchway paths to glide;

The spirits tucked in a graveyard may be more fortunate than the heavy ploughman's thoughts in that they are guided by churchway paths, but Robin and the fairies have appeared onstage to lend more assurance about the path our own spirits have taken during this night's watching of their play:

And we fairies, that do run

By the triple Hecate's team

From the presence of the sun,

Following the darkness like a dream,

Now are frolic. Not a mouse

Shall disturb this hallowed house.

I am sent, with broom, before,

To sweep the dust behind the door.

This house, where lovers have come to look with the eyes, is now hallowed ground like that of Titania's sacred grove (they share the same stage), and we stand to be as transformed as Bottom if we share his vision. Puck has been sent before to sweep the dust behind the door; this is the dust that remembers our mortality and disturbs the heavy ploughman's sleep. The line reads that Robin is sent to sweep the dust. It may be that he will not or cannot sweep up the dust. Rather, it may mean that he will sweep it out of sight for a time. This is our interval for comedy.

That done, Oberon, Titania, and the entire fairy train appear to bless us and our vision. Oberon begins:

Through the house give glimmering light,

By the dead and drowsy fire;

Every elf and fairy sprite

Hop as light as bird from brier;

And this ditty, after me,

Sing, and dance it trippingly.

Oberon is no judge. He's more like a butler giving instructions to the household staff. To amend the fractures of the day, he tells them, each chamber must have light even though the fire has gone out. This light is like the lightness of a fairy, which is the lightness of a bird about its business on a briar or a branch. The heaviness of plowing in the earth is done. Here is light work like dancing and singing, which even a ploughman can do if the spirit moves him.

Titania then reminds the staff that their work to be effective must be disciplined:

> *First rehearse your song by rote,*
>
> *To each word a warbling note.*
>
> *Hand in hand, with fairy grace,*
>
> *Will we sing, and bless this place.*

There's nothing haphazard about what they sing or do. Hand in hand, they are each links in the chain of a great enterprise, and so they sing and dance in the great room of the house.

Once harmonized into one blessing, they all are ready to visit each chamber and Oberon gives his last instructions:

> *Now, until the break of day,*
>
> *Through this house each fairy stray.*
>
> *To the best bride-bed will we,*
>
> *Which by us shall blessed be;*
>
> *And the issue there create*
>
> *Ever shall be fortunate.*
>
> *So shall all the couples three*
>
> *Ever true in loving be;*

And the blots of Nature's hand

Shall not in their issue stand;

Never mole, harelip, nor scar,

Nor mark prodigious, such as are

Despised in nativity,

Shall upon their children be.

A general blessing apparently is not enough. Each chamber, each person, each child about to be conceived must be touched by the blessing because each chamber, each individual within the chamber, including the child yet to be conceived, is a world unto itself and requires individual attention. To this purpose he gives them all a little refreshment to dispense:

With this field-dew consecrate,

Every fairy take his gait,

And each several chamber bless,

Through this palace, with sweet peace.

And the owner of it blest

Ever shall in safety rest.

Trip away; make no stay;

Meet me all by break of day.

This blessing doesn't just magically happen. It takes time, all night in fact as each room is separately visited; it requires a fairy's touch and the anointing of that which is fresh and clear. It's work, fairy work, but it ends in peace and safety.

Like a great building where every stone and every fixture has its place and function, their work, each chamber, every character in the chamber, even those yet to be born are all part of a deep structure. A great cathedral or a structure like the Houses of Parliament requires a deep foundation, and the opening words of Theseus' great speech in "The Knight's Tale" lays the groundwork for Shakespeare's work:

> *The First Great Cause and Mover of all above*
>
> *When first He made that fairest chain of love,*
>
> *Great was the consequence and high the intent.*
>
> *He well knew why He did, and what He meant.*

The structure is a chain of love that is constrained to be earthbound, and yet it lifts itself up into the open. The tension between being earthbound and free to soar upward is reflected throughout both works in the two ways love looks at the world. The obsessive concentration of *cupiditas* weighs the spirit down whereas in *caritas* it is set free. The final scene of *A Midsummer Night's Dream* suggests that this tension has been successfully resolved now that the two governments of Theseus and Oberon have joint custody of the same place. Theseus tends to be deliberate and full of himself whereas the fairies are lightning quick and obedient to the law they serve. Nevertheless, they have collaborated to create a comic ending.

To close out the play, images in the speeches of Puck and Oberon recapitulate the constraint and the freedom that's the tensile strength of the foundation. Setting the stage for Oberon and Titania's entrance into the great hall of the palace, Puck recreates for us the pain of desire, the difficulty of laboring in the earth, the piercing cry of a screech owl, and finally the heaviness of the body wrapped in a shroud and placed in a grave. With a quick turn, these graves all open wide and let forth spirits that are free. They are as light and quick as Puck and the fairies who run by the triple Hecate's team.

He is also quick to do Oberon's bidding, and so he appears broom in hand to sweep away the dust of earth from the scene. Oberon's instructions to the fairies deepen the work that Puck has begun by adding the light and lightness of their labor and the freshness from the vial of field-dew to each several chamber in the palace. He tells the fairies that they are to be as quick as birds hopping from branch to branch within a brier. This brier constrains the power and the grace of uninterrupted flight, but still they are as light as can be about their business. When the work is done, they will trip away and make no stay.

Our Earthly Theater

Throughout these readings I have maintained that the tension between constraint and freedom, between *cupiditas* and *caritas*, provides a structure that gives meaning to the narrative, and the theaters for which Shakespeare wrote his plays suggest that the earthly theater in which we live our lives reflects this structure as well. There's the stage of earthly life, the trapdoor that opens into a grave, and the opening of the "wooden O" into the heavens through which the words of Shakespeare's play will swiftly fly and dance in our imaginations. These final scenes involving Peter Quince's play reveal a structure that's a linked chain of constraint and freedom. It resembles Ptolemy's cosmos that has earth in the middle of many concentric spheres. In Ptolemy's model human beings live an earthbound existence, and yet they aspire to the view from Olympus, the intelligence of a point of view whereby we gain a larger understanding. Pyramus and Thisby are earthbound at the center; the actors and Peter Quince inhabit the first sphere in that they overlook the characters they play; the nobility look at the mechanicals' production from a superior height of royal status and education; the fairies observe all the mortals, actors and nobility alike, with a benevolent amusement; and the audience takes in the whole.

Each actor has his own take on the situation, but the structure reveals the limitation of each take. It's the sport of taking what others mistake.

Pyramus thinks that Thisby is dead, but the play itself provides the intelligence that the lion only bloodies her mantle. The actor Bottom thinks that, as a lover who kills himself for love, he must make the audience cry. As Philostrate predicts, the nobility is moved to tears, but they are tears of laughter as they busily critique the play's hapless verisimilitude. The nobility pride themselves on what they know about matters of representation, but they are spared knowing for now if their child, their representation to the next generation, will be affected by "the blots of nature's hand" that can afflict the issue of a marriage. The fairies make us aware of the issue, but this doesn't shed any light on our own fate or that of our children. Everyman including a nobleman is naked and vulnerable in the presence of those powers that can mar a child with despised marks or untimely death.

Of course, we have doctors, but it's common knowledge that in some cases a body can't be saved. Chaucer paints a picture of the body's vulnerability by including a graphic description of the injury to Arcite's heart:

> Up swells Arcita's breast, the grievous sore
>
> About his heart increases more and more;
>
> The clotting blood, for all the doctor's skill,
>
> Corrupts and festers in his body still,
>
> That neither cupping, bleeding at a vein,
>
> Or herbal drink can make him well again...
>
> All, all was shattered and beyond repair,
>
> Nature no longer had dominion there,
>
> And certainly, where nature will not work,
>
> Physic, farewell! Go, bear the man to kirk!

When nature loses dominion over the body, "Physic, farewell!" Everyman and nature, too, is then in the hands of a greater power. On this night of love the nobility are blissfully ignorant of these chances, but the fairies have been charged not to lose sight of them. And so they have come to sweep the dust of the world and do what is within their powers to secure the health and safety of those in each several chamber.

To Restore Amends

As the Pyramus and Thisby story did, Oberon's pointed reminder about the power of Nature's hand to mar its own work goes against the grain of comedy. Why would he darken the scene right as it's coming to a close? Just when the play has brought us to a point of resolution concerning this generation, Oberon reminds us about all the uncertainties that will attend our care of the next one. The field-dew blessing and the verses he has spoken have the character of a charm and a prayer more than the assurance of a guarantee. From this perspective there's no final solution to the obstacles the actors have overcome. The fairies have their instructions, but when he tells them all to meet him "at break of day," we are reminded that they are creatures of the night, our night.

This darkening of the scene with uncertainties is real enough for any human being in attendance, but the poet is setting the stage for his last sleight of hand—the glimpse of a final freedom that's as much a part of life as sleeping and dreaming. He has Puck appear for a last time to give the epilogue. Editors like Kittredge note that Puck's closing is "a regular apology and promise, conventional in epilogues" to do better next time if the actors' play has displeased.[69] It is that but also so much more. In addition to acknowledging the players' limitations, it offers a final amendment that serves as a chink or a cranny in the constraints he and Oberon readily acknowledge:

If we shadows have offended,

Think but this, and all is mended—

That you have but slumb'red here

While these visions do appear.

Who would be offended by the play? one wonders. All actors make mistakes so it can't have been a perfect performance. Or, there may be some who resent that the blots of nature make an entrance right when they are settling in for a comic ending. Puck's chief critic, though, is probably a realist like Theseus who discounts the four lovers' stories as fairy toys. Although Oberon, Titania, and their trains are fairies, the play treats them realistically, and a serious man might find this more than just silly. A strict Puritan, like those who governed London in Shakespeare's time, might find it dangerous that fairies and their dark arts play the role of Providence. It's a serious charge for which the authorities might censor the play or shut the theaters down. Notice, though, that all this seriousness is conditioned by the all-important "If" with which Puck begins his epilogue.

In addition to the "if" that throws any offense into a kind of limbo, Puck skillfully diffuses it by comparing his play with a dream; even a serious man will have dreams when he's asleep. Puck uses the analogy to make a serious point. The blots and mortality of nature set constraints on our natural life, but these constraints are constrained when they are considered in the light of a dream. The fairies and all the actors of Shakespeare's play have their roles in the dream, but first and foremost there's the dreamer. All the actors, everything we witness in the play, the pain of love, the obstacles to love, even the deaths brought on by love—all these dissipate when we wake at play's end and leave the theater to peep at the world with our own fool's eyes.

Now, though, we have seen wonders, specifically about the way love looks with the mind and drives itself crazy with obsessive loves and hates. We have seen how easily and haphazardly love is induced and how that which frustrates love (and life) is a man-made obstacle. Like Wall in Peter Quince's play, it is but a man dressed up in loam, roughcast, and stone to show a wall; and when the wall's part is discharged, away it goes. Shakespeare's comic structure has provided this opening within what appears to be a tragedy. In the story of our life, Wall is death, but in our comedy it has a limited role to play. Wall, Moonshine, Lion, and the others are all content to play a part in the dreamer's story and then depart. This must be true for one who still lives.

That interval between dreaming and waking is upon the audience, and Puck is there to help us make the transition. For starters, he himself is willing to accept his limitations:

> And this weak and idle theme,
>
> No more yielding but a dream,
>
> Gentles, do not reprehend.
>
> If you pardon, we will mend.

Puck works for Oberon. He's no man's errand boy, yet here and in the previous four lines he's content to be a figment of our imagination. He's content to play that role in a weak and idle play because it will help us to realize our own power as the dreamer of him and all the rest.

Do you object to fairies running around in fairyland? This reprehension yields no more than (is as profitable as) getting angry or upset about a dream. Do you object to the blots of nature that can't be wished away with fairy toys? This reprehension yields no more than (is as profitable as) getting angry or upset about a dream. We may not like the dream or we may not like a part of the dream, but we have to own it, every bit of it. It may appear to be weak and idle, but it's a weakness and idleness that we project. It's easy to see this about a dream, but Puck would have us take that short step to see it about our waking hours as well. Just as a dream belongs entirely to the dreamer, Robin's play belongs entirely to the one who discerns it. This will still be true when the play ends, and we look at the world with our own fool's eyes. The world is wholly ours; this is our autonomy, the heart of the matter.

Theseus has warned us, though, that, from the point of view of one who holds the reins of government (the way Everyman does for we are ultimately all self-governed), a lover's imagination is a power for evil and for good. When governed by *cupiditas*, the mind drowns in desire the way Narcissus drowns in the pool. Though the thing he loves is bright and clear "As yonder Venus in her glimmering sphere," this lover spends himself on possessing his own shadow. When governed by *caritas*, the mind is quiet and looks after things with attention and concern.

In *caritas* love looks at the things of this world minding that "we are their parents and original." Like Titania caring for the Indian boy or like Puck caring for us, we are moved by the transient beauty and the vulnerability of all the people and things that dance and sing their existence before our eyes and ears. This looking is the true basis for self-government. Shakespeare's Titania and Puck may be modeled after Chaucer's Theseus who increasingly involves himself with the orphan son of Thebes, Arcite, right up to when he dresses his earthly remains with his own hands in preparation for the final journey every body must take. Though he comes from the royal line of a bitter enemy, Theseus sees him as his own son. It's this experience, this vision of Arcite, that animates his speech at the end. When love looks this way, it is easier to pardon the people and things of this world, even former enemies, and if we pardon, they will mend. One caveat. Arcite is not Creon; this what Theseus had to learn. Creon's name has a place in our collective memory, but he, like others who live in infamy, cannot be pardoned. He is buried at the crossroads, away from our homes and hearts, as a warning.

There is no Creon in Shakespeare's play. All are guilty only of a pardonable folly, and it's devoutly to be wished that this is true for the audience as well. Having made his case, Puck is ready to leave:

And, as I am an honest Puck,

If we have unearned luck

Now to scape the serpent's tongue,

We will make amends ere long;

Else the Puck a liar call.

Being more versatile than most, Puck stands before us in several capacities, and so the passage can have several meanings. A first reading of it suggests that Robin fears the exile of his audience's displeasure. He's an actor who makes his living by giving his audience what they want, and he wants them to come again to his theater. To escape the hissing of a disappointed audience, he throws his and his company's simple skill on the mercy of their patrons, and he promises that ere long, in the fullness of time, they will do better.

But if we take a second look at the lines and if Robin has remained in character as the chief minister of Oberon, he is making a proposition based on a suspension of disbelief. Robin addresses the fact that human beings suffer from the blots of nature and from the fact that every mortal owes a death in nature as surely as Pyramus and Thisby. Since we suffer these things in his and Oberon's jurisdiction, it would be easy to blame them, but Puck's argument once again is seasoned with the word "if" on which so much depends. If Robin and Oberon and the fairies as representatives of the natural world can escape being hissed at or blamed (in part because they are immune to these blots), and if—because he's an honest Puck—we suspend a belief that there are no benevolent forces at work in the world, then the fairies (including their creator) will make amends for those things in nature that are onerous. He challenges the audience to keep a sharp eye out to see whether this is true by issuing an invitation to revisit him and the natural world in this light. If his promise proves not to be true, then call him a liar. It's an argument that appeals to the audience's sense of justice, common sense, and fair play in relationship. There are many ifs here, but comedy involves not only statements of fact but also a suspension of them along with all the possibilities opened by an "if".

If we take a third look, Robin is referring not just to the amends he and his company will make; instead, there may be something of great good in their performance that's transmitted to us and which informs the amends that "we" will make. Here, Robin drops the pretense of being Oberon's chief minister or of playing an actor trying to please his audience and speaks to us directly as an equal, for we are all mortals playing as a company on a common stage. It's a stage for acting and speaking, and this drama, like a morality play with a good angel and a bad angel (who speaks with a serpent's tongue) at either ear of Everyman, is played out between that which is true and that which is false. If *we*, if all of us have the unearned luck of escaping the temptations of the serpent's tongue (which prompts obsessive desire), then we and those in our company will mend ere long. For that, though, we must learn (in the school of hard knocks) to see things as they are, and that's the goal of comedy. From beginning to end, the play has been acting out the reality of this goal.

Because we are the dreamers of the whole and the creators of his luck, the proof of his argument is in the hands of a greater power. Roughly speaking, it's a spiritual power. We can look at the play with the loving eyes of a parent who has given birth to it or not, but if we do, the truth of what he says will make amends for the disruptions caused by a "lack-love".[70] If we don't look at the world with the loving eyes of one who has created it, then call him a liar and be done with it. One more time, he makes his appeal:

So, good night unto you all.

Give me your hands, if we be friends,

And Robin shall restore amends.

He is addressing the alienation of those who have to be coaxed into giving him their hands; in friendship Robin offers with his hand to restore wholeheartedness. An exile may go through the motions of service to life, and yet be unwilling or unable to affirm it. In this, he is like a troubled man who, at the end of prayers, is unable to say his "amens," (a word that sounds the same as "amends"). In friendship Puck will restore them.

A reader or a person in the audience doesn't have to imagine this exile or his amens to a prayer in order to interpret Robin's line. After Hermia exiles Lysander from lying by her side when they are lost in the wood, she prays that he will love her still:

> as may well be said
>
> Becomes a virtuous bachelor and a maid.
>
> Thy love ne're alter till thy sweet life end!

And Lysander replies:

> Amen, amen, to that fair prayer say I,
>
> And then end life when I end loyalty!

Within minutes, though, his desire having been thwarted, Lysander is chasing after Helena. His half-hearted amens are the same as no amens at all. Robin would restore the amens that live at the bottom of Lysander's or anyone's heart.

Now Robin's play is over. We have passed the time between after-supper and bedtime as if we slumbered here. The iron tongue of midnight has spoken to remind Everyman that all things have an end. These are ironclad restraints, and yet we have it in our power to restore, within these constraints, the freedom love has of looking with the eyes to see another looking at us the same way. Even if he's been gone now for almost four hundred years, those eyes are windows opening on an invitation: make friends with me, and you may make friends with the world and yourself.

Coda

The great hunt that Theseus and Hippolyta enjoy prior to their marriage puts in mind the great hunt for a comic vision that has been the preoccupation of human beings from ancient times. These essays have traced that vision to its conclusion, the way a hound traces a deer (or a dear heart) to its conclusion. From ancient times, poets have found something of great constancy in this quest, and people still seek the something out in works that have stood the test of time. I have borrowed the words "something of great constancy" from Hippolyta's debate with Theseus concerning the dreams of the four young lovers. Because their argument is about the reality not just of fairies but of the comic vision that's the purpose for writing a work that may lighten the heart of another, Hippolyta's response to her husband's skepticism is worth recalling here:

> But all the story of the night told over
>
> And all their minds transfigured so together,
>
> More witnesseth than fancy's images
>
> And grows to something of great constancy;
>
> But howsoever, strange and admirable.

Hippolyta speaks for much more than the story told over by the four lovers. The comic visions of our literature have transfigured minds and have witnessed more than fancy's images for thousands of years as they are told over from generation to generation. The constancy can be found in the comic vision itself where people pledge themselves in love and in the way people continually seek out the sense and sensibility of great comic poets who have gone before them. In these texts they find the friendship of those who love and look in this way.

Robin's plea to give him our hands echoes the final words of Chaucer's

Theseus. Emily, the longtime object of Palamon's passion, signals that she agrees to wed Palamon by giving Theseus her hand, and Theseus turns then to Palamon to say:

I think there needs but little sermoning

To gain your own assent to such a thing.

Come near and take your lady by the hand.

The joining of hands at the end of "The Knight's Tale" and at the end of *A Midsummer Night's Dream* sums up the essence of a comic vision. Like hands that touch, everything we have seen or heard in the play transmits the spirit of comedy and lights a path forward for those who would survive and prosper. Like a hand that holds, it's a spirit that's "catching," for it expresses that which has been passed, like the fire of one candle lighting another, through the generations. Anyone who enters the theater of Shakespeare's play or Chaucer's poem is invited to become a link in this chain.

But this is just another image, out of many, to which poetry must resort. Like fairyland, this image and all the other images in its train trip away at break of day when we get out of bed in the morning and go to work in the world. Notwithstanding, a vision of these images may yet do the business of comedy. Even though it comes and goes like the images of a dream, the vision I have set down has a remarkable durability and constancy. It's like a round and orient pearl set overnight in a small flower or on a slender blade of grass. Even though it will dissolve in the heat of the day, with unearned luck I find it there at dawn for a time, a pearl of great price, mine own and not mine own.

AFTERWORD

An Essay on Significant Influences

In keeping with the informality and the personal nature of my approach, as indicated in the Preface I am including an essay concerning those who have had a significant influence on my reading of these texts. I'll begin with the lectures I attended as a graduate student at the University of Oregon. I took a class on the Pearl Poet given by Dr. James Boren, and it was here that I learned about the centrality of *cupiditas* and *caritas* in Medieval literature. His lectures were models of clarity, and these concepts continue to influence the way I read literature. More than that, they have proved their worth when I'm forced, usually by some kind of screw-up, to interpret my own life. A study of these concepts from Chaucer's time along with Helena's formulation of them in Renaissance terms can foster an awareness that love usually looks, not with the eyes, but with the mind.

I read *Shakespeare's Comedies* by Bernard Evans as an undergraduate at Trinity College, and more than any other book of literary criticism it has shaped the way I read his plays. Evans documents Shakespeare's use of dramatic irony, a device that contrasts the ignorance of a character with the intelligence of an audience that's allowed to see and understand more. I studied this in Evans about Shakespeare but found over time that his analysis could be used to interpret other great comic writers in Western literature, starting with Homer. Shakespeare may have learned this device from any number of authors, especially the Roman comedies he read in school as a student, but he certainly admired Chaucer's mastery of it in *The Canterbury Tales*. I argue in the book that Chaucer and Shakespeare structured their stories around dramatic irony because the device dramatizes the limitations of human intelligence. This insight is critical for their purpose as it establishes a baseline or a "bottom", the way a ship has a bottom, for the mending of the social order.

At Trinity College some of our English professors were deeply influenced by the work of Northrup Frye. In particular, I learned from Dr. Paul Smith in a course on Yeats about Frye's synoptic view of literature and the importance of archetypes. I readily acknowledge that I continue to read literature through this critical lens. It's old fashioned, but the world of archetypes has a great deal of room for different critical points of view. For example, the determinism that's popular in contemporary critical circles has been around in different forms—as fate or fortune—from our earliest literature.

Back in the 80s Freeman Dyson wrote a book about nuclear disarmament called *Weapons and Hope* at a time when the two superpowers were still governed by a policy of mutual assured destruction. His last chapter, "Tragedy Is Not Our Business," includes a description of Odysseus as a comic hero. I read this book when I was first putting together my AP course for seniors, and this chapter, especially the title, expressed what I hoped to teach my students. Dyson is a world-famous scientist still active at Princeton at this writing, but he is unusual in that he has maintained strong ties with the literary roots of our culture. For me he also represents the hope that the folkways and the insights of an older culture and the methods of modern science can be brought more into balance in the world view passed on to our children.

About the same time that I began teaching *A Midsummer Night's Dream* to seniors, PBS brought out a video of a live performance filmed at the Shakespeare Festival in Central Park. I credit the director, Joseph Papp, for engaging hundreds of my students with wonderful farce, the speed and energy of fairyland, and the force of great poetry. Papp's direction of Peter Quince's play at the end reveals it to be comic gold, as I argue in the text. It would be impossible to see that gold when it's buried in a printed text; it takes a master director and live theater.

After I retired from teaching in 2002, I embarked on a self-directed reading program to prepare myself for the book I wanted to write. I read all the plays by Shakespeare that I had never studied along with readings in history, art, architecture, and culture. After attending a lecture by the historian Daniel Boorstin, I read a number of his books beginning with his trilogy, *The Discoverers*, *The Creators*, and *The Seekers*. Boorstin keeps his language simple and straightforward. It's a worthy goal and one to which I aspire as well. Also, he approaches his subject as a storyteller which is what I have done throughout my career in teaching. His history is a vast, interconnected series of biographies loosely grouped into heroes of the natural sciences, heroes of the imagination, and heroes in the search for meaning. At some point I realized that Boorstin's method of presentation was closely linked to his overall argument. He was opposing historicism, the view popular in modern thought that history is an objective supernatural power like Zeus or Providence that can dictate the way things (and people) are in the world. Boorstin humanizes history instead by telling the linked stories of human beings who have added their discoveries and creations and insights about a world that in modern times has exploded to an infinite size and infinite complexity. At the beginning of *The Discoverers* he writes "A Personal Note to the Reader" which touches on this sense that the world will always be a place of wonder for human beings rather than an object acted on by historical forces. He writes:

> *My hero is Man the Discoverer. The world we now view from the literate West—the vistas of time, the land and the seas, the heavenly bodies and our own bodies, the plants and animals, history and human societies past and present—had to be opened for us by countless Columbuses. In the deep recesses of the past, they remain anonymous. As we come closer to the present they emerge into the light of history, a cast of characters as varied as human nature. Discoveries become episodes of biography, unpredictable as the new worlds the discoverers opened to us.*
>
> *The obstacles to discovery—the illusions of knowledge—are also part of our story. Only against the forgotten backdrop of the received common sense and myths of their time can we begin to sense the courage, the rashness, the heroic and imaginative thrusts of the great discoverers. They had to battle against the current "facts" and dogmas of the learned.*

This is another way of describing the comic vision that's been the subject of my book. It's a way of looking that appreciates the greatness of what isn't known, and it's a way of looking that overcomes obstacles created by what we know.

On a trip to California I bought *The Passion of the Western Mind* by Richard Tarnas in a Pasadena bookstore and studied it carefully over a number of years. Bernard Evans' book on Shakespeare describes how a literary device or vehicle creates an intellectual framework or setting that implicitly conveys the poet's theme—that people's thoughts and perceptions are limited. Tarnas' book provides a step by step survey of Western philosophy that enabled me to place the work of Chaucer and Shakespeare within a coherent frame or narrative of philosophical ideas. Throughout his book, Tarnas describes thinkers wrestling with the problem of knowledge, and he concludes with the scenario in modern philosophy that I describe in the Preface and at other points in the text.

Like the pattern in manic depressive behavior, Descartes' manic drive for certainty may be closely related to the depressive nihilism of postmodernism. It's a great irony and a paradox that the modern project to establish certainty has ended up on the other side of the certainty spectrum. I argue that there's an anxious, sometimes hysterical quality about modern and postmodern thought that spills over into our culture and daily lives. It's not particularly helpful or healthy to be in the grip of such a deterministic, fatalistic view, and so *A Comic Vision* offers a critique of these effects by celebrating the wisdom of comedy. Modern thought sees itself as the culmination of a logical and irresistible progression that ends in chaos whereas comedy sees a man foolishly painting himself into a corner.

We think that, as members of a modern culture, we are dealing with problems never faced before, and the outlook is rather grim. The scientific era began in the glow of intellectual certainty and mastery, but scientific conclusions would now persuade us that, as human beings have lost their exalted status in the scheme of things and are immersed along with everything else into the chemistry and the physics of the natural world, the basic relationship reverses to where "Things are in the saddle and ride mankind" instead of the other way around. What a relief it can be, then, to discover authors at a distance of 600 and 400 years who describe with great specificity the same cul de sac and who point the way forward out of the mind-forged prison of fatalism and historicism. And the wisdom tradition is much older than the works of Chaucer. From ancient times it has been the business of comedy to show that the mind, as opposed to fate or historical forces, is at the heart of human survival and prosperity. This will always be the case, but what I refer to as "mind" may not be what a philosopher like Descartes had in mind. I explore this difference in the book.

Along with an indebtedness to Tarnas' overall narrative, specific chapters in his book have shed more light on the way I have read Shakespeare throughout my teaching career. For example, my section on "Devouring Time as Played by Snug the Joiner" derives from a study of Shakespeare's sonnets that I have worked on since I began teaching the advanced placement course in the nineteen-eighties. I knew then that Shakespeare was consistently playing with, and generally trying to dislodge or explode, the concept of time as a thing. I didn't know, as I hadn't studied it, Hume's views about causality. I learned from Tarnas that Hume's skepticism about causality came from finding the Achilles heel of empiricists who would ground all human knowledge in sense experience. Tarnas writes,

> If every valid idea has a basis in a corresponding [sense] impression, then to what impression can the mind point for its idea of causality? None, Hume answered. If the mind analyzes its experience without preconception, it must recognize that in fact all its supposed knowledge is based on a continuous chaotic volley of discrete sensations, and that on these sensations the mind imposes an order of its own.

Having questioned the reality of causation, it was a short step for Hume to question the nature of the self as well, for a sense of self is a creation of time and memory.

Since I read this passage about Hume, I have wondered whether his skepticism could have been suggested or confirmed by reading

Shakespeare's sonnet "Devouring Time" and other works. For example, the chaotic volley of discrete sensations in Tarnas's account sounds like Lear's night on the heath. Without a sense of time in the darkness of the heath, a sense of self slips away as well. Lear is a tragedy, but his night on the heath has the much the same function as a midsummer night in fairyland. They serve as a comic wake-up call for the characters initiated into them. In *A Midsummer Night's Dream* Shakespeare makes the case that the suffering caused by time (the four days and nights, for example, that separate Theseus from that which he desires and which define him in relation to Hippolyta) is a necessary prologue to a comic vision in which the days dissolve seamlessly into night and the nights dream away the time. Despite a skepticism about concepts that human beings employ to orient themselves, neither Hume nor Shakespeare was a nihilist or anarchist. Hume argued, Tarnas points out, that human beings order the world with an opinion. He saw that this opinion was necessary, but as a philosopher he couldn't substantiate it. For the most part, he thought a people's inherited culture reflected that opinion and could be counted on to serve as a basis for a social order. Then again, he lived in England which had long and deep traditions in law and liberty.

Tarnas's chapter on Thomas Aquinas confirmed for me the way I had been reading Theseus' great speech at the end of "The Knight's Tale" even though I wasn't aware at the time of Aquinas' influence on Chaucer. His chapter, "The Quest of Thomas Aquinas," includes a description of his philosophy that is particularly relevant for understanding what Theseus means by "experience" when he refers to it in his speech. Tarnas argues that Aquinas blended the teachings of Plato and Aristotle for his theory of how human beings perceive and know the world. Aquinas, he writes, moves away from Plato and toward Aristotle when he argues that sensible things do not exist merely as "shadowy replications of the Platonic Ideas." Aquinas agrees with Aristotle that the Platonic forms "were genuinely embedded in matter, united with matter to produce a composite whole." Aristotle, however, tends to view nature as existing apart from God, and this is where Aquinas parts company with him. He argues instead that meaningful perception would "connect the created world with God." I quote the next passage at length because Tarnas here explains in philosophical terms what Theseus is telling his people in plainer language:

> To accomplish this [connecting the created world with God], Aquinas reintroduced the Platonic notion of "participation" in this new context. Created things have true substantial reality because they participate in Existence, which is from God, the infinite self-subsistent ground of all being. For God's essence was precisely his existence, his infinite act of being which underlay the finite existence of all created things, each with its own particular essence. The essence of each thing, its specific kind of being, is the measure of its participation in the real existence communicated to it by God. What a thing is and the fact that it is at all are two distinct aspects of any created being.

These passages helped me to interpret Chaucer's text to mean that, "the fact that we can 'sense' the world at all ties us to the whole, the sentience and 'sentence' of the world, from which we derive. Order and meaning take shape in perception itself." (See the section called "Perception: A Glimpse into the Garden, pages 159-165.) When Tarnas writes that "What a thing is and the fact that it is at all are two distinct aspects of any created being," he is phrasing in different words Helena's formulation that there's looking with the mind and looking with the eyes. The one calculates what a thing is; the other appreciates that the thing, and the one perceiving it, is at all. The larger view, the one that looks with the eyes, embodies what I refer to as a comic vision.

I'll close these acknowledgments of Tarnas' work, however, with a disclaimer. While I found Tarnas' narrative persuasive and compelling and the commentaries I have just reviewed were particularly helpful, this is not to say that I agree with his answer to the philosophical problems posed by postmodernism. His second book, *Cosmos and Psyche*, looks to the stars and astrological charts for guidance, whereas I follow the lead of Chaucer and Shakespeare who understood comedy to be a declaration for establishing self-government.

Teaching Western literature in a public school classroom has become problematic due to sensitivities about religious issues being discussed there. This doesn't mean that I ignored religious texts in my own reading. I have studied the literature of the Old Testament and the New Testament to see for myself what Chaucer and Shakespeare learned from them. As my own text indicates (see "The Source of a Noble Respect," pages 487-491), I regard The Book of Job as an indispensable wisdom text. A book by a Tibetan Buddhist, who escaped the Chinese takeover of his country and eventually settled in America, also has had a decisive influence on my reading of "The Knight's Tale." *Cutting Through Spiritual Materialism* by Chögyam Trungpa is a transcription of lectures he gave to students back in the 70s. Once I retired, I began to read his books and discovered that his map of the mind is similar to one I discovered in Chaucer. This has influenced the way I organize several chapters on "The Knight's Tale," specifically the material concerning the birth and development of ego in "Everyman's Story" and the six psychological states that the two knight's experience during the course of "Ego's Sold-Out World Tour." These six states have an uncanny resemblance to the Six Realms as Chögyam Trungpa describes them. The Tibetan system has been worked on for thousands of years, and the insights of these teachers are still revered for their directness and clarity. If Chaucer arrived at similar insights into the human mind, this speaks in favor of a vision that is constant in human beings despite their different languages, history, and culture.

I have obliquely referred to the title of Toni Packer's first book, *The Work of This Moment*, in a section of the Introduction called "The Work." Toni began her teaching life as the dharma successor of Phillip Kapleau at the Rochester Zen Center but eventually left that position to establish her own center for meditation. Her teaching is deeply rooted in the Japanese Zen that was her teacher's discipline, but once on her own she developed a more informal style. Toni was an important influence during the time I was teaching and developing the readings I have set down in book form. In conversations with her I first glimpsed the strong similarities between the central theme of her teaching and the comic insight of Shakespeare and Chaucer. Borrowing Helena's terms to explicate Toni's terms, the work of this moment is to look with the eyes.

Richard Tarnas presents his survey of Western philosophy in *The Passion of the Western Mind* as a series of what he calls "world views." He begins with the Greek or Classical world view, shows how that evolved into a Christian or Medieval world view, and ends with the modern world view which came into being during the course of the Renaissance, the Reformation, and the scientific revolution. The passion he refers to in his title is for ideas that shape the way we look at the world. The way we look at the world endows us with the power to create a world, just as we have the power to create a life in our passion for another. From the beginning comedy has been about this power of creativity so for me this links Tarnas' structural device for telling the story of Western philosophy with comedy which has its origins in fertility rites. Similarly, Tibetan Buddhism is more than just a set of ideas. It's a world, a cosmos that's structured around male and female polarities, and so it's a way of looking at the world that creates a world.

This observation serves as a prologue for a book that shares the approach I have been outlining in these other books. *A Conflict of Visions: Ideological Origins of Political Struggles* by Thomas Sowell is about economics, politics, and culture, but it's structured specifically around two conflicting visions of human nature. Sowell calls them the constrained and the unconstrained view. The first argues that human beings are intrinsically limited as to what they can know of themselves and the world. Because our knowledge is hopelessly inadequate for the task, we cannot be counted on to manage a complex social order, and so those with the constrained view rely instead on well-established institutions and social processes like a market economy and the rule of law. Those with the unconstrained view, on the other hand, believe that gifted and highly trained experts can successfully manage complex economies and societies in an ad hoc manner, and, if given the power to do so, they'll create the best of all possible worlds. Sowell points out that the deep division between those who share the constrained view and those who share the unconstrained view proves that a vision creates a world. Those who don't share that vision in effect inhabit a different world. *A Comic Vision* argues that this conflict of visions doesn't begin in the 18th Century with writers like Adam Smith and the Marquis de Condorcet. If Sowell and Friedrich Hayek are familiar with a constrained view, it's because comic writers have left an enduring and vivid record of it starting with Homer, the father of Western literature. When Helena tells us that love looks, "not with the eyes, but with the mind," she expresses what a great comic writer four hundred years ago had to say about the conflict of visions that Sowell has found at the heart of our economic and political life. This conflict is not just an economic or political problem. We find it in the human heart, in the way we love. The two views would appear to be forever hopelessly in conflict, but comedy puts us on a path to resolving them. This is the point of my book and a reason for writing it.

From the beginning *A Comic Vision* argues that the insights of comedy provide a foundation for self-government. It's easy to observe, along with Theseus in "The Knight's Tale," that there is nothing so foolish as a man in love. It is very difficult, on the other hand, to observe it when that man is oneself. Nevertheless, this is the essential act of self-government. Because the themes of comedy and government are so intimately related in my reading of these stories, I studied the history of our own government as an experiment in self-government magnified in time and space. Edmund Morgan has thoroughly researched the early years of the American colonial experiments in government, and he begins his important book on the subject, *Inventing the People: the Rise of Popular Sovereignty in England and America*, with a quote from David Hume to which I referred earlier in the essay:

> *Nothing is more surprising to those, who consider human affairs with a philosophical eye, than to see the easiness with which the many are governed by the few; and to observe the implicit submission with which*

men resign their own sentiments and passions to those of their rulers.
When we inquire by what means this wonder is brought about, we shall
find, that as Force is always on the side of the governed, the governors have
nothing to support them but opinion. 'Tis therefore, on opinion only that
government is founded; and this maxim extends to the most despotic and
most military governments, as well as the most free and popular.

Morgan agrees with Hume but he alters the statement slightly to read
that government is based, not on opinion, but on a "fiction." It also could
be called a "world view." Some may argue that force is not always on the
side of the many, but the breakup of the Soviet bloc, one of the most brutal
totalitarian schemes in history, and other mass uprisings against police
states tend to reinforce Hume's observation. After beginning with Hume's
quote, Morgan then painstakingly shows that the experiments in
government during the English Civil War in the mid-seventeenth century
illustrate Hume's idea, and he argues as well that the idea found its fullest
expression in the American colonies, the American Revolution, and the
establishment of constitutional government. It is interesting to note that
Ben Franklin met with Hume personally when he visited Scotland in 1758.

Hume's insight into the nature of government and Morgan's research
into the establishment of self-government in England and America make
a compelling case for the role a fiction like "The Knight's Tale" or *A
Midsummer Night's Dream* may actually play in our national life. It suggests
that, at a very basic level, a government is not a concrete fact, like a king
on his throne or a soldier with a gun; it's an opinion. It's the way a man
sees the world and the way he sees himself in the world. Government is
now free to be something other than a trick of fate or a fact of history. This
view of government frees up a space for a play of ideas like that in a play or
in a truly representational government. It's a space that even hard-headed,
skeptical Theseus finally sees for himself in his last words at the end of *A
Midsummer Night's Dream*:

This palpable gross play hath well beguil'd

The heavy gait of night. Sweet friends, to bed.

A fortnight hold we this solemnity

In nightly revels and new jollity.

Edmund's Morgan's presentation of this argument helped me to see the relationship between my work as a student of literature and the authority I sought (and needed in order to effectively teach) at the head of a classroom. Government, he says, is based on a fiction, and what better fiction can we imagine than that we live in a comic world. As in any kind of sorcery, though, there's a great danger in the idea that government is based in a fiction. It could easily lead (and has) to the anarchy of Everyman as his own priest and king or the anarchy of a leader who is king of everything. And so I argue in the marketplace of ideas for something of great constancy in human history, a comic vision.

Bibliography

Ackroyd, Peter. *Shakespeare: The Biography*. London: Vintage Books, 2006.

Boorstin, Daniel J. *The Discoverers*. New York: Vintage Books, 1985.

Chaucer, Geoffrey. *The Canterbury Tales*. Translated by Neville Coghill. London: Penguin Books, 1951.

Cooper, Helen. *Oxford Guides to Chaucer: The Canterbury Tales*, 2nd Edition. Oxford: Oxford University Press, 1989.

Dyson, Freeman. *Weapons and Hope*. New York: Harper and Row, 1984.

Evans, Bertram. *Shakespeare's Comedies*. London: Oxford University Press, 1960.

Homer. *The Odyssey*. Translated by E.V. Rieu. London: Penguin Books, 1946.

Morgan, Edmund S. *Inventing the People*. New York: W.W. Norton and Company, 1988.

Ovid. *The Metamorphosis*. Translated by Arthur Golding. New York: The Macmillan Company, 1965.

Ovid. *The Metamorphosis*. Translated by Horace Gregory. New York: A Mentor Classic, 1958.

Nhat Hahn, Thich. *Living Buddha, Living Christ*. New York: Riverhead Books, 1995.

Packer, Toni. *The Work of This Moment*. Boston: Shambhala, 1990.

Palmer, R.R., Joel Colton, and Lloyd Kramer. *A History of the Modern World.* 9th ed. NewYork: Alfred A. Knopf, 2003.

Chögyam Trungpa. *Cutting Through Spiritual Materialism.* Boston: Shambala, 1973.

---. *Meditation in Action.* Boston: Shambala, 2004.

Robinson, F. N., ed. *The Works of Geoffrey Chaucer.* Boston: Houghton Mifflin Company, 1957.

Sowell, Thomas. *A Conflict of Visions: Ideological Origins of Political Struggles.* New York: Basic Books, 2007.

Shakespeare, William. *A Midsummer Night's Dream.* Edited by George Lyman Kitteredge and revised by Irving Ribner. Waltham, MA: Blaisdell Publishing Company, 1966.

Tarnas, Richard. *The Passion of the Western Mind.* New York: Ballantine Books, 1991.

Warburton, Nigel. *Philosophy: The Basics*, 4th ed. London and New York: Routledge, 2004.

Endnotes

1   Homer, *The Odyssey*, trans. E. V. Rieu (London: Penguin Books, 1946), 3.

2   Ibid., 42. The bench for true judgment is strategically placed, ensuring that anyone who passes through the doors of the ancestral house will encounter it whether coming or going.

3   William Shakespeare, *A Midsummer Night's Dream*, ed. George Lyman Kittredge (Waltham: Blaisdell Publishing Company, 1966). All quotes of the play are taken from this edition.

4   A defining feature of our own time has been shooting sprees like that at Columbine High School in Colorado. In that particular incident, two boys decided to become the army of their own little state, and, following their own foreign policy, they waged a private war against their enemies. On a much larger scale, thousands of civilians were murdered on 9/11 by a paramilitary group. It's a large organization, but it's essentially a private army that does the bidding of its founders. Also, newspapers in mid-sized cities publish stories every few days about an argument or a vendetta or a power play that left someone dead in the street. These actors are people who reject the authority of recognized governments and replace it with the rules of a splinter group or, just as strictly, with their own opinion.

5   There's a story about Socrates attending Aristophanes' play about him. Since Greek audiences usually knew the story before they saw the play, Socrates probably knew that Aristophanes would roast him, but he came anyway. It is said that, with all eyes on him, he stood and acknowledged the crowd.

6   Chögyam Trungpa, *Meditation in Action* (Boston: Shambala, 2004), 70-71.

7   Here's the full text of the poem:

I wander thro' each chartered street,

Near where the charter'd Thames does flow.

And mark in every face I meet

Marks of weakness, marks of woe.

In every cry of every Man,

In every Infants cry of fear,

In every voice: in every ban,

The mind-forg'd manacles I hear.

How the Chimney-sweepers cry

Every blackning Church appalls,

And the hapless Soldiers sigh,

Runs in blood down Palace walls

But most thro' midnight streets I hear

How the youthful Harlots curse

Blasts the new-born Infants tear

And blights with plagues the Marriage hearse

8   I borrow this term from J.R.R. Tolkien and his novels about Hobbits. His character the Gollum called the ring of power his "precious." It became even more precious to him after he lost it to Bilbo Baggins.

9   "The truth hurts" is only half true. Hearing the truth can hurt, but if what is said is true, it is more accurate to say that the pain comes from attachment to the misconception which the truth has now dissolved. The truth in the end is what makes us whole.

10   This scene recalls the Cyclops incident in which Odysseus and his men enter the Cyclops's cave hoping for the host's hospitality. When the host returns home through the mouth of the cave, he rolls a heavy stone in front of it which only he could move. The Greeks are then trapped. Instead of entertaining them with food, the Cyclops eats them.

11   I have imagined the arrow speaking in this way because of what happens at this critical point in the narrative. Odysseus aims his first arrow at the leader of the suitors who has lifted his head to drink one more cup of Odysseus' wine. The arrow strikes the exposed throat of the drinker so that, instead of the usurped wine, he drinks his own blood. It's a powerful image of a person waking up from a drinker's dream to taste the reality of his own life.

12   In the second half of the epic, Odysseus returns to Ithaca disguised as a beggar. The disguise expresses that over the course of his trials he has become Nobody which was how he identified himself earlier when the Cyclops asked for his name. Using his disguise to gather intelligence at the palace, Odysseus finally takes his stand on his own threshold and destroys the mob that usurped his home. Odysseus-as-Nobody reestablishes himself in his home and in his bed, but he still has to deal with the consequences of his actions. He has to confront the relatives of the suitors, and, after only one night with Penelope, he leaves his home once more to placate Poseidon for the blinding of his son, the Cyclops.

13   "Tragedy Is Not Our Business" is the title of the last chapter in Freeman Dyson's book *Weapons and Hope*. I read this book in the same year that I began planning my course in comic literature.

14   When a person is on an extremely narrow ledge on a mountain or a steep gorge, the first step and any other step can move a person into death or life. Gustave Dore's illustration of a scene from Dante's *Commedia* at the beginning of this chapter shows us Dante and Virgil (along with Marco the Lombard) on a narrow ledge. The incident is from *Purgatorio*, Canto 16. The first step recommended here doesn't guarantee a comic outcome, but it's as good as any as a first step. Dore's image also introduces and resonates with the story of Deucalion and Pyrrha on the ledge of a mountain that plays an important role in my interpretation of *A Midsummer Night's Dream*.

15   I have illustrated this chapter with Vermeer's *The Love Letter* which places the viewer quite specifically within the frame of a house. The sense of an interior is increased by the frame of a doorway through which we view the scene. By defining the space so precisely, the artist has put us in the position of this young lady's mother or father who would witness the way she reacts to the letter her maid has brought her. It's a technique much like Chaucer's use of a persona for the telling of his tales.

16   Chaucer's portrait of the Cook in "The Prologue" is one of my favorite examples of Chaucer the Pilgrim's wide-eyed innocence. Members of a guild fraternity have embarked on the pilgrimage to put themselves and their wealth on display:

> *They had a cook with them who stood alone*
>
> *For boiling chicken with a marrow bone,*
>
> *Sharp flavouring-powder and a spice for savour.*
>
> *And he could roast and seeth and broil and fry,*
>
> *Make good thick soup and bake a tasty pie.*
>
> *But what a pity---so it seemed to me,*

That he should have an ulcer on his knee.

As for blancmange, he made it with the best.

Here's Chaucer the Pilgrim at his best! He describes the man with gusto like he's hungry for what he is cooking up. We're in the kitchen as if we're watching a celebrity chef on TV, but then when we take our eye off all the busyness of what he is doing, our attention drops to that ulcer on his knee. Chaucer the Pilgrim says, "What a pity," where most observers would say to themselves or out loud, "OH, GROSS!" Here's this infected thing, brimming with puss, in the middle of the food we are about to eat. For Chaucer the Pilgrim, however, innocent and carefree as ever, the image of the ulcer triggers an association with the cook's blancmange pudding which he makes as well as anyone. This observation by Chaucer the Pilgrim sets up a poetic association for the portrait of the Pardoner that comes shortly after this one. It reminds me of the analogy questions in the verbal part of the SAT exam for which I prepared my juniors. The ulcer is to the body of the cook as the Pardoner is to the body of the Church. Chaucer's patron, John of Gaunt, was a strong supporter of John Wycliffe who opposed abuses like those committed by the Pardoner.

17   Geoffrey Chaucer, *The Canterbury Tales*, trans. Neville Coghill (London: Penguin Books, 1951), 22. All the quotes in modern English are from this translation.

18   Since it can address despair as well as a comfortable complacency, a wake-up call can come at either a bad time or a good time. Mahler has written a musical equivalent of it in the final movement, referred to as the "Great Call," of his Second Symphony. Over the course of the first four movements the music passes alternatively through states of biting anguish and ecstatic beauty, and it's only midway through the final movement that we hear the Great Call as an offstage suggestion. It builds from there to an explosive fanfare coming from all sides as trumpet players have been stationed in the four corners of the theater.

19   There are similarities here with two scenes in Shakespeare's *Hamlet*. First, there's the opening scene when the ghost of Hamlet's father appears out of the mist to Horatio and the guards on duty. These people are terrified of the ghost. Nominally, the play is set in Elsinor, but in effect it is set in a state of fear. Everyone in *Hamlet* is besieged by fear, and Palamon and Arcite are reborn in the same environment. The graveyard scene in act 5, scene 1 of *Hamlet* also contains echoes of this scene from Chaucer, not just in the situation but in the language as well. The clown tells Hamlet that the grave he digs is "Mine." Hamlet objects and explains that a grave "is for the dead, not for the quick. Therefore thou liest." The clown replies, " 'Tis a quick lie, sir, 'twill away again from me to you." The subject, of course, is death which shares with Palamon and Arcite that characteristic of being "neither fully quick nor dead." As a concept, death is an idea and has no life. It's proper place, then, is the grave, and yet as an idea that lives in the mind of one still alive, it is "quick" to affect the behaviors of the living—moving from one mind to another the way Yorrick's famous skull moves (in the clown's hands) from the grave into Hamlet's hands. These are hands, like a mind, that clutch at things.

20   Nigel Warburton, *Philosophy: The Basics,* 4th ed. (London and New York: Routledge, 2004), 138-139. Gilbert Ryle called mind/body dualism "the dogma of the ghost in the machine."

21   Shakespeare's Perdita in *The Winter's Tale* is just such a woman. At the sheep shearing festival Camillo, the steadiest mind in either Sicilia or Bohemia, recognizes Perdita as "the queen of curds and cream." Everyone there, even the king who has cause to hate her, sees in her the "quality" that a heart instinctively loves. (Of course, she is "quality," the daughter of a Leontes, but no one knows that yet.) The egotist king, the father of Florizel who opposes any union with a commoner, sees the threat of those loving arms and warns Perdita off:

—*if ever henceforth thou*

These rural latches to his entrance open,

Or hoop his body more with thy embraces,

I will devise a death as cruel for thee

As thou art tender to 't. (act 4, sc. 3)

If it could speak, this is the authentic voice of Chaucer's tower which instinctively resists the fleeting softness of a lover's arms.

22   In Tom Stoppard's *Rosencrantz and Guildenstern Are Dead* two clowns play a game like this. Stoppard gets the game from Hamlet's antics, and Shakespeare might have found his model for it in Chaucer.

23   My interpretation of *A Midsummer Night's Dream* begins with the autonomy of a consciousness in which "there is no other" and follows that theme right to the conclusion.

24   Shakespeare judged this characteristic of ego to be so important that he adds the character of Bottom in his retelling of Chaucer's tale. During the casting scene for the Pyramus and Thisby production, Bottom would play as many parts as he can.

25   I use the word "prefers" here to anticipate the scene in Shakespeare's play when Duke Theseus prefers the Pyramus and Thisby entertainment over the others on Philostrate's list. To prefer one thing over another is to make a choice.

26   For those who would like a modern instance, this is the dramatic tension with which the TV show *Mad Men* begins and which informs the character of Don Draper throughout the series. Since the formula worked so well with *Mad Men*, the character of Mike Ross on the TV show *Suits* is written around the same dynamic.

27   Here's part of Palamon's original speech:

I am thy mortal foo, and it am I

That loveth so hoote Emelye the brighte

That I wol dye present in hir sighte.

Wherfore I axe deeth and my juwise;

But sle my felawe in the same wese,

For bothe han we deserved to be slayn.

The translator may have had in mind Hamlet's speech when he comes out of hiding to assert that a lover's grief for Ophelia, especially his grief, must be greater than a brother's:

What is he whose grief

Bears such an emphasis, whose phrase of sorrow

Conjures the wand'ring stars, and makes them stand

Like wonder-wounded hearers? This is I,

Hamlet the Dane. (act 5, sc. 1)

Hamlet goes on to claim that forty thousand brothers could not make up his grief. Palamon submits completely to Theseus' power and judgment, but in the lines quoted he also claims for himself the power to do so. By jumping in the way he does (and as Hamlet does), he frames the situation to suit himself.

28   We see this interplay of gods and men at the end of Part Three when an argument breaks out about the boons that the gods have granted their respective

favorites. Saturn has to settle the argument, and this compromise dramatically alters the landscape for the characters.

29   I use the image of eyes opening here to tie this moment in Arcite's life to Helena's formulation in Act I of A Midsummer Night's Dream that love looks, not with the eyes, but with the mind. People usually look with a mind that would possess something, but wisdom literature celebrates those experiences when human beings have on occasion looked with the eyes. These moments, while possible, are elusive, for, as in Arcite's experience, they require relinquishing that which we love the most.

30   Chaucer uses the great chain image at the beginning of Theseus' speech at the end of the tale. The concept derived from Aristotle and was incorporated into the Christian world view. By Chaucer's time it was a well-known figure of speech, and the stratification of people and things was a defining feature of medieval life.

31   The image of spheres surrounding the earth and the people who live on earth comes from the Ptolemaic system with which Chaucer was quite familiar. Jupiter's sphere is the furthest from earth so it encompasses all those that come before it, including that of Mars.

32   Robin speaks these words at a crisis point of A Midsummer Night's Dream: Act 3, Scene 2, lines 92-3.

33   I have illustrated Chapter Six, "The Government of Theseus," with Schiavone's painting "The Marriage of Cupid and Psyche" (p. 94). The two young lovers are the focus, but they are surrounded by the mature figures of other gods. Chief among them is Jupiter, and even though he has his back to us, we sense the power of his government. Like Theseus acknowledging the God of Love in his judgment, Jupiter receives the frontal, naked power of the young couple with an outstretched arm. The arm, hand, and finger (which receives a ring from Psyche) indicate that Jupiter is as taken up by her as Cupid has been. In addition, just as

the God of Love imposes his lordship on Theseus by forcing him to overrule his sentence of death on the lovers, Cupid appears to be the active party in this summit of great powers as he bestows the wreath on Jupiter's head.

34   The character of Polonius in Shakespeare's *Hamlet* lives in the same sort of bubble. Because it's a tragedy, though, Polonius dies before his bubble is burst. The circularity of thought comes out especially in his advice to Gertrude and Claudius concerning the cause of Hamlet's madness. Here's a brief sample:

> *Your noble son is mad.*
>
> *"Mad" call I it, for, to define true madness,*
>
> *What is 't but to be nothing else but mad? (act 2, sc. 2)*

When Shakespeare has borrowed so much from Chaucer in *A Midsummer Night's Dream*, it isn't hard to imagine that a few years later he drew on Aegeus for his Polonius.

35   Gen. 3: 16-24.

36   To contrast the government of Theseus with the government of comedy, I have illustrated Chapter Seven with Van Gogh's "Wheatfields With Cypresses." In Van Gogh's painting, as in Theseus' actions throughout the chapter, the need for human government appears to have been burned away in the intensity and the truth of the vision. As in many of the paintings Van Gogh completed during these last months of his life, there's the presence of an overwhelming energy like that of a god, but it's contained and stabilized by the rootedness and serenity of other powers: the gold of wheatfields ready for harvest, the olive trees bowing in the wind but fixed in the field, the cypresses framing our vision with a vertical stop while mountains rising softly in the distance break through that barrier to keep our vision moving along and up.

37   Helen Cooper, Oxford Guides to Chaucer: *The Canterbury Tales*, 2nd ed. (Oxford: Oxford University Press, 1989), 77. Cooper defines "sentence" here as "the meaning of the poem that controls structure and treatment."

38   Chaucer's Theseus celebrates the greatness of the consequence and the height of the intent when the First Great Cause made that fairest chain of love. Shakespeare's Theseus describes a similar strength of purpose in the government of himself and his subjects near the end of *A Midsummer Night's Dream*. The way to get along with people, for a ruler of men or anyone, is to take what others mistake with equanimity. After all, nobody's perfect. "And what poor duty cannot do, noble respect / Takes it in might, not merit." If we can sense the greatness of the consequence and the height of the intent that lies behind creation, then we may serve that purpose with a noble respect that derives from creation itself. I have used Shakespeare's word "noble" in interpreting Chaucer's text in order to foreshadow this speech in Act 5, Scene 1, lines 89-92.

39   Once again, Vermeer's painting on the title page of Chapter One illustrates the point being made here. We who look at the painting have been positioned in a hallway or an adjoining room, and we see the woman in yellow narrowly framed by an open doorway. The painting captures, the way Arcite's and Palamon's glimpse of Emily through the prison window does, the evanescent beauty of a moment. For the woman, it is as complete a moment as she may ever know, full of unexpected pleasure and anticipation. We share her pleasure, but the painting can only hint at the great world from which the letter has derived. While this is a beautiful painting and she's a lovely subject, the world hinted at in the letter is as much the painting's subject as she is.

40   Here are Chaucer's original lines:

And heer-agayns no creature on lyve,

Of no degree, availleth for to stryve.

The word "this" that appears in the translation is implied; no living creature, whatever its degree, can strive (against this). The implied word "this" refers to what Jupiter has willed in the previous four lines.

41   *A Midsummer Night's Dream*, Act III, scene ii, line 461.

42   The words "airy nothing" are quoted from *A Midsummer Night's Dream*. They appear in Theseus' speech at the beginning of Act 5 where he describes the function of poetry.

43   Chaucer uses the word "slider" in the original, but Coghill's word in the translation has the same associations with something earthbound, something that moves in the mud and dust. Chaucer has chosen the mouse to represent a creature who, like Satan in the book of Job when asked "Whence comest thou?", replies, "From going to and fro in the earth, and from walking up and down in it." (Job 1:7) For me it is significant that Chaucer (Arcite) thinks of an innocent mouse in this context and not the more weighted and freighted symbol of a snake.

44   David Pryce-Jones, *The Closed Circle* (Boulder, CO: Paladin Press, 1990).

45   Shakespeare makes much use of the confusion that derives from two things having the same name in his early *A Comedy of Errors*. The identical twins of a wealthy father both have the name Antipholus, and they each have a servant named Dromio who are also identical twins.

46   See Sonnet # 18.

47   Shakespeare structures his play *As You Like It* around the metaphoric frame of a wrestling match for this reason. The play begins with Orlando wrestling with his older brother for his patrimony, and the government of the state in which they live has been usurped by the younger brother of the rightful duke. These stories in turn recall incidents in the Hebrew Bible like the wrestling of Cain and

Abel, the wrestling between Jacob and Esau for their father's blessing, and Jacob's long night when he wrestled with an angel of the Lord.

48   In the Induction of *The Taming of a Shrew* Christopher Sly would "let the world slip" by watching a play.

49   *Hamlet*, Act III, Scene ii, lines 17-24.

50   "O that he (the sexton) were here to write me down an ass." *Much Ado About Nothing*, Act IV, Scene ii, lines 75-76.

51   *King Richard II*, Act II, Scene i.

52   It's a change of heart that's the focus of "The Knight's Tale" as Chaucer carefully documents the opening of Theseus' heart in relation to Arcite.

53   In keeping with the character of a courtly dance enjoyed by the nobility, I have illustrated this chapter with a painting by Nicholas Lancret of a fete gallante, a subject popular with eighteenth-century French aristocrats. They had tired of the constraints at Versailles, and so they staged elaborate parties outdoors in a natural setting. Shakespeare's play and Lancret's actors (for Camargo was a famous dancer at the Paris Opera) are following a long tradition of pastoral poetry which imagines people living harmoniously in nature. The Garden of Eden in Genesis provides a starting point for a writer interested in this theme, and there was widespread familiarity in Elizabethan England with the *Eclogues* of Virgil based on Greek models. Christopher Marlowe's most famous poem, "A Passionate Shepherd to his Love," is a pastoral, and the smoothness of its iambic lines set a high standard for English lyric poetry. The astute Shakespeare learned from the older poet both a powerful verse form and the powerful attraction a pastoral theme has for audiences.

54   1 Corinthians 15:52.

55   *Hamlet*, Act II, Scene ii, lines 453-541.

56   Paul uses the twinkling of an eye as a measure of that which is impossible to measure. Chaucer and Shakespeare see a twinkle in the eye, which they convey in a tone of voice, as the sign and the standard of a comic transformation.

57   Ovid's *The Metamorphoses*, trans. Arthur Golding (New York: The MacMillan Company, 1965), 67.

58   Ovid, *The Metamorphoses*, trans. Horace Gregory (New York: A Mentor Classic, 1958), 40.

59   It's an echo of Chaucer's "small fowl…making melody" whose hearts are pricked and engaged. See page 323.

60   Peter Ackroyd, *Shakespeare: The Biography* (London: Vintage Books, 2006), 183.

61   *Hamlet*, Act I, Scene iii.

62   Snug the Joiner's role at the end of Shakespeare's play represents what Chaucer's Theseus had to say about time at the end of "The Knight's Tale." (See the sections called "The Source," pages 130-137, and "A Comic Conclusion," pages 137-143.) Chaucer's Theseus presents his insight about time largely in the form of a philosophical essay, and it's a measure of Shakespeare's skill that he found a way to dramatize it in a play.

63   For an initial interpretation of Robin's epilogue see pages 3-5. The enlarged interpretation of Robin's epilogue on pages 448-454 also depends on the prominent role "if" has been given. See also the discussion of Chaucer's chain of love image in the paragraph that begins, "What is Theseus' experience?", p. 122-124.

64   Job 39-42.

65   There are strong parallels in Philostrate's and Hippolyta's reception of the mechanicals with Polonius' reception of the players in *Hamlet*. There, too, *Hamlet* contrasts a socially conditioned merit, which a man like Polonius enjoys, with a man's true worth. See *Hamlet*, Act II, Scene II, lines 546-559.

66   This sentence recalls what Hamlet says to Horatio in Act V, Scene II, lines 230-235.

67   In note 48 I mentioned that in the Induction of *The Taming of the Shrew* Christopher Sly would "let the world slip" by watching a play. Sly is a tinker, and a local nobleman finds him drunk in the street. The nobleman takes him home to his palace and has all his servants treat him as if he were the lord of the manor. Sly at first resists his new identity, but it doesn't take long to convince him that he merely dreamed that he was a tinker and that he is in fact a lord. I have included this allusion to Sly's situation to shed more light on Robin's final lines at the end of *A Midsummer Night's Dream*. Robin plays with the mind of the audience much like the nobleman plays with the mind of Sly. Both are comic inventions, but Robin's epilogue is more kindly meant. Induction, Scene II, line 146.

68   When it's his turn to tell a story in *The Canterbury Tales*, the Pardoner gives a sermon showing that the love of gold is the root of all evil. The Pardoner would have his listeners lighten the burden of their sin by giving the gold to him. Chaucer's and Shakespeare's understanding of *cupiditas* is much broader and deeper than the Pardoner's obsession with gold.

69   William Shakespeare, *A Midsummer Night's Dream*, edited by George Lyman Kittredge and revised by Irving Ribner (Waltham, MA: Blaisdell Publishing Company,1966), 85.

70   This is how Robin described Lysander for not lying by Hermia, p. 271.

Picture Credits

Cover: Art Resource

Introduction: Worthington Scranton Library, Penn State Scranton

Chapter One: Rijksmuseum

Chapter Two: PD-US

Chapter Three: PD-US

Chapter Four: Art Resource

Chapter Five: Art Resource

Chapter Six: Art Resource

Chapter Seven: Art Resource

Chapter Eight: Art Resource

Chapter Ten: National Gallery, Washington, DC

Chapter Eleven: Art Resource

Chapter Twelve: The Phillips Collection

Chapter Thirteen: Bridgeman Arts

Excuse me, but it's my turn.....

Written by Karen Romano Young
Illustrated by Doug Cushman

 CHILDRENS PRESS, CHICAGO

School & Library Edition

ISBN 0-516-09321-5

Titles in the Best Behavior™ Series

Published by Ideals Publishing Corporation

Produced for Ideals Publishing Corporation by
Joshua Morris Publishing, Inc.
167 Old Post Road, Southport, Connecticut 06490

Printed in Singapore

Someone famous once said, "It's not whether you win or lose,
it's how you play the game." Manners have a lot to do with how
you play the game.

Before you make the team. . .

Sports require good manners, before, during, and after the game. This is especially true when you play on a team. First, you may have to try out for a team. Just try to do your best.

Don't make excuses for your mistakes.

Player's from last year's team may have to try out again. If someone tries to upset you, don't pay attention.

I'm ALWAYS the goalie, kid!

Likewise, if you're a member of last year's team, don't show off.

What if you don't make the team? Quietly decide to practice extra hard next time. Give yourself time to get over your disappointment before deciding you'll never play again.

Don't go around complaining about the way the tryouts were run.

Once you've made the team. . .
Take responsibility for being a good team member.

One for all and all for one.

Don't miss practice if you can help it. If you have to miss practice, be sure and call your coach. Don't expect your parents to do it for you (unless you're too sick to come to the phone). Be a team player.

Sorry coach, bu[t] I have to visit my Aunt, so I'[ll] have to miss practice!

Be a team player. Be willing to learn, listen, and try new things at your coach's suggestion.

My soccer coach says to run a mile each day.

Since I made the basketball team, I'll run too!

On the way to the game. . .

Don't distract the bus driver by running around the bus or by singing too loud.

Don't scream out the windows or throw things at passing cars and people.

If you travel in a carpool, be respectful toward the driver. If you need a ride home from the school, field, or pick-up place, ask someone ahead of time if possible.

At the game. . .

Keep quiet about the other team's field, court, town, locker room, etc.

Never make rude comments.

Say 'good luck' to the other team.

Cheer for your team.

If you kick or hit the ball over a fence or into the woods, volunteer to get it yourself.

If you're stuck on the bench, don't sulk. Instead, watch the game and cheer your team on. Be ready to join the game as soon as your coach needs you.

Don't be a star. No one makes a touchdown, goal, or basket without the team behind them. Never brag about yourself!

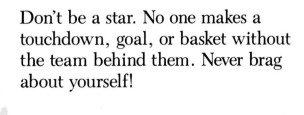

Fans can be difficult. If your parents (or other friends and relatives) make you embarrassed, politely ask them to be more quiet.

Ask your coach to handle problems with other team members, parents, or friends.

If someone is injured, get them the help they need as soon as possible, or help them off the field.

Don't crowd around a hurt person.

Don't discuss the person's injury with others if you really don't know what happened. You could frighten someone or start a rumor.

Many people think it's smart or cool to argue with the referee or umpire. In almost all cases, the ref will not change their mind. Besides, arguing is against the rules of most games. You could be thrown out or forced to give up the game to the other team.

Never cheat.

If you suspect someone of cheating, quietly mention it to your coach. Let the coach speak to the referee or handle the problem himself.

Never. . .

. . .use bad language,

. . .fight with the other players,

. . .insult other players,

. . .tackle or bump someone in order to hurt them.

These things are impolite, and they show that you are a poor sport. What's more, they're against the rules.

After the game. . .

Shake hands with the other players and coaches, or give them a team cheer.

Be a gracious winner,

Even if you're the most valuable player, the win belongs to the wh team.

Be a brave loser. Don't complain about the rules, the coach, the other players, or the field. Instead congratulate the winners.

If possible, smile.

Be considerate of the person who cleans your uniform. Hand it over as soon as possible after the game.

Other sports. . .

Some sports have fewer rules. Still, manners are important.

Play where you won't disturb anyone. Whether you play on a school playground or in a public park don't hog the whole area.

Don't hog equipment meant to be shared by all.

Let others join you if they want.

Generally, the people who start the game set the rules. If you join in the game later, don't argue about the rules.

When Hiking. . .

. . .follow marked trails,

. . .stay with your group, don't wander off by yourself,

. . .don't litter or destroy any plants or trees.

. . .be considerate of other hikers. Don't make too much noise or frighten other people.

When Skiing. . .

. . .stay on marked trails,

. . .ski at a safe speed,

. . .don't cut into the lift line.

If you save a place for a friend, ask the people behind you if they mind if your friend joins you.

When swimming. . .

. . .pay attention to the lifeguard,
. . .don't run around the deck of the pool,
. . .don't push people into the pool for fun,
. . .watch out for the other swimmers, expecially younger children.

When jogging. . .

Stay to the side of a busy sidewalk or road. Better yet, find a place that isn't crowded.

Oops! Think I'd better stop!

If you're behind a group that is blocking your path, slow down and call out "Excuse me." If they don't move, stop and walk around them.

Using manners as part of sports doesn't mean you can't have fun. It means that everyone can enjoy themselves in their own way!